# The Zimbabwean Crisis

This book is part of the Peter Lang Political Science, Economics, and Law list.
Every volume is peer reviewed and meets
the highest quality standards for content and production.

PETER LANG
New York • Bern • Berlin
Brussels • Vienna • Oxford • Warsaw

# The Zimbabwean Crisis

## Perspectives, Paradoxes and Prospects (1997–2017)

C. Luthuli Mhlahlo and
Levar Lamar Smith, Editors

PETER LANG
New York • Bern • Berlin
Brussels • Vienna • Oxford • Warsaw

**Library of Congress Cataloging-in-Publication Data**

Names: Mhlahlo, Corwin Luthuli, editor. | Smith, Levar Lamar, editor.
Title: The Zimbabwean crisis: perspectives, paradoxes and prospects
(1997–2017) / C. Luthuli Mhlahlo and Levar Lamar Smith, editors.
Description: New York: Peter Lang, 2020.
Includes bibliographical references.
Identifiers: LCCN 2019045830 | ISBN 978-1-4331-5644-1 (hardback: alk. paper)
ISBN 978-1-4331-5645-8 (ebook pdf)
ISBN 978-1-4331-5646-5 (epub) | ISBN 978-1-4331-5647-2 (mobi)
Subjects: LCSH: Zimbabwe—Politics and government—1980– | Zimbabwe—Social
conditions—1980– | Zimbabwe—Economic conditions—1980–
Classification: LCC DT2996 .Z567 2020 | DDC 968.9105—dc23
LC record available at https://lccn.loc.gov/2019045830
DOI 10.3726/b13512

Bibliographic information published by **Die Deutsche Nationalbibliothek**.
**Die Deutsche Nationalbibliothek** lists this publication in the "Deutsche
Nationalbibliografie"; detailed bibliographic data are available
on the Internet at http://dnb.d-nb.de/.

The paper in this book meets the guidelines for permanence and durability
of the Committee on Production Guidelines for Book Longevity
of the Council of Library Resources.


29 Broadway, 18th floor, New York, NY 10006
www.peterlang.com



Printed in the United States of America

For Doc “Khulu” Mhlahlo
&
Africa’s leaders, present and future

# Contents

# *Figures*

# *Tables*

# Preface

Depending on how one perceived and understood it, the socioeconomic and political situation in Zimbabwe between 1997 and 2017 was widely known by different nomenclature or rather, phrasing. To some, it was geopolitically the Zimbabwe crisis. To such, I gathered what was happening in the country-was a national crisis inflicted less by economic geography and more by poor governance of the nation-state of Zimbabwe. To these, it was sorrowfully "Zimbabwe's lost decade" (Sachikonye, 2010). To others, it was tellingly the crisis in Zimbabwe.

From this second group, one got the impression that, in their view, what was happening was a remote problem, something to observe at a distance. As far as those in this group were concerned, they were far removed from what was happening and content to be so. To them, Zimbabwe was a distant country and they were nothing more than detached, occasional spectators to the occurrences in "that country". To some others, however, it was thought–provokingly the Zimbabwean crisis.

To these, I conjectured, the crisis had acquired a human face, a character—a kind of personaone that was, and rightly so, uniquely Zimbabwean. To such, I got the impression the crisis was all about Zimbabweans, it was "theirs". After all, they had caused it, were suffering because of it and so must take ownership of it. This group put responsibility for the crisis and the impact it was having on Zimbabweans. To these ones the crisis was personal. However, much as they wanted to dismiss or create some distance from it, the crisis remained both affective and emotive. To a large extent, I, identified with this group.

In my view, as long as the people of Zimbabwe and their leadership remained the main cause of, and the most impacted by the crisis, then it was correct to call it a Zimbabwean crisis. This is especially as doing so, also brought into play issues of Zimbabwean identity and being Zimbabwean both in Zimbabwe and in a global context. As far as I was concerned therefore, what was an issue in Zimbabwe was more than just a tangible socio–economic and political crisis. It was also one of intangibles, of identity, of the human spirit, traditions and ethics. If this is what the latter group meant, then we agreed.

However, if by calling and giving the crisis a wholly Zimbabwean identity, this group simply sought to apportion total responsibility for the crisis on Zimbabweans alone and saw them as its apathetic victims, then we disagreed. This is because, from my perspective, and as it later turned out, some of the contributors to this volume, while some Zimbabweans and their actions were arguably the impetus of, and most affected by the crisis, they were not its only cause and neither were they apathetic to it. Regional, continental and international actors, actions and forces had either directly or indirectly contributed, manipulated, fanned and exacerbated the crisis to its dizzy heights. Heights to and at which some Zimbabweans were agentive.

Yet other differing points of view were: whom the crisis was affecting and their responses to it. To the casual observer, the crisis was indisputably affecting those Zimbabweans within the country's borders. After all, they will argue, it is they who were its daily "victims". However, to the more analytical, all Zimbabweans, both in and outside the country, private and public were suffering the crisis—but perhaps just not to the same extent. Similarly, neither were they all passively baring the crisis. Instead, as this study reveals, both the government and some private citizens actively formulated varied strategies in the fervent hope of surviving the crisis.

Aside from how best to phrase the crisis, other questions of interest and contestation have been asked over the years. Aligned to what I have touched on above, some of these have included: how and when exactly the Zimbabwean crisis started? Did it start at the end of 1979 with the signing of the Lancaster House Agreement, or in the early 1980s when the Zimbabwe National Army's North Korean 5th Brigade embarked on an operation code-named *Gukurahundi* (a chiShona word for a wind that blows away the chaff before spring rains) and perpetrated untold atrocities in parts of Matabeleland and the Midlands? Or do the answers to these questions lie in the 1990s when the country embarked on the Economic Structural Adjustment Program (ESAP)? Or was it when then President Mugabe paid unbudgeted gratuities to war veterans and thereafter embroiled the country's army in an equally costly war in the Democratic Republic of Congo (DRC)? Could the answers perhaps lie in 1999 and the 2000s with the formation of the Movement for Democratic Change (MDC) opposition party and the victory of the "No" vote this encouraged during the country's Constitution Referendum? Could it have been the "land invasions" which the referendum result "ignited" and that the Mugabe government tacitly supported? Just how many crises in Zimbabwe were there anyway? The exasperated asked of this complex yet, in some ways, simple Zimbabwean crisis.

Besides the questions above, the question that has become most pertinent is: what the present and future hold for both the country and its people? Since the military's intervention in Zimbabwe's governance, the resignation of Robert Mugabe in November 2017, the ascension of Emmerson Dambudzo Mnangagwa to the presidency and the July 30 2018 elections, some of the questions foremost on many people's lips remain whether the military intervention was a coup and if the crisis is now over? As Zimbabweans and certainly the world await a post-Mugabe government and era, this four-part multidisciplinary volume, most of whose contributors lived through and had first-hand experience of the crisis, reflects on, shares their perspectives, seeks to provide answers, and provokes more questions and imaginations about the Zimbabwean crisis, the people and country of Zimbabwe. To those who witnessed, experienced and responded to the Zimbabwean crisis between the years 1997 and 2017, not enough can ever be written on or about it. Nonetheless, it is my hope and the contributors' that this contribution adds value to the other book projects that have preceded it. That, as traumatizing and life-changing as the crisis was, the confusion, agony, economic and human losses, which those both inside and outside the country's borders suffered, were not and have not been in vain.

This offering has painstakingly taken a decade of research, reflection, writing, revision, editing, proofreading, shelving, more research, additional writing, editing, compilation, dismantling, compilation, editing, proofreading and finally, yes finally—submission and publication. For me, it has indeed been a labor of love, hate, patience, extreme endurance, growth, maturity and self–discovery.

My sincerest thanks to all the contributors for their patience and anxious enquiries when the "dust took too long to settle" and it appeared this volume would never be "done and dusted" let alone see the light of day. I am forever grateful to you all for selflessly sacrificing your time in ways only those emotionally, philosophically, spiritually, intellectually and academically dedicated to Zimbabwe could have. Without you, the import of the crisis's origins, its course and impact to 2017 could never have been this volume.

Where would we all be without family? I cannot thank our families enough for the support they have given and shown throughout the course of this project. *Garai kure nemoto*! (do not sit too close to the fire). Do not come to any harm. May our families, both immediate and extended, not tire in their continuing support, comfort and encouragement of us all. In this regard, my heartfelt thanks go to my "girls", Celeste-Esther "Celz" and Memory Tatenda "Memz" for their loving understanding, assistance and patience when they deserved some family time and I could not spare it. I love you for it girls.

To the people of Zimbabwe, it is my cherished hope that as the crisis lingers and new ones arise and threaten, that you remember always that "*hapanachisingaperi*" (there is nothing that does not finally end). As we await that final end, in the meantime may this volume help us take stock of where we have come from, what it is that we have learnt from the crisis, where it is we are going, but want to go, and how we can get there—now, tomorrow and into the future. Lastly, to all who will encounter and read this collection, may it probe us all to take responsibility and make the world a better place than we found it.

Gweru, Midlands., Zimbabwe
C. LUTHULI MHLAHLO

# Contributors

***Lere Amusan*** is a political scientist by education and inclination. He has published extensively on Third World politics and established his career at Osun State University, Osogbo in Nigeria. He is currently a professor and senior lecturer in the Department of Politics and International Relations at North-West University in South Africa.

***Munamato Chemhuru*** obtained his PhD in Philosophy from the University of Johannesburg in 2016. In 2017, he was awarded the Global Excellence Stature Fellowship (GES) for a post-doctoral research fellowship by the University of Johannesburg's department of Philosophy, Faculty of Humanities. He is now Senior Lecturer in Philosophy at Great Zimbabwe University where he has been teaching Philosophy for over a decade now. He is also Research Associate in Philosophy in the Humanities Faculty with the University of Johannesburg, South Africa. His research focuses on various social, political and ethical issues in African Philosophy stemming from concepts such as African governance and democracy, African communitarian philosophy and the idea of *ubuntu*. He has published in some central journals like *Philosophia Africana, South African Journal of Philosophy, Journal on African Philosophy* and *Phronimon*.

***Dennis Masaka*** was born and raised in Zimbabwe. He holds a PhD in Philosophy and is a senior lecturer in philosophy at Great Zimbabwe University in Zimbabwe. He has had papers published/accepted by journals such as *South African Journal of Philosophy, Philosophical Papers, Journal of Black Studies, African Study Monographs, Journal of Negro Education*, and *CODESRIA Bulletin*.

***C. Luthuli Mhlahlo*** is an Africanist Zimbabwean. He has resided in Zimbabwe, South Africa and the United Kingdom. From 2007 to 2012, he pursued a PhD in English Studies specializing in Zimbabwean literature at the University of the Witwatersrand where he was awarded numerous scholarships and awards among them the Postgraduate Merit Award (PMA). He holds an MA in English specializing in Gender and Identity from the University of South Africa and a Postgraduate Diploma in Education (PGDE) from the University of Zimbabwe. He also holds academic degrees in English and Economic History and professional diplomas in Business Administration and Marketing Management from Zimbabwe and the UK, respectively. His academic and conference papers have been published both locally and internationally in peer-reviewed journals. His current affiliations include the Department of Culture, Communication and Media of the University College London (UK) where he is a graduate student as well as Comecinc Communications and Strategic Solutions Services Incorporated, a multidisciplinary consultancy in South Africa where he is Associate Senior Consultant.

***Samson Rwadzi (Lwazi) Mhlahlo*** held a PhD in Geography (Midlands State University) and an MA in Geography (UCL, University of London). He was passionate, researched, wrote and published on housing in Zimbabwe in refereed journals. Formerly a Geography lecturer at the then Gweru Teachers' College, he subsequently became Lecturer and Chairperson of the Department of Geography and Environmental Studies at Midlands State University in Gweru, Zimbabwe. He was later appointed Executive Dean: Faculty of Social Sciences, the post he held until his untimely death at the end of 2017.

***Fortune Sibanda*** is Associate Professor in the Department of Philosophy and Religious Studies, Great Zimbabwe University, Masvingo. He has widely published articles in refereed journals and book chapters on various themes from a religious perspective, which include New religious movements, the Land question, Indigenous ways of knowing, Human rights issues, and the Environment and Power dynamics in the African context. He co-edited: *Power in Contemporary Zimbabwe* (2018). Prof. Sibanda is a member of the African Consortium for Law and Religion Studies (ACLARS), African Theological Institutions in Southern and Central Africa (ATISCA), Association for the Study of Religion in Southern Africa (ASRSA) and African Association for the Study of Religion (AASR).

***Levar Lamar Smith*** is an African–American with a keen interest in African affairs and developments on the African continent. He completed both his

MA and PhD in Political Science at Miami University in 2009 and 2017, respectively. He also holds an MS in International Affairs from Sam Nunn School of International Affairs, Georgia Institute of Technology that he received in 2007. His research interests focus on political development, international political economy, and democratization in Sub-Saharan Africa.

# Introduction

## "(...) by reflection, by some other things": Tracking, Reflecting and Taking Responsibility for the Zimbabwean Crisis

C. Luthuli Mhlahlo[1]

Even during prelapsarian times, humanity has often found it difficult to take responsibility for its actions or the condition it has found itself since then. Over the years, Africa has experienced more than its share of crises. None, however, has arguably been as severe and enduring as Zimbabwe's almost two-decade-long crisis. Reminiscent of just before and after the Fall of Man, no one has been keen to take responsibility for it. During the Robert Mugabe administration, he and the then ZANU-PF government blamed the British government for reneging and inadequately financing land redistribution and the European Union (EU) countries for imposing economic sanctions on Zimbabwe. Conversely, it accused the U.S. government of attempting an illegal regime change by enacting and enforcing the Zimbabwe Democracy and Economic Recovering Act (ZIDERA) on the country's leadership and inadvertently, the Zimbabwean economy itself.

Equally, some Zimbabweans, both inside and outside the country, blamed the country's socioeconomic and political condition on either the ZANU-PF led government or some western countries for imposing sanctions on Zimbabwe. Thus, for instance, although the final decision to embark on Zimbabwe's Economic Structural Adjustment Program ultimately was the decision of the government of the day, Mahoso was, however, of the view that: "The purpose of the Economic Structural Adjustment Programme (ESAP) and the illegal sanctions (ZIDERA) which followed was to engender self-defeating values, perceptions and practices among the people (...) ESAP contributed to the crisis which illegal sanctions intensified" (2013, p.D2). As such, based on his reading and interpretation of Naomi Klein's *The Shock Doctrine: The Rise of Disaster Capitalism*,[2] Mahoso likened the socioeconomic suffering some Zimbabweans experienced between 2007 and 2008 to "a period of economic torture and terror (…) the same way militarily targeted populations experience what the Nazis called 'blitzkrieg.' This is a situation in which war becomes pure event which is not accompanied by any narrative explanation." What Mahoso and others like him, however, seemed to sidestep or be unaware of is that the crisis' economic terror had a narrative explanation—one that had most of its origins in Zimbabwe and Zimbabweans themselves.

It is perhaps for this reason that both the U.S. and U.K governments in turn blamed the crisis on, among others, the rampant corruption in the ZANU-PF government. Blessing-Miles Tendi's interview of Zimbabwean academics and intellectuals at the height of the crisis, for instance, revealed that primarily on their own cognizance, many of them had since "abandoned the ideals of scientific and scholarly research in favor of foreign–funded projects intended to deepen the western–sponsored regime change agenda against Zimbabwe" (Mahoso, 2014, p.D2) in pursuit of financial gain. As one female academic from the University of Zimbabwe almost boasted, "I do consultancy work for NGOs and I bend my analysis to please them (…) That way they will come again next time for my analysis and even bring me new clients" (Tendi, 2010, p.62). To some outsiders looking in, like then South Africa's President Thabo Mbeki, however, Zimbabwe was thought provokingly and as far as they understood the country's situation, actually not in a state of crisis at all. "The Zimbabwe crisis, what crisis?" they rhetorically questioned.

A lexical definition of the word "crisis" as derived from various dictionaries can be paraphrased to delineate a crisis as a "crucial or decisive point or situation"; especially one involving an impending abrupt change. It is a turning point in political, social, economic, or military affairs. The Merriam-Webster dictionary defines "crisis" as: "an unstable or crucial time or state of affairs in which a decisive change is impending; especially, one with the distinct possibility of a highly desirable outcome, a situation that has reached a critical phase." (Crisis, n.d.)

Based on which one of these descriptions one chooses to understand the word, Zimbabwe has over the years arguably and paradoxically, like many other countries over the same period, alternated between a state of crisis and not a state of crisis. That is primarily as it can be argued that every significant event in the life of a nation-state, be it independence from repressive minority/democratic rule, an election, the impeachment or death of a sitting head of state, a unity government, a liquidity crunch, the introduction of a new currency, a *coup d'etat*, a national strike, an uprising, a civil war, or the transition from military to civilian rule—all can and have the potential to lexically constitute a crisis—in which case Zimbabwe could, therefore, be said to have over the last 20 years arguably experienced various crises within a crisis.

It is in view of the above understandings of "crisis", that in this volume, while a crisis is recognized as comprising some of the lexical elements outlined above, in the context of Zimbabwe, it is to be further comprehended as entwined with forfeitures of traditional, personal[3] and leader identity[4] for the sake of existence. Subsequent to which is "a situation whereby socio-economic equilibrating mechanisms have broken down, and some force external to the prevailing systematic logic must be invoked to restore stability" (Bond, 2001, p.25). Against such an appreciation of what constitutes a crisis, this volume concludes the situation Zimbabwe and Zimbabweans found themselves in, and to some extent still find themselves,constituted and constitutes a Zimbabwean crisis. Just to what extent it is such a crisis called and calls for reflection.

A wise saying goes, "the eye sees not itself, but by reflection, by some other things" (Shakespeare, *JuliusCaesar*, Act1, ii). Indeed, the impossibility of the eye to look at and analyze itself necessitates that it be aided by a mirror or other media, "some other things" to enable it to do so. Similarly, if an individual, more so a people are to critically look at and see themselves, they crucially require some other thing(s) to reflect an image of what they are or have become. Such a reflection is in my view of paramount importance if people, in this case Zimbabweans, are to "see themselves", take responsibility for and ownership of what has happened in the past, is happening in the present, and need to be corrected in future.

The speed with which Zimbabwe's socio–economic and political condition unraveled had academics, scholars, and writers both inside the country, and across the globe documenting, researching, writing, and publishing. Consequently, from the turn of this century, the Zimbabwean crisis possibly became the most topical global African subject since the end of apartheid and the advent of a democratic South Africa. In the years that followed, global attempts to unpack and make sense of the crisis resulted in both literary and academic output. The crisis inspired poetry, novels, conferences proceedings, journal and book publications.

Of the research output published, partly based on, what in my opinion was the first phase of the Zimbabwean crisis, the years between 1999 and 2009, prominent among them is a volume by Patrick Bond and Masimba Manyanya entitled: *Zimbabwe's Plunge. Exhausted Nationalism,*

*Neoliberalism and the Search for Social Justice* (2002). Its critique of the different phases of Zimbabwe's macroeconomic development immensely assisted contributors to this volume and proved invaluable for the statistical, analytical and informational trove it captured. The same is equally true of volumes edited by Amanda Hammar, Brian Raftopoulos, and Stig Jensen entitled: *Zimbabwe's Unfinished Business: Rethinking Land, State, and Nation in the Context of Crisis* (2003) and another by Brian Raftopoulos and Alois Mlambo titled *Becoming Zimbabwe: A History from the Pre-colonial Period to 2008* (2009). A decade after Raftopolos and Mlambo's edition, this volume reflects, rethinks, captures, builds on and extends the story of Zimbabwe and Zimbabweans' crisis.

Although both African and Zimbabwean literature such as Ayi Kwei Armah's *The Beautyful Ones Are Not Yet Born* (1968) and Dambudzo Marechera's *The House of Hunger* (1978) respectively, had years earlier ominously predicted socio–economic conditions akin to the Zimbabwean crisis, post–2000, the country's literary fraternity was not as quick to publish on and about the crisis. However, as emigration from Zimbabwe rose and Zimbabweans established themselves as diasporans, most notably, Brian Chikwava's enigmatic *Harare North* (2009) launched a scathing satire on the country's immigrant population in the United Kingdom, the violent exploitation of youths by the ruling ZANU-PF party and its resultant psychological impact on the former. In the same year, Petina Gapppah's *An Elegy for Easterly* (2009) particularized "the stories of ordinary people what it meant, on a day–to–day basis, to be part of a crisis that has gripped the attention of the world" (Conversations with Writers, 2009, para. 22). The literary world, rather late, finally launched commentary on the crisis.

After a decade of widespread dystopian decay, decrease, death, and the setting in of fatigue over the Zimbabwean crisis, the signing of the Global Political Agreement (GPA) in September 2008 and the installation of the country's Government of National Unity (GNU) in early 2009 finally saw the crisis abate but not recede. By 2010, the crisis had for many researchers and commentators lost its luster. The once plethora of media, academic, and creative voices largely fell silent. Others adopted a "let's wait and see" attitude, and others did not. As far as they were concerned it was finally over. For the latter, it was time to assess and evaluate the damage the crisis had caused and make pronouncements. Of particular interest, the year 2010 saw the publication of *Zimbabwe's Land Reform: Myths and Realities* (2010) by Ian Scoones et al. Their volume appraised the credibility of the Land Reform Programme's deliverables. This was followed by Lloyd Sachikonye's: *Zimbabwe's Lost Decade* (2010). In it, Sachikonye explored how Zimbabwe's difficulties impacted

Western business and politics as well as debates solutions to the country's rising poverty levels. However, just as "Sachikonye guides us all to the reality that the African and Zimbabwean poor will always be with us" (Codling, 2012, np), the crisis too also proved it was not over. As time revealed, the Inclusive Government (IG) or Government of National Unity (GNU) years had been an interregnum, a pause if you will, a phase or stage in an ongoing crisis. Thereafter, analyses of the IG tenure and the success or lack thereof of the Land Reform Program (LRP) took center–stage of much that was published about the country's crisis at the start of what I consider the second phase of the Zimbabwean crisis, the years 2010—2017.

The volume: *Zimbabwe in Transition: A View from within* edited by Tim Murithi and Aquilina Mawadza followed in 2011. In their compilation, Murithi and Mawadza sought to assess the functionality and inclusiveness of Zimbabwe's Government of National Unity as well as whether the country was indeed in transition. Considering that Zimbabwe's ex-combatants or war veterans of the country's liberation have since the mid-1990s played a significant role to the trajectory and course of the country's post-independence history. Sadomba's publication: *War Veterans in Zimbabwe's Revolution: Challenging Neocolonialism and Settler and International Capital* was therefore an interesting and welcome addition. In his book, Sadomba rightly or wrongly: "Traces the roots of Zimbabwe's well–known, but little analysed, revolution of 2000 to the 1970s guerrilla war" (Sadomba, 2011 back cover). Particularly curious, and something which I question in Chapter One of this volume, is to what extent in Sadomba's view, the war veterans in the year 2000 challenged neo-colonialism, settler and international capitalism in their "ongoing bottom–up struggle against colonialism"(Sadomba, 2011, back cover). When in essence, they could be said to have, to some extent, actually aided and abetted neo–colonialism, settler and international capitalism. It is such perceptions, paradoxes and possibilities, that this book in some measure seeks to highlight and critique.

However, an understanding of a crisis as complex and multifaceted like the one Zimbabwe is experiencing cannot be handled effectively by a singular group of specialists.Consequently, this four-part multidisciplinary volume linearly tracks, reflects on, explores, and analyzes the proceedings and internal mechanisms of Zimbabwe's ongoing socioeconomic and political crisis to 2017. It does so via eclectic theoretical lens, ethnocentric, empirical research findings, and indigenous knowledge systems to explore and at times further illuminate the country's seemingly permanent state of crisis.

Whereupon, it primarily argues that while during the colonial era, some western governments were and could indeed be implicated and held complicit for the adverse developments and under development in Zimbabwe, postcolonial, mainly from 1997 to 2017, Zimbabweans individually and collectively also need to scrutinize their condition objectively and the country's situation and, where convicted, hold themselves accountable for some of it. In this regard, this tome urges that contemporary understandings of Zimbabwe need to transcend blind patriotism, the tendency to focus solely on the dynamics of leadership and governance by equally interrogating the relationships between and among nation-states, the citizenry and their local and indigenous knowledge systems as has never been done before.

Equally recommending this collection is that it fortuitously comes shortly after the "military intervention" in that country and the installation of Emmerson Dambudzo Mnangagwa as interim president that followed. Most significantly, it follows immediately after the ZANU-PF party's parliamentary and presidential election victory in the country's July 30, 2018, harmonized polls. It is one of the few that engages in Zimbabwe's present political moment, for which literature is still limited. This gives it the advantage of hindsight that enables it to critically reflect on Zimbabwe's tumultuous decades of crisis from informed fresh perspectives. An opportune and enabling position to offer alternate explanations, reappraise, reevaluate earlier assessments about the crisis, and make pronouncements on how best the country, the continent, and indeed the world can reengage with it. To this end, the work has as much as possible, drawn together and on the perceptions and informed, critical reflections of new black Zimbabwean voices' as arrived at via, among others, ethnographic, sociological library-based research, historical data analysis, indigenous knowledge systems, and some theories of the Global South.

The contributors featured here are relatively young, aspiring researchers and emerging academics based in Zimbabwe, the continent and abroad. Through this collection, this "reflection, and other things," they bring together here their recollections, experiences, emotions, alternative explanations, reappraisals, divergent opinions, and constructive thoughts; about Zimbabwe's and Zimbabweans' seemingly perpetual crisis state as arrived at utilizing the numerous abovementioned research approaches. As can be expected, given the controversy and conversations that happenings in Zimbabwe sparked, and continue to elicit, not all readers will agree with the views, assessments, and evaluations offered here.

In this vein, the chapters contained here should not be read as a form of alternative political activism. Instead, they should be taken in the spirit that they have been offered—subjective perceptions which seek to contribute to the robust debate about Zimbabwe's past, present, and, more importantly, its future. As such, the purpose of the volume is not only to acquaint readers with facts about the course and nature of the crisis. It also seeks to familiarize them with both documented and undocumented underlying factors about the country's past which are perceived to have significantly contributed to the present and are vital to Zimbabwe's search for solutions and paths to its future. In view of the gravity of the undertaking, without papering over the crisis, an attempt has, as much and as far as possible, been made to offer some new insights to it while maintaining verity, objectivity, and impartiality.

The resultant tome spans 20 years of the crisis. Understandably, it tackles numerous aspects of the nation's socioeconomic and political spheres during that period. In order to comprehensively manage what the collection offers, it has been divided into four parts or segments of not less than three chapters each. Each segment concentrates on a specific theme about an aspect of the crisis. For instance, the first segment attempts to trace and theoretically illuminate the origins of the crisis by deploying theory to discuss an aspect the contributor perceives was a catalyst of Zimbabwe's crisis. The second segment explores the survival strategies of those who stoically and commendably remained within the country's borders and of those who opted or were forced to migrate. In doing so, it surveys the agentic acts and practices they resorted to for them to survive and evaluates the impact such survival strategies had on such agentic ones, their families, Zimbabwe, and their host countries. The third segment, in hindsight, weighs and analyzes Zimbabwe's most recent past. It covers the post–GNU years which it debatably perceives as again rehashing the kind of humanitarian crisis that previously resulted in a GNU and might, this time around, bring it to yet another watershed moment. This is especially so, taking into account the military intervention in November 2017 and the sudden depature of President Mugabe from power. The last segment however, audaciously hopes the best for Zimbabwe going forward. It recommends how best the country can navigate to a stable and prosperous future in the waters ahead.

Overall, the result has been a four-part volume of a minimum of three and a maximum of four chapters. These range from theoretical attempts to explore and illuminate the origins of the crisis to strategies Zimbabweans resorted to survive it, as well as suggestions about how best to restore, develop, and regrow the country and its human capital to their former glory.

## *PART 1: Causing Crisis: Theorizing the Origins of the Crisis*

In an age when there have been calls and attempts towards Africanizing the African curriculum, this section attempts to show how this can be done by basing theory on people's history, traditions, indigenous knowledge systems and responses to their socioeconomic and political situation. What however remains theoretically challenging is not necessarily the nomenclature for the "African theory" that is then put forward. Somewhat, what remains a challenge is how best to explicate and illuminate it solely as it is without relying on the tenets of conventional western theory to do so. In this regard, this collection to some extent, and where possible, attempts to marry Zimbabwean precolonial history, traditions, and indigenous knowledge systems with some tenets of conventional western theory into an eclectic lens through which to explore, theoretically analyze, and reflect why crisis transpired in Zimbabwe and why it has persisted for so long.

In an opening chapter that briefly traces the historiography of Zimbabwe's land issue, C. Luthuli Mhlahlo asserts that the country's unresolved land question, though, arguably politically expedient at the time it was undertaken, was a genuine grievance that had been the cause of generational despair and ought to have been effectively addressed at the onset of the 1979 peace negotiations. However, because it was not, C. L. Mhlahlo posits that, examined via an eclectic mix of Zimbabwean precolonial history and Shona indigenous knowledge systems illuminated via an existentialist lens, Zimbabwe's decline over the years is possibly attributable to some Zimbabweans' disobedience during the land re–appropriation period of an order given by the legendary Mbuya Nehanda over a hundred years ago.

During the First *Chimurenga*, Nehanda had reportedly ordered that those involved in *chimurenga* should only take possession of the land and not the white settlers' personal belongings.[5] In disobedience and contravention of this, however, at the time of the country's Third *Chimurenga*, some of those who had liberated the country from colonial rule during the Second *Chimurenga*, some war veterans and peasants had defied *chimurenga* tradition and disobeyed Nehanda's admonition. Instead, of following tradition regardingan adversary's personal possessions, they had embarked on actions which Mhlahlo sees as assuming near existential and existentialist-like proportions. This is especially taking into account that the land re–appropriation was often accompanied by usufruct violence and looting in an existential bid to transcend the postcolonial despair which had been instigated partly by the ZANU-PF government's economic policies and the country's unresolved land issue. Consequent to the "land invaders'" existential actions, Mhlahlo conjectures that the ancestors had turned their backs on the nation—what Shona tradition terms *kupfuratirwa nevadzimu*—literally to be given the ancestors' back in a kind of ancestral abandonment. As such, Mhlahlo concludes that akin to Adam and Eve's disobedience in the garden of Eden, it was some Zimbabweans' disobedience that was a catalyst of crisis and despair. The culmination of which was yet more existentialist acts in search of being. So, if Zimbabwe is today in crisis, those who disobeyed Nehanda's order must take responsibility for it and set mattersright.

Conversely, in a chapter that theoretically holds the first ten years of Zimbabwe's crisis against Samuel P. Huntington's (1968) thesis about modernization and political consciousness, Lere Amusan attempts to explain the possible reasons for the dire straits the country found itself. He argues that the crisis can be best understood as an outcome of larger global processes and responses beyond Zimbabwe. In this vein, Amusan argues that in addition to Zimbabwe's historical and domestic circumstances, external forces such as South Africa's "quiet diplomacy," Britain's historical relations and policies, as well as the varied responses to the events in Zimbabwe were all contributory to the country's deterioration and near collapse. Amusan concludes by making some recommendations as to how the country and the international community can best move forward.

Zimbabwe's political economy is largely seen as having been the catalyst to the country's crisis. Throughout human history, whenever and wherever a command economic system has been applied, the ramifications have been disastrous.[6] The implementation of a command economic system in Zimbabwe was no exception. At the turn of the millennium, the Zimbabwean government's intensified regulation of the economy reactivated a command economic system as a corrective measure to a declining economy. In a chapter whose fundamental premise is that a market economy is preferable to a command economy, Dennis Masaka proffers that the government's command system and its prominent component of price controls were eventually the cause of the country's ruinous and endemic economic and social crisis. That is especially since, in Masaka's view, it was the Zimbabwe government's regulation of the economy which, among others, led to business disinvestment, devastating shortages of commodities, and an unprecedented shrinkage of the economy. He sees the perilous economic situation Zimbabwe has faced since, as yet another illustration of the viability of a free market system over a paternalistic one. He concludes by firmly advocating and applauding the country's return to a free market system as the panacea to Zimbabwe's currently fragile economic situation.

Masaka's view is to some extent supported by Levar Lamar Smith. Smith's chapter surveys Yoshiko Herrera's imagined economies against dimensions of state–control in Zimbabwe. He argues that the case of Zimbabwe from 1999 onwards illustrated authoritarian state politics in the ruling party's dismantling of intense political opposition and the reinvigoration of race-based nationalism. In this regard, Smith demonstrates how in the case of Zimbabwe the ruling party recognized and manipulated several characteristics of an imagined economy, namely the presence of a politically stable and active civil society and the external influences of the international community in the domestic affairs of the state. In Smith's view, it is the presence of these in Zimbabwe that ultimately led and enabled the interpretation, perception, and control of Zimbabwe's economy from the center, eventuallyleading to crisis.

## *PART 2: Surviving Crisis—by All and "any means necessary"*

Crises challenge individuals and countries to think outside the proverbial box and embark on new directions and experiences. The Zimbabwean crisis was no different. However, the nature of the Zimbabwean crisis was such that it created victimizers and victims—a "survival of the fittest" of a different kind[7]. So, while some national, regional and international media houses capitalized on, overdramatized and superficially reported from outside the country's borders the impact the crisis was having on Zimbabweans and Zimbabwe, what often went unreported was how individuals and families did not wallow and succumb to the crisis, but instead strategized and reinvented themselves in search of both survival and existence.

Part 2, therefore, recognizes that some Zimbabweans were not passive victims of the crisis. Instead, it demonstrates how some of them depended on their agency by paradoxically adopting multiple, opportunistic, manipulative, and extortionate survival strategies. In this way, the active and agentic "cannibalized" on the weaker and less so, making the latter double if not triple victims of the crisis. Survival strategies were however not some private Zimbabweans alone. The Mugabe-led government equally resorted to its mix of diplomatic and strategic policy maneuverings to ensure it stayed afloat. In view of the diverse private and public survival strategies that emerged, this segment to some extent paradoxically commends but simultaneously chastises the agency of both the then Mugabe-led government and those Zimbabweans who refused to be victims and instead devised strategies to survive the crisis by manipulating the opportunities it presented and by so doing, ruthlessly "cannibalized" on the unfortunate others.

Contributors to this segment deploy, among others, survival strategy and ethnographic approaches to analyze some Zimbabweans' responses to the crisis. In their respective chapters, the late Samson R. Mhlahlo and C. Luthuli Mhlahlo explore and discuss different survival and livelihood strategies some Zimbabweans, both inside and outside the country's borders, resorted to in order to survive the socioeconomic challenges the crisis had immured them.

From an international relation perceptive, Lere Amusan examines how the then government of Robert Mugabe's foreign policy of reciprocity ensured its continued survival during the crisis. Conversely, Fortune Sibanda and Dennis Masaka from the angle of domestic politics examine and evaluate Zimbabwe's Inclusive Government/Government of National Unity from 2009 to mid-2013. They conclude that it was equally a ZANU-PF and the MDC parties' political and power survival strategy that paradoxically ended up being both a convenience and an inconvenience. To some extent, the chapters in this section correct some misconceptions and highlight other facets about the crisis that often went unreported by the media.

In a chapter that revolves around housing during the period 1999–2009 and mostly draws on findings from in-depth interviews with heads of households in Gweru's townships of Mtapa, Ascot, and Senga, Samson R. Mhlahlo reports that adding to the pressures of the crisis was an urban housing backlog. Focusing on Gweru, Zimbabwe's third largest city, he argues that, as the crisis escalated some restrictive housing policies, disinvestment in new housing projects and government's intolerance towards illegal shelter led to a dire demand for accommodation as both low to middle-class housing dwindled to desperate levels. He reveals how amid such a dearth of housing and rental accommodation, Zimbabwean landlords based both locally and abroad, made their fortunes and sustained themselves and their kith and kin by demanding ever-rising exorbitant rentals. S. R. Mhlahlo concludes his chapter with housing solutions and strategies to ameliorate the nation's housing backlog.

From the late 2000s, the decades' old trickle of black Zimbabwean immigrants entering South Africa became a flood. When between 2007 and 2008 this immigration reached its zenith, animosity, reminiscent of the apartheid era, grew towards African immigrants, most of whom were Zimbabwean. The culmination were the so-called intermittent xenophobic attacks that targeted African foreigners generally and Zimbabweans in particular. Based on ethnographic, participant observations and unstructured interviews, C. Luthuli Mhlahlo reflects on the lives of some Zimbabwean immigrants in South Africa. He examines the survival strategies some of them adopted given the hostile reception some of them received as foreigners from an infamous neighboring country. With his focus on Ndebele-speaking Zimbabwean immigrants, C. L. Mhlahlo argues that because of the ancestral, linguistic similarities and traditional backgrounds some Ndebele-speaking Zimbabwean immigrants share with Zulus in South Africa, some of them were able to assume "Zulu masks" as it were, by mimicking Zulu identity and culture to blend into South African society and thus survive. He concludes that apart from such a survival strategy reuniting clansmen long–separated by the historical *Mfecane*[8] (time of crushing/trouble) and enabling them to survive in South Africa, what also emerged amongst such immigrants are ambivalent personal identities and cultures that often vacillated between what is already known and something that must of necessity be anxiously and, at times, exaggeratedly repeated for survival's sake.

It was, however, not only a crisis in governance and some extortionate Zimbabweans that wrought socioeconomic suffering on the population. Some would argue that terroristic international interference which turned the country into a pariah state, also contributed. Given Zimbabwe's pariah status from 1999 onwards, the ZANU-PF government embarked on a defensive foreign policy in order to counter the country's ostracization and so remain in power. Apart from seeking to counter its ostracization by the West, what Lere Amusan terms the ZANU-PF government's politics of reciprocity mainly sought to divide the United Nations' Security Council. In a chapter that analyzes Zimbabwe's foreign policy during the crisis, Amusan reveals how, snubbed by the West, in a move that served as a litmus test to 21st-century international politics, the Zimbabwean government strategically looked East towards Asia and specifically China for recognition and investment. As Amusan explains, by so doing, the ZANU-PF government's intention was so that China's investment forays into the country would asphyxiate the West's anti-Zimbabwe posture, while strong ties with President Mbeki ensured South Africa's geostrategic location and membership in the African Union (AU) ruled out aggressive action against what the West perceived as an illegal government. Conversely, the solidarity clause in the AU's Constitutive Act also warranted that the organization stood by the country in the event of any acts of aggression. Assured of its international and continental alliances, the Harare government continued to enjoy the patronage of some AU and other trans-Atlantic states right through the crisis. That accomplished, the ZANU-PF government thereafter turned its attention to securing its political survival on the domestic front.

On the domestic front, as hyperinflation and socioeconomic instability reached terrifying levels, the post-June 2008 ZANU-PF government initially sought its political and governance survival by unleashing "degrees of violence"[9] on its political main political rivals, the MDC formations. But when that did not improve neither its international image or the economic situation, it strategically settled for a negotiated GNU. For the MDC formations, aside from the IG possibly solving the crisis, the GNU was, strategically for them, an opportunity to savor governmental power that had thus far somehow eluded them—even if it meant sharing it. At the stroke of a pen, it appeared all involved would have what they wanted. It was, however, not to be.

In a chapter that draws parallels between the GNU and the traditional processes of a Shona marriage, Sibanda and Masaka reveal how the GNU instead laid the foundation of an uncertain political future for both the MDC formations and the country. This especially since the power-sharing deal conferred significant governmental control to both Mugabe and ZANU-PF by way of the former remaining president and the governance deal being a mediated negotiation rather than an outright electoral victory. In this respect, the two argue that the GPA legitimatized a political process that somehow negated democratic processes of electing governments into power. Severally considered, therefore, the duo of Sibanda and Masaka conclude that the eventual winners of the Inclusive Government (IG) arrangement were Mugabe and the ZANU-PF party and not the ill–fated MDC formations. Despite this, however, the two contributors assent that GNU had its significant successes much as it had its challenges.

## *PART 3: Crisis Watershed—Retreat or Surrender*

Post-GNU, in 2013 the ZANU-PF party electorally obtained the sole mandate to govern Zimbabwe. After that, though the country did not decline to pre-2009 socioeconomic and political crisis levels, Zimbabwe was again gripped by challenges that paradoxically stemmed from some of the solutions that the GNU had implemented as solutions to the crisis' liquidity crunch. Primary among them, the introduction in 2009 of a multi-currency system as legal tender in the absence of vibrant export receipts was soon fueling "the already tight liquidity conditions in Zimbabwe" (Dlamini & Mbira, 2017, p.213). Secondly, the rampant corruption within the socioeconomic fabric and leadership that largely paid lip–service to eradicate it, and yet was occasionally implicated in it, worsened Zimbabwe's economic performance.

In addition to the above, nonagenarian Mugabe's apparent reluctance to either groom a successor or hand over power to a younger and more capable woman or man spelled a leadership crisis for Zimbabwe. The result was divisive factionalism and succession intrigue within the ZANU-PF party. The premise of Part 3 is such that towards the end of 2017, with the removal of President Mugabe and installation of Emmerson D. Mnangagwa, the Zimbabwean socio–economic and political crisis could be described as close to a watershed—one that would see it either abate or exacerbate after Zimbabwe's elections on July 30, 2018—leading to either the glorification or final admission and political surrender of those in power to the crisis.

Loomba (2005, p.173) writing about a different context notes that, "the 'nation' itself is a ground of dispute and debate, a site for competing imaginings of different ideological and political interests." Often, when such disputes and debates are not effectively managed and contained, it results in the "competing imaginings of different ideological and political interests" grouping themselves into numerous factions. Factionalism has been synonymous with Zimbabwe's political parties since the formation of its first black nationalist party in the late 1950s. In a chapter that traces factionalism in Zimbabwe's body politic from the country's preindependence, but mostly to its post-independence era, C. Luthuli Mhlahlo argues that factional fighting, particularly in the years 2008 and 2013–2017 coupled with the country's liquidity crunch eventually became the fuel at the epicenter of Zimbabwe's deadly socioeconomic and political decline. He concludes that unless checked, the two remain the country's biggest challenge and threat to the country's recovery and survival.

Crisis by its nature has a sociological impact that, often culminates in some form of artistic and satirical response. In the second installment of Part 3, C.Luthuli argues that the various political and socioeconomic challenges that emanated from the Zimbabwean crisis, particularly during 2007–2009 provoked Zimbabweans' sociological imaginations both within and without the country's borders to both artistically and satirically respond to the goings–on in the country. He demonstrates how using electronic and digital media, Zimbabweans creatively produced images that expressed their perceptions, emotions, and attitudes towards some of the instigators, actors and drivers of events that were happening in the country. In the days before the advent of WhatsApp©Twitter© and Instagram©, these creative, but critical images were often emailed as attachments to family, friends, relatives, and fellow countrymen who in turn then forwarded and shared them with others far removed from their initial recipients. This ensured that such forwarded emails had a wider audience and so spread what C. Luthuli Mhlahlo calls: "ZForwards" from and about crisis-ridden Zimbabwe. In the absence of a critical framework within which to critically analyze and evaluate ZForwards, C. Luthuli deploys Irele's (1971) sociohistorical perspective to analyze the ZForwards selected.

The adage goes that: "Behind every successful man is a woman." In a chapter that demonstrates that while this was to some extent true of Zimbabwe's former President Robert Gabriel Mugabe, it paradoxically also was not. C. Luthuli Mhlahlo argues that so too were Mugabe's leader identity—in particular his age, Africanist views and African modernity. At which point C. L. Mhlahlo then paradoxically also counter-argues that while these factors might initially have been at the forefront of Mugabe's rise and popularity as prime minister of newly independent Zimbabwe, by 2017 they could equally be said to have eventually contributed to his presidential demise. That is especially considering the role of Mugabe's second wife Grace Mugabe, Mugabe's increasingly radical Africanization agenda, his much-advanced age, and the African modernity he had cultivated amongst most urbanite Zimbabweans through the provision of a robust education system.

Events in Zimbabwe from 14–21 November 2017 left many asking whether what had happened was a coup, a popular rebellion, or a constitutional change of power. In a chapter that traces the events of what has now become one of Zimbabwe's most memorable week, C. Luthuli juxtaposes, compares,and contrasts the events of that memorable week against elements of what over the years has defined and characterized coup d'états, popular rebellions, and, lastly, constitutional changes of power. At which point he concludes that what transpired over that week can best be described as a coup that was but paradoxically was not.

## *PART 4: Beyond Crisis: Walking and Working Away from a Pariah Status*

Human beings cannot change the past. The best they can do is learn from it and be guided by what it has taught them in order to make the future better. Post Mugabe's presidency and proceeding into the 21st century, what visions light the Zimbabwe's path? Is it to determinedly march blindly forward, stagger and grope in the dark? Or alternatively, will it be to show that it has learned from its torrid past, assumed responsibility for it, and strategically chart its course into the future? In this last segment of the volume, Fortune Sibanda, Dennis Masaka, C. Luthuli Mhlahlo, and Munamato Chemhuru share their ideas on how best Zimbabwe can learn from its crisis experience and chart its way forward from its present sociopolitical and economic condition. They suggest resonant ways and paths Zimbabwe might consider using to both walk and work away from the pariah status of a crisis–ridden nation–state that has been bestowed upon it over the last twenty years.

Many social, political, and economic formations the world over consciously or unconsciously aspire to and cherish modern liberal democratic principles such as majority rule and good social governance. In a chapter that reimagines Zimbabwe's governance beyond the July 30, 2018 elections, Munamato Chemhuru suggests that if ever democracy, good governance, peace, and development are to be achieved in Zimbabwe, and indeed Africa, there is the need to revisit the sociopolitical and economic structures of traditional Zimbabwean and African societies, rather than continuing to rely on borrowed liberal democratic principles which are incompatible to the country's sociopolitical culture. Difficult as consensus might be to achieve in any form of democracy, Chemhuru develops his thesis on the premise that there is some good in both African and Zimbabwe's traditional societies which have since the advent of colonialism, been superficially portrayed as democratically inept. In Chemhuru's opinion, all that is required is an analysis of the both the continent and country's traditional systems of governance and the adoption of what is acceptable within them. Chemhuru's research and analysis of some of them leads to the conclusion that a non-party consensual democracy is a *sine qua non*-option for Zimbabwe if a semblance of Zimbabwean appropriate democracy, good governance, and development are to be achieved beyond the country's 2018 elections.

In a chapter that partly speaks to Chemhuru's, C. Luthuli Mhlahlo highlights the need for Zimbabwe to, among others, seriously consider its traditional values and indigenous knowledge systems in its search for socio-economic recovery, national healing, development, and growth. For instance, because of the political violence that accompanied the period 1999–2009, C. L. Mhlahlo urges that the country's Organ of National Healing and Reconciliation be revived and recommends that some form of traditionally acceptable atonement be made to both victims and their survivors. Similarly, considering what he perceives to have been a deviation from Nehanda's principles on Chimurenga, C. L. Mhlahlo suggests that white commercial farmers be adequately compensated for the loss of their personal belongings such as houses and their contents which were looted during the land reappropriation exercise. In the political sphere, C. L. Mhlahlo calls to an end to partisan bickering and insults by all political parties and their engagement in the participatory governance of Zimbabwe. In pursuit of this, he proposes the setting up of a strategic government relations initiative if lost trust, communication, reconstruction, stability, development and growth are to be achieved and sustained. Failure to which socioeconomic and political challenges will reemerge in future and continue to plague the country.

Due to the rampant corruption and moral decay that have bedeviled and inculcated themselves in most Zimbabweans during the crisis, conducting ethical and sustainable business practices remains a challenge for most Zimbabwean persons and businesses. That is mainly because the country's drawn out crisis gave rise to a plethora and culture of immoral business practices as extortionate businesses took advantage of the unaccountability and near lack of legal and moral sanctions in the economy. From Aristotle's perspective of moral virtue, Dennis Masaka philosophically reflects on the challenges Zimbabwe's business sector has had to face during the crisis. He argues that because the crisis led and ingrained unethical business conduct, there is a dire need for the reintroduction of ethical business practices. Therefore, if Zimbabwe's business climate is to resuscitate and stabilize, issues around customer service, honest dealings, marketing, fair labor practices, transparency, accountability, social responsibility, and sustainability rigorous ethical conduct must again be revived and prioritized by all entrepreneurial players. In this vein, Masaka calls for virtue ethics as a panacea to Zimbabwe's malpractices in business if the country is to regain credibility and goodwill moving forward.

Let those with ears hear, eyes see, hearts feel, minds think and re–imagine a reconstructed and prosperous Zimbabwe. Only time will tell.

## Notes

1. Affiliation: Department of Culture, Communication & Media, University College London, & Comecinc Communications and Strategic Solutions Services Incorporated.
2. 2007, New York: Metropolitan Books.
3. Defined as "the concept you develop about yourself that evolves over the course of your life" (see https://study.com/academy/lesson/what-is-personal-identity-definition-philosophy-development.html)
4. Philosophically defined as "the sum of how others view you as a person., your leadership behaviours, skills and willingness to work with others and the impact of all your behaviors as judged by others." (vivoteam.com, 2017, np). See vivoteam.com/2017/8/16/leader-identity/identity-definition-philosophy-development.html
5. Reported in Shona oral tradition and the mythological *Nehanda* (1994) by Yvonne Vera.
6. For example, those of Cuba, former East Germany, and the USSR during the 1980s.
7. Not to be confused with Charles Darwin's process of natural selection.
8. A period during the early 1800s when generals of the Zulu king Shakadefected from him with their tribes and trekked north into what are now Zambia, Zimbabwe, Mozambique and Malawi.
9. Part of a boastful quote attributed to President Mugabe towards the rerun of the June 2008 Presidentialelection run-off elections. See https://www.thezimbabwean.co/2008/05/qwe-have-degrees-in-violenceq/ for more details.

## References

Armah, A.K. (1968). *The Beautiful Ones Are Not Yet Born*. Boston: Houghton Mifflin Harcourt.

Bond, P. (2001). Radical rhetoric and the working class during Zimbabwean nationalism's dying days. In B. Raftopoulos & L. Sachikonye (Eds.), *Striking back: The labour movement and the post-colonial state in Zimbabwe 1980–2000*. Harare: Weaver Press.

Bond, P., & Mandinyanya, M. (2002). *Zimbabwe's plunge, exhausted nationalism, neoliberalism and the search for social justice*. Harare: Weaver Press.

Chikwava, B. (2009). *Harare North*. London: Jonathan Cape.

Codling, R. (2012). Zimbabwe's lost decade by Lloyd Sachikonye. *National European Literary Scene Examiner*, June issue.

Conversations with Writers. (2009). An Interview with Petina Gappah. Retrieved 2018, June 30, 2018, from http://www.pambazuka.org/governance/interview-petina-gappah

Crisis. (n.d.). Retrieved August 4, 2018, from https://www.merriam-webster.com/dictionary/crisis.

Dlamini, B., & Mbira, L. (2017). The current Zimbabwean liquidity crisis: A review of its precipitates. *Journal of Economics and Behavioural Studies*, *9*, 3, July, 212–219.

Gappah, P. (2009). *An Elegy for Easterly*. London: Faber & Faber.

Hammar, A., & Raftopoulos, B. (2003). Zimbabwe's unfinished business: Rethinking land, state, and nation. In A. Hammar, B. Raftopoulos, & S. Jensen (Eds.), *Zimbabwe's unfinished business: Rethinking land, state, and nation in the context of crisis*. Harare: Weaver Press.

Huntington, S. P. (1968). *Political order in changing societies*. New Haven & London: Yale University Press.

*The labour movement and the post-colonial state in Zimbabwe 1980–2000*. Harare: Weaver Press.

Loomba, A. (2005). *Colonialism/postcolonialism: The new critical idiom* (2nd ed.). New York: Routledge.

Mahoso, T. (2013). Zim currency story will not go away. (22–28 December). *The Sunday Mail In–depth*, Opinion, p. D2.

Mahoso, T. (2014). Pitfalls of using foreign currency. (5–11 January). *The Sunday Mail In–depth*, Opinion, p. D2.

Marechera, D. (1978). *House of Hunger*. London: Heinemann African Writers Series.

Murithi, T., & Mawadza, A. (Eds.). (2011). *Zimbabwe in transition: A view from within*. South Africa: Fanele/Jacana Media and The Institute for Justice and Reconciliation.

Raftopoulos, B., & Mlambo, A. (Eds.). (2009). *Becoming Zimbabwe: A History from Pre–colonial Period to* 2008. Harare: Weaver Press.

Sachikonye, L. (2010). *Zimbabwe's lost decade: Politics, development and society*. Harare: Weaver Press.

Sadomba, Z.W. (2011). *War veterans in Zimbabwe's revolution challenging neo-colonialism &settler &international capital*. Harare: Weaver Press.

Scoones, I., Marongwe, N., Mavedzenge, B., Mahenehene, J., Murimbarimba, F., & Sukume, C. (2010). *Zimbabwe's land reform: Myths and realities*. London: James Currey.

Tendi, B. (2010). Making history in Mugabe's Zimbabwe: Politics intellectuals & media. Nationalisms Across the Globe.

# *Part 1: Causing Crisis*

# 1 Nehanda's Order and the Existentialist Transcendence of Despair

C. Luthuli Mhlahlo[1]

The spirituality of Zimbabwe's land is central to understanding the country's past, present and, indeed, future. In this chapter, I begin with a historical overview of how the country's black inhabitants lost possession of it. After which I posit that this dispossession of land not only caused generational despair among most black Zimbabweans, but it also culminated in a spiritual loss of identity. A spiritual loss of identity that during the country's land reappropriation resulted in both an existential and a kind of existentialist transcendence when some black Zimbabweans transgressed the spirit medium Nehanda's principled order regarding *chimurenga* or struggle for liberation and white settlers' moveable personal possessions. The result of that violation I conjecture was not only *kufuratirwanevadzimu*, a kind of ancestral abandonment of the country and its people, but also an international one, as Zimbabweans were left to battle the effects of sanctions and ostracization, alone. The result of which Zimbabwe hurtled into and became entrenched in a socioeconomic and political depression that, for over twenty years now, has forced some Zimbabweans into further existential and existentialist-type survival acts.

## Land Occupation, Mbuya Nehanda's Order and Chimurenga

The 1890s white occupation of vast tracts of land of what is modern-day Zimbabwe culminated in the deep despair of its black inhabitants. This is because, since precolonial times, black Zimbabweans, especially the Shona have held strong traditional beliefs about the sacrosanct relationship between themselves, their ancestors, their identity as a people and the land. As Vambe

(2004) explains, to the Shona, "The ownership of (...) land also presupposed a stable identity. Loss of land signalled loss of identity" (p.26). Chivaura succinctly and emphatically illustrates this relationship thus, "We cannot live our lives as Africans without control of our land as a God-given heritage (......) the beauty of being African is inseparable from our land from our land" (2012, p.14). In October 1890, therefore, when members of Cecil John Rhodes' Pioneer Column who had initially entered the country in July gradually began occupying parts of Mashonaland in search of gold, anguish set in amongst the blacks. It intensified as additional whites arrived to occupy more land in Mashonaland.

The misery that till 1892 had been the Shonas' soon became that of the Ndebele. In November 1893, war broke out between white occupiers and the Ndebele over the latter's raids into Mashonaland. Within a short time, the white occupiers' superior weaponry had defeated the Ndebele. Matabeleland's more favourable land and cattle were distributed amongst those who had financed, volunteered and participated in what is now known as the Ndebele's War of Dispossession. Alienated from their land, the Ndebele joined the Shona in their deep resentment of the white arrivals and sought to dislodge them at the earliest possible opportunity. Such an opportunity arose in 1896.

White occupiers' discovery that both Mashonaland and Matabeleland did not contain as much gold as they had initially anticipated had resulted in them turning their attention to agriculture. To ensure a steady supply of cheap labour for these prospectors-cum-farmers, Cecil John Rhodes British South Africa Company (BSAC) imposed head, hut, cattle and even wife taxes on both the Shona and Ndebele (Magirosa, 2012, p.13). This introduction to and incorporation of the Shona and Ndebele into a monetary system thus far alien to them both intended to either force them to work for the occupiers or sell whatever livestock they had left. Most were forced to work in order to meet their tax obligations resentfully. The late Solomon Mutsvairo's novel, *Feso* (1957), imagines and articulates the Shona people's 1896 suffering and supplication in an ode. In it, they lament their ordeal since the arrival of white occupiers. An old man bemoans that:

> Today the wealth of the land has been taken/The top-dogs, the kindred of *Pfumojena* (whites), share the spoils./Today they are eating the fat of the land,/ And we are reduced to eating the pus of our wounds./Today they are as fat as fat pigs./And we are lean as diseased dogs./Today they live in willful freedom/And we are gagged, strangled with bindings. (Mutsvairo, 1957, p.66)

The Shona and Ndebele's despair finally came to a head when in addition to losing their land, livestock and resentfully providing labor, they were befallen by natural disasters.

In early 1896, drought and an outbreak of the contagious cattle disease, rinderpest, befell the land. To its ancestor-venerating black inhabitants, the two occurrences were interpreted to be signs that their *vadzimu* or ancestors were displeased with the white occupiers' presence. To better appreciate their interpretation, an understanding of both the Shona and Ndebele's mediumistic religion is necessary. According to Moyo (1988), amongst:

> The Shona, *Mwari*, [or God] literally 'He who is' or the Ndebele's *uMlimu* is believed to be active in both the everyday lives of people and even in politics. Generally, people communicate with *Mwari* through the *vadzimu* (in Shona), or *amadhlozi* (in isiNdebele). These are deceased ancestors. The *vadzimu* are believed to constitute an invisible community within the community of the living, always around their descendants, caring for them and participating in their joys and sorrows. Spirit mediums communicate with the *vadzimu* on behalf of the people. (p.199)

When, therefore, both drought and an outbreak of rinderpest occurred in the same year, both the Shona and Ndebele supplicated to their spirit mediums to invoke their ancestors and enquire from them about the catastrophes. Charwe Nyakasikana, a spirit medium, emerged as one of their spiritual guides.[2]

From May 1896, Charwe Nyakasikana directed the people of northern and central Mashonaland to take up arms and fight the white occupiers off the land. At the beginning of what was to be known as the First *Chimurenga*, it is reported that Nyakasikana stringently ordered the fighters not to take the personal possessions of the white occupiers. Both Zimbabwean oral history and literature attest to this fact. For instance, world acclaimed Zimbabwean novelist, the late Yvonne Vera in her historical and yet mythologized novel *Nehanda* (1993) imagined and literarily documents Nehanda's order thus:

> Do not take anything that belongs to the stranger (…) Take only guns. If you touch anything else that belongs to him, even the spirits shall be offended. *The spirits will abandon you for such a travesty.* Take only the things that will also protect you, not the things that will destroy you. *The stranger can only bring ruin and evil among us. Do not covet anything of his* (…) *It is the envying eye that will destroy us, that will change us entirely* [my emphasis]. (pp.61, 66, 79)

By October 1897, both the Shona and Ndebele had been defeated by the white occupiers' superior weaponry and "the arrival in Bulawayo of imperial soldiers under the command of General Sir Fredrick Carrington" (Baxter, 2011: np). Some Ndebele fled to the spiritual Matopo Hills until Cecil John Rhodes "initiated overtures to the amaNdebele leadership, and (…) negotiate[d] a peace that saw the end of hostilities and the acceptance of the amaNdebele of the inevitable" (Baxter, 2011: np). The price of peace for the Ndebele was not only the further loss of more cattle to the settlers but also more arable land. Much to their despair, many were driven into arid reserves of Gwaai and Shangani; others became the now settlers' servants.

In the meantime, the Shona's uprising had continued. However, with the subjugation of the Ndebele, the colonial forces' wrath could now be concentrated on the Shona. Those caught hiding in caves were reportedly bombed while still inside (Sweetman, 1984). Nehanda and Kaguvi, the spiritual leaders of the revolt, were eventually captured, tried and subsequently hanged in 1898. Nehanda's last words were reportedly: "my bones shall rise again'" (as cited in Matshobana, 2003, 1). Chiwome (2002, p.180) and Bull-Christiansen (2005, p.204) inform how Mbuya Nehanda and her dying words later became the inspiration for the country's Second *Chimurenga* for liberation. For now, however, white settlerism intensified.

Following the Shona's military conquest, the country's white population grew. In 1930, this necessitated the now self-governing colony of Southern Rhodesia to enact the Land Apportionment Act. Under its provisions, most of the country's arable land was allotted for white occupation and settlement. Blacks could not purchase land outside their allotted area and neither could they permanently reside in the colony's emerging urban towns and cities. Blacks' predicament and despair were, however, far from over.

After World War II, Southern Rhodesia experienced an influx of immigrants from Europe. Their arrival further increased the demand for land. In response, the government passed the Land Husbandry Act of 1957. Enactment of the Act "saw the systematic removal of blacks from land earmarked for white occupation and their concentration into native reserves" (Baxter, 2011, np). Such further losses of ancestral lands widened the hiatus between blacks and their land. The response of some nationalist blacks was to seek civil and political redress. However, while in Malawi and Zambia, "the usual strategy of civil unrest [...] had brought freedom" (Baxter, 2011, np) when in November 1965 the Prime Minister of the then Southern Rhodesia declared the country's unilateral independence, civil and political agitation had failed. Resorting to armed struggle remained the only option.

On April 28, 1966, seven gallant black freedom fighters engaged and fought Rhodesian soldiers in the then Sinoa[3] area. Because they were outnumbered and outgunned, the seven were swiftly defeated and killed in what is now famously known as the Battle of Chinhoyi. The bones of Nehanda had risen. The battle marked the beginning of black Zimbabweans' Second *Chimurenga* against colonial rule and oppression. As with the First *Chimurenga*, the Second *Chimurenga*'s main objectives were primarily to liberate blacks from white colonial rule and reclaim the land for the country's black masses. Akin to Fanon (1967) writing in a different context, the country's black nationalists seemed to have concluded that, "only violence can truly free the native from his inferiority complex, his despair and inaction [as it] is the key to freedom, self-identity and self-respect" (p.74). Thus in support of the war effort, from 1967 onwards, black nationalists such as the late Josiah Magama Tongogara of the Zimbabwe African National Union (ZANU) and its military wing the Zimbabwe African National Liberation Army (ZANLA) left the country for military training in communist China. Others like the late Nikita Mangena of the Zimbabwe African People's Union (ZAPU) and its military-wing the Zimbabwe People's Revolutionary Army (ZIPRA) left for military training in Russia. In the meantime, some Black Nationalist leaders such as Joshua Nkomo, Ndabaningi Sithole and Robert Mugabe were arrested and imprisoned and political parties banned.

A protracted war of liberation waged by those of the country's black women and men who sought to restore the land to the black majority followed. Military and refugee bases were initially established in Zambia to receive those who were trekking out of the country to join the liberation struggle. However, when Mozambique attained independence from Portuguese rule on 25 June 1975, this opened an eastern warfront. More military and refugee bases were established in that country and the Second *Chimurenga* gained momentum.

The struggle against the white supremacist Rhodesian government intensified. As it did so, the memory and spirit of the eponymous heroine Nehanda and *Chimurenga* served as an inspiration and guide. Vambe (2002) explains how, to the freedom fighters, "The spiritual world of ancestors [......] operate[d] as a cultural sieve for retrieving cultural memory [......and] energize[d] opposition to colonialism" (p.130) in search of its demise. By 1979, with the war's intensification and its cost's escalation on the one hand and international sanctions strain on the Rhodesian economy on the other, the Rhodesian government was forced to call a ceasefire to negotiate peace. The culmination was the Lancaster House Agreement.

## *Zimbabwe's Land Issue, ESAP and the Existentialist Transcendence of Despair*

The first objective of the Second *Chimurenga* was finally achieved on 18 April 1980 when Zimbabwe finally attained political independence. The second—the return of the country's land to its black inhabitants—would, however, not be as easy. In adherence to a constitutional clause of the Lancaster House Agreement, the new Zimbabwean government could only acquire the country's white-owned farmland on condition of a "willing buyer, willing seller". In this regard, it could only acquire land based on an individual white landowner's willingness to sell it at a price deemed appropriate for it and the black government's willingness to buy the said land, at its stipulated price. In order to enable the new government to buy white-owned land, the British government pledged to finance the country's land redistribution program. Over time, however, changes in British governments between 1980 and 1999, ever-increasing farmland prices, maladministration, financial mismanagement and corruption in the Robert Mugabe–led government reportedly ensured that the return of black Zimbabweans' ancestral land remained elusive. Consequently, most descendants of those who had been dispossessed of the land remained in the reserves and Tribal Trust Lands (TTLs) allocated to them after 1897, 1931 and 1957. For these, despair over the land continued to fester.

From 1980, the Zimbabwean government embarked on a socialist economic model to governance and development. This policy saw the new black government spend most of the country's revenue on social services such as free primary education and healthcare, the building of schools, clinics, hospitals and bridges. The public service created employment and absorbed the unemployed. The government's salaries bill more than doubled. Massive expenditure on social services at the expense of income-generating projects resulted in the stagnation and eventual contraction of the country's economic growth. By 1990, the country was failing to service its external debt. In response, the country's main creditors, the World Bank (WB) and International Monetary Fund (IMF) advised the Zimbabwean government to implement an Economic Structural Adjustment Program (ESAP). The projection was that such a program would reform and redress the problem of the country's contracting economy. Accordingly, the country's economy was liberalized. This required the streamlining of companies to make them more efficient and competitive.

Between 1991 and 1995, the Zimbabwean government's implementation of ESAP saw the retrenchment of thousands of employees from both the country's public and private sectors. Some of the governments' public enterprises were restructured or privatized to make them more profitoriented and less of mere social services.Of the employees laid off, most were given early retirement incentives and packages to enable them to either set up their own businesses or permanently retire. Many opted to retire to their rural homes in the reserves and TTLs work, the now-exhausted land long cultivated by their forefathers since the 1930s.

Post-Zimbabwe's independence, the land issue, once the backdrop of the country's two *Chimurengas*, had intermittently surfaced and submerged in the psyche of older and more historically conscious Zimbabweans. This had exacerbated such Zimbabweans' despair over land. More so, when reminiscent of the late 1890s, during most of the early and late 1990s, the country suffered bouts intermittent and severe drought—to Zimbabwean traditionalists long considered a harbinger of the ancestors' displeasure but the result of the El Nino effect to westerners and modernists. The yet unresolved land issue, coupled with joblessness and drought, worsened and deepened the despair of those affected.

After independence, freedom fighters of Zimbabwe's nationalist armies of the ZANLA and ZIPRA who had waged war against colonial oppression under the banners of ZANU and ZAPU were demobilized. Those who were not co-opted into the country's unified army were given pensions ranging from Z$150 to Z$400 to enable them to reintegrate into society and rebuild their lives. Seventeen years later, in 1997, South Africa's first black president, Nelson Mandela, allegedly awarded former cadres of the African National Congress' military wing *Umkhonto weSizwe* (Spear of the Nation) with demobilization packages of ZAR50,000 each. In what can be seen as more than just an existential response, Zimbabwe's veterans across the Limpopo demanded they also be awarded gratuities of Z$50,000. In my view, their demand for monetary compensation for fighting in the Second *Chimurenga* went beyond the existential, was past the mercenary and closer to the existentialist.

Existentialism emerged in Europe after the devastation of World War II in 1946. Consequent to people's experience of war, their belief systems had been left dehumanized. Religion no longer held the luster it once had. The war's destruction had undermined people's confidence in religious faith and God. It is, therefore, the despair of postwar Europe; a factor that is common to all existentialists, that led to the establishment of existentialism as a philosophy. Lexically and concisely defined, therefore, the term "existentialism" is a "twentieth-century philosophy emphasizing the active participation of the will rather than reason in confronting the problems of a non-moral or absurd universe" (Funk and Wagnalls, 1997). To existentialists, a human being is the total of one's actions and nothing else. This is because to them, there is no God and so "we must accept individual responsibility for our own becoming" (Bigelow, 1961, p.9). As such, humans are in their view "self-interpreting animals" (Taylor, 1985, p.45) where the interpretation of what one is, "is constitutive of the interpreter" (Taylor, 1985, p.45) and no other external power. In the light of what the Second *Chimurenga* had spiritually signified and the nature of some war veterans' and later, liberation war restrictees and collaborators' demands in the late 1990s as well as into the 2000s and most recently in 2016[4]; I am of the view that the war veterans, war restrictees and collaborators' financial demands can be read as an existentialist-like attempt at transcending despair. To understand the thrust of this argument, the spiritual link between Shona cosmology and the modern day nation-state of Zimbabwe is vital.

The 1966 Battle of Chinhoyi was and still is perceived as an extension of the First Chimurenga. This is such that Zimbabwe's freedom fighters and later liberation war veterans had both, during and after the Second *Chimurenga* been seen and considered the fulfilment of Nehanda's declaration that: "my bones shall rise." This is especially because it was a pronouncement that Zimbabwean traditionalists and nationalists had been interpreted to mean that the people of the country would in future again rise and fight to liberate their land. Consequently, when other black sons and daughters of the then colonially oppressed country had streamed into Mozambique, Zambia and beyond, in search of military training, they had been seen to signify Nehanda's "bones rising" to liberate the land. Fighting for Zimbabwe thus came to be regarded as a spiritual calling—the rising of Nehanda's spirit and bones.

In 1997, however, the Zimbabwe National Liberation War Veterans Association (ZNLWVA) formed in 1989 by some of ZANU-PF's 35 000 men and women veterans of the Second *Chimurenga* came under the leadership of the now late Dr. Chenjerai Hunzwi. Under his guidance, the ZNLWVA was soon incredulously agitating for hefty gratuities from the government for its members' participation in the country's war of liberation. The once spiritual role and function of war veterans as Nehanda's bones risen to liberate Zimbabwe reduced to the existential. From revered spiritual "bones" of Mbuya Nehanda, they lowered their spiritual contribution and themselves. Aside from the fact that Zimbabwe's economy was undergoing economic structural adjustment, the war veterans' request had existentialist hues.

Until *UmkhontoweSizwe* veterans' alleged receipt of monetary gratuities, never had it been fathomed that African freedom fighters could receive a gratuity for their participation in the struggle against colonial oppression. I am of the opinion that, by demanding to be compensated for liberating the country the perceived 'spiritual agents' of the ancestors were renouncing this belief and their perception as such and like common mercenaries reducing themselves to guns for hire. Over time, consequent to the display of such existential and existentialist acts and tendencies, when "the failure of ESAP in the 1990s brought with it a descent into authoritarian politics" (Raftopoulos, 2009, p.231), this was to have the backing of the self-same war veterans.

The year 1997 was economically a memorable year for Zimbabwe. The country's agro-based economy was boosted by a generous rainy season, and most regions of the country anticipated bumper harvests. This as it was, however, the economy generally had not been performing well since the early 1990s. The country's adoption of ESAP had resulted in severe austerity and massive retrenchments. The Zimbabwe Dollar, at one time stronger than the British Pound after independence, had since been steadily weakening and eroding the purchasing power of most Zimbabweans. Besides, while the South African economy could afford to make huge payouts to its relatively few liberation struggle cadres, Zimbabwe's could ill-afford to pay its estimated 35 000 war veterans. This was especially also considering the Zimbabwe government's unbudgeted involvement in the Democratic Republic of Congo's civil war that was then engaged in was rapidly exhausting the country's treasury. Given this context, the gratuities the ZNLWVA were demanding were too high and, more importantly, had also not been budgeted. Despite all of the above, however, the then hefty gratuities of Z$50 000 each were paid to members of ZNLWVA.

Consequently, on what has now infamously become known as Black Friday, the country's currency drastically depreciated against major world currencies. The payment of unbudgeted gratuities to war veterans had a knock-on effect on the whole Zimbabwean economy. The government's selling of the country's foreign currency reserves and its borrowing from domestic and foreign markets in order to raise enough money for members of ZNLWVA resulted in lowered domestic and foreign investor confidence. The depreciation of the country's currency against the world's major currencies made importation expensive. Fuel, electricity and raw materials, all essential to both the manufacturing and domestic sectors, began to dwindle and became increasingly difficult to restock.

Inflation is crudely defined as too much money chasing too few goods. The price of commodities steadily rose and subsequently inflation with them. Exacerbating the rise in inflation was the increased availability of money in the country—the war veterans' gratuities that sought to purchase steadily fewer goods. By 1999, Zimbabwe's steadily rising inflation had eroded both the war veterans' once immense gratuities and the retrenchment packages of those who had been retrenched and turned to peasant farming. Zimbabwe's urban dwellers, peasantry and war veterans were steadily sliding into socio-economic hardship and despair.

During Zimbabwe's liberation struggle, freedom fighters had at times held *pungwes* or night vigils with the peasantry. The purpose of such vigils was often for the latter's politicization and indoctrination about the liberation struggle. During such vigils, the then freedomfighters talked about reclaiming the land of Zimbabwe and returning it to the people once the war was over and the country won. However, by the dawn of this millennium and 20 years since the end of the Second *Chimurenga*, the land was still not returned. The country's rising economic hardships revived memories of the second primary objective of Zimbabwe's liberation struggle, the reappropriation of the land.

Although the sunset clause of the Lancaster House constitution that had curtailed the government's acquisition of farmland from white farmers had expired in 1990, by 1999, a decade later, little progress had been made towards land acquisition and resettlement. Since the 1980s, both the government and some black Zimbabweans had purchased some farmland for purposes of resettlement. Of the land acquired by the government, some of it had reportedly been leased out on 99-year leases to politically connected individuals or handed over to cooperatives.

Regarding the latter, some had reportedly been successful and others unsuccessful cooperative ventures. On the whole, however, by 1999 most of the country's fertile farmland was still white-owned. Consequently, nearly 20 years after political independence, though the land issue had been at the heart of the liberation struggle, the ZANU-PF government still had not comprehensively and adequately addressed it. The impact of what appeared to be government's slow response or unwillingness to settle the country's land issue was in 2000 responded to by what has infamously become known as Zimbabwe's land invasions and at times land occupations. I however consider and prefer to refer to them as land reappropriations some of which by their existentialist-like defiance of Mbuya Nehanda's order became invasions.

Various books and hypotheses have been raised and written regarding the dynamics behind the reason why peasants and war veterans invaded white-owned farms in 2000.[5] Among these is the argument that the invasions were the result of the emergence in 1999 of the opposition Movement for Democratic Change (MDC) that was allegedly being funded and supported by some white commercial farmers and Western governments. In retaliation against some white farmers and other funders of the MDC therefore, it is thus often perceived that in the face of emerging political opposition, the ruling ZANU-PF party's campaign strategy for the June 2000 elections became that of finally settling of Zimbabwe's land issue. Equally famous has been the notion that the farm occupations were instigation of the ZANU-PF government after its first ever political loss during the February 2000 referendum over a new constitution.[6] On its part, the Zimbabwe government argued that it was the peasants' "hunger for land" that led to the farm occupations.

Of particular interest to this author is Sadomba's 2011 contribution that traces the roots of Zimbabwe's 2000 land revolution "to the 1970s guerrilla war". While I concur with Sadomba (2011) to some extent, in this chapter, I however tacitly question to what extent war veterans' leadership challenged neo-colonialism, settler and international capital when a closer analysis reveals that they instead imbibed these forces' spirit and were unconsciously complicit. This is especially as I am of the opinion that akin to the 1940s post-war Europe, it was some war veterans and Zimbabweans' existential despair over socioeconomic developments in the country's during the later 1990s, the over prolonged resolution of the country's land issue and an existentialist-like greed whose hues were first displayed by some war veterans from 1997 onwards, that can be attributed to the farm occupations which eventually spawned the crisis the country finds itself. It is against this background, therefore, that I fortuitously also answer Sadomba's intriguing question: "what are the people of Africa trying to free themselves from and what are they trying to establish?" which, in my view, was also behind Zimbabwe's crisis. The contribution of war veterans to nation-building or the lack thereof calls for exploration and closer analysis.

D.E Cooper (1999) reveals that in existentialism the individual's starting point is characterized by an 'existential attitude', a sense of disorientation and confusion in the face of an apparently meaningless and absurd world. Zimbabwe at the turn of the millennium was characterized by mounting hyperinflation, rising poverty levels, disgruntlement with the government of the day, persistent drought in some parts of the country and food shortages. It was a state and condition that one can safely assume resulted in an 'existential attitude' comparable to that of European existentialists in the mid-late 1940s. The war veterans had in 1997 already displayed such an existential attitude by bringing their recognition as Mbuya Nehanda's rising bones into disrepute. In the year 2000, the trait now manifested itself among some Zimbabweans in the way they, supported by the country's already existential and existentialist-like war veterans, looted white farmers' personal possessions in transgression of Mbuya Nehanda's earlier order.

During the land reappropriation period, some peasants and war veterans' existential attitude and existentialist transcendence of their despair were, in my view, apparent in the *modusoperandi* some farm invasions assumed. In such instances, a crowd reportedly wielding knobkerries, hoes, axes, adzes and okapis, amongst others, would march to or arrive at a designated farm in lorries, mini-buses and trucks, issue the white farmer a few hours ultimatum to leave with whatever he could take with him. After that, the crowd would later return to ransack and loot the farmhouse of its goods and the farmer's clothing and effects. In some cases, local chiefs, the people's custodians of tradition, " 'the burden bearers for people hence (who) should exhibit selfless and exemplary leadership' " (Minister of Rural Development, Protection and Preservation of National Culture and Heritage, Abednego Ncube as cited by

Ncube, 2017, S6) reportedly took possession of farmhouses and their contents, booty from some of their subjects and some war veterans' resumption of the Second *Chimurenga*—cum—*jambanja* (violent disorderliness)[7]. Those farmers who were found to be still on the premises after the expiry of the ultimatum were in some cases reportedly beaten, chased off the farm empty-handed and in others, even killed.

Although most white farmers were in possession of guns and related weapons, the so-called land invasions never escalated into neither protracted battles nor civil war. Much to some observers incredulity, most affected white farmers instead opted to either leave for their homes in the urban areas or went overseas. Unknown to the new occupants of the farms, the land they had dramatically reappropriated technically already belonged to their relatives via banks within the country. Albeit headquartered in overseas capitals, most local international banks where the majority black population had their money deposited was in essence there for onward loaning to, among others commercial farmers. Over the years, most white farmers had mortgaged their farms and used such loans to develop and make the land productive. Some of it had been invested abroad in real estate, mining, offshore currency accounts, stocks and bonds. As such, when some white commercial farmers "left empty-handed", they paradoxically did, though, in principle, they actually did not. This is because what some of them were left is actually debt free—the land invasions debatably liberated some of them from the debts they owed to various financial institutions .

Such conjectures aside, however, insofar as the Second *Chimurenga* was a continuation of the first, so too was the reappropriation of Zimbabwe's land at the turn of the last century. This is such that, Zimbabwe's former President Mugabe writing on the land reappropriation period in 2001 poignantly and pointedly titled his book: *Inside the Third Chimurenga: our land is our prosperity*. In this respect, all those who looted furniture, domestic appliances and other personal possessions of some white farmers did so in blatant disobedience and violation of the primary principle of *chimurenga* as instructed by Mbuya Nehanda during the First *Chimurenga*.

Sartre (1943:564) observes that "[w]e always have a choice [and in choosing], we define ourselves." By choosing to transgress Mbuya Nehanda's order, I am of the opinion that those who chose to act existentially in order to satiate their material desires in the name of the people of Zimbabwe did so at the people's expense. This especially as I am of the view that by doing so, the choice of such existential–existentialist invaders, as forewarned by Nehanda, alienated black Zimbabweans' from their ancestors and severely compromised what until then had been an intensely spiritual project. It is an intensely spiritual project which Chivaura (2012, p.14) encapsulates well when he writes: "The beauty of being African lies in our existence in harmony with our land and people past, present and future" By choosing to demand and receive hefty gratuities, Zimbabwe's war veterans I will argue sowed the seeds of disharmony between themselves, the ancestors and the land.

They likewise set aside the spirituality of their earlier spiritual self-sacrifice and redefined not only themselves but also the country Zimbabwe's destiny and that of the relationship between the country's black people and their ancestors. In what follows, I demonstrate how because of what I perceive as the existentialist-type actions of some black Zimbabweans, the people's relationship with their ancestors became characterized by a subalternating silence or what the Shona describe as *kufuratirwa nevadzimu. Kufuratirwa nevadzimu* translated means to be given the ancestors' back in a kind of ancestral abandonment. I argue that this ushered in a period during which the country's ancestors left their descendants to their existentialist devices.

To me, what Shona tradition terms *kufuratirwa nevadzimu* is somewhat akin to a literal understanding of Sartre's existentialist notion of 'abandonment'. The difference is however that when existentialists speak of 'abandonment', they "mean to say that God does not exist and that it is necessary to draw the consequences of his absence right to the end" (Sartre, 1989, p.6). To them, such a scenario means "that we ourselves decide our being" (Sartre, 1989, p.8). Conversely, Shona tradition believes that when life is not progressing well in an individual's, a family or community's life, then their ancestors have turned their backs on them and are no longer watching over—abandoned them—because of some offense or oversight committed by their descendants. When this occurs, an individual's, family or community's life becomes plagued by misfortune. So, while occasional hardship can be tolerated, recurrent misfortune as has plagued Zimbabweans for close to 20 years is often considered an indicator that the ancestors have turned their backs on their descendants, hence their hardship, suffering, pain and poverty. In such cases, the ancestors' silence and kind of "abandonment" is a cosmological discontinuance but not necessarily that of their spiritual presence in its varied forms.[8]

Recalling and reflecting on Zimbabwe's socioeconomic and political state from 2001 onwards still fills one with sorrow at a people's increasingly hard existence, bewilderment and despair. As the years progressed, it became glaringly apparent that the government had been overtaken by events as no apparent logistics for an immediately productive land reform program had been fore planned. Although its intervention in the land invasions had seen A1 (small-scale) plots of land and A2 (commercial farms) being given to some members of the general public, the larger farms had been allocated mainly to ruling party cadres, most of whom had a dearth of farming knowledge. This fact, combined with a lack of inputs, capital and the vagaries of weather rendered most allocated land virtually unproductive.The government had, in economic terms, not factored the productivity implication into the matrix.

In those cases where the government provided inputs of seed and diesel to plough with, the existential spirit of some persisted. Some newly resettled black smallholder and commercial farmers reportedly opted to instead sell the inputs on the country's booming black market. Drought in Africa and other parts of the world has traditionally been a harbinger of the cosmos' displeasure, sporadically revisited the country. Subsequently, the redistributed land yielded, if any, minimal raw materials for the country's manufacturing industries. Zimbabwe turned from an exporter of agricultural produce to a net importer of food products and manufactured goods.

The explicit absence of a coherent post-land reform program, some resettled farmers' existential sabotage of agricultural productivity and the withdrawal of lines of credit by most Western financial institutions also severely impacted the commercial farming sector, Zimbabwe's traditional source of exports and, as such, foreign currency. This scenario accelerated the country's economic decline and marked the demise of the industrial sector. By 2005, the number of Zimbabwe's unemployed stood at an estimated 70% and lived below the poverty datum line. Inflation reportedly rose to an estimated 2 million per cent. By the end of 2017, an estimated 1.5 million jobs had been lost.[9] Over the years, the country's socioeconomic scenario led to further existential and existentialist type modes of transcending despair.

*Self-making Amid Nothingness: Virtual and Christian Existentialism*
Another of Sartre's contributions to existentialist thought lies in his analysis of the notion of 'nothingness'. In *Being and Nothingness* (1943/1992) Sartre pronounces human life to be "a 'negation', a void, a nothingness (Sartre, 1992, p.9)." In his view: "If man, as the existentialist sees him, is not definable, it is because, to begin with, he is nothing. He will not be anything until later, and then he will be what he makes of himself" (Sartre, 1989, p.3). It is for this reason that in existentialism existence is self-making in a situation (Sartre, 1992) where one was initially nothing.

Amid rising unemployment, hyperinflation, food shortages and an increasingly worthless currency, some Zimbabweans had by the end of 2007 been reduced to virtually nothing. In a bid to make something of themselves, between 1999 and 2008 an estimated three million Zimbabweans left the country. They spread across the globe in search of opportunities to self-make.

In response to the despairing economic malaise that the country had fallen into, a sizeable percentage of the population migrated to both neighboring and overseas countries in search of employment and business prospects. Among them were teachers, scientists, engineers, lecturers, accountants, technicians, academics, nurses and doctors. For many, the objective was to seek economic refuge.

In search of a better life, some dared perilous situations. Due to financial constraints and a lack of proper travel documentation, some either jumped the border into neighboring South Africa and Botswana in existential hope of what they possibly might become if they made it. The migration of skills resulted in a "brain-drain" that left the country bereft of skilled expertise vital to the developing country's resurgence and future development. Depopulation also reduced the country's market potential and reproduction rate, as mainly young people migrated in the hope of later remitting money home so their families could live.

Sartre expands and makes universal what constitutes 'nothingness' when he writes that: "When we go about the world, we have expectations which are *often* not fulfilled [my emphasis] (Sartre, 1992, 9)." Notably, the word 'often' suggests some people's expectations are at times fulfilled and and at others, not. Because of some Zimbabweans' academic qualifications, business acumen and willingness to work hard at both formal and menial jobs, several managed to become what they aspired to. Apart from securing employment abroad or in a neighboring country, various Zimbabweans, particularly those in the United Kingdom and the United States of America existentially took advantage of the country's weakening currency and purchased houses in some of the country's most affluent low-density suburbs. In 2008, at the height of Zimbabwe's socioeconomic and political crisis, when essentials were scarce, and hyperinflation rendered local currency worthless, it was on those Zimbabweans outside the country's borders that relatives within the country relied on for remittances in cash and kind. It was, however, not all Zimbabwean migrants who were able to do so.

Not all Zimbabweans in neighboring countries and the Diaspora were, however, able to realize their aspirations. Due to their host country's immigration policies and requirements, some were unable to work, while others were underemployed in various menial capacities. A number of them became and remain illegal immigrants in their host countries. Sadly, in some cases, this has forced such immigrants to resort to crime or street begging in order to survive. For most, financial constraints, the shame of failing to accomplish something, the fear of reprisals from the present government on those who fled as opposition party cadres and the perceived instability of the country's current political and economic state, as reported by some independent houses, have made returning to Zimbabwe not an option. Interestingly, it is the reporting of what was and has been happening in Zimbabwe since 2000 by media houses both inside and outside that also gave rise to a different kind of existentialist Zimbabweans—virtual existentialists who sought to transcend a different kind of despair.

Dallas Darling (2008) terms virtual existentialism "the continual absorption of the mass media (such as television, radio, movies, internet, video games, etc.), and then basing your beliefs on and living your life through these electronic existences" (p.1). In 2002, the then parliament of Zimbabwe enacted the Public Order and Security Act (POSA) and the Access to Information and Protection of Privacy Act (AIPPA). Aimed at curtailing civil unrest and the independent media, the two pieces of legislation severely trammeled Zimbabweans' civil liberties and regulated all forms of media activities within the country. Conversely, the result was ultimately not only the regulation but also the suppression of the independent media. This left the state-owned public broadcaster, the Zimbabwe Broadcasting Corporation (ZBC) and its ZTV as the sole sources of news and entertainment. Listening to or watching most of the national broadcaster's content, however, became depressing and unbearable for most primarily due to unbalanced news and the excessiveness of the state's propaganda.

In response to government censorship and its authoritarian control of the country's print and electronic media, some Zimbabweans still within the country's borders resorted to virtual existentialism. Satellite dishes rapidly replaced television aerials as those who could afford it resorted to satellite television for news about what was happening in the country and the rest of the world. Pay per view decoders such as DSTV and free-to-air decoders like Fortec and Wiztech that aired BBC News, CNN, News24 and Al Jazeera news networks at no charge rapidly replaced the ZBC as most urbanites' source of news. At a time TelOne, the country's leading telecommunications provider, had just introduced Asymmetric Digital Subscriber Lines (ADSL) to those with landlines, and who could afford it, the internet became an alternative source of news, electronic communication and entertainment. Since then other pay-per-view decoders such as the recently introduced *Kwese TV* and internet broadband have become available. The escapism offered by the programs of such televisions, radios and the internet became and remains a necessity rather than a luxury. Those who could not afford internet in their homes initially relied on internet cafes or simply tuned their radios to such offshore broadcasts as *Voice of America* (VOA), SW Radio, Studio 7 and Radio Nehanda for alternative news and views.

However, because such news sources were oftentimes sponsored by interests biased against the Zimbabwe government and its Land Reform Program, for the country's virtual existentialists, it soon became a case of exchanging national propaganda for half-truths and misinformation from international media. Also, such virtual existentialism became and remains largely the preserve of those who could and can afford to have satellite television, internet installed or purchase smartphones. Given the state of the country's economy though, this has meant a small percentage of the urban population and even then, the country's erratic power supply at times curtailed the effectiveness of this mode of existentialist self-expression. Despite this, it is to the Zimbabwe government's credit that over the years, it rarely explicitly interfered with citizens' virtual, nor their Christian existentialism.

In 2008, as Zimbabwe's socioeconomic and political crisis deepened, many were thrown into a spiritual quandary. Because of the country's crisis state of affairs, some pondered and questioned if God was indeed still with them. Considering the severity of the socioeconomic hardships the country was experiencing, there are those who lost faith and belief in God. Cases of Satanism and the occult became topical and were reported in the media.[10] It was rumored that in pursuit of wealth, some desperate Zimbabweans were resorting to such dark practices as robbing graves in a bid to become financially successful. Stories of abductions, ritual murders, the eating of human flesh and the rearing life-sapping *tokoloshes*, evil gnomes that supposedly could make their owner wealthy, were similarly reported. Conversely, other Zimbabweans turned to Christian existentialism.

In contrast to Sartre's atheist existentialism, Kierkegaard's Christian existentialism focuses on the relationship between the individual and God. It argues that despite one's doubts, an individual can take a leap of faith and believe that God exists and that He is good. This leap of faith was for Kierkegaard a choice that an individual must make to help him or herdefine his or her life. As with atheist existentialism, Kierkegaard's Christian existentialism does not impose meaning on the individual; instead, the individual makes a choice to take action and make meaning of his or her life. This type of Christian existentialism was arguably behind the rise in anumber of independent churches during the crisis.

Karl Marx (1843/1970) antithetically described religion as "the sigh of the oppressed creature, the heart of a heartless world and the soul of soulless conditions. It is the opium of the people."[11] As Zimbabwe sunk deeper into crisis, some turned to the various churches that seemed to mushroom every day. Largely Pentecostal and charismatic by nature some had such interesting and inspiring names as: Kingdom Prosperity Ministries (KPM),

Authentic Church of God, End Time Message, Hope in Christ Ministries, His Presence International Ministries, United Family International Church (UFIC), Prophetic Healing and Deliverance Ministries (PHD), RMG End Time Message and Goodness and Mercy Ministries. Most were a response to the socioeconomic and political situation in Zimbabwe. In this regard, they were and, although some have fallen by the wayside, they are still led by apostles, prophets, pastors, evangelists, bishops and ministers to name a few who preach the message of overcoming economic struggle and achieving financial prosperity. Prognostication and miracle manifestations became the order of the day. In return for congregants' purchasing anointed water, oil, bangles, T-shirts and "planting seed money", they can "reap and experience breakthrough" in their lives. This is so long as they have faith in God, tithe and take action by participating in an income generating project. As the crisis took on dystopian dimensions of despair, therefore, some Zimbabweans unconsciously supplanted conventional Christianity and traditional spirituality with either atheist or Christian-type existentialism.

Amid the deepening crisis and the rise of new independent churches, religious fervor took root in the most unlikely places—prisons. Bulla reported how Harare Central Prison had become "one religious jungle" as "in a bid to survive the tough prison conditions inmates (had) resorted to different religions" (2017, S1) such as Christianity, Islam, Rastafari and African tradition. In these, the prisons' inmates confessed to having found solace. One inmate explained that, at a time when the crisis had resulted in a frugal diet for prisoners, while "people of other faiths complain that we don't have meat in our diet. But as a Rastafarian, I am not bothered by diet because we are vegetarians" (Bulla, 2017, S1). The prisoner's explanation helps to demonstrate the subjectivity of what constitutes and can be deemed a crisis.

On their part, the more Orthodox and some Pentecostal churches perceiving the country to be in crisis engaged the government and its leadership by embarking on what some construed as unholy liaisons with the State. The amity between some senior representatives of religious institutions' such as the Anglican and Apostolic Churches with the State led to the politicization of such churches. In what perhaps reflected the public's perception of some in Christendom, in his letter to the Editor of *The Chronicle* Hayes Mabweazara from Tshabalala in Bulawayo wrote:

> Interestingly and in fact more painfully, the extended period of indifference to the disintegrating socio-political fabric by the clergy has also been characterized by an upsurge of a coldhearted breed of church ministers whose key agenda has been to forge the interests of evil-doers to perpetuate the status-quo which is benefiting them(…) As they continuously flattered for purposes of self-gain.

In some cases, this drove a wedge between such churches' leadership and their congregants. At times it resulted in fisticuffs within church premises. Factionalism commonly associated with politicians reared in some churches and paradoxically breakaway denominational factions either sought the mediation of the courts or left to start new churches. The blare between spiritual and existential pursuits was, however, not only evident among members of the clergy, but it also appeared among some spirit mediums.

In 2008, Nomatter Tagarira, a self-proclaimed woman witchdoctor and spirit medium, Nomatter Tagarira professed that the ancestors had directed her to a diesel-producing rock. She approached the ZANU-PF government with the claim that she had indeed discovered such a rock. In return for her discovery, Tagarira wanted money and a farm. She reportedly received both from the government. However, when it was later discovered that Tagarira's 'find' was, in fact, a hoax, the spirit medium absconded. This incident exposed not only the existential desperation of Tagarira but also that of the crisis-ridden government of the day.

## *Conclusion*

Knowledge and some understanding of Zimbabwe's precolonial traditions and beliefs regarding the country's land, its people's relations with it and their ancestors is pivotal to an appreciation of the country's past, present and future. This is because it is such aspects of Zimbabwean life that have shaped, and in some respects continue to influence the course of this fascinating and spiritual country past and present. It is in this ambit that it is my view the war veterans' demands and acceptance of gratuities in 1997 not only spiritually sullied their service to Zimbabwe but significantly contributed to the crisis the country finds itself in today. This is primarily because it was an existential and existentialist act that opened the way to similar action amongst some of their contemporaries. As I have posited and attempted to demonstrate here, their disobedience or disregard of Mbuya Nehanda's warning given during the First *Chimurenga*, in my view, subsequently led to the country's ancestors falling silent and turning their backs on their descendants in a kind of abandonment. So, while the reappropriation of Zimbabwe's arable land was in keeping with the goals of *Chimurenga*, the existential and existentialist manner that in some cases accompanied land reappropriation of land compromised the country's future socioeconomic and political development.

Secondly, influenced by the actions of some of their erstwhile liberators, as the country socioeconomic and political decline progressed, more Zimbabweans embarked on various existential and existentialist acts in search of existence. Many uprooted themselves from their ancestral land and migrated beyond the country's borders, paradoxically to both the short- and long-term detriment and yet benefit of the country and those they left behind. Of the latter, as the crisis further deepened, some turned to a Christian or virtual kind of existentialism. While in some cases, others embraced Satanism in the hope of transcending the country's socioeconomic and political quagmire.

## *Notes*

1. Affiliation: Department of Culture, Communication & Media, University College London, & Comecinc Communications and Strategic Solutions Services Incorporated
2. Later famously and reverentially known as Mbuya Nehanda, Charwe Nyakasina is at times considered to have been both myth and historical reality. Sweetman, however, attests to her historical existence at "a rocky sanctuary in the Mazoe Valley" (1984, p.91).
3. After Zimbabwe's independence Sinoa was renamed Chinhoyi.
4. In 2016, the remaining war veterans were again demanding US$500 000.00 each. Follow the link for story https://www.voazimbabwe.com/a/war-veterans-demand-500000-gratuities-each/3595710.html
5. See B. Raftopoulos & A. Mlambo (Eds) *Becoming Zimbabwe: A History from the Pre-Colonial Period to 2008* footnote 1 for a comprehensive list of books on the subject.
6. In February 2000, the ruling ZANU-PF for the first time experienced electoral defeat when the country's electorate rejected its draft constitution by voting against it.
7. See R. Magosvongwe, A. Nyamende & T. Gwekwerere (2013) Black Zimbabwean women and 'jambanja' in Eric Harrison's *Jambanja* (2006): An Africana Womanist exegesis for a detailed unpacking of the term.
8. It is believed the ancestors take various forms.
9. This is a March 2018 estimate by Zimbabwe's finance minister Patrick Chinamasa.
10. Visit https://relzim.org/tag/satanism/ for more on Satanism in Zimbabwe.
11. In Karl Marx's Critique of Hegel's Philosophy (1843/1970).

## *References*

Baxter, P. (2011). A brief history of Rhodesia. Retrieved December 7, 2017, from http://www.peterbaxterafrica.com/a-brief-history-of-rhodesia

Bigelow, G. E. (1961). A primer of existentialism. In *College English*. December: 207.

Bulla, F. (2017, May 28). Harare prison's religious jungle. *The Sunday Mail*, pS1.

Bull-Christiansen, L. B. (2005). Yvonne Vera: Rewriting discourses of history and identity. In R. Muponde & R. Primorac (Eds.), *Versions of Zimbabwe: New approaches to literature and culture* (pp. 203–217). Harare: Weaver Press.

Chivaura, V. G. (2012, November 16–22). The beauty of being African. *From Rhodesia to Zimbabwe, The Patriot* 14.

Chiwome, E. (2002). A comparative analysis of Solomon Mutsvairo and Yvonne Vera's handling of the legend of Nehanda. In R. Muponde & M. Maodzwa-Taruvinga

(Eds.), *Under the tongueandqithout aname. Sign and Taboo perspectives on the poetic fiction of Yvonne Vera* (pp.179–189). Harare: Weaver Press.

Cooper, D. E. (1999). *Existentialism: A reconstruction* (2nd ed.). Oxford, London: Wiley-Blackwell.

Darling, D. M. (2008). *The Other Side of Christianity*. Maitland, Florida: Xulon Press.

Fanon, F. (1967). *The wretched of the earth*. London: Penguin Books.

Funk and Wagnalls. (1997). *Standard dictionary of the English language*. International Updated Edition.

Hallencreutz, C., & Moyo, A. (Eds.). (1988). *Church and state in Zimbabwe*. Gweru: Mambo Press.

Kaufman, W. (Ed.). (1965). *Existentialism from Dostoyevsky to Sartre* (pp.345–352). Cleveland: Meridian Publishing Company.

Magirosa, M. J. (2012, November 16–22). Poll tax: The exploitation of a people. *Decolonising the Mind, The Patriot*, 13.

Magosvongwe, R., Nyamende, A., & Gwekwerere, T. (2013). Black Zimbabwean women and 'jambanja' in Eric Harrison's *Jambanja* (2006): An Africana Womanist exegesis. *South African Journal of African Languages, 33*(2), 125–132.

Marx, K. (1970). *Critique of Hegel's Philosophy of Right*. Oxford: Oxford University Press.

Matshobana, E. (2003). Bulawayo history. Retrieved December 7, 2017, from http://www.Bulawayo1872.com/history/history/nehandambuya1.htm

Moyo, A.M. (1988). Religion and political thought in independent Zimbabwe. In C. Hallencreutz & A. Moyo (Eds.), *Church and state in Zimbabwe* (pp.197–249). Gweru: Mambo Press.

Mugabe, R.G. (2001). *Inside the ThirdChimurenga: our land is our prosperity*. Harare: Jongwe Press.

Muponde, R., & Maodzwa-Taruvinga, M. (Eds.) (2002). *Sign and Taboo perspectives on the poetic fiction of Yvonne Vera*. Harare: Weaver Press.

Muponde, R., & Primorac, R. (Eds.). *Versions of Zimbabwe: New approaches to literature and culture*. Harare: Weaver Press.

Mutsvairo, S. (1957). *Feso*. Cape Town: Oxford University Press.

Ncube, D. (2017, May). Chiefs central to social justice. *The Sunday Mail: Society Religion*, S6.

Raftopoulos, B. (2009). The crisis in Zimbabwe 1998–2008. In B. Raftopoulos & A. Mlambo (Eds.), *Becoming Zimbabwe: A history from the pre-colonial period to 2008* (pp.201–232). Harare: Weaver Press.

Raftopoulos, B., & Mlambo, A. (Eds.). (2009). *Becoming Zimbabwe: A history from the pre-colonial period to 2008*. Harare: Weaver Press.

Sadomba, Z.W. (2011). *War veterans in Zimbabwe's revolution challenging neo-colonialism & settler & international capital*. Harare: Weaver Press.

Sartre, J. P. (1943/1992). *Being and nothingness*. Translated and introduced by H. E. Barnes. New York: Washington Square Press.

Sartre, J. P. (1946). Existentialism is humanism. In W. Kaufman (Ed.) (1965), *Existentialism from Dostoyevsky to Sartre* (pp. 345–352). Cleveland: Meridian Publishing Company.

Sweetman, D. (1984). *Women leaders in African history.* London: Heinemann.

Taylor, C. (1985). Self-interpreting animals. In *Philosophicalpapers1: Human agency and language.* Cambridge: Cambridge University Press.

Vambe, M. (2002). Spiritual possession and the paradox of postcolonial resistance in Yvonne Vera's Nehanda. In R. Muponde & M. Maodzwa-Taruvinga (Eds.), *Under the tongueandwithout aname. Sign and Taboo perspectives on the poetic fiction of Yvonne Vera* (pp.127–138). Harare: Weaver Press.

Vambe, M. T. (2004). *African oral story-telling tradition and the Zimbabwean novel in English.* Pretoria: Unisa Press.

Vera, Y. (1993). *Nehanda.* Harare: Baobab Books.

# 2 The Globalization of Domestic Politics in Zimbabwe: 1999–2009

Lere Amusan[1]

## Introduction

This chapter is based on the view maintained by Meredith (2005, p.634–635) when she writes that, "for the end of the 1990s Zimbabwe was in dire straits." With this in mind, I test Samuel P. Huntington's (1968) thesis about modernization and political consciousness against what characterized Zimbabwe over the ten years under consideration in an attempt to explain the possible reasons for the dire straits the country found itself. At which point I argue that in addition to Zimbabwe's historical and domestic circumstances, there also emerged external forces such as South Africa and Britain's historical relations and policies that eventually contributed to the country's near collapse. The chapter concludes by making some recommendations as to how the nation and the international community can best move forward.

## Early Political Developments in Zimbabwe: 1980–1999

Although to Claude Ake (1979, p.77) "western theories of political development are nothing but an attempt to promote bourgeois ideology and foster capitalist values", in my view, Huntington's political modernization theory to a large extent helps animate Zimbabwe's crisis between 1999 and 2009. Defining political modernization, Huntington sees it as:

> [A] change in the attitudes, values, and expectations of people from those associated with the traditional world [......as] a consequence of literacy, education, increased communications, mass media exposure, and urbanization. (1968, p.33)

Twenty years into Zimbabwe's independence, the scenario described above to some extent characterizes the stage of political development the country had been aspiring to and more or less attained. However, much as political modernization also includes and, "involves increased participation in politics by social groups throughout society. In many cases, office and power are distributed more by achievement and less by ascription" (Huntington 1968, p.33); the country's politics was such that it had not reached such a level of political modernization.

Huntington sees in a country's political development, different times for the centralization of authority, national integration and social welfare. When the ideological, political system of the then Union of Soviet Socialist Republics (USSR) collapsed and could no longer support its surrogates in Eastern Europe and the rest of the Third World States (TWS), a non-polarity international system evolved as the uni-polarity system receded (Haass 2008, p.44–56). In Zimbabwe, this heralded many political changes in the country's domestic politics. As early as the 1980s, Robert Mugabe had sought to consolidate himself as life president when, in line with the ideology of his mentors North Korea and China, he had advocated for a one-party socialist state and stifled the main opposition party, the Zimbabwe African People's Party (ZAPU). However, Gorbachev and Yelstin's neutralization of communism by their introduction of glasnost and perestroika and the eventual mixed economic system in China compelled Mugabe to a *de jure* multi-party system. This saw the formation of the Zimbabwe Unity Movement (ZUM) by the former ZANU-PF stalwart and now late Edgar Tekere and the Zimbabwe Union of Democrats (ZUD) of the once ZANU-PF cadre, Margaret Dongo.

Huntington (1968, p.33), perceives a country to have reached political modernization when 'Democracy, stability, structural differentiation, achievement patterns, national integration-often is dubious at best.' By 1999, the ZANU-PF government, which was largely supported by the majority Shona, had ruled Zimbabwe as a *de facto* one-party state since 1980. Ever since independence, both Mugabe and his ruling party had not faced any major political challenges from Joshua Nkomo's ZAPU, supported mainly the county's minority Ndebele. A political party was neutralized by ZANU-PF by 22 December 1987 through Unity Accord signed between Mugabe and Joshua Nkomo, which brought about Patriotic Front (PF), hence ZANU-PF (Meredith, 2005, p.625).

However, from 1982 to 1985, it was alleged that ZAPU was sponsoring dissident activities. This allegation came after caches of arms were discovered on ZAPU-owned farms. The opposition party's leader, Joshua Nkomo, was branded "Father of dissidents" and forced to flee the country to England. To quell the dissident activities, a North Korean–trained brigade of the Zimbabwe National Army (ZNA), the Fifth Brigade embarked on the military operation *Gukurahundi.* It was dispatched to parts of rural Matabeleland and Midlands provinces. The then state Police Commissioner, and now late Enos Nkala, apparently supervised the Fifth Brigades operations (Meredith, 2005). The culmination was the death and disappearance of an estimated twenty thousand people in what has infamously become known as the *Gukurahundi* atrocities.

In 1987, after a state of near civil war, Zimbabwe's then main political parties ZAPU and ZANU signed a Unity Accord on 22 December. Under the accord, the two opponents agreed to form a coalition to be called the Zimbabwe African Nationalist Union-Patriotic Front (ZANU-PF). The then Prime Minister, Robert Mugabe, was to be transformed into an executive president with executive presidential powers. The country's ceremonial president, Canaan Banana and Joshua Nkomo, were to be twin vice presidents. The result of the Unity Accord was effectively the cessation of micro-nationalism at national level and the entrenchment of political power in the new executive president. A sense of unity and stability returned to Zimbabwe. From then onwards, the political situation in the country was such that President Mugabe could be life president if he so wished.

## *Mugabe's Foreign and Domestic Policies and the Rise of the MDC: 1999–2009*

Until 1999, Mugabe had adhered to the provisions of the Lancaster House Constitution of 1979. However, this soon changed when a new political threat, the Movement for Democratic Change (MDC), introduced prebendal politics to Zimbabwe. Headed by the then Zimbabwe Congress of Trade Unions (ZCTU) secretary-general, late Morgan Tsvangirai, the formation of MDC was mainly a response to Mugabe's unpopular foreign policy which adversely impacted the country. Topmost was his involvement of Zimbabwe in the Democratic Republic of Congo's civil war on the side of Laurent Kabila (Amusan 1999, p.28–29). The country's unbudgeted involvement in the DRC led to the further devaluation of the Zimbabwe dollar and the unconfirmed loss of hundreds of military personnel.

Due to the state's involvement in the civil war in the DRC, the country was reportedly incurring an estimated $2 million a day in the war that had no direct effect on the already ailing economy (Amusan 1999, p.29). Tsvangirai's promise was to withdraw Zimbabwe's 11,000 troops from the DRC if voted to power; he won his party supporters among the middle and junior military officers who saw no reason to fight a war that had no direct positive impact on the nation's economic development to have a rethink on their involvement in the war. This threat to the Mugabe government came on the heels of the war veterans' accusation of their neglect by the government since their demobilization at the end of Zimbabwe's war of liberation. Subsequently, in late 1997 the ZANU-PF government had paid the war veterans unbudgeted gratuities. It was a move that had led to the initial sharp devaluation of the country's currency and the ruling party's decline in popularity.

The Economic Structural Adjustment Programme (ESAP) earlier introduced at the command of the IMF had resulted in high unemployment, in response to the country's worsening socioeconomic situation. In late 1999, partly in response to the National Constitutional Assembly's (NCA) call for constitutional reform, Mugabe attempted to officially mutate himself into a president for life by setting up a constitutional commission to review the then Lancaster Constitution in his favor. Comprised mainly of Mugabe's party members, the Constitutional Commission was headed by the then High Court Judge, Justice Godfrey Chidyausiku (Musavengana 2009:26). The Commission recommended among others that the incumbent president get a ten-year term, and all future presidents have terms of five years each. The arrangement was to allow Mugabe to remain president *ad infinitum.*

In a further bid to ensure Mugabe remained president and to garner the support of black voters in the upcoming constitution referendum and mid-2000 elections, the ruling ZANU-PF party, without consultation with the Commission that had drafted the new constitution, introduced a clause nationalizing white-owned land without compensation. The onus was put on Britain to compensate the dispossessed farmers. In early 2000, the draft new constitution was put to a national referendum in what was to be the first acid test of ZANU-PF's popularity since the formation of the MDC.

Besides the fact that the draft constitution was not an accurate reflection of what the people had enunciated when the time finally came to vote on the referendum, the Zimbabwean electorate was negatively disposed towards ZANU-PF. This is because the MDC, white commercial farmers, civil society and various international organizations such as the International Monetary Fund (IMF), the World Bank, European Union, USA and UK had rallied against the proposed constitution. The referendum also coincided with high unemployment among the youth. According to Meredith, by 2000:

> The unemployment rate [in Zimbabwe] had risen to more than 50 per cent. Only one-tenth of the numbers of pupils leaving school were able to find formal employment. [......] The value of wages in real terms had fallen over ten years by 22 per cent. On the average, the population of 13 million was 10 per cent poorer at the end of the 1990s than at the beginning [...] More than 70 per cent [of

> Zimbabweans] lived in abject poverty. Hospitals were short of drugs and equipment; government schools of funds; state corporations were bankrupt; the public transport system was decrepit; fuel supplies were erratic; scores of businesses had closed. (Meredith, 2005, p.634–5)

Recalling Huntington's (1968) observation that the higher the levels of education amongst the unemployed, alienated or otherwise dissatisfied, the more extreme the destabilizing behavior of the masses is likely to be. These added to the votes against the new draft constitution.

Huntington further notes that a country's "level of economic development is the *sine qua non* to political stability and the same determines peaceful coexistence in a state" (1968, p.33). Economic well-being is therefore associated with political order and violent unrest and extremism with poverty and underdevelopment. In fact, when economic prosperity is lacking in an urban context, opposition parties tend to have more followers than in the rural areas where the populace is mostly ignorant of political developments in the country. Zimbabwe's growing poverty, fuel shortages, factory closures, crumbling public services, corruption in the military and civil service, the military's unpopular involvement in the DRC's civil war did not work in favor of the ZANU-PF government. Moreover, contrary to Huntington's observations that rural dwellers have a low political culture and a parochialism that emanates from their lack of information about political developments outside the rural environment, the 1990s Zimbabwe's rural voters proved to have politically matured along with the political modernization of the state. Historically ZANU-PF's support base abstained from voting during the referendum, and 55% of those who did voted against it.

However, just as Huntington also highlights, in the context of less developed states, the *nouveau riche* (newly wealthy) always find means of containing the masses by employing acts of violence such as arson, assault and intimidation against their political opponents. After the loss of the referendum, Meredith (2005, p.636) reports that mayhem was let loose against rural dwellers suspected to have voted for the MDC. War veterans and ZANU-PF youths reportedly perpetrated violence against rural folk and cowered them into submission. After that, they were re-indoctrinated about the ZANU-PF and the country's war of liberation.

The period was also one when the ZANU-PF government embarked on its land-grabbing politics partly to regain the support of the rural population. Foreign investors pulled out their funds from the country's stock exchange; the Zimbabwe dollar plummeted against major currencies. Inflation rose to over 70% and the government's lack of transparency in its management of the economy, fast-track land reform and governance saw the IMF cut aid to the state (Amusan, 2008b). The supplies of electricity, fuel, fundamental and infrastructural amenities were stretched to the limit and became scarce. The citizenry, especially the poor who bore the brunt of it all, quietly wished for change.

Mark Hertsgaard (2002), Michael White (2005) and Stephen Armstrong (2008) once noted that because of developments in technology, instruments of violence had readily become available to governments bent on oppressing its citizenry. The private media came under censorship and brutal state attack. The state-controlled media placated the masses with the ruling party's propaganda and dwarfed the reality on the ground. After the referendum, Zimbabwe's elections were conducted in an atmosphere fraught with intimidation. During the June 2000 parliamentary elections, for example, election monitoring groups such as the Violence Monitoring Unit (VMU) reported widespread violence. In the 2002 elections, an EU observer was summarily expelled, attracting further Western sanctions on the country. The government reportedly perpetrated additional terror attacks on the masses in both rural and township centers. Opposition political parties such as the MDC were not given the opportunity to air their political agenda via the print and electronic media.

Despite the Supreme Court of Zimbabwe's ruling against the state's monopoly of broadcasting, independent radio stations were closed down by the state police. Though Capitol Radio began secret broadcasts, incessant raids of its offices and arrests of its staff and the lawyers representing them were rife. Joy TV in which war veterans had an 11% stake was also closed down by the Information Minister, Professor Jonathan Moyo, when it invited an MDC member to a talk show it had organized.

Mainly due to such developments in Zimbabwe, when the June 2000 parliamentary elections were announced, ZANU-PF had narrowly won 51.7% (62 seats) to the MDC's 47.5 (57 seats). Without a sizeable majority, this made it difficult for the ZANU-PF government to amend the constitution. The newly formed MDC had begun to make inroads into the country's political landscape and to redraw the political map of the state. In response, Mugabe and his ZANU-PF party having earlier stooped to physical violence against the opposition resorted to verbal abuse and the intensification of its controversial land reform program.

Dowden highlights that:

> [L]and had been at the heart of Zimbabwe's liberation war. Far more than human rights, democracy or self-rule, people had fought for their stolen land. However, under the independence settlement, if the government wanted land, it had to pay full compensation in a currency of the seller's choice. (2009:148)

Consequently, for close to twenty years, the Mugabe government had done little to correct the massive discrepancy in the country land ownership. Instead, it had allowed the principles of the 1931 Land Apportionment Act and the Lancaster House Agreement to perpetuate. Both pieces of legislation had reserved 48 million acres of Zimbabwe's land for white commercial farmers and less than 25 million acres for the country's 1 million black farmers. So, whereas at independence in 1980: "6000 white commercial farmers [had] held 39 per cent of the land, by 1990, only 8 per cent of this commercial land had come under black ownership" (Dowden 2009, p.148). Mugabe had "not done much about the land issue because he did not want to upset the delicate negotiations going on over the future of South Africa" Dowden (2009, p. *ibid.*). This was despite the British government's alleged provision of 44 million pounds sterling for land reform in Zimbabwe (Boateng, *The Star* 18 June 2007). The money was meant to offset the issue of payment in the seller's currency of choice, training and support, avail agricultural inputs and financial succor for potential farmers. However, since Zimbabwe's independence, only fifty farms had reportedly been bought using the £44 million disbursed.

When the Lancaster House Constitution's ten-year grace period to white farmers expired in 1991, the ZANU-PF government had not grabbed the window of opportunity that opened. Instead, it mooted a law which if passed would have enabled it to acquire land without compensation. However, "the process was slow and still had to be referred to the courts. Not much land changed hands by the end of the decade" Dowden (2009, p. *ibid.*). Until 2000, the country proceeded without a functional policy on land redistribution.

Consequent to the 2000 referendum result, politics of the land became ZANU-PF and Mugabe's best opportunity to win the June 2000. Initially penciled for April, the 2000 parliamentary elections were moved to June of the same year partly due to ZANU-PF's shock defeat in the February referendum. By the first week of March, those who had over the years benefited from the largess of the party and government intensified the eviction of white farmers from farms. Against the advice of various international financial institutions, the Mugabe government was bent on fast-tracking land reform at whatever cost (Amusan, 2008a; Landsberg, 2004).

Two schools of thought emerged as to the reason behind the Zimbabwe government's land reform. On the one hand, the ZANU-PF party, as the country's democratically elected government, saw it as its right to correct land ownership that favored a white minority. On the other, those opposed to the ZANU-PF government perceived as an orchestrated cheap political maneuver by the ruling party to regain lost credibility and popularity. Whatever the reason, war veterans and unemployed youths were reportedly employed and encouraged by state security agents to invade white commercial farms. Some of these were later subdivided into small pieces of land and shared amongst participating peasants and war veterans as A1 plots. The peasantry and other qualified middle-class black farmers in whose name the land had been reappropriated were primarily denied access to the prime farmland.

Instead, some of it was divided mainly amongst ZANU-PF politicians, civil servants and senior military officers. Thus, most of the country's prime land ended up in the hands of cabinet ministers, government officials and politically connected urbanites that had little or no knowledge and experience of farming. This new crop of farmers was later dubbed "cell phone farmers"as they ran their farms by phoning those working on the pieces of land to find out how things were progressing on the ground (Amusan, 2011). Corruption and cronyism defeated equitable land redistribution.

Of the peasant farmers who were allocated plots of land, most of them eventually abandoned their new plots and returned to their old, barren ones in the communal areas. This was mostly because of government's failure to provide them with much-needed farm inputs. Equally problematic was the fact that the farm inputs and especially fuel was in short supply and only available mainly on the black market for exorbitant prices. Also, the new resettled farmers' lack of documentary title to the land meant they had no collateral with which to secure loans. This was despite Agricultural Minister, Joseph Made's January 2006 declaration that commercial banks extend loans to the new farmers. The lack of inputs, an unfavorable and erratic rainy season, incoherent agricultural policy and the withdrawal of lines of credit by international finance houses meant an unsuccessful start to the country's land reform program.

Land reform took its toll on Zimbabwe's economy. The country's currency depreciated, inflation escalated and food shortages set in. Tourist inflows markedly declined, and investors' confidence slumped by as much as 80% subsequent to violence such as when some Britons and some Swedish investors were beaten by ZANU-PF militia when they occupied a game lodge. Amid the socioeconomic decline, the opposition MDC gained much political support, especially among the unemployed urban youth. Together with the fast fading middle class of the urban centers, they were most critical of the ruling party and wanted change to the *status quo*.

In response to the ruling party's loss of popularity, as the years progressed and crisis entrenched itself, state terror visited those in the country's townships, urban centers and countryside. In spite of the callous incidences of violence against some of the citizenry, the police did little to intervene. Many MDC officials were arrested for questioning and perceived supporters of the opposition party were arrested or allegedly killed. In mid-2001, the Mugabe government adopted a strategy whereby company directors who laid off workers due to the scarcity of foreign currency exchange to import raw materials were forced to reabsorb their retrenched workers and to financially support ZANU-PF in exchange for political support (Africa Today June 2001:26). On 11 March 2007, the leader of the opposition, Morgan Tsvangirai, was beaten and tortured by the Mugabe security agents resulting in both domestic and international condemnation of the act. Members of the opposition who sustained series of injuries were not allowed to travel abroad for medical treatment.

Towards the 2008 elections, micro-nationalism and factionalism, the banes of African politics, evidenced themselves in both the MDC and ZANU-PF formations. In ZANU-PF, on one hand, Emmerson Mnangagwa, Mugabe's one time security minister during the *Gukurahundi* atrocities, later justice minister and Mugabe's military/coup d'état option should the MDC ever win elections in the country formed a faction against co-Vice President Joyce Mujuru and her now late husband ZANLA supremo, Retired-General Solomon Mujuru. On the other, stood former ZAPU members headed by the now late co-Vice President John Nkomo.

Since Simba Makoni's tenure as one of Mugabe's youngest cabinet ministers in the early 1980s, he had been mooted to succeed the aged leader. Makoni's achievements as the first Southern African Development and Coordination Conference (SADCC) executive secretary in the mid-1980s made him a credible candidate for the position. After the June 2000 elections, Mugabe had removed some of his senior cabinet ministers and appointed technocrats in economic-related ministries. Makoni had been appointed finance minister in the hope of attracting Western financial institutions. The appointment had further reinforced perceptions of Makoni as Mugabe's possible successor.

However, Makoni's anti-graft war against politicians and senior military officers coupled with his proposed macroeconomic solutions to the country's financial crisis vis-a-vis that of the Zimbabwe Reserve Bank (ZRB) of printing of more banknotes had made him unpopular in government and discredited him as a likely successor (Gono 2007, p.16). Makoni was eventually dismissed as finance minister because of his popularity in the ZANU-PF and senior military officers' negative attitude towards him.

Against the advice of SADC and Nigeria to step down before the 2008 elections, President Mugabe reportedly coerced the party's politburo and imposed himself to run for another five-year term. He was apparently of the opinion that he was still relevant to ZANU-PF and Zimbabwe. Mugabe's nomination and appointment as the ruling party's presidential candidate ended speculation within the ZANU-PF party and the country generally that he would relinquish power before the 2008 elections.

Perceptions that the first secretary of the ruling party was determined to transmute himself to a president for life put some members of his political party into a quandary. In 2008, Makoni left the ZANU-PF party and availed himself to lead the MDC into Zimbabwe's 2008 general elections. The MDC did not however totally accept Makoni as leader. Instead, its secretary general, Welshman Ncube, invited former student leader and activist, Professor Arthur Mutambara, to lead the party. The move saw the split of MDC into MDC–Tsvangirayi (MDC-T) and MDC-Mutambara (MDC-M) and Makoni running as an independent presidential candidate against Mugabe, Tsvangirai and Mutambara. To date, both Makoni and Mutambara are considered to have split the vote and cost Tsvangirayi the presidency.

Towards the 2008 general elections, reminiscent of Ian Smith's alternative plan B of 1979 (i.e., handing over power to a trusted military) Zimbabwe military's service chiefs announced they would not recognize anyone likely to reverse the gains of independence. Implied by the announcement was that they would not pledge allegiance to an MDC leader and government. As part of the political elite that had immensely benefitted from ZANU-PF rule and the fast-track land resettlement program, high-ranking military officials stood to lose the commercial farms, wealth and political power they had accumulated.

Conversely, while senior military officers implicitly pledged their allegiance to the ZANU-PF government, junior officers of the ZNA reportedly held different views. Because they were sidelined from the politics of prebendalism, it was suspected they were planning a coup. The alleged purge of both senior and middle-rank army officers that followed in 2007 was an apparent attempt by the state to consolidate its precarious security. The harmonized March 2008 elections were held in an atmosphere of peace and relative fairness. Problems only arose later when the announcement of the final presidential result was delayed for some weeks. When they were eventually announced, neither of the front-runners, MDC-T and ZANU-PF had a clear majority of 51% of the vote. As initially agreed before the election, this necessitated a presidential run-off election.

Political violence has been described as "the act of political children without the patience to operate constitutional machinery" (Dowse & Hughes, 1986, p.363). Due to the support of the MDC by foreign media, the government imposed 70% tax of their selling cost before allowing them into the state. Towards the run-off, a campaign of political violence and torture erupted as ZANU-PF reportedly embarked on another round of criminalizing the state's security agents and war veterans. Tsvangirai was eventually forced to withdraw from the race. Thus, by the time the run-off presidential election was held in June 2008, Mugabe was the sole candidate. However, despite this, the run-off went ahead, and Mugabe emerged both "winner" and president of the country. The socioeconomic situation in the country further worsened to frightening levels.

## South Africa's "quiet diplomacy" and the International Community's Mixed Responses

Although the noninterference clause in the internal affairs of the African Union (AU) member states (Ar. 4(g)) is no longer sacrosanct in 21st-century African international relations, Africa's response to Zimbabwe's crisis was flat-footed. The rebirth of the AU on 1 October 2002 had come with innovations aimed at enabling it to confront the challenges of globalization and the nonpolarity of the international system (Haass 2008: 45). In this regard, Stephen David Krasner (2004) and Mario Blaser (2001) point out that the Constitutive Act of the AU (Ar. 4(h&J)) and the birth of the NEPAD made interference in the internal affairs of member states, when necessary, feasible and a reality.

In addition, the formation of the African Peer Review Mechanism (APRM) to actualize the objectives and principles of the AU as stated in Articles 3 and 4 aimed at the general development of the continent. However, despite both these instruments, some states in Africa were hesitant to interfere in the internal affairs of Zimbabwe constructively. For instance, the South African parliamentary observers sent to Zimbabwe to monitor the country's 2000 elections reportedly took more than 10 weeks to come with a report favorable to the Zimbabwean government. The Violence Monitoring Unit (VMU) set up by NGOs to publicize the torture, rape, murder, mass beatings and intimidation by the ruling party was ignored by the South African delegation. South Africa's infamous quiet diplomacy andtacit support for Harare's politics of violence contrary to the AU's and SADC's objectives was because of several reasons.

The economic benefit of the state is germane to its relationship with other nations. Historically, Zimbabwe and South Africa have always been close trading partners. The economic decline of Zimbabwe meant the growth of trade in South Africa's favor. Zimbabweans trekked south across the border in search of food and other essentials scarce in their own country. This is to the extent that even though Western states had conjectured that because of South Africa's strategic import to Zimbabwe, Pretoria would impose comprehensive sanctions on the Mugabe government, which never happened. South Africa's investment, colonial linkage, cultural affinities and contiguous politics did not allow Pretoria to embark on the western type resolution of Zimbabwe's crises. Besides, since 1995 it had been South Africa's foreign policy to be courteous to other African countries and their issues (Amusan, 2006: p.232–243).

Due to the crisis in Zimbabwe, educated, skilled and unskilled Zimbabwean labor flowed across the country's southern border and boosted South African agricultural, educational and industrial sectors. In addition, most investment capital fleeing Zimbabwe also found a home in the South African economy. So long as South Africa remained the primary beneficiary of Zimbabwe's crisis, both Presidents Thabo Mbeki and Jacob Zuma's administrations avoided taking swift and decisive action against the Mugabe regime.

In 2008, many white Zimbabwean farmers took the state to the sub-regional court. The Southern African Development Community (SADC) Tribunal confirmed the illegality of the land invasions that had taken place but would not impose its decision on Mugabe government as states such as South Africa did not support the recommendations of the judiciary. In the meantime, the effects of the crisis such as the refugee crisis, an increase in crime and pressure on the social amenities (Amusan 2008a, p.139) were borne by South Africa.

When in the late 1990s and early 2000s President Mugabe started seizing white farms, concern over political and economic developments in Zimbabwe was internationalized as various western governments and civil society reacted. The ambitious $1 billion the ZANU-PF sought to settle landless Zimbabweans and revive the country's ailing economy was not forthcoming from donors and representatives of various international financial institutions. The £44 million earlier given to the Mugabe government as part of a £100 million aid package for land resettlement could not be accounted for. The British stopped the disbursement of the remaining £56 million.

In response to Zimbabwe's land invasions and President Mugabe's call that the farmers be compensated by the British, Clare Short, the UK Secretary of State for International Development, made it clear that the new Labor government in Britain was not obligated to meet the costs of land purchase in Zimbabwe. Short retorted: "We are a new government from diverse backgrounds without links to former colonial interests." In support of this assertion, on 10 June 2004, a spokesperson for the British embassy in Harare,

Sophie Honey again enunciated that the UK had not reneged on commitments made at Lancaster House. In her view, even at Lancaster House, the British government had made it clear that the long-term requirements of land reform in Zimbabwe were beyond the capacity of any individual donor country. As such, while the UK remained a strong advocate of effective, well-managed and pro-poor land reform, fast-track land reform had "not been implemented in line with these principles and [Britain] cannot support it." The British's stance contributed to the Bretton Woods institutions' lack of interest in Zimbabwe's agricultural revolution and future economic development.

As with Britain, the US's policy position is also often that of the IMF, the World Bank and by extension the European Union's financial clubs. Economic and smart sanctions were slapped on Zimbabwe. The comity of nations' reaction of comprehensive and smart sanctions aggravated further the country's crisis. Their actions further reduced the erstwhile darling of the West in Africa to pariah status and isolated a leader who already felt victimized by Western powers. President Mugabe was accused of human right abuses according to the Alien Tort Claims Act which allows foreigners to file civil suits in US courts for violations of international law. While attending the 2000 United Nations' Millennium Summit, there was an attempt to serve him with papers for a civil lawsuit. Such was the furore over Zimbabwe's land reform that some developed states reportedly considered a military strike as against the country. It was, however, an option which would have severely undermined international law, the sovereignty of a nation-state and set a terrible precedent on the continent.

The fact that the European Union was not united over Zimbabwe also determined the extent to which other western countries could go. States such as France and Germany prevaricated on developments in Zimbabwe. In 2007, when Gordon Brown, the then British Prime Minister proclaimed that he would not attend the EU-Africa Strategic Partnership in Lisbon if Mugabe was invited, German Chancellor, Angela Merkel, supported the Harare government's attendance. The Chinese government's policy of non-interference in the internal affairs of other states and its historical relations with the ZANU-PF government saw it contribute to the country militarily, economically and diplomatically. In its bid to recapture its 1980s' lost glory among the Third World States (TWS), so too did Russia. This affected the voting system in the United Nations Security Council and explains why the United Nations, the quasi-world government, did not act in unison on Zimbabwe's deterioration.

The implication of international and continental responses or the lack thereof to Zimbabwe's crisis was that by the end of 2008, life expectancy for Zimbabwean males was 44 years and 43 years for females (World Health Organization 2009 Report). Besides, a United Nations Index which combines health, knowledge and standard of living ranked Zimbabwe 151st out of 177 countries. The World Food Programme (WFP) estimated that by April 2010, 2.8 million (out of an estimated 13 million) Zimbabweans would be recipients of humanitarian assistance.

Zimbabwe's capital, "Harare, once renowned as one of the cleanest cities in Africa, was noted now for debris on the pavements, cracked cement pavings, broken street lights, potholes, uncollected refuse and burst pipelines" (Meredith 2005, p.635). The country's health care system was in disarray and medication in short supply. Cholera broke out in many parts of the country. By the time it had been officially brought under control, an estimated 4,200 people had reportedly died and more than 100,000 people affected. Most of these were in the country's low-income group.

To Huntington (1968), the relation between literacy and stability is unusually high. In the case of Zimbabwe, the crisis proved this to be relatively accurate. Despite Zimbabweans being subjected to some of the harshest socioeconomic conditions imaginable, the populace did not revolt and civil war did not break out. The same would not have been said in less learned societies. In this respect, Zimbabwe's internationally acclaimed education system can be partly attributed to the social peace that prevailed during the crisis. The government's promotion of education, literacy and to some extent urbanization before 1999 produced a politically conscious and rational citizenry that prioritized self-preservation above all else.

*The Inclusive Government and Zimbabwe's future.* In mid-September 2008, with Zimbabwe near collapse and rumors of secrettalks between the country's main political players South Africa's Thabo Mbeki finally brokered a negotiated power-sharing agreement between ZANU-PF and the two MDC parties. After close to a decade of partisan violence, kidnappings, disappearances and imprisonment of the opposition, the negotiations had been held under a climate of tension and mistrust. The role played by the now South African former president had been blighted by accusations of favoritism against the negotiator towards the incumbent ZANU-PF government. However, the popularity of the MDC and the realities on the ground, namely runaway hyperinflation, a worthless currency, deteriorating infrastructure and broken citizenry could no longer be ignored nor denied. The culmination of the 15 September 2008 agreement was the inauguration of the Zimbabwe Coalition Government (ZCG) on 13 February 2009. In this Inclusive Government, Mugabe retained the presidency and Tsvangirai was appointed Prime Minister.

As can be expected, given the coalition principals' divergent socioeconomic and political goals, it soon encountered hurdles. Of primary contention became how best to share critical government ministries such as Home Affairs. Accusations and counter-accusations flew between ZANU-PF and MDC-T. Roy Bennet, a white opposition politician and treasurer of the MDC-T formation, was accused of attempting to overthrow the government when firearms were allegedly found on his farm. ZANU-PF viewed Bennet's appointment as Deputy Agriculture Minister as an attempt to return to *status quo ante.* President Mugabe's unilateral appointments of Attorney-General Johannes Tomana and his retention of Gideon Gono as the head of the Reserve Bank shook the new Inclusive Government. The new arrangement was further destabilized when the MDC-T's Deputy Minister for Youth, Thamsanqa Mahlangu, was arrested in August 2009 on a charge of stealing a mobile phone. Though this charge was later dropped, the incident signified the new government's instability.

In going forward, respect for the rule of law, private property rights and other civil liberties is necessary for Zimbabwe's future prosperity. The comity of nations expects that the ZANU-PF government will enunciate clear-cut land and investment policies and publish them internationally. Failure to do so will only keep both domestic and forcign investors skeptical about investing in the country. In this regard, adherence to the country's new 2013 constitution and the institution of a transparent judicial system is vital. Although under Article 6 of the Global Political Agreement (GPA), there was room for secret constitutional negotiations amongst the three parties forming the coalition, it is heartening that the constitution-making process did not prioritize political elites at the expense and exclusion of civil society. The new constitution was drafted and voted for after consultation with Zimbabwe's citizens.

A new constitution has since been signed into law. It must now be religiously observed and in future, guide the election and installation of a transparent system of government where the power and terms of the president are rigidly adhered to and curtailed. No administration should continue *ad infinitum.* Equally urgent is the need to use the constitution to restrict the power of the country's security agents. This also applies to the power that over the years has been accorded to the war veterans.

The last decade saw war veterans often taking the law into their own hands in the name of the ZANU-PF party and government. Their often spontaneous and continuing disruption of the remaining white-owned farms needs to be adequately addressed if there is going to be any meaningful and stable economic development in Zimbabwe. Instead, strategies that the government failed to adopt earlier, such as taking away unused land, regardless to whom the land belongs to and/or imposing taxes based on land size should be implemented.

The official acceptance by both economic fundamentals and the GNU in February 2009 that the state currency had been rendered worthless by the events of the last ten years and needed to be replaced by more acceptable tender in the form of the US dollars and South Africa Rands was sound economic policy. This markedly lessened what had become hyper-inflation to about 7.7% and resuscitated sane business transactions and activities. The Government Work Programme (GWP) backed by MDC-T to redeem the state from its pariah status and achieve peace, stability, sustainable growth and prosperity for all was a move in the right direction and should be maintained. Unfortunately, the coalition government was not a blessing for MDC-T as political elite within the party also embarked on corruption like their senior partner in the government of national unity as, Olusegun Obasanjo (2014, p.206) opines that MDC-T's "five years in office has also shown… (that the party) had their own corrupt, inefficient, poorly performing-members in the government as well".

The crisis in Zimbabwe will not have a lasting solution as long as the country continues to be ostracized by the international community through past and personality politics. Despite the then Mugabe government's name-calling of some western powers, the international community needs to work towards normalizing relations with Harare government diplomatically as dialogue is the only way to salvage itself from its socioeconomic doldrums successfully.

## *Conclusion*

Huntington's (1968) position on stages of development as they obtained in Europe and America may not precisely apply to either an African or a Zimbabwean situation. However, his theory does, to some extent, manage to illuminate the situation that unfolded during Zimbabwe's decade of crisis and proves itself not alien to an African situation. Indeed, as this chapter has demonstrated, events that unfolded in Zimbabwe between 1999 and 2009 illustrated the stage the country had achieved according to Huntington's (1968) theorization of political modernization. The ZANU-PF government's use of the land redistribution program as a weapon on a literate population by the Mugabe government only made its party widely unpopular and, coupled with the globalization of Zimbabwe's domestic politics, the result was socio-economic and political instability.

## Notes

1. Affiliation: Department of Politics & International Relations, North–West University, South Africa

## References

*Africa Today*. (2001). June 7(6).

Ake, C. (1979). *Social science as imperialism: The theory of political development*. Ibadan: Ibadan University Press.

Amusan, L. (1999). The great lakes imbroglio: Analysis of the Congo crisis. *Nigerian Forum*, *20*, 7–8.

Amusan, L. (2006). *South Africa as an object of Nigerian foreign policy: 1960–1999*. (Unpublished D.Litt. et. Phil), University of South Africa.

Amusan, L. (2008a). *Politics of contiguity in international relations*. South Africa.

Amusan, L. (2008b). Politics of congruity in international relations: South Africa–Zimbabwe in Perspective. *Nigerian Journal of International Affairs*, *34*(2), 119–146.

Amusan, L. (2011). When solidarity and brotherhood among African states are questionable: Zimbabwe's exportation of insecurity to the rest of Africa. *Journal of Alternative Perspectives in the Social Sciences*, *3*(2), 279–319.

Armstrong, S. (2008). *War PLC: The rise of the new corporate mercenary*. London: Faber and Faber.

Blaser, M. (2001). Development and changing sovereignties: An analysis of structures in motion. *International Relations*, XV(5), 65–77.

Boateng, P. (2007). Zimbabwe broke land reform deal. *The Star Newspaper* (Johannesburg) 18 June.

Dowden, R. (2009). *Africa: Altered states, ordinary miracles*. London: Portobello Books.

Dowse, R. E., & Hughes, J. A. (1986). *Political sociology*. Chichester: John Wiley & Sons.

Gono, G. (2007). Zimbabwe will not die. *NewAfrican*, 465.

Haass, R. (2008). The age of nonpolarity: What will follow U.S. dominance. *Foreign Affairs*, *87*(3), 44–56.

Hertsgaard, M. (2002). *The eagle's shadow: Why America fascinates and infuriates the world*. London: Bloomsbury.

Huntington, S. P. (1968). *Political order in changing societies*. New Haven & London: Yale University Press.

Krasner, S. D. (2004). Sharing sovereignty: New institutions for collapsed and failing states. *International Security*, *29*(2).

Landsberg, C. (2004). *The quiet diplomacy of liberation: International politics and South Africa's transition*. Johannesburg: Jacana Media.

Meredith, M. (2005). *The state of Africa: Ahistory of fifty years of independence*. Johannesburg: Jonathan Ball Publishers.

Musavengana, T. (2009). How Zim politicians hijacked the constitution-making process. *The African Org*, Issue 3 October-November.

Obasanjo, O. (2014). *My watch: Now and then volume three.* Lagos: Prestige.

White, M. (2005). *The fruits of war: How military conflict accelerates technology.* London: Simon & Schuster.

# 3 *Zimbabwe's Paternalistic Command Economy and the Crisis*

DENNIS MASAKA[1]

## *Introduction*

Prior to the formation of the Inclusive Government (IG) in February 2009, Zimbabwe was infamously the country with the world's highest annual inflation rate. At some 489 000 000 000% and its month-on-month 'official rate' pegged above 231 000 000%, its situation was unfathomable. In January 2009, independent analysts estimated hyperinflation at 6.5 quindecillion novemdecillion, the highest for a country not at war (Makochekanwa and Kwaramba, 2009, p.3; Hanke 2008). To observers, Zimbabwe's economic freefall was unprecedented in contemporary economic history and exhibited signs of: "[S]uffering from war-like trauma" (Makochekanwa and Kwaramba, 2009, p.3). Despite Zimbabwe's earlier vibrant, promising and diversified economy, in 2005 Clemens and Moss wrote:

> Today is a country in deep crisis, and the signs of collapse are everywhere. The economy has contracted in real terms in each of the past five years, inflation is in triple digits, the local currency has lost 99% of its value, and almost half of the country faces food shortages. Unsurprisingly, up to one-quarter of the population has fled the country. (Clemens and Moss 2005, p.1)

What had happened to this once economically buoyant beacon of Southern Africa? This sudden and "drastic shrinkage of the economy has been attributed to the collapse of the key contributors to the country's GDP [...] following the introduction of the government's contentious fast-track land redistribution programme in 2000" (The Solidarity Peace Trust 2007, p.7). However, in this chapter, I argue that it was mainly the Zimbabwe government's adoption of a full-fledged command and control approach to the economy that had happened. I do so by showing how at the turn of the new millennium, the government's adoption of a paternalistic economic system weakened and disincentivized the country's manufacturing sector from producing enough for both local and export requirements, building a healthy foreign currency reserves and enabling the country to service its foreign debt (Bond 2001; 2007; IMF Country Report No. 09/139, 2009, p.6). The result of which was the social devastation and economic woes (Bracking and Sachikonye, 2009, p.3) the country manifested and the world witnessed.

## *Mistrust and ZANU-PF's Interventionist Policy: Paternalism and Its Consequences*

In 1990, the Zimbabwe government had at the behest of the Bretton Woods institutions abandoned its socialist command and control approach to the country's economy and adopted a quasi-free market system. Ten years later, however, it reverted to its earlier command approach. The reasons for this are manifold. Ayittey reports that most African regimes are statists where statism is:

> [S]tate hegemony in the economy and the direction of economic activity or development by the state through such devices as price control, legislative acts, regulations, state ownership of means of production, and operation of state enterprises. (Ayittey 1998, p.49)

The reason for such statism stems from the fact that at independence, some African governments, "...misidentified capitalism with colonialism and opted for socialism" (Ayittey, 1998, p.160). The perceived danger posed by an unfettered market system, particularly in third world countries, thus solicited a heavy-handed response to capitalist activities by some governments. For example, it is for this reason that the late Julius Nyerere of the then socialist Tanzania once said: "It is the responsibility of the state to intervene actively in the economic life of the nation so as to ensure the wellbeing of all the citizens" (Ayittey 1998, p.160). At the turn of this century, the Zimbabwean government readopted the same view.

For the Zimbabwe government to embark on a land reform program in 2000, it had perceived, and to some extent rightly so, that the activities of critical economic players within the country, particularly those in the private sector, were not only morally scandalous but also bent on inventing a socio-economic crisis that would eventually oust the ZANU-PF government from political power. In response, the ZANU-PF government paternalistically adopted a command approach to the country's economy in order to protect the country's vulnerable consumers in the context of its seizure of land from white commercial farmers (Bond and Manyanya 2003; Raftopoulos 2001) and shrinking agricultural productive.

At about the same time, the ZANU-PF government and the Bretton Woods institutions also had a falling out. The reasons for this ranged from the disputed land reforms that the country had embarked on to the Zimbabwean government's failure to timeous service its loans with the International Monetary Fund. However, this as it may be, it would be unfair and too simplistic to arrogate all blame for Zimbabwe's socioeconomic meltdown only on internal and external opposition forces alone. Indeed, to do so would be to blight a rational dissection and discussion of what I perceive to be a third dimension to the country's crisis and as such, a misdiagnosis of its panacea. In this chapter, I argue that to have been the ZANU-PF government's open distrust of the utility of a free market system and its re-adoption of a command economic system. Moreover, instead of such a command economic system giving the government of the day control, it went horribly wrong and landed the country in a perilous crisis.

A command economy is a system in which a single authority or its appointed bodies make the decisions about production and the consumption group (Grant, 2000:21; Wonnacott and Wonnacott, 1990). Under a command economic system, the government is the single authority responsible for appointing and communicating such decisions to employees of a bureaucratic system in the form of enforceable commands or directives. Thus, a management group communicates to divisions what they are supposed to produce and what products each division will supply to the other divisions. A command economic system can be extended to an entire economy (Velasquez 2002:174) as once pertained in the former Soviet Union.

The command economic system is at times also referred to as a centralized, planned or collective economy (Grant, 2000:21). In it, all critical decisions on what to produce, how to produce and who gets it revolve around the state. Unfortunately, the danger of such a command and control approach to the economy is that decision-making processes become not only bureaucratic, but decisions, at times, centralized in the hands of political cadres who may lack some requisite skills to direct the critical operations and economic activities. Because of some such reasons, a command economic system is usually undesirable (Smith, 2002a) as it slows down economic growth.

Despite this, the fundamental logic for a command economic system is often a desire for a fairer distribution of income and wealth among the citizens of a given nation-state. Endemic in this economic system is severe fear and suspicion that private ownership of the means of production leads to unfair enrichment of the owners of capital and their accumulation of excessive economic power at the expense and impoverishment of the have-nots. Consequently, throughout history, the command economy and its fundamental component of price controls have been an economic ideology predicated on economic control and interference by government vis-à-vis letting market forces determine the course business should take.

Price control refers to the fixing of prices by a government or its appointed bodies to below market value. The primary objective of price controls is to prevent price inflation and to cushion the generality of consumers (Spinello, 2002). It is, however, a truism that throughout the world, those countries that have aggressively intervened in business within their borders have often not achieved economic growth. Holding the price of a commodity below its market value typically brings about two unfortunate consequences.

The first one is that it increases demand for the controlled commodities (Sowell 2002). Since under a price control regime goods will be effectively cheaper, profiteers make bulk purchases and hoard them for resale when the commodities are no longer available.

In this vein, Sowell (2002) highlights that the second upshot of price controls is a sharp decrease, if not absence, of the commodities once prices reduce to sub-economic levels. The reason for this is partly because as the commodities are quickly bought, discouraged manufacturers stop the now unprofitable controlled goods' production. Moreover, as philanthropy is not the primary objective of enterprise in a free market system, in due course, such commodities vanish from warehouses, wholesalers and, eventually, shop shelves. Price controls can, therefore, have dire penalties on not only the growth and stability of an economy but also its citizens, as Zimbabweans experienced from 2000 onwards.

The free market system borrows heavily from the ideas of Locke (2002), Smith (1991) and Friedman (1983). The two pillars of private property and voluntary exchange maintain it. A free market system is only possible if: " property laws (including contract law) assign to private individuals the right to make decisions about goods they own and reassigns these rights when individuals exchange their goods with each other" (Velasquez 2002:175). In such a market, a business is free to exchange its goods and services with others businesses and its customers at prices advantageous to it.

In such an environment, a businessperson is motivated to engage in the production and selling of a given product based on the attraction of expected incentives. The reason for this being that in a free market economy, the function of business is "fundamentally to produce sustained high-level profits and that is consistent with its own survival as an economic system" (Levitt

1983:83). Participants in a free market system must, therefore, be free to come together in the "market" to voluntarily exchange with each other without undue interference from government and its appointed bodies. In a free market economy, therefore, market forces take precedence over governmental decrees that ascribe value to commodities.

In this respect, a free market economy advocates an individualistic society in which the role of government is limited to the fundamental roles of protecting private property, enforcing contracts and ensuring that the marketplace remains as open and competitive as possible. Fundamental to the economic system's thesis is that governments must have as minimal a role in business as possible and only justifiably intervene in a free market when business practices threaten public health and safety. Even today, the question: What type of role and to what extent a government should play in its country's business sector remains debatable?

Advocates of command economic systems, on the one hand, maintain their position by pointing out the defects of the free market system. They argue that an unregulated market system is defective because:

> it cannot deal with the annoying problems of recession, inflation, ensure open and fair trade, equal opportunities, poverty, the need to foster long-run basic research and innovation and ensure national security. (Velasquez 2002, p.172)

For such reasons, proponents of the command system see it as the only system that can adequately address the ills that free market systems fail to address. It was partly because of this that post-2000 the Zimbabwe government re-embarked on a command approach to the country's economy.

From the year 2000, the ZANU-PF government's negative attitude towards a free market system re-emerged in the way it addressed the land question. Aside from its limitation of maintaining the status quo of resource disequilibria between the indigenous and white settlers, the "willing-seller-willing-buyer" model of land reform (Moyana 2002:187) was predicated on the free market premise that market forces ought to determine the price of land. Initially, this made it difficult for the Zimbabwe government to purchase the farms offered for sale.

Via its fast-track land reform program, the ZANU-PF government sought to negate and circumvent the free market system's right to private land ownership and market forces in determining the price of land. Therefore, instead of paying for the land at prevailing prices, some of Zimbabwe's veterans of the liberation struggle and civilian sympathizers had invaded some white commercial farms and taken control of them. Thereafter, the promulgation of the Land Acquisition Act in 2000 had effectively obliterated the provision of "willing-seller-willing-buyer" in favor of settling "the last colonial question heavily qualifying our sovereignty" (President R.G. Mugabe, in Moore 2005, p.ix). A pattern of the Zimbabwe government's paternalist intervention from the 1980s had been re-engaged and would continue into the 2000s.

Subsequent to resorting to a commando approach as a socioeconomic strategy, the country's economic decline worsened. Gross domestic product (GDP) went down by 40% from 1999 to 2003 and continued to decline at an alarming rate (The Solidarity Peace Trust, 2007, p.7). In addition, as the mining and export sectors steeply declined:

> Manufacturing, which at its height [had] constituted 16% of GDP, [...] shrunk by more than 35%. Unemployment hovered near 80%. The Zimbabwean dollar [became] worthless from hyperinflation. Tourism earnings, once Zimbabwe's second-biggest source of foreign currency, declined from US$198 in 2004 to US$98 million in 2005, a decline of 49%. (The Solidarity Peace Trust, 2007, p.7)

The government paternalistically stepped in. Its response to the deepening economic situation was the implementation of a command economy approach as a panacea. For example, this involved attempts to stop manufacturers' "price madness" that had since the beginning of the land reform exercise seen almost 95% of Zimbabweans living below the Poverty Datum Line (PDL). With the country's economic situation worsening yearly, state intervention in the running of the economy markedly became more pronounced in June 2007.

The ZANU-PF government's price blitz code-named Operation *Dzikisai Mitengo* (Reduce Prices) was instituted against the backdrop of a world record inflation rate officially pegged at more than 4500% as of May 2007 (*Financial Gazette*, July 2007, p.1). In June 2007, with Zimbabwe's economy facing imminent collapse, the country's business sector was ordered to revert to pre-June 18, 2007 prices. To government, this meant businesses slashing the price of their commodities by 50%. The implementation of Operation *Dzikisai Mitengo* incapacitated producers, wholesalers and retailers from operating and severely compromised the country's credit worthiness.

Historically, price controls have been predicated on the need to make available goods cheaper than they otherwise would be in a free market. Cox (2007) argues that: "[P]rice controls are the political solution to stop price inflation." However, price controls do not only make goods scandalously cheaper;in fact, they also result in shortages of those goods, as the demand will be higher than supply. The reaction of Zimbabwe's business community to what it perceived as an open violation of its right to sell their commodities at economically viable prices was immediate. Some of the country's critical private manufacturing industries suspended production of commodities whose prices had been designated. Both existing and potential investors literally fled the country for other investment destinations such as neighboring South Africa and Botswana.The result of Operation *Dzikisai Mitengo* was the virtual disappearance of whatever remained of goods on the formal market.

Of the companies that remained operating in the country, most virtually stopped producing or scaled down production. This further strained the supply side of the economy. The severe shortage of critical components such as foreign currency with which to import machinery, raw materials and spares, electricity and fuel vital to the smooth operation of the manufacturing sector worsened the situation. The price blitz of June 2007 practically grounded the country's industry and commerce to a standstill. Subsequently, production capacity and productivity receded to record lows and severely strained the shortages already facing the country's retail sector. Many economic players in Zimbabwe ran out of stock and would not restock and sell at the non-viable prices they were being forced to charge. This left store and shop shelves empty even in some of the country's leading retail outlets such as OK and TM.

The widespread shortages of essential commodities, goods and services only prompted the Zimbabwean government "to cause havoc in the belief that its interventionist measures will wrap it in the mantle of a knight in shining armour" (*The Standard* Comment, 2–8 September 2007, p.19). It tightened price controls. Chitambara reported that: "government…threatened to take over companies defying the price freeze through the resuscitation of the defunct Zimbabwe State Trade Corporation" (*Financial Gazette*, July 12–18, 2007, p.15). Such government threats to confiscate firms that defied its price slash and freeze of June 2007 were an assault on private property in a free market system. They would continue into the future at the risk of the economy. A few business owners and executives were alleged to be selling their wares at prices that were higher than those which had prevailed before June 18, 2007 and imprisoned. In addition to being forced to deploy their economic resources for significantly less economic returns unprofitably, such drastic action left business disincentivized.

Despite the above, the ZANU-PF government intensified its control of the economy. It suspended its privatization drive that had produced such notable success stories as the Commercial Bank of Zimbabwe (CBZ), Rainbow Tourism Group (RTG), Cotton Company of Zimbabwe (CCZ) and Dairibord. Bloch (2007, p.12) bemoaned that: "…government's entrenched craving for absolute control of anything and everything has motivated it to pay naught but lip service to its further privatisation policy statements." The position of the government on privatisation became one of intransigence as it argued that privatisation would only "hand wealth to the rich, [and] usher in the increased impoverishment of the masses that rely on services provided by parastatals" (ibid). Even though the said public enterprises were tottering on the brink of total collapse, overburdened with debt and insolvent, dismally failing to deliver social services and bolster economic growth.

Paternalistic moves against free enterprise had tragic consequences to an economy already in the doldrums. Economic crimes and widespread immoral business practices crept in as business matched wits with central government management of economic activities. For instance, in order to compensate for the below-market value of goods and services that they were being forced by the government to offer, some manufacturers resorted to offering scandalously low-quality products and undersized products at consumers' expense. Food, fuel, goods and basic commodities became acutely scarce on the formal market, only to resurface on the parallel market where they were being sold at fraudulently exorbitant prices. There were allegations that even some of the country's biggest retail chains had turned to the black market where their commodities traded at viable prices and suspected that some of their employees were purchasing whatever stock was ordered and reselling it on the parallel market. Such uncouth business practices betrayed the lawlessness that had crept into Zimbabwe's commercial sector because of the central government's intervention in the country's economy.

The parallel market refers to the selling of goods and services outside the normal channels of transacting business. Zitha (2007, p.3) reports that profiteers reacted to the slashing and freezing of prices of commodities with absolute joy as it enabled the hoarding of goods from shops for resale later on the black or parallel market. There the law of supply and demand determined prices legally prevailed as government's price decreed did not extend to it. As a result, the parallel market was abundant with essential commodities, though at punitive prices.

Through it all, the Zimbabwean consumer whom the government had hoped to protect by calling for price slashes and freezes suffered most from the fallout. In addition to an informal hyperinflationary environment, consumers now had to endure the misery of literally hunting for almost all basics on the parallel market at above market prices. Aside from causing shortages, price controls made goods more expensive than they would otherwise have been in a free market economy. They also led to time wasted in long queues, encouraged bribery, unethical practices and severely violated consumers' right to choose. Zimbabweans had to endure the rigors of buying basic needs only from the avaricious parallel market where they were available. Price controls and pronounced government intervention in the running of the economy thus stifled not only free market forces and consumers rights but also generated new and worse challenges for the Zimbabwean consumer.

The internationally condemned Operation *Murambatsvina* of 2005 had constituted the ZANU-PF government's third jibe at the country's free market system. Ostensibly embarked on to deal with, among others, unsanctioned urban structures meant for habitation and business operations such as informal trading (Tibaijuka, 2005, p.205) it had an adverse impact on the free enterprise. More so, taking into account that some of the informal structures in question had mushroomed as a result of enterprising unemployed workers retrenched after the 1990s Bretton Woods initiated Economic Structural Adjustment Programme (ESAP) (Tshuma, 1997:122). As a result of the operation, a significant number of Zimbabwe's labor was reportedly forced to migrate to regional and international destinations (Clemens and Moss, 2005:4) such as South Africa, UK, Canada and USA in search of work and a living wage.

Between the years 2005 and 2008, the sum total of Zimbabwe's economic situation became that of an economy that due to a substantial government command presence was failing to meet economic growth and cater for the country's public welfare. Clemens and Moss (2005:1) report that: "[T]he purchasing power of the average Zimbabwean in 2005 [...] fell back to the same level as in 1953". Such a great fall in the country's economy translated "directly into sickness and death" (ibid). A humanitarian crisis threatened as the economy continued to shrink and people's daily needs of food, medication, clean drinking water, electricity and fuel ran out. The standard of living of most Zimbabweans drastically lowered.

The food shortages and near mass starvation that followed caused thousands of Zimbabweans to seek "alternatives in the context of economic collapse and repressive authoritarian nationalism" at home (Zimbabwe Torture Victims Project, 2005, p.3). An estimated three million left the country in search of the proverbial greener pastures. By the end of 2008, an estimated 60% to 70% of Zimbabwe's economically active population had left the country due to the country's hostile socioeconomic and political environment.

Historically, the particular or holistic implementation of price controls has always disastrously failed. Indeed Rothbard (1995) writes that: "[I]n every age, in every culture, price controls have never worked. They have been a disaster." From Hammurabi, Babylon, and the Roman Empire to the 1970s "experiences of the United States, Japan, Canada, and Australia, price controls have been tried [and...] have been found wanting" (Pharmaceutical Manufacturing Association 2002, p.105). Therefore, arm-twisting business people in a free market towards price control defies business logic as they will stop producing and selling commodities as long as doing so translates into a loss-making venture.

It is perhaps because of such reasons that Cox (2007) makes an analogy between price controls and "plugging a thermometer so that it never can read greater than 72 degrees even though the actual temperature may be higher." The reality of price-fixing often reveals itself in a vibrant black market, a reduction in the quality of products produced and valuable time lost by consumers as they queue for hours to access commodities that are unavailable. As has been pointed out elsewhere, this is because price controls "create artificial scarcities, resource misallocation, and a black market. Large bureaucratic structures for administration are in such cases necessary. Problems of enforcement and equity arise" (Pharmaceutical Manufacturing Association, 2002, p.104) as indeed the aftermath of Zimbabwe's price slash and freeze proved.

The implementation of command economic measures in Zimbabwe again demonstrated that they are catastrophic to economic growth and stability, and human welfare and well-being. Consequently, Mberi (2007) likened Zimbabwe's Operation *Dzikisai Mitengo* to the economic folly of the Roman Emperor, Diocletian. Faced with hyperinflation in AD 301, "Diocletian ordered that merchants halve prices. He then set maximum prices for a range of basic goods" (*Financial Gazette*, July 12–18, 2007). However, instead of reducing inflation as Diocletian had hoped, the controls only managed to drive commodities onto the black market and created severe shortages.

Akin to Diocletian and others before him, the ZANU-PF government soon learnt that price controls have only short-term political gains. Because of its attempts to control the economy, it has often noted Zimbabweans, both black and white, voted with their feet. Mass emigration heralded the fall of the country's economy to unprecedented levels in the history of contemporary economies outside the war zone. The emigration of people to neighboring countries to look for jobs (AfDB/OECD, 2003, p.368) and other opportunities led not only to a breakdown of the social fabric but also started an irreversible hemorrhage of the country's skilled workforce from the shrinking and tottering economy. Services sectors such as education and health were mainly left compromised as skills left the country and companies could no longer sustain their social responsibilities.

Events and Zimbabweans' experiences particularly between 2007 and 2008 testified to the disturbing complications a government's populist intervention in an economy can cause. The specter of business' supposed political machinations resulted in even more hardships for consumers and the Zimbabwean economy. By the end of August 2007, the suffering of

Zimbabwean citizens had become so acute that the ZANU-PF government made a U-turn on the price blitz, "in the interests of the general public". The business community was once again permitted to hike prices to economically viable levels. The policy shift from a command economy to a quasi-free market system testified that a free market is a better economic alternative to a command approach. It is unfortunate that it had taken so much suffering and displacement for this to be acknowledged.

As observed by Rockoff (2002) writing in a different context, "controls only postpone the day of reckoning, converting what would have been steady inflation into a period of slow inflation followed by more rapid inflation." Indeed, other countries' experiences have been such that "when controls have been ended, inflation typically has equaled or exceeded the rate which would have been reached without controls" (Pharmaceutical Manufacturers Association 2002:104). The market-oriented prices instituted by business caused a steep rise in commodity prices and a subsequent meteoritic rise in inflation. An upward spiral in inflation and a steep rise in prices of commodities followed the government's marginal relaxation of price controls. By October 2007, the PDL had risen to close to fifty million Zimbabwe dollars (*The Zimbabwean*, October 2007).

The ZANU-PF government's blinkered belief that the country's economic woes were solely the result of Western governments' calculated machinations to destabilize the country blinded it to its own economic miscalculations as the cause of the crisis' hyperinflation. As Maanda and Tsunga pointed out, the:

> order by the government for business to reduce prices and sell their commodities at prices that prevailed before June 18, 2007, was ill-conceived and was executed without regard to the consequences that have since proved to be dire for the economy. (Maanda and Tsunga 2007, p.7)

The aftermath of the June 2007 price blitz once again testified to the fact that though the command and control approach coercively manages to suppress inflation to respectable levels, once removed, the reality has dire consequences to the whole economy. It is perhaps because of this that Bloch (2007:12) reminded that "recurrent political interventions are contrary to sound business decision-making and constructive operational procedures." The clarion call was for the ZANU-PF government "…to disinvest from its enterprises, so that market forces govern the future operations of those enterprises in a competitive environment" (ibid). If government indeed transparently disinvested from its public enterprises in a free market atmosphere, this would lead to their better economic performance and sustainable production levels commensurate with the nation's needs.

## *Zimbabwe's Economic Future Lies in the Past: The Free Market Economy*

In light of the catastrophic collapse brought in by a commando-economic approach in Zimbabwe, a return to a free market economy is advisable. Traditional Western economics extols free trade and believes that a government's minimal intervention or non-interference results in the best economic outcome for all concerned, but it also makes universal business sense. Among others, firms benefit from their countries' natural endowments or comparative advantages. Writing on free enterprise, Levitt highlights that:

> capitalism, as we like it, can thrive only in an environment of political democracy and personal freedom. These require a pluralistic society where there is division, not centralisation, of power; variety, not unanimity, social, and spiritual function. (1983, p.83)

Parallel to Block (2007), Levitt (1983) is strongly against bureaucratic bungling in a free market. In his view, governments need not unnecessarily peg prices of commodities and determine the manner in which participants in a free market should transact business. As such, Levitt takes great exception to: "[A]n omnipotent state because it creates a dull and frightening conformity-a monolithic society" (1983:83) in which there is "one locus of power, one authority, one arbiter of property" (ibid). Where such conditions prevail, Levitt advises that:

> business should fight off any threats of government controls of its operations that are unwarranted if business organisations are to achieve their mandate of profit-making through the provision of goods and services to society. (1983:83)

Levitt thus recommends the liberalization of a country's market to enable participants to freely transact without government fixing prices of commodities in the market to levels that are economically nonsensical.

British empiricist and political philosopher, John Locke, also strongly argued for unregulated markets where free individuals or business organizations trade their wares free from undue state interference. (De George 2006) Locke's argument for unregulated markets derived from his belief that human beings have certain natural rights that can only be preserved by free markets. In Locke's view, one such right was every individual's freedom to "voluntarily exchange commodities with others free from the intervention and coercive power of government and legislative impediments" (Matson, 1987, p.322). The massive presence and involvement of government in economic activities were, therefore, contrary to the notion of unregulated markets and also an open indictment to business people's right to voluntary and profitable free trade.

Adam Smith, a Scottish moral philosopher and famed "father of modern economics" (Beardshaw, Brewster and Ross, 2001:127) strongly support Locke's view concerning free markets. In his utilitarianism argument, Smith supports the free market system. He states that only those actions that bring about the greatest net happiness of the people affected by the action have the greatest utility (Velasquez, 1997). It is Smith's belief that in a free market this is when people are left to pursue their self-interests are led by the "invisible hand" to promote public welfare (Wonnacott and Wonnacott, 1990:46). To Smith, the "invisible hand" was the unintended or accidental fulfilment of the needs and wants of people by participants in the market.

One prominent feature of a pure free market system is a competitive environment in which private businesses compete with each other for the same customers. The law of supply and demand helps to prevent sellers from becoming ruthless and cruel profiteers (Shaw, 1999:135) by ensuring that commodities are available at prices that are fair to both the seller and consumers. It was Smith's understanding that such competition would eventually lead to businesses' allocation of their economic resources to ventures that would best maximize returns and incidentally contribute the most to social utility. Hence, Smith's famous remark:

> It is not from the benevolence of the butcher, the baker, and the brewer that we expect our dinner, but from their regard for their own self-interest. We address ourselves not to their humanity, but to their self-love, and never talk to them of our own necessities, but of their advantage. Nobody but a beggar chooses to depend chiefly upon the benevolence of his fellow citizens. (Smith 1991, p.125)

In Smith's view, business persons' promotion of social utility is not primary to their endeavors but is incidentally congruent to their pursuit of profits.

There are, however, instances when a government can justifiably intervene in a free market system. For instance, when unscrupulous manufacturers deliberately produce structurally defective goods that are potentially harmful to consumers or threaten the environment or act illegally, it is the government's responsibility to intervene and enforce adherence to relevant standards. Other than that, it is incumbent on government to ensure that businesses operate in an environment devoid of unnecessary government intervention.

In 2007, then as now, a significant portion of Zimbabwe's manufacturing industries and its means of production were in the hands of foreign-owned corporate organizations headquartered in foreign nations. Partly due and as a response to the government's land reform program, together with some retail outlets, they reportedly colluded to reduce production and fix the prices of commodities. Such actions ruled out competition, and prices became unilateral. Inflation escalated, and prices were changed daily and even hourly. It no longer was right that the self-interested motives of private individuals and organizations in a free market system inevitably lead to the maximization of social utility. In all fairness, the government was forced to act in order to protect the populace. However, it was the action it decided to take, that of controlling prices and ultimately the economy that became the catalyst for more problems.

In deciding to control prices and Zimbabwe's economy, the Zimbabwean government believed that certain businesses in the country had been deployed to engineer economic decline and unemployment levels. If left unchecked, it was indeed a situation that could lead to the collapse of the economy and eventually social and political unrest. The ZANU-PF government thus felt it was legally justified to interfere with the operations and activities of Zimbabwe's free-market economy, and correct economic injustices that it perceived were the result of irresponsible and irrational price hikes which had as their political agenda, regime change (The Financial Gazette, 2007, July 12–18, p.15). In the ruling party's view, some form of economic despotism was necessary to promote social utility and nip the specter of irresponsible business practices in the bud.

Subsequently, just as other countries had done at some stages of their history, (Rockoff 2002) the Zimbabwe government took some quick-fix measures to arrest the worsening economic situation. Unfortunately, while the intention was commendable, the action to institute the June 2007 price blitz was in the view of this researcher not the best and only accelerated the country's economic decline. Particularly as the government's economic policies post-2000 became more for political rather than economic expediency.

The merits of a free market economy manifested themselves in Zimbabwe with the installation of the country's Inclusive Government in 2009. The gradual deregulation of the economy and currency to be used as tender saw the country gradually return to a sound economic footing. Business organizations ability to charge economically viable prices for their commodities spurred higher production levels, competitive pricing and the maximization of social utility. Essential commodities that had virtually disappeared from shop shelves between June and August 2007 returned to the shelves.

The availability of essential commodities on the local market and the adoption of stable multiple hard currencies, among other positive economic changes, improved the general standards of living of people in the country. For the first time in about a decade, a "credible record of strong policy implementation to ensure macroeconomic stability, [and] entrench reforms" (Itam cited in IMF Country Report No. 09/1392009, p.4) returned to Zimbabwe. Concerning Zimbabwe's return to a free market economy, the IMF Country Report No. 09/139 (2009) noted that:

> Against [this] background of the economic and humanitarian crisis, the new administration has rapidly taken several macroeconomic and supply-side policy actions in the fiscal, monetary, financial, and structural areas aimed at maintaining low inflation, halting and reversing the economic decline, and improving social conditions. The new administration's Short-Term Emergency Recovery Program (STERP) articulated this. Through strict fiscal discipline and appropriate monetary policy, macroeconomic stability is must be restored, and inflation contained (IMF Country Report No. 09/1392009, 2009, p.1).

Indeed, economic developments in Zimbabwe's economy following the formation of a government of national unity bore witness to the actuality that a return to the fundamentals of a free market system is the panacea Zimbabwe's two-decades-long economic freefall had been waiting. The country's prudent fiscal policy shift that the then ZANU-PF- MDC-T government introduced breathed life into the economy and gave some confidence to otherwise highly skeptical investors.

From mid-2009 onwards, Zimbabwe's transitional political arrangement and return to a free market approach halted and began a reversal of the country's decade-long economic freefall. It countered "the tightening of price controls and exchange restrictions [which had] exacerbated the deterioration in business climate" (IMF Country Report No. 09/1392009, 2009:1). This economic policy shift and reform agenda helped transform and bring stability to Zimbabwe's once-battered economy, ignited by a command approach to it. This chapter advocates that government continue to nurture sound free-market principles predicated on non-to-minimal interventionist approaches to the country's economic affairs. Any future economic policy changes should, therefore, be implemented for the sake of Zimbabwe's economic stability, sustainability, greater social utility and with a view to incentivizing both local and foreign investors to invest in the country.

## *Conclusion*

Zimbabwe's blatant flirtation with a command system arguably led to the country's economic crisis. The years 2000–2009 proved that a paternalistic approach to an economy is suicidal and does not bring about a sustainable solution to skyrocketing inflation. Events after the infamous June 2007 price slash and freeze in the country testified to the fact that an unregulated market is a better alternative to a command economy. Price controls caused the flight of existing investors and scared potential foreign direct investment away as they arbitrarily tempered with free-market economic efficiency. Subsequent to which the economy and Zimbabwean consumers' welfare suffered as price controls accompanied by widespread shortages, the emergence of parallel trading, exorbitant prices and the specter of corruption resulted in widespread hardship.

Undeniably, the case of Zimbabwe during the crisis once again showed how coercive interference by government in the operations of private enterprises, more often than not, stifles competition in the market (Smith, 2002b). It bore true to the fact that individual business organizations are not motivated to employ their economic and human resources to the fullest when faced with economically unviable price decrees. As a result, during 2007 and 2009, production levels of the country's manufacturing industries drastically slumped and shortages set in, leading to the suffering of consumers and the collapse or migration of both business and consumers. Of those businesses that remained, the prevailing situation forced them to compromise quality in order to remain viable, and the absence of competition did not justify improvement.

On a political level, price-fixing and coercive interference in the operations of a free market system by the ZANU-PF government demonstrated the short-term political gains and long-term consequences that accrue from controlling an economy. However, as the chapter has also highlighted, political intervention is at times justified. It should just not be the institution of price controls. At best, it should take the form of government, business and labor concurring on a social contract administered along free-market economic principles. In the absence of such a consensus by all stakeholders, the unilateral implementation of a command economy by any government can definitely be a monumental disaster of sheer socioeconomic insanity, political retardation and instability, as Zimbabwe's experience demonstrated.

## *Notes*

1. Affiliation: Department of Philosophy and Religious Studies Great Zimbabwe University

## *References*

African Economic Outlook. (2003). *Zimbabwe*. AfDB/OECD.

Ayittey, G. B. N. (1998). *Africa in chaos*. New York: St Martin's Press.

Beardshaw, J., Brewster, D., & Ross, A. (2001). *Economics: A student's guide.* Harlow: Prentice Hall.

Bloch, E. (2007, September 7–13). Foolhardy rejection of privatisation. In *The Zimbabwean independent.* Harare: Zimind Publishers (Pvt) Ltd.

Bond, P. (2001). Radical rhetoric and the working class during Zimbabwean nationalism's dying days. In B. Raftopoulos & L. Sachikonye (Eds.), *Striking back: The labour movement and the post-colonial state in Zimbabwe 1980–2000.* Harare: Weaver Press.

Bond, P. (2007). *What today's looting of Africa tells us about tomorrow's looting of Zimbabwe* (pp.1–10). Harare: A New Zimbabwe Lecture for the Zimbabwe Research Foundation, 31 July.

Bond, P., & Manyanya, M. (2003). *Zimbabwe plunge: Exhausted nationalism, neoliberalism and the search for social justice.* London: Merlin Press.

Bracking, S., & Sachikonye, L. (2009). *Development finance, private and public sectors in Zimbabwe: Sustainability or odious debt?* (BWPI working paper 84, pp. 1–22). Manchester: Brooks World Poverty Institute.

Chitambara, P. (2007, July 12–18). Of price controls and the social contract. In *The financial gazette.* Harare: Fingaz.

Clemens, M., & Moss, T. (2005). *Costs and causes of Zimbabwe's crisis* (pp. 1–4). Washington: Centerfor Global Development.

Cox, J. (2007). The concise guide to economics. http://www.FreedomKeys.com/bkecon.htm

De George, R. T. (2006). *Business ethics.* Upper Saddle River, NJ: Pearson Prentice Hall.

Friedman, M. (1983). The social responsibility of business is to increase its profits. In Snoeyenbos, M., Almender, R., & Humber, J. (Eds.), *Business ethics and corporate values and society.* New York: Prometheus Books.

Grant, S. J. (2000). *Stanlake's introductory economics.* Essex: Pearson Education Limited.

Hanke, S. H. (2008). *Zimbabwe: From hyperinflation to growth.*Washington: The CATO Institute, June 25, No. 6, 1–36.

International Monetary Fund. (2009). *Zimbabwe: 2009 article IV consultation-staff report; public information notice on the executive board discussion; and statement by the executive director for Zimbabwe.* Washington: International Monetary Fund Publication Services, IMF Country Report No. 09/139, 1–49.

Levitt, T. (1983). The dangers of social responsibility. In T. L. Beauchamp & Bowie, N. E. (Eds.), *Ethical theory and business.* Englewood Cliffs: Prentice-Hall, Inc.

Locke, J. (2002). Of the state of nature. In L. P. Hartman (Ed.), *Perspectives in business ethics.* New Delhi: Tata McGraw-Hill Publishing Company Limited.

Maanda, T., & Tsunga, A. (2007, September 7–13). Price war driven by malice. In *The Zimbabwe independent.* Harare: Zimind Publishers (Pvt) Ltd.

Makochekanwa, A., & Kwaramba, M. (2009). *State fragility: Zimbabwe's horrific journey in the new millennium* (pp. 1–36). Accra: A Research Paper Presented at the European Report on Development's (ERD).

Matson, W. I. (1987). *A new history of philosophy* (Vol.11). Orlando: Harcourt Brace & Company.

Mberi, R. (2007, July 12–18). The emperor's new clones: Govt latest stroke of economic genius borrowed from ancient times. In *The financial gazette*. Harare: Fingaz.

Moore, D. S. (2005). *Suffering for territory: Race, place, and power in Zimbabwe*. Harare: Weaver Press.

Moyana, H. V. (2002). *The political economy of land in Zimbabwe*. Gweru: Mambo Press.

Pharmaceutical Manufacturers Association. (2002). Price controls in the economy and the health sector. In L. H. Newton & M. M. Ford (Eds.), *Taking sides: Clashing views on controversial issues in business ethics and society*. Guilford: McGraw-Hill/Dushkin.

Raftopoulos, B. (2001). The labour and the emergence of opposition politics in Zimbabwe. In B. Raftopoulos & L. Sachikonye (Eds.), *Striking back: The labour movement and post-colonial state in Zimbabwe 1980–2000*. Harare: Weaver Press.

Rockoff, H. (2002). The Concise Encyclopedia of Economics: Price controls. Retrieved September 19, 2014, fromhttp://www.ecolib.org/library/Encl/PriceControls.html

Rothbard, M. N. (1995). Making economic sense. Retrieved September 19, 2014, from http://www.FreedomKeys.com/bkecon.htm#sense

Shaw, W. H. (1999). *Business ethics*. Belmont: Wadsworth Publishing Company.

Smith, A. (1991). *The wealth of nations*. London: David Campbell Publishers Ltd.

Smith, A. (2002a). An inquiry into the nature and causes of the wealth of nations. In L. Newton & M. M. Ford (Eds.), *Taking sides. Clashing views on controversial issues in business ethics and society*. Guilford: McGraw-Hill/Dushkin.

Smith, A. (2002b). The wealth of nations. In L. P. Hartman (Ed.), *Perspectives in business ethics*. New Delhi: Tata McGraw-Hill Publishing Company Limited.

Sowell, T. (2002). An ancient fallacy: Price controls. In H. Hazlitt (Ed.), *Economics in one lesson*. http://www.FreedomKeys.com/bkecon.htm

Spinello, R. A. (2002).Ethics, pricing and the pharmaceutical industry. In L. H. Newton & Ford, M. M. (Eds.), *Taking sides: Clashing views on controversial issues in business ethics and society*. Guilford: McGraw-Hill/Dushkin.

The Solidarity Peace Trust. (2007). *A difficult dialogue: Zimbabwe-South Africa economic relations since 2000*. Solidarity Peace Trust, 23 October, 1–45.

The Standard Comment. (2007, September 2–8). *The standard*. Harare: Standard Press (Pvt) Ltd.

Tibaijuka, A. K. (2005). *Report of the fact-finding mission to Zimbabwe to assess the scope and impact of operation Murambatsvina by the UN special envoy on human settlements issues in Zimbabwe* (pp. 1–100). Harare: UN.

Tshuma, L. (1997). *A matter of (In) justice: Law, state and the Agrarian question in Zimbabwe*. Harare: SAPES Books.

Velasquez, M. G. (1997). Ethical principles in business. In K. A. Getz (Ed.), *Business, ethics and society*. Needham Heights: Simon & Schuster Education Group.

Velasquez, M. G. (2002). *Business ethics: Concepts and cases.* New Delhi: Pearson Education, Inc.

Wonnacott, P., & Wonnacott, R. (1990). *Economics.* New York: John Wiley & Sons.

Zimbabwe Torture Victims Project. (2005). Between a rock and a hard place: A window on the situation of Zimbabweans living in Gauteng. *idasa*, 1–11.

Zitha, B. (2007, September 13–19). Black market thrives...as minister threatens. *The Zimbabwean.* Hythe, London: The Zimbabwean.

# 4 *Herrera (2005) and the Role of Imagined Economies in State-Controlled Zimbabwe*

LEVAR LAMAR SMITH[1]

## *Introduction*

This chapter deploys concepts of Yoshiko Herrera's Imagined Economies thesis to explore how social constructions of the economy can be used by authoritarian-inclined governments such as that of ZANU-PF to centralize power under the guise of nationalism. In my view, from 1999 Zimbabwe became an excellent example of some dimensions of Herrera's imagined economies with regards to its government's use of nationalism and the economy as forms of state control.

### *Orthodox and the Consolidation of Post-independent Zimbabwe*

Herrera's pioneering *Imagined Economies* (2005) thesis confronts several critical assumptions regarding the connection between nationalism and economic interests. Her main argument focuses on how economic factors are constructed around particular social values and cultural affinities. In Herrera's view, the presence of external influences on the economy creates advantages and disadvantages that are imagined by state actors at the national or regional level. On the basis of how the collapse of the Soviet Union undermined the career paths of local elites who had depended on the delegation of authority from the center for their affirmation and legitimization, for instance, Herrera (2005) posits that the political disintegration at the center and the struggle over legitimacy at the regional level by local elites coincide with and result in institutional decline.

For this reason, Herrera (2005, p.76) believes that if the centralization of power within a nation collapses or fails to provide beneficial economic services coincidental with regional needs and demands, then the push for geographical separation is likely. As such, the contribution of the imagined economies framework is:

> to bring previously established insights regarding the constructed nature of the economy and economic interests to the literature on movements for greater sovereignty including, nationalism, regionalism, and separatism. The imagined economies framework suggests that (1) economic structural variables alone do not determine economic interests; (2) economic facts are subject to multiple understandings; and (3) benefits and external conditions are mutually constituting (Herrera, 2005, pp.94–95).

Because the dynamics of the imagined economy are a multifaceted part of society's political and cultural histories, an understanding of imagined economies is dependent on multiple, legitimate interpretations of data or economic information by the state and its actors. This makes any perspective of the economy derivable from the preexisting state's common beliefs.

In the imagined economies framework, a state's monopoly on dominant values is viewed as the *doxa*, "a thought construct that often exists unquestioned by those in society" (Herrera, 2005, pp.88–89). Challenges to the existing *doxa* either result in the reaffirmation of the *orthodox* (defense of established beliefs) or the emergence of the *heterodox* (social change and disruption) as competing forms of social understandings. The process of imagined economies takes into account both the *heterodox* and *orthodox* perceptions about the state of the economy based on each group's knowledge of localized social, political, cultural, and historical factors. These then either reinforce institutional perceptions or lead to the development of new political and economic systems (Herrera, 2001). Beginning with racial confrontations over economic growth, during Zimbabwe's post-independence period of 1999–2009, this process occurred at several junctures.

At first glance, the literature on Zimbabwe's economic malaise and hyperinflation suggest it to be the consequence of the country's land seizures on the domestic economy. However, surveyed and guided from and by Herrera's imagined economies theory, it is clear that in the post-independence period, the country's historical roots of economic inequality continued to fuel existing animosities between white commercial farmers and predominately black society. This is because, characteristic of Herera's notion of the *orthodox*, after a challenge to the *doxa*, the foundation of Zimbabwe's statehood continued to rest on the recognition of race-based economic rights from the country's colonization in 1897 to its independence from Britain in 1980.

As part of a negotiated settlement between the British government, Robert Mugabe's Zimbabwe African National Union (ZANU) and Joshua Nkomo's Zimbabwe African People's Union (ZAPU), Zimbabwe's new black government inherited a defeated settler state with hostilities towards it and a strikingly racially unequal agricultural system (Herbst, 1989). At independence, more than two-thirds of the country's most arable land was in white hands and because of some provisions of the Lancaster House agreement, could only be reappropriated by the new black government on the basis of "willing buyer, willing seller". The policy of reconciliation pursued by the Mugabe government soon after independence from white minority rule sought to diffuse the underlying racial and economic tensions and their potential to destabilize the country. In this regard, the new Zimbabwe had attempted to create a government committed towards development than around questions of race and land. In his first speech during the country's independence celebrations, the then Prime Minister Mugabe had focused directly on racial harmony:

> If ever we look to the past, let us do so for the lesson the past has taught us, namely that oppression and racism are inequities that must never again find scope in our political and social system. It could never be a correct justification that because whites oppressed us yesterday when they had power, the blacks must oppress them today because they have power. An evil remains an evil whether practiced by white against black or by black against white. Our majority rule could easily turn into inhuman rule if we oppressed, persecuted or harassed those who do not look or think like the majority of us. We have abundant mineral, agricultural and human resources to exploit and develop for which we need perfect peace. Given such peace, our endeavors to transform our society and raise our standard of living are bound to succeed. We already have a sophisticated infrastructure. Our expertise is bound to increase as more and more educational and technical institutions are established to transform our skilled manpower (Mugabe, 1980, inaugural speech).

By all intense and purposes, it seemed Mugabe truly believed it "was time to beat our swords into plowshares so we can attend to the problem of developing our economy and society" (Raftopolous, 1996, pp.169). However, the reason for the reconciliation policy was also partly to prevent the flight of white skills as had previously occurred after Angola and Mozambique's independence from the Portuguese in 1975.

By reaching out to the predominately white large-scale commercial settler farmers, the new black government retained the "technological expertise necessary to foster economic development and preserved economic stability in the country through the protection of minority white property in exchange for political authority" (Norman, 2004:83). Looked at from another angle, however, by deciding to follow a policy of reconciliation, the black government, together with the Lancaster House Agreement, further perpetuated white farmers' control of the land. Twenty years later, this would play a significant role in the dynamic interaction between history, ideas, data, and the centralization of power by the Zanu (PF) government.

In the meantime, the Zimbabwean government embarked on what can at best be described as an unofficial populist policy of Africanization. From 1980 onwards, the government commendably provided beneficial social services mainly in health and education. They were geared towards gaining the support of civil society at large while at the same time pushing the moral imperatives of the black government. During the initial years of independence, the Mugabe government showed its seriousness in addressing the needs of the country's impoverished urban and rural black citizens. Its Africanization thrust saw the establishment and implementation of new legislation to confront racial inequity in education and the civil service. As an economic and ideological doctrine, Africanization tapped into the *orthodoxy* of *Chimurenga*, the Shona word for "revolutionary struggle." Developments within the country became connected to the ruling party's historical consciousness of resistance and self-determination (Shaw, 2003). Similarly, some twenty years later, Zimbabwe's land reform programwould be branded the *Third Chimurenga* (Mugabe, 2001), the continuation of Zimbabwe's historical fight to end colonial occupation to promote black economic and social development.

To ensure that its Africanization development programs garnered support, after independence, the government's expressions of political and economic autonomy were popularized. This was done through the state's media outlets that were sympathetic to the government's Africanization rhetoric. For example, the majority black staff of the weekly newspaper *The Sunday Mail* focused on social issues despite the lingering skepticism of the new regime's ability to continue providing social services (Kinloch, 2003). Promotion of nationalism through media outlets allowed ZANU-PF to develop its political allegiances amongst the population, mainly in the country's rural constituencies. Thus, by way of its rural development policy and the media, the ruling party managed to remain active in the context of nominally democratic institutions (Gandhi, 2007).

The politics of resource allocation and patronage often blur the line between the private and public (Rutherford 2004). In the context of Zimbabwe, land and its tenure as sources of economic sustainability and patronage are also critical to understanding the country's story. Before 1980, the Native Land Husbandry Act of 1951 had granted chiefs parcels of land to distribute as recognition of their power (Nyambara, 2001). Post-independence, therefore, the existent smallholder land tenure in the country's rural areas was that which had been established by some of the colonial government's appointed chiefs. This had resulted in peasants' dependence on their traditional leaders.

After independence, the ZANU-PF government established and implemented the Land Reform and Resettlement Program as well as propagated the District Councils Act. Under the two, the government sought to control the distribution of land through the formation of rural-based administrations. With ZANU's political allegiance concentrated mainly within the country' rural areas, the establishment of District Councils created for the ruling party a top-down channeling of resources from the center to cadres at the local level. The new system replaced the old chieftaincy-style authority (McGregor, 2002). The power of traditional leaders diminished, though they remained part and parcel of the state. This enabled land distribution by chiefs to continue as some of them found new ways to bypass official channels and sell land to members of their communities.

At the state level, akin to a limited form of land redistribution, the Zimbabwean government gave some political elites ninety-nine-year leases to some commercial farms purchased for the resettlement program. The result was all a manner of patronage. In response, these political elites utilized their leases not only to maximize land rents and wealth accumulation, but they also used them to make political connections as well as means to create additional opportunities for themselves in the private sector (Brett 2005:97). This is especially when after 1987, government cemented the influence of newly formed Zimbabwe African National Union-Patriotic Front (ZANU-PF) over the economy and its executive right to rule. Parastatals and agricultural control regimes such as the Grain Marketing Board (GMB) and the Agricultural Rural Development Authority (ARDA) responsible for the resettlement of communal area farmers and households were politicized. After that, ZANU-PF's policy approaches regarding land resettlement, economic inequality, and poverty alleviation became an attempt towards nationalizing industrial capital while appeasing the emerging African comprador class within the country.

As a result of an average economic growth of 4% from 1980 to 1990, the government advocated greater public ownership modeled on socialist policies. This was apparently to ensure that: "[T]he private sector did not fall prey to the economic, foreign influence of countries such as South Africa" (Herbst, 1989, p.77). Import substitution industrialization and tariffs protecting state-owned enterprises from foreign competition were also revived or instituted. Agricultural price controls gave commercial farmers cheap credit while food subsidies reduced urban food prices (Thomas, 2003). By the end of the first decade of independence, the State's intervention had consolidated power through additional subsidies in education and health. In so doing, it had benefitted from reigning in various sections of the economy in exchange for ideological and political access to its citizens. This was, however, to decline throughout the 1990s as a direct result of both the United States and the Soviet Union scaling back economic aid and the country's political support of many African states.

## *Economic Structural Adjustment and the Decline of the Nation-state*

From independence, the government had steadily assumed the role of main employer. Over the years, this had led to the expansion of the civil service at the government's expense. The country's wage bill had substantially added to its mounting external debt. The International Monetary Fund's Economic Structural Adjustment Policies (ESAP) that began in Zimbabwe from 1990 ended the country's socialist economic system. It was believed that ESAP would introduce competitiveness, prevent financial crisis, and promote stability not only in Zimbabwe but also throughout Africa. Its implementation encouraged the ZANU (PF) government to eliminate economic subsidies, actively involve itself in the economy, and liberalize trade.

The imposition of neoliberal reforms on a country with an inefficient market economy and ill-equipped to deal with foreign intervention led to and exacerbated the nation's economic and societal ills. Ideological contradictions between the government's socialist leanings and the realities of capitalist structural adjustment came to a head when social services and civil service jobs that since independence had been provided by the state were curtailed. Government cuts in the civil service led to public sector strikes primarily among nurses and teachers. In response, the Civil Service Reform Program was instituted in 1996 as a negotiated settlement between the government and the public sector to increase salaries by more than 60%. However, when civil servants demanded even higher wage increases, (McGregor 2002, p.13), protests against ESAP not only challenged the structural adjustment program but governmental efficacy as well. The government was prompted to resort to repression against civil service workers.

The Zimbabwean government's failure to provide concessions to the civil service immensely affected the Mugabe government's ability to retain its widespread support among urban elites. Its reduction of food, education, and agricultural subsidies further undermined its ability to maintain economic patronage to elites and the rural poor. Negative economic growth occurred as cuts in government spending impeded on the growth of new business ventures. Besides, ESAP's impediments to Zimbabwe's industrialization coincided with the cancellation of trade and tariffs with the South African government.

Conversely, the United Kingdom's failure to deliver on its 1988 pledge to provide economic aid contributed to the devaluation of the national currency and the inefficiency of the GMB entrusted with, among others, the collection and distribution of grain throughout the country. Due to structural adjustment, the GMB's ineffectiveness hampered black peasant and small-scale farmers from accessing agricultural information and technical services regarding inputs and food production. This was also partly because, despite the government's policy of reconciliation, the economy and, as such, credit and investment facilities continued to be controlled by a white minority. Limited access to lines of credit, financial and agricultural markets, water rights, and arable land undermined black peasant and small-scale farmers' ability to be and remain an integral part of the nation's agricultural productivity in comparison to their white counterparts.

By 1994, food prices in Zimbabwe had risen by more than 225% (Thomas, 2003, p.699). The Zimbabwe National Liberation War Veterans Association (ZNLWVA) and the Zimbabwe Congress of Trade Unions (ZCTU) emerged from the shadows and tabled other structural adjustment–related issues. The ZNLWVA came out to demand gratuities, land, and greater political participation for war veterans. While for its part, the ZCTU to push for a living wage for ESAP stressed Zimbabweans. The culmination was the mobilization of civil society against the ZANU-PF government. Calls by the ZCTU for work stayaways were obeyed, and the economy adversely affected.

In 1980, the Zimbabwean government had implemented war provision legislation that legitimized the role of war veterans and granted disability pensions of Z$400 to ex-combatants who had not been incorporated into the new army (Kriger 2003). In addition to the incorporation of some war veterans into the national army, a few cooperative programs had focused explicitly on retraining and educating other ex-combatants. In the case of some individual war veterans, their appointment to senior posts in the military and civil service had taken priority over the development of comprehensive policies towards reintegration and demobilization (Raftopolous, 1992:64) of the others.

In 1989, the second phase of the war provision legislation had given additional recognition to war veterans already on state pensions. This had allowed ex-combatants who had been part of the uniformed services to count their years of military service towards their retirement pension. Although these reforms had worked to appease those war veterans already within the civil service, they did little to alleviate the isolation of war veterans left to work on farm cooperatives or engage in subsistence farming. These developments around war veterans set the foundation for future disgruntlement and widespread unrest.

The establishment of the Zimbabwe National Liberation War Veteran's Association (ZNLWVA) in the 1990s brought to new heights war veterans' long struggle for recognition, compensation, and benefits from the ZANU-PF government. Led by the charismatic leadership of Dr. Chenjerai Hunzwi, a polish trained medical doctor, the association of the country's former freedomfighters initially sought to represent its members' demands for greater pensions rather than land rights (Chan and Primorac, 2004, p.70). In the late 1990s, the ZNLWVA mounted both legal and extralegal protests against the government's apathy to its members' plight in the face of economic structural adjustment constraints. To appease the ZNLWVA, the government's War Veterans Act of 1997 granted more than 70,000 ex-combatants veterans' concessions in the form of substantial cash gratuities, healthcare, education provisions, and monthly pensions. Government's inability to secure external loans and its payout of the unbudgeted gratuities significantly impacted the Zimbabwean dollar. In the face of falling world commodity prices for Zimbabwe's exports of gold, tobacco, and steel, the country's participation in the Democratic Republic of Congo's civil war, intermittent drought and recent economic mismanagement, the country's currency collapsed against other major currencies and firmly put the country on the path to economic decline.

The creation of the Zimbabwe Congress of Trade Unions (ZCTU) in 1980 had provided the government with trade unionism as a corporatist solution to labor issues. Since its inception, therefore, the ZCTU had faced difficulties distancing itself from the government primarily because of its lack of democratic structures and financial independence (Raftopoulous, 1992). Consequently, over the years, the labor organization had been plagued with low worker participation and diminishing credibility. The ZTCU's public perception worsened when in 1990, the ZANU-PF government capitalized on the labor movement's weakness by not allocating it any of the twenty seats formerly reserved for whites parliamentarians under the Lancaster House Agreement. The labor movement was effectively put at the margins (Raftopoulous 1992, p.58). Thus, due to its lack of collective and political will, the ZCTU would throughout most of the 1990s continue to operate in its historical role of more or less a cleavage of the State. Towards the end of the 1990s however, this changed.

The rise of the Zambian labor movement and the ascension of its leader Frederick Chiluba as president of Zambia in the mid-1990s to some extent influenced the ZCTU's political activism. On the other hand, the negative impact of ESAP and the end of Zimbabwe's corporatist economy in the 1990s ensured an end to the labor movement's political apathy. The ZCTU's membership benefited from a decline in employment, the "professional status of civil service workers, declining purchasing power, and reduced wages within the public sector" (Raftopoulos, 1992, pp. 59–60). Together with other civil society formations, the ZCTU clamored for democratic governance and the removal of corrupt leadership amid a declining economy and a waning government. They embarked on strike action to ensure they achieved their goals. The labor movement's mobilization, in particular, it calls for "stayaways" or illegal leave in favor of greater social welfare policies, enhanced the organization's autonomy and responsiveness within urban areas, and helped bridge class divisions among city-dwellers. By the end of 1999, the ZCTU had firmly set the foundation for its transition from a civil society–based organization concerned solely with economic issues, to one increasingly involved in Zimbabwe's political transformation. The culmination of this was the Movement for Democratic Change (MDC).

The rise of the MDC as ZANU-PF's political challenger can primarily be attributed to the implementation of structural adjustment policy without public consultation and its effects. Comprising mainly the ZCTU's top echelon, the labor movements' membership and elements of civil society, the MDC rose quickly to accentuate urbanites' grievances. A factor in its growth was, to some extent, the politicization of ethnicity emergent from the preferential treatment of those from the indigenous Shona group over the Ndebeles (Raftopoulos, 2005). In this case, deep-seated resentment for the Mugabe government was residual from the *Gukurahundi* era when Ndebele tribal groups in parts of Matabeleland and Midlands had been massacred after the war of independence. This attack on civilians had sparked when in response to government's regionalist post-independence rural-urban development style, some former freedomfighters of Ndebele origin had turned dissident and utilized local nationalism and regional inequality to improve their group's rights by rejecting governmental authority.

The emergence of the MDC not only revealed the rise of discontent and growth of social organizations, but it also pointed to urbanites disillusionment with nationalist political parties. The new millennium saw the government's increasing inability to support its vulnerable citizenry. Similar to Herrera's argument, the failure of state institutions to protect citizen interests at both the rural and urban levels had led to regionalism. While political elites corruptly accessed the country's wealth, the masses suffered under ESAP's austerity measures. This *heterodoxy* of post-independence Zimbabwe culminated not only in regionalism but also political dissent and racial tension. Support for the MDC spread in both urban and rural areas and undermined the power of ZANU-PF and its authority over the state.

Both local and external interests and conditions constitute Herrera's thesis. In it, Herrera animates how movement within civil society and at the local level can emerge in the worst of economic times, devoid of the ideologies which often stifle liberation movements. The Zimbabwe crisis illustrated the mutuality that can arise between local and external interests to mobilize civil society against a regime. In February 2000, amid escalating unpopularity, a strong and organized political opposition, and a deteriorating economic situation, a beleaguered President Mugabe and ZANU-PF advocated reform through a referendum on a new draft constitution (Shaw 2003:76). Zimbabwe's differing interest groups united against ZANU-PF and the draft constitution. White liberals, white commercial farmers, and white business allied with MDC. In the face of Zimbabwe's economic woes, voters rejected the draft constitution and galvanized support for the MDC.

Herrera (2005) undermines the nature of state control and the centrality of the state in its manipulation of historical, cultural, and political experiences. Zimbabweans' 2000 referendum nay vote on the country's new draft constitution indicated ZANU (PF)'s waning popularity and the emergence of a strong civil society sponsored by privileged white capital and external Western donors. Because of this, ZANU-PF's lingering dominance and control of the nation-state found a scapegoat in white farmers and the MDC's external Western donors. The ruling party used its control of state media to permeate into Zimbabweans' daily lives and disseminate propaganda. Race-based interpretations of the economy and its woes emerged and with them racial tension as ZANU-PF fought to retain its hold on political power. The result was the resurgence of political, racial, and economic contestation in the country's quest for economic policies that sought to intervene in the country's deepening economic malaise, with some disastrous consequences. The stage for the state's use of political violence and racial manipulation was set and unraveled in itself in the form of illegal land seizures by disenfranchised war veterans.

*Heterodox and the reimagining of Zimbabwe's economy* In the late 1990s, the Zimbabwean government's earlier *orthodox* that, for stability and continuity's sake, the white minority should continue to control the country's land and by default, its economy, came under attack. The government was not the only entity challenging it, but also some of those in the country's main rural communities,namely the peasantry and war veterans. Despite the fact that Zimbabwe's liberation struggle had primarily been fought over land, the government's first phase of the Land Reform and Resettlement Program that in 1980 had aimed to acquire more than 8.3 million hectares of land and to resettle 163,000 families had by 1990 only succeeded in relocating and resettling a little more than a third of its targeted families (Thomas, 2003, p.697). National dependence on foreign aid from Britain for the resettlement program as pledged under the Lancaster House Agreement and allegations of misappropriation of the money already provided stifled resettlement initiatives.

The "willing seller, willing buyer" provision within the Lancaster House Agreement ensured that whites in most cases sold land which they deemed undesirable and offered it for sale at their own pace. The purchase and partition of land by government often resulted in small plots of a poor quality suitable only for subsistence farming. Thus, twenty years after independence, extensive land reform and meaningful redistribution had still not taken place in the country. The Mugabe government focused on and conceptualized Zimbabwe's future around the country's 4 000 white commercial farmers.

Tensions around land and its redistribution had surfaced as early as 1985 when isolated incidents of squatting had occurred. In regions such as Gokwe, for instance, Rural District Councils (RDCs) had been established to deal with the problem that had commonly become associated with immigrants, invisible traders, anti-government job seekers, and social outcasts (Nyambara, 2001). In 1999, however, as relations between ZNLWVA and the government see-sawed and peasants increasingly become disgruntled with the slow pace of land resettlement, as a demonstration of their hunger for land, the Svosve people invaded a farm that previously had been a part of their ancestral land. After that, land invasions and squatting escalated and spread throughout the country.

By the year 2000, the ZNLWVA's membership had grown in numbers and strength. This made it a potential incubator for radical political activity. The ZANU-PF government recognized this and manipulated the association's capacity as a political wand to transform its party's political predicament. Notably, therefore, from the 2000 referendum onwards, more than fifteen illegal farm invasions of commercial farms occurred with the implicit support of ZNLWVA members (Thomas, 2003, p.670). In response, then President Mugabe argued that:

> What we reject is the persistence of vestigial attitudes (…) of a master race, master color, master owner, and master employer. Our whole struggle was a rejection of such impervious attitudes and claims to privilege—the process of land

> delivery has been slow and frustrating—land reform is the last colonial question, we are determined to resolve it once and for all. Equally, the resources which the British and American governments had pledged to make available at Lancaster House either stopped or reduced to a trickle. Even after removing the constitutional barriers we were still faced with the issue of diminishing resources against ever-rising prices (Mugabe, 2001).

By articulating Zimbabwe's grievances with the ill-fated Lancaster House accords and admonishing both the United States and Britain's failure to fulfill their promises to compensate white commercial farmers, President Mugabe gave legitimacy to the war veterans' actions.

The alliance between ZANU-PF and ZNLWVA legitimized the war veteran's land seizures and gave them the right to exercise their authority in the name of the ZANU-PF party and government. This and the apparent collusion between white commercial farmers and the international community emboldened peasants, war veterans, and some ordinary Zimbabweans to reclaim the land, at times with impunity. To bring some semblance of legality and order to the agricultural sector, the continuing disorderly invasions forced the government to implement the second phase of the Land Reform and Resettlement Programme. This entailed government's compulsory designation and acquisition of large-scale commercial farms on the understanding that the British government would compensate the affected farmers.

By way of the radical land redistribution, the Mugabe government envisioned the economic advancement and sustainability of Zimbabwe's black majority. Land seizures were thus presented as a "necessary evil" if the disparities between black and white, rural and urban economic development were to be bridged. After all, as far as ZANU-PF was concerned, establishing self-determination through the promotion of black economic and social development had been one of the goals of the liberation struggle (Shaw 2003:80) and the country's economic transformation agenda.

Although thousands of Zimbabwe's peasantry and urban poor were indeed allocated small to large A1 plots of land, the country's best A2 commercial farmland went to the ruling elite. It is mainly government officials, senior party cadres, traditional chiefs, key war veterans, and the black petty bourgeoisie that benefitted the most from the land redistribution exercise. Such state patronage highlighted the use of the economy as an extension of authoritarian politics (Raftopoulous and Savage, 2005) than sustainable broad-based economic empowerment. As a result, in the years that followed agriculture and agricultural activities were severely disrupted, the economy eroded, and millions of Zimbabwe's citizens impoverished. It soon became evident that the ZANU-PF government had not had a clear policy as to how to proceed after redistributing land. New black farmers remained mostly unsupported, and the country's agricultural output plummeted.

By the end of 2000, the ZANU-PF government's land reform program had accentuated Zimbabwe's racial and economic differences but helped the party maintain political power. The MDC and the international community were left questioning the legitimacy of the land seizures. To dilute the force that had become the war veterans, the MDC helped form the Zimbabwe Liberators' Platform for Peace and Development (ZLPPD), a group of "true veterans" who had not engaged in land invasions (Kriger, 323). The establishment of the ZLPPD and the distinction between "true" and "fake" veterans by MDC was meant to counter and challenge the legitimacy of the ZNLWVA as well as garner support for the opposition in rural areas. This MDC strategy rested on the depiction of ZANU-PF as a violent political party that had outlived its usefulness by it revitalizing nationalist sentiment, yet fostering little economic development or political openness.

Unfortunately, in the MDC and ZANU-PF's attempts to define the parameters of their political power, both parties polarized nation. In his famous but divisive speeches, President Mugabe and his supporters depicted the MDC as contrary to the country's economic interests. In his book the *Third Chimurenga*, Mugabe wrote:

> The MDC should never be judged or characterized by its black trade union face; by its youthful student face; by its salaried black suburban junior professionals; never by its rough and violent high-density lumpen elements. It is much deeper than these human superficies; for it is immovably and implacably moored in the colonial yesteryears and embraces wittingly or unwittingly the repulsive ideology of return to white settler rule. MDC is as old and as strong as the forces that control it; that converge on it, that drive and direct; indeed that support, sponsor, and spot it (Raftopoulos and Savage, 2005).

This denigration of the MDC to "puppets of western imperialism" over the years often coincided with a campaign to utilize the historically laden land issue as a means of recovering support for ZANU-PF in urban areas. The land's connections with both race and nationalism allowed the government to delegitimize the MDC as a viable political alternative and to parade the opposition as scapegoats for Zimbabwe's economic decline, hyperinflation, and poverty.

Consequently, while often in the face of growing economic malaise, authoritarian regimes steadily weaken and eventually give way to what is supposed to be the will of the people or majority, this did not happen in Zimbabwe. Instead, a nationalist ZANU-PF government continued to hold onto power. This serves to illustrate that while aspects of the imagined economies framework can illuminate the Zimbabwe crisis, there is need to adopt and amalgamate various theories if one is to explicate the sociopolitical and economic development of African states fully.

Over a decade later, the Zimbabwe government of Robert Mugabe was seen as having a deleterious effect on the country's reimagined economy. When it has sought to resuscitate national economic development through its political institutions, the government has faced external fiscal constraints from the international community. The subsequent erosion of parastatal economies within Zimbabwe has been comparable to the economic decline of some former Soviet Republics. Legacies similar to those of some post-communist Soviet Union states have since the turn of the century become present in contemporary Zimbabwe in the process of its attempts to foster democratic, equal development amid a global market economy. Such factors continue to complicate the country's role in the global economy as well as its prospects for productive state-building and political development..

The dynamics surrounding power-sharing in Zimbabwe and its challenges were also crucial towards understanding how a government of national unity can be hindered and at worst, be rendered ineffective. It is in the light of this that literature on economic and political transitions in the post–Cold War era such as Herrera's is helpful to get an understanding and provide possible roadmaps to some of the difficulties Zimbabwe was facing post-2009. On its own, the country offers valuable insight into some socioeconomic and political processes and errors to be avoided by other countries within the continent[2].

## Conclusion

A comparison of Herrera's imagined economies framework, in particular, its notions of *doxa*, *orthodox*, and *heterodox* to some extent explicate the cause and course of Zimbabwe's crisis. The ZANU-PF government's policy of reconciliation in pursuit of economic stability and development coupled with certain provisions of the Lancaster House Constitution maintained, sustained, and retained power in the hands of a white minority. In return, the country remained economically buoyant, received donor funding, and concentrated its efforts on a socialist-style Africanization program. This saw the exponential growth of education, social services, and ballooning civil service. Only when the Bretton Woods institutions called for economic structural reform did the country's economic realities unravel. As the austerity measures of economic structural adjustment set in, many were retrenched, left unemployed, and social services curtailed. In response, active civil society and the formation of political oppositional emerged. For the ruling party, its earlier orthodox position had to be reversed if it was to remain in power.

In an illustration of Herrera's notion of *heterodox*, the ruling party resorted to its ability to draw multiple historical and cultural understandings of the economy and used it to rally the peasantry and war veterans to liberate their land from postcolonial economic domination. Both local and external interests mutually constituted and mobilized the entire Zimbabwean society, in one way or another, against the Mugabe regime. However, the ability of central government to forcibly articulate its views on various media platforms, combined with the failure of opposition groups to mobilize popular opinion ultimatelycarriedthe day. The state's invocation of the past and a possible return to that past convinced and mobilized some in the country that despite the ruling party's flaws, it was better than the specter of foreign intervention, regime change, and loss of sovereignty. The culmination was that despite the violence that accompanied some of the land seizures, there is no denying that the country's land has been restored to the black majority, however skewed the restoration. This has resulted in the emergence of a nationalist ZANU-PF party that continues to hold onto the reins of power firmly.

## Notes

1. Affiliation: Department of Political Science, Morehouse College, Atlanta
2. South Africa particularly comes to mind.

## References

Brett, E. (2005). From corporatism to liberalism in Zimbabwe: Economic policy regimes and political crisis 1980–97. *International Political Science*Review, *26*(1), 91–106.

Chan, S., & Primorac, R. (2004). The imagination of land and the reality of seizure: Zimbabwe's complex revolutions. *Journal of International Affairs*, *57*, 63–80.

Gandhi, J. (2007). Authoritarian institutions and the survival of autocrats. *Comparative Political Studies*, *40*, 1279–1301.

Herbst, J. (1989). Political impediments to economic rationality: Explaining Zimbabwe's failure to reform its public sector." *The Journal of Modern African Studies*, *27*, 67–84.

Herrera, Y. (2001). "Imagined Economies." Paper presented at annual Miami University Havighurst center symposium for Russian and post-soviet studies, Oxford, Ohio, March 22–25.

Herrera, Y. (2005). *Imagined economies: The sources of Russian regionalism*. London: Cambridge University Press.

Kinloch, G. C. (2003). Changing racial attitudes in Zimbabwe: Colonial/post–colonial dynamics. *Journal of Black Studies*, *34*(2), 250–271.

Kriger, N. (2003). Zimbabwe: Political construction of war veterans. *Review of African Political Economy, 30*, 323–328.

McGregor, J. (2002). The politics of disruption: War veterans and the local state in Zimbabwe. *African Affairs, 101*, 9–37.

Mugabe, R.G. (2001). *Inside the ThirdChimurenga: our land is our prosperity.* Harare: Jongwe Press.

Norman, A. (2004). *Robert Mugabe and the betrayal of Zimbabwe.* London: McFarland and Company.

Nyambara, P. S. (2001). Immigrants, 'Traditional' Leaders and the Rhodesian State: The Power of 'Communal' Land Tenure and the Politics of Land Acquisition in Gokwe Zimbabwe, 1963–1979. *Journal of Southern African Studies, 27*(4), 771–719.

Raftopoulos, B. (1992). Beyond the house of hunger: Democratic struggle in Zimbabwe. *Review of African Political Economy,* 57–66.

Raftopoulos, B. (1996). *Zimbabwe: Race and nationalism in a post-colonial state.* Harare: SAPES Books.

Raftopoulos, B., & Savage, T. (2005). *Zimbabwe: Injustice and political reconciliation.* Harare: Weaver Press.

Rutherford, B. (2004). Desired publics, domestic government, and entangled fears: On the anthropology of civil society, farm workers, and white farmers in Zimbabwe. *Cultural Anthropology, 19*, 122–153.

Shaw, W. H. (2003). They stole our land debating the expropriation of white farms in Zimbabwe. *Journal of Modern African Studies, 41*, 75–89.

Thomas, N. H. (2003). Land Reform in Zimbabwe. *Third World Quarterly, 24*(2), 671–712.

# *Part 2: Surviving Crisis*

—by all and "any means necessary"

# 5 *Zimbabwe's Housing Shortage:* **Murambatsvina** *and Small-Scale Landlordism*

Samson R. Mhlahlo[1]

When white colonial governance ended and ushered in a black political dispensation in April 1980, all legal and institutional constraints on movements to towns and cities no longer applied. Subsequently, the country experienced rapid urban migration and growth in the context of relative post-independence prosperity. Despite such developments, however, the Zimbabwe government and its urban municipalities continued to adhere to pre-independence housing policies. These made it both increasingly difficult and expensive for low-income urban residents to access and comply with legal housing requirements. The housing shortage and its twin seed, small-scale landlordism was thus planted.

The late-1990s began a disastrous economic decline that made house ownership ever more difficult. Potts (2006) explains that this was because of "the crippling economic hardships caused by the Economic Structural Adjustment (ESAP) adopted by the Zimbabwe government from the World Bank and International Monetary Fund (IMF) that caused widespread unemployment and underemployment" (pp.526–551). When at the end of the last millennium, declining economic growth, restricted land supply and the country's "land invasions" devastated the livelihoods of the country's urban and rural population,this was exacerbated. Consequently, as Zimbabwe's economic crisis worsened and poverty intensified into the early 2000s, the cost of housing equally became increasingly unaffordable for most urban poor. In response, many economically struggling low-income urban residents housed themselves in rented one rooms or illegal backyard shelters. Small-scale landlordism as a means of surviving the economic crisis manifested itself. Backyard shacks mushroomed as they quickly became a survival strategy for some enterprising house owners living in most of the country's urban centers. Then, both the Zimbabwe government and its urban councils seemed tolerant of such goings-on. That is until 2005.

In 2005, the then Zimbabwe government launched what it termed Operation *Murambatsvina*, literally Shona for "Does not want dirt/filth", among other translations[2]. Although different hypotheses as to the operation's impetus, aims and objectives abound[3], however coming as it did on the tail-end of the ruling party's poor showing in the March 2005 parliamentary elections, the government's official narrative was that it had become intolerant of illegally built shelter and structures which had sprung across the country in recent years. The United Nation's protocols and the Habitat Agenda outlaw the arbitrary demolition of inhabited shelter without providing alternative housing to the affected. The consideration and adherence to this during and after Operation *Murambatsvina* is not evident. Consequently, at the end of the operation, mostlythe low-income former occupants of the illegal shelter and structures were left with nowhere to shelter in the longterm. The only options open to themwere either return to their rural homes or to seek private rental rooms. At a time when unemployment was high in the country's urban areas, some returned to the rural areas[4]. Others opted to remain and instead move into rental accommodation. Renting out rooms inside one's house exponentially and paradoxically became Operation *Murambatsvina* and the crisis' survival opportunity for most house owners. This witnessed the expansion of private rental shelter in most Zimbabwean towns. In Gweru, Zimbabwe's third largest city, many capitalized on it. Demand for accommodation soon outstripped supply; so muchso that rentals escalated to astronomical levels as landlords exploited the country's housing shortage to survive the economic crisis.

## *Background: Rural-Urban Migration and Postcolonial Housing Policies*

Between 1966 and 1979, many people living in areas close to the then city of Gwelo (now Gweru) abandoned their rural homes fleeing Zimbabwe's liberation war. The rural to urban migration brought much pressure on the city's housing demands. On occasions, city authorities provided rental housing, but since the war refugees often arrived without financial resources and jobs were not easy to come by, the immigrants could not afford to pay for such housing and its related services. In the majority of cases, they could only rent a room. The renting of rooms set a trend that would perpetuate post-independence.

In 1980, all legal and institutional constraints on movements to Zimbabwe's urban areas lifted. This intensified rural-urban migration to the country's cities of Harare, Bulawayo, Gweru and Mutare. Spurred on by the country's periodic droughts, the migrants answered to the cities' proverbial opportunities of employment, higher education, electricity and other socioeconomic infrastructure that purportedly waited.Unknown to them, the reality was that the capacity to shelter citizens which the Gweru City Council inherited in 1980 was and with the crisis remains inadequate. Over the years, the city has not been able to satisfy the demand for housing. The stack reason for this is mostly because, since colonial times, Gweru City Council's housing policy trajectory has not changed—over three decades into independence. If anything, the policy has during the last thirty years, worsened. Sadly, Gweru's physical residential planning typifies the residential set-up in most, if not all, of Zimbabwe's main cities and towns. It is in this regard that the city becomes an appropriate case study to explore the country's housing issues generally and specifically private rental shelter during the country's crisis.

Post-independence, the then socialism-geared Zimbabwe government encouraged all local authorities to offer all High-Density Area (HDA) houses for home ownership. Together with the city of Gweru, it built and provided public sector houses for workers working and living in the city. Most of these houses were constructed in the city's HDAs of Mkoba, Mutapa and Senga. In some cases, such houses were built by the government for the local authority under a 25-year lease agreement. When the leases expired, the houses were then handed over to Council (Satterthwaite, 2003). On the other hand, individuals or companies also built private houses in both the city's low- and high-density residential areas. Some companies based in Gweru contributed by constructing houses for their graded employees.

Zimbabwe's official and, some would say, populist policy of financing, constructing and facilitating access to housing continued through the 1980s and into the mid-1990s. After that, with the onset of ESAP the government's construction and delivery of housing virtually came to a standstill. For most Zimbabweans, this resulted in housing affordability constraints. More so, when despite Gweru's continuing rapid rural-urban migration, the city's council maintained strict enforcement of the Urban Councils Act 29:15 (Section 222:1) revised in 1996. This piece of Zimbabwe's legislation prohibits the construction of informal housing within city precincts. Consequently, Schlyter's 1989 study of housing affordability in Zimbabwe found that due to the prohibitive costs, even the cheapest houses were unaffordable. Instead, the majority of urban dwellers then depended on extended family housing rather than the other alternatives of owning, squatting and shack dwelling prevalent in such countries as South Africa and Kenya.

While this author is not an advocate of informal housing, he is of the opinion that the absence of an option to construct informal housing in the context of the 1990s and continuing economic slump, the rise in rural-urban migration gravely exacerbated accessibility and warranted some form of response regarding shelter provision. Especially taking into cognizance the glaring fact that by 1996, there were already 29 851 families on the city of Gweru's housing waiting list (Mhlahlo, 2005: 40). Moreover, considering that for one to be eligible for inclusion on the waiting list, an applicant must be legitimately employed or have proof of self-employment; this means the housing waiting list automatically excluded unemployed people, the unemployable, those in the informal sectorand recent rural arrivals. As such, one can, therefore, argue that what the waiting list reflects at any given time is an inaccurate representation of the demand for housing and easily only the tip of the iceberg.

Aside from this, what is equally alarming is that during the decade 1985–1995 housing production in the formal public sector had already rapidly declined to less than 600 houses. The reason given for such a drastic reduction was that: "the guiding policy in Council with regards to public housing units is that housing is a social service, not a business" (Director of Housing and Community Services Report, City of Gweru 2006). This is because as Gweru's City Council progressed through the 1990s, housing being a social service and not a business, it stopped being a priority. More so, when from the late-1990s began a disastrous economic decline in Zimbabwe that made house ownership even more difficult.

The Economic Structural Adjustment Programme (ESAP) adopted by the government during the 1990s and turbulence in Zimbabwe's agricultural sector accelerated the country's economic decline. By the early 2000s, as the country's economy continued to weaken, most of Zimbabwe's urban areas witnessed an upsurge in the number of unemployed, underemployed and homeless people. A spike in poverty meant the cost of housing themselves increasingly became unaffordable for most urban poor. As the new millennium progressed, more of them housed themselves in illegal backyard shelters. The same pertained in the country's city of Gweru, which houses about 300 000 people (Central Statistical Office Report, 2008).

Mhlahlo (2007, pp.121–126) perceives the purchase or construction of a house as a significant investment in the life of a family. In his opinion, purchasing a house should, therefore, be any family's most massive expenditure and most prominent investment in an urban setting. After the year 2000 however, Zimbabwe's economic policies further disenabled housing affordability and accessibility in the country's major towns and cities. In addition to the country's economic crisis, the resultant economic stress led to the withdrawal of mortgage facilities by most building societies and banks. The withdrawal of mortgages made it both difficult and expensive for most middle-class and low-income urban residents to acquire houses, let alone invest in housing. After 2000, therefore, housing for Zimbabwe's low- to middle-income earners residing in urban areas dwindled to desperate levels. In response, Gweru's lower to middle-class urban dwellers turned to private rental rooming. Interesting, such a scenario had been envisioned elsewhere, seven years after Zimbabwe's independence. Doebele (1987, pp.7–22) writing in a different context had earlier warned that: "The realities of the future will more probably be a housing market in which a much larger proportion of the poor dwell in rental units and for whom the hope of ownership of land and house will become increasingly remote." By the early 2000s, lodgers overcrowded the city's accommodation services system. Other low-income urban residents housed themselves in illegal backyard shelters. In most of Zimbabwe's urban centers, backyard dwellings mushroomed. Local authorities generally seemed to have accepted as a panacea to the housing shortage and so increasingly tolerated. For a while, backyard dwellings became the solution to the country's housing shortage. It was a trend that would continue into the new millennium and amid the thralls of economic crisis, fortuitously offered valuable financial assistance to the city's small-scale landlords. That is until mid-2005.

Midway through the first decade of this millennium, the Zimbabwean government's tolerance of illegal housing and related structures, especially in the country's capital city of Harare, seemed to have waned. Its intolerance became evident when in June of 2005 central government embarked on an operation code-named: *Murambatsvina/*Restore Order. *Murambatsvina*, which translated from Shona also literally means, "Refuse rubbish", aimed to eradicate all illegal and informal housing. Consequently, during the operation, all illegal backyard structures were demolished. Tibaijuka (2005) estimated that between 650 000 to 700 000 people from mainly informal and low-income households were left homeless. As Potts (2006) later commented, Operation *Murambatsvina* became "A *Tsunami* for the urban poor" in its devastating effects on the low-income households. It left thousands of Zimbabwe's poor urbanites without shelter. Instead of restoring order, *Murambatsvina* had caused more disorder.

Instead of order, the result was the almost exponential ballooning of the housing shortage in most urban areas. Rehousing those displaced by the then government's slum clearance became a significant problem. The difficulty of accessing shelter manifested itself in many ways. Left available to them were overcrowded private rental shelter located in mostly high-density suburbs and those housed in dilapidated low-density houses, garages, illegal extensions and storerooms. Those who could not find or afford a place to rent resorted to squatting on open land, garbage dumps and public pavements. Others of the displaced opted to either return to their rural homes or to seek private rental rooms. Those formally and informally employed in various capacities in the city that opted to remain created further demand for formal and informal rental housing. The dire urban housing shortage that Operation *Murambatsvina* tremendously aggravated provided some of Zimbabwe's landlords with a means of livelihood and surviving the country's crisis.

## *Small-Scale Landlordism as a Mode of Survival*

The *Sunday Business News* of 29 October 2008 reported that inflation in Zimbabwe had at that time soared from 47% in July 2005 to 231000000% in August 2008. During that period, an unquantifiable number of Zimbabweans lost their jobs and, in some cases, their houses. Research evidence gathered during 2008 in sample areas of Gweru revealed that 126 people who had failed to meet their monthly mortgage repayments had lost their homes to various banks due to the drastic economic downturn and retrenchment. As can be expected, rates of owner-occupancy declined as more and more people turned to renting private rooms.

Accessing shelter became further aggravated by the fact that as recorded by the Director of Central Statistics Office (CSO) in August 2008, about 83% of Zimbabwe's urban population was already living below the Total Consumption Poverty Line (TCPL). For example, persons earning less than the equivalent of US$110 per month at the time did not qualify and found themselves financially excluded from participating in low-income housing projects. As a result, most of the shelter built through the legal housing market had as its target market upper- and middle-class consumers only. Mhlahlo (2005, pp.43–47) observed that in the face of such exclusionary barriers, more than two-thirds of Gweru's urban families could not afford even the cheapest new houses available in the city at the time.

As for those wishing to purchase a house during Zimbabwe's then hyper-inflationary climate, the cost was astronomically prohibitive. Most urban residents, in particular, low to middle-income households could neither afford to buy or build a decent house. Instead, it was some of those working in the diaspora and earning in such foreign currency denominations as the Pound Sterling and United States Dollars who could afford to purchase or build houses. To some such migrants, the purchase or construction of a house was considered an investment. More so since the money could be recouped from the tenant's rentals. The advantages of this were manifold. In due course, the purchase price of the house or the costs of the building materials and for the construction would be passed on to the tenants in the form of exorbitant rentals collected by relatives back in Zimbabwe. These would, in turn, be able to survive on the collected rentals and not always resort to asking for money from relatives outside the country. Such a phenomenon is quite common in the continent but in different forms.

Edwards (1990, p.162) reveals how in Africa, the pattern of landlordism is variable but is usually a small-scale phenomenon. To Aina (1990), however, in the cities of Nairobi and Lagos, it can also be on a largescale and more exploitative, especially in situations of high shelter demand. In Zimbabwe's city of Gweru, this researcher found private rental housing to exist in two categories. Firstly, it takes the form of formal private rental housing which is leased through estate agents such as Trevor Dollar, Central Cattle Sales, commonly known as CC Sales, Midlands Property Estates and FitzGerald. Secondly, it takes the mold of open private rental rooms. Private rental housing is mainly for Gweru's lower middle to middle-class households. It is to be found in the Low-Density Areas (LDAs) as found in eastern, northern and southern Gweru, the formerly white–only suburban areas. On the other hand, open private rental rooms are found in the High-Density Areas (HDAs) to the west of the city and are primarily for lower middle- to low-income households.

Private rental shelter in Gweru is best described as "informal" because of the way it operates. There is little participation by formal actors such as Gweru City Council or estate agents. On this score, Gweru's private rental housing has also become mostly informal. The reason for this is that while characteristics which often dictate where one would like to reside such as neighborhood, availability of health, education and community-related activities are essential, in the context of Zimbabwe's housing shortage, such considerations became secondary to selecting private rental accommodation. In Gweru, renting became increasingly about availability and affordability rather than the choice of amenities available. Indeed, as demand outstripped supply, field surveys in the city confirmed that the majority of middle-class income earners had become so desperate that they were willing to forgo formalities and prioritize availability.

The informality of the city's private rental shelter is, however, more pronounced in that lease agreements are usually oral and between landlords and tenants. It is unregulated by contracts and mainly exists outside the law. Such rental shelter thrives on an informal network of information as to its location, terms and conditions of lodging. Such informal private rental room accommodation is associated with low-income households and new urban arrivals. It is prevalent in Gweru's HDAs, historically former African Townships or 'blacks only' residential areas. High density informal private rental shelter consists of houses, rooms and parts of rooms rented to individuals and families. Lodgers of such rental shelter find their private rental rooms by word of mouth or by walking around and searching on their own. In both LDAs and HDAs, rental housing is a complex phenomenon involving many actors. At times, landlords are the tenants' relatives, friends and, in rare cases, even employers.

During the crisis, the character of these actors increasingly became ruthlessly avaricious as some of them sought economic survival at the expense of their tenants and lodgers. Amid the crisis' dearth of income, private rental housing and shelter became a livelihood for small-scale landlords. In this chapter, these private landlords are referred to as small-scalelandlords and small-scalelandladies, as some of them were women. Despite, in most cases, the avarice of both at times; I see their activities as agentic modes of livelihood survival strategies.

Kumar (1996, pp.769) describes a small-scale landlord as a "petty landlord who is renting out part of one's house to other tenants'. While Bond and Manyanya (2002) correctly report that such small-scalelandlords often live on the same property as their tenants. In the Zimbabwean context, such small-scalelandlords are unnecessarily the legally registered owners of the house they are deriving an income. In Gweru's townships of Mtapa, Ascot, Mambo, Senga, and Mkoba, a large number of private rental rooms were operated on a small scale of up to three rooms by low-income landlords. The rented rooms were located either in council or company housing which had been transferred to home ownership as part of a retrenchment package or belonged to absentee relatives of the low-income small-scale landlord. House owners who over the years had managed to acquire houses practically put their homes to work as it were.

Due to the severe shortage of accommodation in the city, room rentals increased sharply, and acquiring private rental rooms became more competitive. Landlords and ladies capitalized to the extent of charging the equivalent of US$50 for a standard single room (Trevor Dollar Estate Brochure, 2008, np). Depending on the size of the house and the number of its rooms, one to eight tenants were taken in to supplement the unemployed or retired landlord's income or his/her other informal income generating ventures. As one of the low-income landlords commented, *"My house is the second breadwinner."*

As the housing shortage worsened, the full import of the landlord's comment became evident. Middle and higher income seekers of shelter financially outbid their lower income competitors out of the houses in which they had been renting rooms. Consequently, some 77.5% of the city's small-scale landlords/ladies who participated in this research had tenants from different income brackets occupying either a whole house or one to two of their rooms.

Countrywide landlords capitalized on the housing crisis and escalated rentals to astronomical levels through exorbitant monthly rent increments. In the larger cities of Harare and Bulawayo, at a time when many low-income people were earning very little, rentals for a single room were already not less than the equivalent of US$50 plus. Offering rental accommodation became a lucrative business to participate in, and more households sought to be landlords. According to McGarry (2005), even before Operation *Murambatsvina*, private housing initiatives accounted for more investment in housing units than any other.After it, housing provision intensified as "a mechanism for wealth accumulation and distribution, a consumer good, a framework for family liaison, a status symbol, an indicator of social relations, a potential source of power and profit" (Mhlahlo, 2004, p.107). Field investigations and observations confirmed inflated rentals, overcrowding, noise and restricted services. Restricted water use and the lack of adequate toilet doors were common complaints.

The reason for this was because, despite their apparent greed, most small–scale landlords were themselves poor. Often, an enquiry revealed they occupied one or two rooms in their dwellings as a way of supplementing their meagre pensions, if any. Investigations in Gweru's high-density residential areas concluded that without tenants, life would have been more difficult. So, while White (1985, pp.505–528) portrays the landlords of high-density lodgings in Senegal as "capitalist savages' whose sole objective is to accumulate wealth at the expense of their poor tenants", Mwangi (1997, pp.141–159) on the other hand, rightly observed and argued that only a few of Nairobi's landlords are wealthy because most are just as poor as their tenants, as in this case. Of those who are relatively well off, investigations discovered that they were so because, for quite a few small-scalelandlords, deriving an income from the rental property was not their only livelihood survival strategy. Instead, they had what has Owusu termed multiple modes of livelihood survival strategies (MMLS)—the practice of relying on more than one source of income.

Owusu (2007, pp.450–465) observed that livelihood strategies in many African cities involve participation in multiple economic activities in both formal and informal sectors. In the Multiple Modes of Livelihood Survival Strategy framework, people's strategic responses to economic crisis are analyzed with a focus on the urban poor and other marginalized populations in their desperate attempt to survive. Analysis of the small-scale landlords encountered revealed that quite a few of them also operated multiple other income-generating projects. These included local tuck-shops, informally selling cigarettes from their windows, vegetables, sweets at their gates, and in rare cases, operated a *kombi* or emergency taxi. Besides, at a time when essential commodities like soap and candles were scarce and electricity erratic, some had also ventured into soap and candle-making.

Interestingly, in a few other cases, this researcher discovered that employed small-scale landlords rented accommodation somewhere else in the city in order to be close to their places of work and rented out their homes located far from their workplaces. I found this to be the case in Gweru's South East Mtapa which is located less than one kilometer from the city's light industrial site. The tenants in East Mtapa and yet are landlords elsewhere in the city. For such landlord-tenants, I learnt that letting rooms in their homes had become an essential part of consolidating their various incomes during the time of crisis.

Gilbert and Varley (1991) noted that savings and earnings from private rental rooms often provide capital to construct additional rooms for the satisfaction of low-income household lodgers and tenants. Before the crisis intensified, in rare cases some of the rental income derived from the house would then be forwarded to the house owners wherever they were, but mainly if they were still resident in Zimbabwe. However, as the crisis intensified some house owners based in the diaspora urged the custodians of their income property to build multiple-roomed structures within the yard to accommodate as many tenants and lodgers as possible. As noted by Gilbert (2003), I discovered that some small-scale landlords had used rent accumulated to extend the same or build other houses. This way, the custodians or relatives "lording it" over the property relied on the rental income to sustain themselves as well as the house owner's kith and kin still resident in the country.

In order to maximize, landlords who had extended their houses continued to share a house with their lodgers or tenants while either owning other properties in the same area or another residential area. The additional income would then be used to build amenities and outbuildings to house more tenants. In some cases, money for extensions did not always come from rental income. Instead, it came from relatives in the Diaspora. It is such money, which would then be used to extend the existing house, build a new one or purchase another. In the majority of cases, however, house or room letting was the only source of regular income for most landlords. For such small-scale landlords, as long as Zimbabwe's housing crisis persists and depending on the number of rooms they rent out, they will continue to make substantial profits after paying rates and utilities.Consequently, the viability of private rental shelter coupled with multiple modes of livelihood survival strategies during Zimbabwe's crisis witnessed the expansion of private rental shelter in most of the country's cities and towns as all income groups strove to survive.

Accompanying private rental shelter was private rental housing. Private rental housing operated mainly in the medium to LDAs. Field research evidence in Gweru revealed that low-density lodging in the city occurs mainly in those houses where the owners had left the country, purchased the house from outside the country, been transferred elsewhere by their employers or retired to their rural homes leaving their property under the care of friends and relatives. In such circumstances, the friends or relatives of the absentee landlords turned the house under their care into rental accommodation and found tenants or lodgers to either rent the whole/"full–house" or single rooms within it.

Generally, however, remarkably few house owners in LDAs offered private rental rooms. Usually, all habitable rooms within the house were rented out to either one family or one or two single persons. Besides, although many homeowners would not admit to the practice, in some LDAs residents also rented out the servants' quarters-cum-cottage located at the rear of their yards. This research identified that the majority of servants' quarters and enclosed garages in the LDAs had been converted into rental rooms.

In central Gweru, private rental housing was also made available by subdividing of buildings. Typically these were buildings in inner city areas initially built by wealthy landlords for owner occupation and abandoned upon either a decline in wealth, the departure of adult children to set up their own homes, the migration of the owner or only because of the owners' preference to move and live in the suburbs. They would then rent out their homes to mainly single middle-class tenants plying their trade in the city's Central Business District (CBD). Conversely, in the city's old central business district near Gweru's railway station, such houses were converted either into offices or sleeping/boarding rooms for rent to passengers in transit. Tipple's (2005, pp.611–632) empirical studies in New Delhi and Pretoria established that a house could also be a place of home-based informal enterprises. Just as owning a house during the crisis enabled some householders to pursue multiple modes of livelihood strategies by using their homes informally as business premises, so too did their lodgers. Not to be outdone, tenancy or lodging also enabled tenants and lodgers to eke out some income at their places of residence. During field observations in Gweru's Ascot high-density township, this researcher observed that while some landlords used private rental rooms as their main survival strategies, their lodgers or tenants also pursued other informal economic activities with or without their landlords' knowledge and consent.

The more enterprising tenants used some areas within and without the house as make-shift "workshops and small factories" for income generation. Informal businesses, often referred to as *siyaso*, literally "just leave it like it is, we will fix it", sprung up in front or at the back of houses and provided a livelihood to lodging handy-men and artisans who ran them as workshops. It is from such workshops and small factories that mechanics fixed cars and welders manufactured window frames. In order to contribute to family incomes, some housewives reared chickens in backyards for sale, braided hair, sold vegetables or imported merchandise mainly from South Africa, Mozambique and Zambia.

Also, my field survey found that some tenants who are renting full houses in both high- and low-density residential areas also tended to sublet their rented accommodation in order to earn some extra income or merely subsidize their rent. For them, subletting became a win-win survival strategy whereby tenants either earned extra income or subsidized their rent while for some small-scale landlords it assured the timeous receipt of rent. The savings from the shared rent cushioned such tenants and lodgers' overall livelihoods.

To counter landlords' often exorbitant rentals that did not match the size and living conditions the rooms provided, some lodgers and tenants, particularly students and bachelors at times resorted to subletting parts of their own rooms to a friend or relative. In so doing, they shared the burden of rent for the room with them. Such subletting of private rental rooms afforded and enabled students, low-income households and lumpen proletariat access to shelter while cushioning them from the effects of paying full rent. Good as this may have been, to deter subletting, landlords later resorted to charging a fixed amount per occupant of a room found subletting. Owning a home became the desire of most lodgers and tenants.

Community-Based Organisations (CBOs) in the form of cooperatives have since the late 1980s played an indispensable role in housing provision. Amid the housing shortage and the rental incomes being earned by small-scale landlords and landladies, many aspiring home-seekers joined housing cooperatives in the hope of eventually owning a house of their own. Based on the understanding that through loyal monthly contributions to the cooperative a member would eventually be assisted to acquire a house, the period from 2005 to 2008 saw some cooperatives defying the crisis and delivering "more houses than the Government itself" (Gotora, 2014, p.C2). Consequently, from 2009, CBOs "were given the platform to showcase their capabilities and lobby for policies and regulations (…) for them to actively participate in housing delivery" (Gotora, 2014, p.C2). The culmination was the Revised 2012 National Housing Policy that acknowledged the pivotal role of CBOs in housing delivery in Zimbabwe.

However, although some housing cooperative members managed to deliver houses to some of their members, there were those that dismally failed. In the context of crisis and human nature, some housing cooperatives were founded by unscrupulous individuals who, aware of the desperation of some home-seeking members, capitalized on it and embezzled their contributions. In other cases, bad governance issues arose as some cooperative leaders made themselves " 'life' chairpersons in these cooperatives where there are no elections held to choose the new administration or to produce audited books." (Gotora, 2014, p.C2) As can be expected, corruption and its companions—greed and nepotism followed. Gotora reports how there "was nepotism and corruption in the allocation of stands and lack of transparency and accountability" in resource utilization (2014, p.C2).In the meantime, invisible to all, low-income earners and the unemployed who were unable to join cooperatives were forced to find accommodation of the worst type.

Edwards (1990, p.259) observed that renting increases in cities which have a high growth rate and the government's policy is intolerant to squatting. Faced with ever-escalating rent, on the one hand, and yet strongly committed to urban life, on the other, some low-income households had by the year 2008 finally decided to squat. In Gweru, small squatter camps emerged in Mtapa Township, Bata Estate, the Gweru River valley, along the Mvuma Railway line and outside the city's Forestry Commission. The structures have been destroyed several times, only to reappear after a few weeks.To both local authorities and individual low-income households, lodging in private rental rooms remains the only legal coping mechanism for Gweru's lack of housing and affordability.

In Harare, low-income households and the unemployed also "resorted to constructing their own 'fantasy city' (…) on unsanctioned open spaces" (Mwase & Matabvu, 2015, p.9). By 2015, in low-income households, there reportedly were 63 slum settlements around Zimbabwe's capital city. Until 2015, the city's response to this apparent provocation was to demolish the structures only to have them put up again. The challenge for that city's council, indeed as for others in Zimbabwe, therefore, remains "the need to provide all residents with decent accommodation and restore sanity in the housing sector" (Mwase & Matabvu, 2015, p.9). Given the country's current crisis, which encompasses its housing shortage that has lent impetus to small landlordism, what then is the way forward for housing provision in Zimbabwe?

*Tackling Zimbabwe's Housing Shortage: Some Considerations* Zimbabwe's housing backlog is unacceptably estimated to be between 1 250 000 000 and 1 500 000 000. The provision of shelter is one of many fundamental human needs and rights, but also because "housing [has become] a major contributor to national socio-economic development" (Potts 2006, p.270) it needs urgent priority. As Amis (1995, pp.145–157) points out, lack of housing is a highly visible dimension of poverty in areas where it is inadequate. So, while Zimbabwe is understandably in a crisis state, it can ill-afford to neglect housing provision. The provision of housing should and must remain a prominent feature of both the national and local governments' agendas.

In most countries, housing provision is the most regulated activity in any urban area. Often it is spearheaded by government. Over twenty years ago, Teedon and Drakakis-Smith (1986) researching Harare's then vibrant housing situation noted that suppliers of shelter included the state, corporations, local authorities, private institutions, private commercial companies and individuals. Then, the government's official policy of financing, constructing and facilitating access to housing continued into the 1980s and until the mid-1990s. Since the onset of the crisis, however, it and most, if not all, of these players have disinvested from housing provision.

To the State's credit though, the Constitution of Zimbabwe's Amendment Number 20 recognizes the provision of housing as a fundamental human right. In its 2012 National Housing Policy, the Zimbabwe government, at both central and local levels, supportively undertakes to forge vertical and horizontal partnerships with CBOs. Then in 2016 the Apex Council comprising state officials and civil service representatives resolved that government workers should "pay a minimum monthly contribution of US$150 under the Civil Service Housing Scheme" (Matabvu, 2017, p.4). The money collected is to be used in the construction of model flats in Harare, Bulawayo and other national cities. Matabvu reports that "over 75 000 civil servants have registered" (2017, p.4). Just how able they will be to consistently contribute US$150 when most of them on average earn US$400 is to be seen. On the whole, the Government's role has over the years confined itself to policy statements and alternate implementation. Such a role is maybe as it should be.

Mwangi (1997) advises that governments should focus on facilitating the self-help or self-managed process of housing production undertaken by middle- to low-income households. The crisis has mostly resulted in private initiatives accounting for more investment in housing units than government (McGarry, 2005). Varying from 100% rental accommodation to 100% owner-occupation, individuals, cooperative groupings and diverse forms of collective groups took action to develop their housing. In the fifteen years from 1980 to 1995, the number of housing cooperative societies increased from 83 to 175 (Musekiwa, 1993). Between then and the crisis, land buying cooperative societies such as Destiny for Africa, land buying and development companies such as Heritage Housing Trust and building societies like the Zimbabwe Building Society have risen in Gweru and other cities in the country and are offering both upmarket and low-cost housing. Such initiatives have immensely contributed to housing production through the sale of plots at affordable prices and must be commended, supported, encouraged and emulated in other parts of the country. However, while housing cooperatives are helpful, they need strict professional monitoring, to ensure accountability checks and balances adherence.

Information sharing and multilateral cooperation are crucial to housing provision. The City of Harare's Vision 2025 envisages the construction of 105 000 housing units by 2018. Towards this vision, in 2012 the Harare City Council resolved that "the demolition of (slum) structures was not the solution to ending housing problems and adopted a strategy to developing existing slums" (Mwase & Matabvu, 2015, p.9). The council has partnered with the Bill and Melinda Gates Foundation and other developmental partners to formalize slum-dwellings in that city's Dzivarasekwa area by upgrading them into low-cost housing units (Mwase & Matabvu, 2015, p.9). Known as the Slum Upgrading Program, the initiative is being made " 'sustainable by creating micro-finance clubs which will see other communities borrowing money from the revolving fund to construct houses and later repay amounts borrowed over a period' " (Bill & Melinda Gates Foundation outgoing deputy director for special initiatives qtd in Mwase & Matabvu, 2015, p.9). The tripartite cooperation shown above is a welcome solution in a credit deficient economy as Zimbabwe's where housing provision has, since the crisis, been perenniallyaffected by lack of funding.

Research findings in selected residential areas across Zimbabwe revealed that while some citizens have stands on which to build, their primary constraint is a lack of access to credit finance. Therefore, a national construction bank should be set up to loan building materials to stand-holders. As Chenga highlights, ownership of "residential land is an asset representative of creditworthiness", and as such, its possession as "an asset that offers credible security to access lending" (2016, p.11) must be considered as crucial to stand servicing and development. It is more so when the recipient is of an economically skilled profile and sound credit standing.

In Zimbabwe today, despite the crisis gripping the country, mines remain among the few business operations making any meaningful profits. In the past mines built and provided housing in such mining towns as Kwe-Kwe,

Shurugwi and Zvishavane, arguably except for Zimplats, most no longer do so.The current housing shortage necessitates the reentry of private sector commercial entities such as mines to participate in housing provision as they have done in the past. Government through local authorities should reengage mining houses and provide incentives to them and related investors in order forthem to participate in housing provision again. Only then can private rental housing be alleviated and the wheels towards housing provision for all start turning again. However, such housing provision also needs to be acceptable development housing trends and affordable.

Various factors influence what is meant by affordable housing. In Zimbabwe, as in many other parts of the world, the cost of accommodation is primarily influenced by the economic environment, the cost of building materials and a house's location. In Gweru and most towns in the country, due to colonial urban planning, most high-density areas are situated in the west of the city where industry's pollution blows due to prevailing winds. Consequently, houses located in the western direction of the city are comparatively cheaper to buy or rent as they frequently experience air pollution. Because of this, the western suburbs are more crowded than the low-density areas in the east. Such colonially determined affordability is not the housing affordability the country should be pursuing.

In developed countries, housing affordability often involves the capacity of households to consume housing services. Specifically, it involves the relationship between household incomes, housing prices and rentals. An often quoted rule of thumb is that households should spend no more than 25–30% of their income on housing unless they choose to do so. Using such a standard to measure affordability is, however, further complicated by the inability to determine whether a household spends more than 25–30% of their income on housing by necessity or by choice. So, although no definition of housing affordability considers household satisfaction with shelter, price and rent, quality and housing services, these must of necessity be factored into affordability. In this vein, Nelson et al. (2004, pp.117–145) broadly defined affordable housing to include housing services, especially "the role of housing in providing shelter, storage, assembly, and access to work". It is towards a combination of both local and international housing affordability that as a country we must aspire.

Vast tracts of land, labor and alternate construction materials all prerequisite to the construction of affordable housing are available in Zimbabwe. However, if our ever-growing population is affordably and adequately provided with shelter, housing perceptions, product types and housing delivery systems need to be shifted. Zimbabwe mainly needs to be aware that housing provision is a complicated process involving various issues. In centuries before the twentieth century, a house offered a household shelter from the social pressures of the outside world. With the advent of the twentieth and twenty-first centuries, however, the term "house" has acquired a broader-based understanding. Whereas in years past a house primarily afforded its users access to shelter against the natural elements, in the twenty–first century, housing provision is no longer just about providing physical shelter. It has become more about providing adequate quantities and appropriate housing types. Such appropriate housing must be capable of meeting the diverse physical, social and even psychological needs of its inhabitants.

As early as 1976, Peil noted that "in the lives of urban dwellers, housing should encompass numerous cultural elements over and above that of physical shelter (1976, pp.155–166)." In the twenty-first century, therefore, a house need not only provide a family with the privacy to carry out daily functions such as sleeping, bathing, preparing food and eating. According to Yu (2006) writing in a different context, it must also cater for economic and livelihood activities. As the country moves forward, an urban house should ideally fulfil many other needs and developments which are complementary to those of basic shelter. It must be within a neighborhood which, in addition to incorporating roads, a clean water supply, shops and educational facilities, must also accommodate recreational and technological access. Its network of pipes, culverts, drains, waste and water disposal systems need to aesthetically blend into the surroundings and be friendly to the Zimbabwean environment. In short, future housing must take into consideration the country's landscape and what it offers regarding local materials that can encapsulate and enhance what constitutes a Zimbabwean house. Cognizance of such must, however, be kept at a balance and accommodated bearing in mind their impact on housing affordability and thus access to shelter in the urban and peri-urban environment.

The Land Reform Programme (LRP) provided more than enough land for both primary and globally acceptable residential development trends. What is now required is to peg and service residential stands for housing development. It remains for innovative and sustainable ways of financing affordable housing if the more vulnerable sections of our population are to be housed and extricated from the clutches of small-scale landlordism.

## *Conclusion*

The crisis in Zimbabwe has affected all spheres of life. The country's shortage of housing notably heightened the crisis for home-seekers and yet provided a survival strategy for those with access to housing who were willing to let it out. For such ones, house ownership proved an economic asset and an essential aspect of wealth-creation, self-empowerment and poverty alleviation, especially so, when Operation *Murambatsvina* and credit deficiency spiked a high demand for shelter. The culmination of it was the birth of an insatiable demand for private rental shelter and private rental rooms. Small-scale landlordism filled the gap. Letting out rooms by some landlords became the only source of regular income. Many were prepared to give up some living space in their houses for it. For others owning a house opened up to possibilities of earning an additional steady supplementary income from rentals. Small-scale landlordism became not only a critical economic survival strategy during the crisis, but it also spoke to the severity of Zimbabwe's housing shortage.

Not to be outdone, lodgers and tenants also devised their survival strategies, both in response to the socioeconomic crisis gripping the country as well as in response to their landlord's survival response to it. So while landlords and landladies turned to cooperatives to finance their future homes, their lodgers and tenants turned to subletting and informal trading. The buoying rental market encouraged the elusive dream of home ownership. For those fortunate enough to be generating income, housing cooperatives assisted them to acquire houses. In some cities, urban councils, philanthropic organizations and CBOs jointly proactively and innovatively tackled the housing provision challenge despite the prevailing economic difficulties. For the less fortunate, the low-income earners and unemployed, slum-dwelling or squatting became the only means of escape. Paradoxically, for some their gateway to owning a house came by way of squatting.

For the majority, however, diverse strategies which call for multilateral and multi-sectorial players are required. The government, home-seekers, the private sector and civil society need to communicate, strategize and implement for their mutual benefit, that of housing the nation. However, such housing need not only shelter nor be targeted only at the middle- to high-income bracket of Zimbabwean society, but must also be affordable to the country's majority low-income earners. In this respect, future housing projects need to take into account the affordability and modern trends in housing provision.

## Notes

1. Faculty of Social Sciences, Department of Geography & Environmental Sciences, Midlands State University, Gweru (Zimbabwe).
2. As far as Government was concerned, Operation *Murambatsvina* was its response to illegal and unsanitary structures which were a potential health disaster and crime. However, it coming soon after Zimbabwe's hotly contested March 2005

parliamentary elections, the Operation was seen by some as the ruling party's way of getting back at the urban poor for voting en masse for the opposition Movement for Democratic Change (MDC). The Times Online of 5 June 2005 carried the story with the title: *Mugabe regime lays waste to buildings in new terror tactic.*
3. The word has also been translated "Restore Order" and "Move the Rubbish."
4. David Coltart, the then MDC legal affairs spokesperson was later to describe "the operation as a sinister pre-emptive strike designed to remove the maximum possible number of people from urban areas to rural areas" *Wikipedia.*

## References

Aina, T. (1990). Petty landlords and poor tenants in a low-income settlement in metropolitan Lagos, Nigeria. In P. Amis & P. Lloyd (Eds.), *Housing Africa's urban poor* (pp.87–101). London: Manchester University Press for the International African Institute.

Amis, P., & Lloyd, P. (Eds.). (1995). *Housing Africa's urban poor.* London: Manchester University Press for the International African Institute.

Bond, P., & Manyanya, M. (2002). *Zimbabwe's Plunge: Exhausted Nationalism, Neoliberalism and the Search for Social Justice.* Durban: University of KwaZulu–Natal Press.

City of Gweru: *Annual reports of the director of housing and community services for the years* ended June 1990–February 2008.

Chenga, C. (2016, October). On residential stands, align social justice with productivity. *The Sunday Mail,* Open Economy, p. 11.

Doebele, W. (1987). Land policy. In Rodwin (Ed.), *Settlement and development* (pp.110–132). Boston: Allen and Unwin.

Edwards, M. (1990). *Rental housing and the urban poor: Africa and Latin America compared.* In P. Amis & P. Lloyd (Ed.), *Housing Africa's urban poor.* Manchester University Press.

Gilbert, A., & Varley, A. (1991). *Renting a home in third world city: Choice or constraint?*

Gilbert, A. (2003). *Some observations on what might be done about rental housing in South Africa.* In F. Khan & T. Petal (Eds.), *Housing Policy and Practice in Post Apartheid South Africa.* Heinemann Johannesburg.

Gotora, P. (2014, January). Cooperative approach key to housing provision. *TheHerald,* C2.

Kumar, S. (1996). Landlordism in third world urban income settlements: A case for further research. *UrbanStudies, 33,* 753–782.

Matabvu, D. (2017, July). US$150 for civil servants housing. *The Sunday Mail,* p.4.

Mhlahlo, S. R. (2004). The impact of housing provision policy on housing problems inGweru before and after independence. *TheDyke, 1,* 107–113.

Mhlahlo, S. R. (2005). The problem of housing affordability and its economic and social effect on the city of Gweru, Zimbabwe. *EASSRR, 21*(2), June: 39–51.

Mhlahlo, S. R. (2007). Assessment of urban governance in Zimbabwe: Case of the city of Gweru. *EASSRR, XX111*(1), January: 107–126.

Musekiwa, A. (1993). *Low-income Housing Development in Harare.A Historical Perspective.* In L. Zinyama, D. Tevera, & S. Cumming, (Eds.), *Harare: The Growth and Problems of the City.* Harare: University of Zimbabwe Press, 51–59.

Mwangi, I. K. (1997). The nature of rental housing in Kenya. *Environmental Urbanization, 9*(2).

Mwase, E., & Matabvu, D. (2015, April). Slum dwelling, gateway to house ownership. *The Sunday Mail*: Extra, p.9.

Nelson, A.C., Pendall, R., Dawkins, C. J., & Knaap, G. J. (2004). *The Link Between Growth Management and Housing Affordability: The Academic Evidence.* In A. Downs. (Ed.), *Growth Management and Affordable Housing. Do they Conflict?*Washington, DC: Brookings Institution Press, 117–145.

Owusu, F. (2007). Conceptualizing livelihood strategies in African cities. Planningand development implications. *Journal of Planning Education and Research, 26*, 450–465.

Peil, M. (1976). African squatter settlements: A comparative study. *UrbanStudies, 13*, 155–66.

Potts, D. (2006). All my hopes and dreams are shattered': Urbanization and migrancy in an imploding African economy- the case of Zimbabwe. *Geoforum, 37*, 537–551.

Satterthwaite, D. (2003). *The ten and a half myths that may distort the urbanpolicies of governments and international agencies.* Institute for Environment and Development.

Teedon, P., & Drakakis-Smith, D. (1986). Urbanization and socialism in Zimbabwe: The case of low-cost urban housing. *Geo forum, 17*(2), 307–329.

Tibaijuka, A. (2005). *Report of the fact-finding mission to Zimbabwe to assess the scope and impact of Operation Murambatsvina, by the UN special envoy on human settlements issues in Zimbabwe.* Nairobi: UN-Habitat.

Tipple, G. (2005). The place of home-based enterprises in the informal sector: Evidence from Cochabamba, New Delhi, Surabaya and Pretoria. *Urban Studies, 42*(4), 611–632.

White, P. (1985). The Impact of policy conflict on the implementation of a government assisted housing project in Senegal. *Canadian Journal of African Studies, 19*(3), 505–528.

Yu, Z. (2006). Heterogeneity and dynamics in China's emerging urban housing market: two sides of a success story from the late 1990s. *Habitat Intrnational, 30*(2), 277–304.

# 6 The Zulu Mask: Surviving "Xenophobia" in "Post–Apartheid" South Africa

C. Luthuli Mhlahlo[1]

## Introduction

Since the early 1900s, some African men from countries such as the then Nyasaland (present-day Malawi), Rhodesia (now Zimbabwe) and Moçambique (now Mozambique) had temporarily and, in some cases, permanently come to South Africa in search of work in the country's mines. Between 2000 and 2008, as Zimbabwe's economy deteriorated, and crisis set in, the decades' long trickle of black migrants from South Africa's northern neighbor steadily increased. Comprised of some affluent white commercial farmers whose farms had been appropriated during Zimbabwe's land reform program, the new immigrants were mostly black, multi-cultural, both male and female, literate and illiterate. All of them were migrating for various reasons. These ranged from political to economic, familial to academic, commercial to criminal. For many, however, the main reason was to seek political and economic refuge in South Africa.

Based on ethnographic observations, participant observations and unstructured interview, this chapter traces the lives of some black Zimbabweans who immigrated to South Africa during the crisis. It mainly focuses on those Zimbabwean immigrants of Ndebele descent and examines the survival strategies some of them adopted because of the hostile reception black foreigners from the continent sometimes received. After which it argues that because of their ancestral and therefore linguistic and traditional backgrounds, some such immigrants were able to assume "Zulu masks" in the form of Zulu identity and culture and cases, mimicked them in order to survive. The chapter concludes that the result of this among some Ndebele immigrants was ambivalent identities and cultures which at times vacillated between what is already known and something that must of necessity be anxiously and, at times, exaggeratedly repeated.

## *Push and Pull factors: Zimbabwe's Decline and South Africa's Gain*

The 2000 farm occupations by war veterans and land-hungry peasants in Zimbabwe severely disrupted the country's supply chains. Citizens' subsequent food demands on the incapacitated supply chains destabilized prices initiating the country's now notorious hyperinflationary environment of the 2000s. As the socioeconomic plight of most Zimbabweans steadily worsened those able to migrate to more stable climes did so. For most black and white migrants alike, this mainly meant neighboring South Africa.

In 2000, post-apartheid South Africa was already in its sixth year of democratic rule. The country's economy was stable and growing quite rapidly. That was mainly because of the post-apartheid government's adoption of the policy of reconciliation and a dominantly liberal economic path. South Africa's first democratically elected president, the late Nelson Mandela and the Truth and Reconciliation Commission's conciliatory stance had assuaged white South Africans' earlier fears of reprisals from the African majority. As a result, the potential outbreak of an all-out civil war that had already seen the flight of some white skills and expertise from South Africa to Australia, Britain and New Zealand had not materialized. The skills that had emigrated and South Africa's expanded and growing economy needed both replacement and addition, respectively.

During the apartheid era, the regime's system of Bantu Education had deprived black South Africans of critical skills to run the country's relatively developed economy. In comparison, the Smith supremacist regime in the then Rhodesia (Zimbabwe) had offered the country's Africans a relatively better and yet equally selective and restrictive education system "with a minimal choice of subjects and training possibilities for African students" (Veit-Wild, 1993:183). In a bid to address such anomalies, at Zimbabwe's independence, the ZANU-PF government had embarked on a policy of mass education and training for the country's black citizens. The rapid expansion and provision of world standard mass education that ensued had facilitated and enabled most Zimbabweans' acquisition of sound academic education and technical skills training.

When between 2000 and 2008 Zimbabwe's socioeconomic and political situation alarmingly deteriorated, some of the country's skilled and semi-skilled citizens responded to South Africa's skills requirements. Thousands of Zimbabweans migrated to South Africa in search of employment as teachers, accountants, engineers, doctors, technicians, artisans and lawyers. The arrival of Zimbabwean immigrants in possession of such requisite skills tremendously alleviated the country's skills shortage. Zimbabwe's loss became South Africa's economic gain. Apart from seeking employment in the country, some skilled Zimbabweans saw in the crisis an opportunity for personal, academic development and migrated to further their studies in the country's institutions of higher learning. Often, all such immigrants on work, study and quota permits were accompanied by their immediate family members or had them join later.

Other than skilled labor and academics, South Africa also witnessed the arrival of political-cum-economic refugees. Starting in 2000, these comprised Zimbabwe's former white commercial farmers and asylum seekers. After the country's June 2000 elections, the post-election violence between some supporters of the ruling ZANU-PF party and opposition Movement for Democratic Change (MDC) had resulted in many of the opposition party's members; both real and falseseeking asylum in South Africa and neighboring countries. Their numbers had drastically increased in 2007 when hyperinflation caused the government to control prices leading to massive food shortages. It reached its zenith when towards the June 2008 Presidential run-off election, supporters of ZANU-PF reportedly unleashed terror on their MDC opponents. Fearing for both their lives and futures, Zimbabweans left the country for neighboring countries and abroad in droves.

Zimbabwe's emigration was exacerbated by the country's food shortages, hyperinflation, factory closures, mass unemployment and increasing poverty levels. As manufacturing industries relocated or failed due to the country's unfavorable economic climate, Zimbabwe's socioeconomiccondition further deteriorated. Commercial immigrants arose and inflated the volume of Zimbabwean immigrants into South Africa. These commercial immigrants comprised two major groups whom Zimbabweans termed: cross-border traders and cross-border shoppers.

Cross-border traders are mostly small-scale entrepreneurs who capitalized on their knowledge of what was scarce or in demand on all sides of the Zimbabwean border. On this basis, they, for instance, took crocheted tablecloths, artifacts, arts and craft, paintings and carvings to countries bordering Zimbabwe such as South Africa and Botswana. Once in these countries, they would then sell them either door-to-door, to galleries, at robots or to the customers who had ordered them. Thereafter, using the proceeds of their sale, cross-border traders would purchase items which they knew to be scarce or unavailable in Zimbabwe (e.g., boxes of green bars of washing soaps, car parts, sundries, cell-phones, technological gadgets and *mazitye* (bales of second-hand clothing) for resalein the country at very exorbitant prices. Cross-border traders were, however, differentiated from cross-border shoppers.

As the word "cross-border shoppers" suggests, these were Zimbabweans who at the height of the country's commodities shortages travelled mainly to neighboring countries for purposes of shopping for essential commodities such as: sugar, cooking-oil, salt, candles, matches, bath soap, toothpaste, mealie-meal, for either their personal use or resell to neighbors and on Zimbabwe's blackmarket. In addition to selling goods on the black market, both cross-border traders also sold some of the foreign currency they brought with them into the country and retained the rest for future excursions across the border.

In order to avoid Zimbabwe's import duties and controls, both cross-border traders and shoppers sometimes engaged *malaichas* (Zimbabwean small-scale long-distance transporters) to transport or smuggle them and their goods across the two countries' border posts. Some bus drivers and conductors notably played a pivotal role ferrying food and goods into the country on behalf of cross-border traders, shoppers and migrants, albeit at inflated almost extortive rates. The cost of bringing such goods into the country was often passed on to Zimbabwean consumers in the form of exorbitant prices. Subsequently, it was cross-border traders and shoppers that contributed to fueling Zimbabwe's hyperinflation.

For many Zimbabweans, the situation became so unbearable and the need to travel so high that thousands of passport applicants daily inundated the offices of the country's Registrar-General. Corruption reportedly set in as citizens without passports resorted to desperate measures in order to acquire the travel document. To ease the demand for passports, the offices of the Registrar-General resorted to issuing an Emergency Travel Document (ETD). However, as ETDs were valid for only six months, they proved an inconvenience for many migrants once the six months had elapsed. Subsequently, some ETD holders never returned to Zimbabwe to renew the ETDs. Instead, some simply overstayed or applied for refugee status in their host countries.

For some impatient and poor Zimbabweans, applying for ETDs let alone for a passport was economically not an option. That forced them to "border-jump" or cross illegally into neighboring countries, either on foot or using unscrupulous long-distance bus, truck or taxi drivers. The proximity, prosperity and porosity of South Africa's borders made the country the preferred destination of the majority of "border-jumpers." Stories abound of how some such immigrants were attacked and eaten by lions or crocodiles while crossing the Kruger National Park and Limpopo River, respectively. Those who survived this often perilous entry into South Africa became the country's estimated 3 million undocumented immigrants. The presence and prevalence of Zimbabweans in South Africa was such that some sensationalist media houses dramatically likened their immigration into the country to a *tsunami*. Although a tsunami is usually a cataclysm resulting from a destructive sea wave caused by an earthquake or volcanic eruption, in this case, the insinuation was that the Zimbabwean human *tsunami* was being caused by the crisis north of the Limpopo River and affecting South Africa because of its porous northern borders. To date, there is no credible and no factual evidence to have estimated Zimbabwean immigrants at 3 million. If indeed this was so, not all of them were in the country illegally.

Unknown to most, the figure of Zimbabwean migrants in South Africa often fluctuated and was most likely smaller. That is because many of those in the countrywere on various temporary residents' permits. For example, both cross-border traders and shoppers would often have a thirty-day visa for continuous stay in South Africa. Often, such migrants would be in the country for only a few days or weeks' trading or shopping and then return to Zimbabwe, engage in other economic activities and perhaps return to South Africa a few weeks later to trade and shop before the expiry of their visas. It is undeniable that sometimes holders of such visas did not return to Zimbabwe. Instead, they overstayed in South Africa after the expiry of their visas and resorted to illegal border crossings such as border-jumping, being smuggled across the border and bribing some corrupt immigration officials.

Conversely, temporary residence's permits for students and those undertaking study or work in the country ranged from a minimum of two to a maximum of four years. Holders of such permits usually were in South Africa for most of the year and only returned to Zimbabwe over the festive season. After that, depending on whether their permits were still valid, they would then return after the festive season. Those whose permits had expired the previous year but still had proven commitments in South Africa could enter the country on a thirty or ninety-day visitor's visa and renew their temporary residence permits. In some cases, Zimbabwean migrants had family connections in South Africa who had attained permanent residence status or even citizenship. The acquisition of permanent residency or citizenship was possible based on, for instance, marriage, proven kinship or descendancy with or from a South African citizen, the holding of excellent academic qualifications and the possession of scarce skill sets. Zimbabweans able to prove any of the above could enter and stay in South Africa when and for as long as they wanted.

The crisscrossing of the Zimbabwe-South Africa border by Zimbabweans, coupled with the fact that other African migrants such as Mozambicans, Malawians, Kenyans and Zambians were sometimes mistaken for Zimbabwean helped contribute to the perception that over 3 million Zimbabweans were in South Africa. That is to the extent that by mid-2008 the migration of Zimbabweans particularly into South Africa had reached 3 million, about a quarter of the country's population. It is against such perceptions of Zimbabweans' immigration into South Africa that based on personal experience, ethnographic observations, unstructured interviews and literature review; I share my findings of some South Africans' responses to African immigrants generally.

### *"Go back to Zimbabwe!" Some South Africans' Responses to African Immigrants—the May 2008 and April 2015 "xenophobic" attacks*

South African society is molded on perceptions and stereotypes cultivated over 300 years. Therefore, despite the country's democratic dispensation, a satisfactory transition to a post-apartheid era has been difficult. Residues of the country's discriminatory past and its effects manifested themselves in some of its citizens' responses to African immigrant arrivals. That was evident at the country's Beitbridge border-post, the entry port of most surface immigrants from neighboring Zimbabwe and those from as far afield as Malawi, Ethiopia and Somalia.

Aside from socio-economic reasons, the selection of South Africa as the preferred destination of most African immigrants from Malawi, Mozambique, Ethiopia, Zambia and Zimbabwe is historic. This was also because during the apartheid years, the Frontline states of Botswana, Zimbabwe, Mozambique, Zambia, Malawi and Angola had trained *Umkhonto weSizwe* (Spear of the Nation), the military wing of the then exiled ANC and/or harbored black South African refugees and provided them with political, economic, educational, military, logistical and moral support.

In response to the Frontline states' spirit of pan-Africanism, African brotherhood and *ubuntu* (African collective consciousness), South Africa's racist regime had launched several covert and overt military operations, retaliatory raids and bomb attacks in pursuit of black South African freedomfighters and exiled political activists (Evans, 1984). Such extraterritorial military escapades had at times caught nationals of the host African country in cross-fire resulting in numerous casualties. Post-1994 therefore, by migrating to the newly democratic South Africa, some Africans sought black South Africans' reciprocation of the spirit of pan-Africanism, African brotherhood and *ubuntu* earlier shown to some of them during the dark days of apartheid.

The spirit was, however, primarily found wanting. As testimonies of some African immigrants who entered South Africa by land attested, their reception was less than hospitable. Some immigration and security officers' treatment of African immigrants, the majority of whom were Zimbabweans was at times abominable. Not only did some of them endure the verbal abuse of being told by irate officers to 'go back to Zimbabwe!' they sometimes suffered the indignity having their passports thrown at them or of being hosed down with hot water. Other corrupt immigration officers reportedly requested bribes in order to facilitate entry into South Africa.

Cultural and linguistic diversity is today a feature of most nations. The events that unfolded in Zimbabwe and the influx of immigration into South Africa from the rest of Africa resulted in the further diversification of an already very multicultural people. As the economic situation in the north of its border deteriorated further and the crisis pushed Zimbabweans south, the South African Department of Home Affairs set up special immigration units called Internal Tracing Units (ITU). Incorporating members of the South African Police Service (SAPS) and immigration officers and reminiscent of apartheidera Internal Stability Units, the units patrolled the streets. Their task was to identify African migrants, stop them and verify whether they were in the Republic legally. The spinoff of this and increased African immigrant arrivals from as close as Zimbabwe and as far and as varied as the Democratic Republic of Congo (DRC) and Nigeria was emphases and interest by some South African officials and citizens in the phenotype, linguistic features, local language performance and dress of black people they encountered in everyday life.

Perceptions of what South African culture and ethnic identityconstitute became essentialized as hallmarks and yardsticks of black South Africanness. Thus, for instance, an African having a very dark skin, round, broad face and nose and of above average height was often suspected of being an immigrant. As Morris explains, Nigerians and Congolese, for example:

> are easily identifiable as the 'Other.' Because of their physical features, their bearing, their clothing style and their inability to speak one of the indigenous languages, they are in general distinct and South African residents are easily able to pick them out and scapegoat them. (Morris, 1998, p.1125)

In order to verify their "suspicion" of a black person being an immigrant, therefore, some South African police officers and some citizens would often engage the "suspect" in Zulu, Sotho or Tswana, the most common of South Africa's eleven official languages. At times, the "suspect's" failure to respond in a South African language often resulted in the use of English. At others, attitudes suddenly changed. Service sometimes became forced, strained and even hostile because a black person had turned out to be an immigrant, a *kwerekwere* (African foreigner). African immigrants from North, East, West and Southern Africa such as Zimbabweans, Mozambicans Malawians, Zambians, Burundians, Somalis, Cameroonians and Nigerians collectively became known as *makwerekwere*, a term that is perceived as derogatory and derived from the phonetic sounds African immigrants make when speaking in their native languages. In the case of some members of the ITU, failure to respond in a local language or a response in English confirmed foreignness. An officer would thus request to see a passport rather than the usual green South African Identity Document (I.D) book a citizen or permit resident would have had to produce. Failure to do so often led to questioning and worst, detention and deportation.

Similar to other countries' IDs the world over, the South African green ID book generally serves to corroborate its holder's citizenship or permanent residence status in the country. At the height of Africans' migration to South Africa, the country's ID book became the preferred foil to an African passport and helped inculcate a new politics of separateness amongst the country's blacks. Owning a South African green ID book and the ability to fluently speak at least one South African language resulted in narcissistic supremacy amongst some South African ID holders. To such citizens, South Africa was disparate from the continent, and so, such South Africans treated African nationals they encountered with either pity or both contempt and hostility. That is such that African migrants not conversant in any local language hesitated to converse in public spaces such as taxis and other public transport for fear of being identified as foreign. Indeed, such was the "power" of the South African green ID book that some immigrants sought integration into South African society, by any means necessary.

The apartheid regime's racist system sought to break black people's sense of self-worth by undermining their humanity.Possessing a passport from the continent and not a South African ID sometimes became a black immigrant's qualification to be mistreated or alienated from one's humanity. It was tantamount to absence where possession of a South African ID or the ability to speak local language meant presence; humanity. Within South Africa, being the holder of an African passport became reminiscent of the apartheid regime's passbook that had caused so much discontent amongst black South Africans and caused the 1960 Sharpeville massacre.

From 1948 South Africa's apartheid government had formalized racial segregation by instituting systematic laws such as the Prohibition of Mixed Marriages Act, Act Number 55 of 1949, Registration Act, Act Number 30 of 1950 and in 1952 the Natives Act Number 67, more infamously known as the Pass Law. Under this latter law, black people had been forced to carry with them a passbook as identification with them at all times. Very much like a passport, inside it was a photograph of the bearer, details of place of origin, employment record, tax paymentsand encounters with the police. It was a criminal offense to be unable to produce a pass when required to do so by the police.

Although the Pass Law had been repealed in 1986, it was unofficially revived by ITU members' equally discriminatory demands that blacks whom they suspected to be immigrants always present and have their passports with them. The foreigner identification methods employed by the ITU also evoked the apartheid regime's identification methods it used to identify black South Africans' tribe of origin and race. According to Minaar and Hough (1996) in trying to establish whether a suspected immigrant is illegal or not,

> members of the internal tracing units focused on many aspects. One of these is language: accent, the pronouncement of certain words (such as Zulu for 'elbow,' or 'buttonhole' or the name of a meerkat). Some were asked what nationality they are and if they reply 'Sud' African this is a dead giveaway for a Mozambican, while Malawians tend to pronounce the letter 'r' as 'errow' (Minaar & Hough, 1996, pp.166–7)

Harris expounds that, "appearance is another factor in trying to establish whether a suspect is illegal -- hairstyle, type of clothing worn as well as actual physical appearance." (2002:173) Thus, apparently, in the case of Zimbabweans and Mozambicans stereotypically,

> a dead give-away is the vaccination mark on the lower left forearm ... [while] those from Lesotho tend to wear gumboots, carry walking sticks or wear blankets (in the traditional manner), and also speak slightly different Sesotho. The biological-cultural features of hairstyles, accents, vaccination marks, dress and physical appearance can be read as indexical markers or signifiers. They signify difference and point out foreignness in a way that is immediately visible. (Harris, 2002, p.173)

Writing on the same, Boullion also adds that: "Dress and hair [were also used in...] the 'sniffing out' methods adopted by the Internal Tracing Units of the South African Police" (Boullion 1996, p. 10). African immigrant men and women caught displaying such typecasts and found to have entered or staying in South Africa illegally, at times, reportedly paid ITU officials bribes to evade arrest or were put in *nyalas* (steel canopied police trucks) parked in the sun as punishment for those inside. Once the *nyala* was full, the illegals would then be trucked to Lindela Repatriation Center where some of them would reportedly be subjected to all sorts of horrors before final deportation.

The "sniffing tactics" of the ITU and the arrogant treatment some African immigrants endured reduced them to worse than third-class citizens and encouraged some South Africans' disdain for non-South African Africans. That left some African migrant groups prone to discrimination, exploitation and random violence due to their "foreignness" and inability to speak a South African language. Before the relaxation of immigration restrictions on Zimbabwean nationals wishing to enter South Africa in April 2009, South Africa was according to the International Organization for Migration (IOM) "deporting an average of 3,900 illegal Zimbabwean migrants every week." However, despite the treatment some such migrants suffered, their desperation often proved stronger, and they would be back in South Africa less than 24 hours after repatriation.

The late president of Mozambique Samora Machel once described racism as " 'a permanent crime against mankind, depriving a man of his personality and dignity, humiliating him to the point where he believes he is inferior because of the color of his skin' " (Smith & Simpson, 1981, p.164). Racism is often perpetrated by those who cannot accept racial equality. The same can also be said of xenophobia. The only difference being, instead of race, xenophobia targets one's country of origin, language and cultural background. According to Tawengwa (2015) "Xenophobia refers to a phobic (anxious) attitude foreigners" (p.10). Among some of "the causes of xenophobia are The perception of foreigners as a threat to physical security, racism, radical nationalism and political scapegoating" (Tawengwa, 2015, p.10). In this vein, Wetherell and Potter writing on xenophobia note that "patriotism and pride are the "positive" face, and xenophobia and chauvinism the unacceptable face of nationalism" (1992, p.141). In May 2008 and April 2015, cultural chauvinism and intolerance blossomed among some black South Africans when animosity towards African immigrants grew and culminated in what has debatably been called xenophobic attacks.

Various research (*see* Simpson et al., 1992; Hamber, 1997; Hamber and Lewis, 1997; Harris, 2002) highlight what has been termed South Africa's "culture of violence." To date, there are many schools of thought as to what exactly sparked these May 2008 and April 2015 xenophobic attacks against some African foreigners. Among the reasons given by the afrophobe attackers, African immigrants were stealing South Africans' women, jobs and RDP houses. As early as 2002, Harris had, for example, reported that:

> Hostility towards foreigners can be explained in relation to limited resources, such as housing, education, health care and employment, coupled with high expectations during the transition. (Harris 2002:171)

Other reasons for the attacks allegedly ranged from instigation by taxi bosses, taxi drivers and the media to the machinations of a "hidden hand or third unidentified force." On the basis of complaints made to the press ombudsman and the South African Human Rights Commission (SAHRC) at the end of May 2008 however, factually corroborative is that on 13 May 2008, the *DailySun* of South Africa had headlined with a story entitled: "War on Aliens" after black South African residents of Alexandria attacked African immigrants staying in the township. The daily had earlier similarly described an African immigrant attacked and set alight by a vigilante crowd in Diepsloot for allegedly stealing.

To some ordinary South Africans living in the townships and informal settlements, the newspaper's attitude towards the attack seemed to be sanctioning violence against the so-called "aliens." They had, therefore, attacked other African immigrants staying in different parts of Johannesburg. In the weeks that followed, attacks on black immigrants spread to the coastal cities of Durban and Cape Town. After that, reports of attacks came from parts of the provinces of Mpumalanga, Orange Free State, Northern Cape and North West.

Ironically, the "sniffing out" *modus operandi* of the ITU, what Morris terms, a biocultural hypothesis of xenophobia on account of it basing xenophobia on the visible differences of 'physical, biological factors and cultural differences exhibited by African foreigners in the country' (Morris, 1998:1125) were deployed to identify African immigrants. For those who were "sniffed out" or "discovered," the results were either a severe beating or death. Hundreds more were displaced and temporarily sheltered at police stations.

Close to a hundred immigrants, among them, Pakistanis, Bangladeshis but mostly Africans are known to have died. The death of some foreigners from outside the continent of Africa has led to contention as to whether it is correct to call the attacks "xenophobic" or riots. Especially so when one takes into account that lexically defined, the term 'xenophobia' is defined as a 'hatred or fear of foreigners' (*South African Pocket Oxford Dictionary of Current English*, 1994). However, considering that South Africa has foreign immigrants from other racial groups who went unscathed and that even some black South Africans from the country's Limpopo Province also died, it has been deemed erroneous to call the May 2008 attacks xenophobic. Since the attacks took the form of black on black violence, the nomenclature Afrophobia and Afrophobic violence as opposed to xenophobia and xenophobic violence have more recently been used to describe them.

Of the Zimbabwean immigrants who were harassed and attacked, those from the country's Shona tribe suffered the most. Fourteen Zimbabweans residing mostly in South Africa's high density and shanty towns lost their lives. In the aftermath, thousands more are estimated to have decided to return to Zimbabwe. On the other hand, immigrants from the country's Ndebele tribe fared better. What survival strategies had they adopted for them to survive and mostly go unscathed? The answer lay in pre- and post-colonial history.

*Reconnecting the Disconnected: Some Zimbabweans' reclamation of "Zuluness"* For the whites who migrated from Zimbabwe to South Africa between 2000 and 2008 integration into South African society had been relatively simple. The reason for this was mainly because of their whiteness, the favorable perception whiteness vis-a-vis blackness the apartheid era seems to have instilled in black South Africans, their kinship with some white South Africans, the dominantly white areas they had settled in, their ability to speak English and/or Afrikaans as well as their historical links with South Africa. Although the same is not so of those Zimbabweans who are of Shona descent, it was, to some extent so of those of Ndebele descent. Albeit bereft of a South African ID book, Zimbabwean Ndebele immigrants had for decades been relying on their ancestral and therefore linguistic and traditional backgrounds to integrate into South African society. To better understand how a brief overview of the origins of the Ndebele people of Zimbabwe is necessary.

During a turbulent period of Zulu history known as the *Mfecane* (the time of crushing) in the early 1820s, Mzilikazi, one of King Shaka's generals, together with his Khumalo clan, fled from Zululand and headed north into what is present-day western Zimbabwe. Once there, Mzilikazi had set about founding what was to be known as the Ndebele kingdom. To ensure the survival and growth of his fledgling kingdom, Mzilikazi incorporated and acculturated some local Shona clans. By the time of Mzilikazi's death in 1868, the Ndebele kingdom had grown to comprise those of the original Khumalo clan from the southeast and the kingdom's highest social class, the *mzansi* (southeast). The Sotho and Tswana people Mzilikazi had defeated and assimilated during his migration to north occupied the second highest status in Ndebele society, that of the *enhla* (higher up/upcountry).[2]

Some Shona clans which Mzilikazi had battled with, subdued and absorbed into Ndebele society on arrival constituted the kingdom's largest group, the *hole* (crippled/paralyzed) social class (Dent & Nyembezi 2006:378). Over time, *hole* women had inter-married with men from the *enhla* and *mzansi* classes, resulting in kinships amongst them. Although the Ndebele kingdom was later destroyed by the British South Africa Company (BSAC) in 1893, Zimbabwe's modern-day Ndebeles, directly and indirectly, share a kinship, language and tradition with the Zulus and to some extent, the Sotho of South Africa. So, while Zimbabwean Ndebeles are technically "foreign," ancestrally, these Northern Ndebeles, as they are known in South Africa, are to a large extent not and could be considered cousins to some South African Zulus.

When from the early 1920s the *Chibaro/Chibalo* (Shona for rape, or Portuguese for forced labor) system had begun recruiting African men from the region to work in South African mines, Ndebele man had been among the majority of them. To such men, coming to South Africa came to be regarded as "returning home from exile" after their ancestor's flight from Zululand during the *Mfecane*. In the years that followed, some Ndebele males had come to regard coming to work in South Africa as almost a rite of passage to manhood. Often, these Ndebele migrant men headed to Johannesburg or Durban where South Africa's black population is mostly Zulu, language and traditions similar, and integration more natural.

The third wave of Ndebele migration to South Africa had occurred when post-Zimbabwe's independence, some Ndebele ex-combatants had in the early 1980s embarked on dissident activity against the new black government resulting in the army's Fifth Brigade perpetrating atrocities against mostly Ndebele communities. That had seen some Zimbabwean Ndebeles seeking refuge in South Africa. Similarly, when from the beginning of the new millennium Zimbabwe began sliding into crisis, some of the country's Ndebeles were among the first to trek to South Africa. Evocative of the 1900s, some of these Ndebele immigrants also headed to Johannesburg and Durban and akin to their predecessors, also assumed what I would like to call, "Zulu masks," the performance of Zulu identity and culture, the mimicry of Zuluness.

Language is central to cultural identity. It is pivotal to the expression of culture as a means of communicating values, beliefs and customs. In South Africa, Zulu language (*isiZulu* to the Zulu) is the language of the country's southeastern peoples[3]. It is widely spoken in KwaZulu-Natal (81% of the province's population are Zulu first language speakers), Mpumalanga (26%) and Gauteng (21%). It is the most widely spoken home language in South Africa with about 24% of the population speaking it and understood by over 50% of the country (Ethnologue, 2005). Second to Zulu is Xhosa, the Eastern Cape's predominant language. Xhosaand Zulu are to some extent mutually intelligible (Ethnologue, 2005).

When Mzilikazi and some of his clan fled Zululand in the early 1800s, they had taken with them the Zulu language and tradition. Consequent to the migrations Shaka's *Mfecane* instigated, therefore, different dialects and traditions of the Zulu are today practiced in parts of Zimbabwe, Malawi, Mozambique and Zambia. Thus from the year 2000, 200 years after *Mfecane*, when crisis descended on Zimbabwe, the ubiquity of aspects of Zuluness in South Africa and its relation and intelligibility to Zimbabwean Ndebeles counted in their favor. As descendants of the Zulu and speakers of Northern Ndebele, a dialect of Zulu, this made it easier for them to communicate with Zulu-speaking South Africans, be accepted and integrate into South African society.

To ensure their integration, some Zimbabwean Ndebeles mimicked observable aspects of Zulu culture such as language and dress. For instance, some tried to "zulufy" their Ndebele as much as possible by, for example emphasizing the distinct click consonants and tonal aspects of the Zulu language. Other Zimbabwean Ndebeles also used such "Zulu" colloquial expressions as, *neh* (isn't) and *mara* (but) as part their Zulu mask repertoire.

In a 2007 *Bona* magazine interview, the then emerging South African songstress Lira was asked what advice she would give to a visitor to South Africa. Her response was for one to dress like a South African. In her opinion, "It is an exhilarating feeling to realize that it is not a matter of discovering who you are so much as deciding what you want to be, and then becoming it." For some Zimbabwean Ndebeles, the choice and freedom to assume a Zulu identity and become it through linguistic performance were enhanced by their dress.

South African fashion trends as popularized by the country's music and hip-hop culture are carefully followed and associated with "Durbanites and Jo'burgers," the people from Durban and Johannesburg. Subsequently, in addition to *isiZulu*, some Zimbabwean immigrants also made dress a part of their "Zulu masks." Thus, clothing brands such as Adidas, Soviet, Supergas, Levi and Zulu accessories as well as hairstyles which are popular in South Africa were also adopted by some Zimbabwean Ndebele immigrants. Accordingly, in addition to their ability to speak a dialect of *isiZulu*, Zimbabwean Ndebeles' outward physical appearance as achieved by clothing, jewelry, hairstyle and personal demeanor, heralded a South African Zulu.

Zimbabwean Ndebeles' mimicry of Zulu idiolects, dress and other South African fashion trends accompanied some notions of what they perceived as South African custom. For instance, in South Africa, when one embarks on a "taxi"—or what Zimbabweans would commonly call a commuter or ET (emergency taxi), it is customary for the commuter embarking to greet all the commuters that are already aboard. Indeed, in a bid to avoid being identified as immigrants, some Zimbabwean Ndebeles outperformed their South African hosts in this regard and if illegally in the country, camouflaged themselves against detection, harassment, detention and deportation.

In pursuit of South Africanness, other Zimbabwean immigrants also not only clothed themselves following South African fashion, but they also ensured that their motor vehicles were registered in the country so that they bear South African rather than Zimbabwean number plates. That is especially since, in some cases, cars bearing foreign number plates reportedly became the target of car hijackers or drew the ire of South African traffic officials. In this regard, Gauteng Province (GP) issued number plates became the plates of choice for their commonality and distinctly South Africanness.

In *Black Skin, White Masks*, Frantz Fanon (1963) demonstrates how colonialism, oppression and even comic books and cartoons cemented "the idea that blackness is associated with evil" (Murombedzi, 2014, p.L9). During the apartheid era, classification of South Africans was according to color. Negative perceptions accompanied pronounced blackness. It was such that, at times, black children would be separated from their siblings for being lighter than their intensely black pigmented family members. The result of this was that the lighter family member would be classified colored and the darker one categorized African. Reminiscent of the apartheid government's classification system, post-apartheid, being a light-skinned black South African became synonymous with South Africanness, wealth and beauty, while a deep black complexion became associated with African immigrants and at times stigmatization.

The result of some South Africans' sensitivity to African skin colors was that despite "the dangers associated with using skin lightening creams" (Murombedzi, 2014, p.L9), some African migrants took to lightening their skins with creams containing skin bleaching chemicals such as hydroquinone and mercury. They aimed to lighten their dark skins and so not arouse any "suspicions" from some ITU officials or attract negative attention from locals. Thus, in the words of Shaun Irlam writing in a different context, "the New South Africa has ushered in an era of identity mongering and separate development on a scale that South Africa's old bosses incessantly promoted at an ideological level" (Nuttal, 2009, p.158). Some immigrants' desires to alter their identities did not, however, stop at lightening their skins.

Probably the greatest mimicry of the "Zulu mask" some Zimbabwean Ndebele immigrants' performed was the alleged fraudulent acquisition of South African ID documents. The prevalence of such Zulu surnames such as Dube, Khumalo, Ncube, Ndlovu, Mhlanga, Moyo, Mahlangu, Mpofu,

Mhlongo, Sibanda and Tshabalala among some Zimbabwean Ndebeles reportedly resulted in them either stealing or fraudulently acquiring authentic South African IDs from some corrupt immigration offers. Not to be outdone, some non-Ndebeles but Ndebele-speaking Zimbabweans allegedly also purchased stolen South African IDs from criminal syndicates and changed their identities to their new Zulu aliases. In extreme cases, other African immigrants allegedly paid South African women to marry them so that they could acquire a South African permanent residence and eventually citizenship.

Some South Africans' decisions to distinguish, differentiate, categorize and exclude African immigrants to the country led to the pursuit and promotion of sameness or monoculturalism at the expense of multiculturalism. Multiculturalism refers to "promoting retention of various cultural divisions for the sake of diversity (...) at the scale of an organization such as a school, business, neighborhood, city or nation."[4] Due to the sometimes xenophobic and hostile reception of African migrant groups within South Africa met, they resorted to hiding their Africanness. For example, some African migrants refrained from dressing in traditional attire when visiting black townships, public areas such as taxi ranks and stadia for fear of easy identification as coming from the continent.

According to the siteRacismNoWay, "[d]enying cultural expression means limiting the expression of unique perspectives on life and the transmission of knowledge from generation to generation"[5]. Akin to living in a racist environment, some African immigrants' deployment of survival strategies in order to "fit into" South African society prevented the further diversification and multicultural composition of the country. In the case of sections of Zimbabwean immigrants, depending on the space they occupied at a particular time, the result was ambivalent, flexible and fluid identities. The irony of it all is that the history of Bantu migration informs that all Southern Africans are from south of the Equator.

Migration to South Africa and other countries enabled some Zimbabweans to escape their country's crisis and variously added to their host countries socioeconomic growth. In the case of some Zimbabwean Ndebeles, ancestral, historical and familial links were revived and restored. Disconnected relatives and family members reconnected and integrated into South African society. Ndebele and Ndebele-speaking men and women's ability to better integrate into South African society put them at a comparative advantage to other Zimbabwean migrants.

In contrast to those Zimbabwean Ndebeles who reconstituted their identity and integrated themselves into the mainstream South African culture and society, non-Ndebele and non-Ndebele-speaking Zimbabweans at times found it more challenging to integrate and blend into average black South African society seamlessly. For instance, staying in black townships and informal settlements, as did some poor Zimbabwean Ndebeles, often left them more susceptible to societal discrimination and victimization in comparison to their Ndebele compatriots. As a result, when the xenophobic attacks had broken out in May 2008, the ability of some Ndebeles and Ndebele-speaking Zimbabweans to reinvent themselves by putting on Zulu masks and mimic Zuluness had resulted in some of them escaping attack. When confronted by xenophobic attackers, some such Zimbabwean Ndebeles had successfully resorted to their Zulu masks and thus camouflaged themselves against muggings, harassment, severe beatings and death.

By 2009, mainly because of Zimbabwe's proximity to South Africa, Zimbabweans were inarguably South Africa's largest immigrant nationality. Depending on their level of education, skills training and nature of visa, some of them were able to find stable formal jobs or start businesses in various sectors of South Africa's economy. The skillset of some Zimbabwean immigrants saw them fill vacancies in such diverse fields as technology, accountancy, engineering, medicine, law, education and training. By 2011, it was estimated that "more than 5,400 foreign teachers work in South Africa's public schools" (News24, 2011), most of them Zimbabwean Mathematics and Science teachers.

However, the less educated and those in South Africa illegally had to compete for survival with South African locals in the country's informal sectors. A study by Africa Check found that "International migrants in South Africa are more likely to take jobs that locals are not willing to take or find work in the informal sector" (Migration Debate Takes, 2014, pp.21). In the case of unemployed Zimbabweans in South Africa, some stood at robot crossings and looked for menial work or sold trinkets, arts and crafts. Others even begged from the drivers of passing cars. A few "practiced" as traditional healers and prophets, some genuine, others bogus.

Other Zimbabwean immigrants though educated professionals but in South Africa, either illegally or without a work permit, worked as domestic workers. At times, the desperation such immigrants often opened them to extreme abuse and exploitation as some South African employers overworked and paid them a pittance. Amongst some South African citizens, some exploited Zimbabweans were called "Mugabe's people" and used to undercut and undermine domestic labor. Even after the May 2008 attacks, the notion of Zimbabweans as intruders rather than victims lingered and a repeat of the 2008 xenophobic attacks always feared.

## *Conclusion*

Since the 1920s, the migration of Zimbabweans to South Africa has been a feature on the subcontinent's landscape. The steady decline of the Zimbabwean economy from 2000 saw a spike in immigrants from Zimbabwe. Some ordinary South Africans' response to the influx revealed a resilient prejudicial past and ignorance of the historical ties between the two countries. In contrast, some Zimbabwean Ndebele immigrants manipulated their close ancestral ties to South Africa and adorned "Zulu masks" by mimicking Zulu identity and culture. Thus, when discriminatory identification practices reminiscent of South Africa's apartheid years emerged, such immigrants enacted what they traditionally already knew, at times, exaggeratedly mimicked and feigned Zuluness as a survival strategy. The result was not only the promotion of monoculturalism but also the emergence of ambivalent, flexible and fluid identities amongst sections of Zimbabwean immigrants.

## *Notes*

1. Affiliation: Department of Culture, Communication & Media, University College London & Comecinc Communications and Strategic Solutions Services Incorporated
2. See the history of the Matabele people on http://en.wikipedia.org/wiki/Matabele_people
3. For a greater appreciation of this, see http://www.sa-venues.com/sa_languages_and_culture.htm
4. For further discussion on multiculturalism, see http://en.wikipedia.org/wiki/Multicultural
5. Visit https://www.racismnoway.com.au/about-racism/understanding-racism/the-importance-of-culture-language-and-identity/

## *References*

Bornman, E., Van Eeden, R., &Wentzel, M. (Eds.). (1997). *Perspectives on aggression and violence in South Africa*, 3–20. Pretoria: Human Sciences Research Council.

Boullion, A. (1996). 'New' African immigration to South Africa. Unpublished paper presented at the conference of the South African Sociological Association, Durban, 7–11 July.

Branford, W., & Thompson, D. (1994). *South African pocket Oxford dictionary of current English.* Oxford: Oxford University Press.

Dent, G. R., & Nyembezi, C. L. S. (2006). *Scholar's Zulu dictionary English-Zulu, Zulu-English.* Cape Town: Shuter & Shooter.

Ethnologue report on Zulu. Retrieved, November 21, 2016, from https://www.ethnologue.com/language/zul

Evans, M. (1984). The front-line states, South Africa and Southern African security: Military prospects and perspectives. *Zambezia, 5*, xii.

Hamber, B. (1997). Dr. Jekyll and Mr 'Hide': Problems of violence prevention and reconciliation in South Africa's transition to democracy. In E. Bornman, R. Van Eeden, & M. Wentzel (Eds.), *Perspectives on aggression and violence in South Africa* (pp. 3–20). Pretoria: Human Sciences Research Council.

Hamber, B., & Lewis, S. (1997). An overview of the consequences of violence and trauma in South Africa. *Johannesburg: South African Journal of Psychology, 30*(1), 14–22.

Harris, B. (2002). Xenophobia: A new pathology for a new South Africa. In D. Hook & G. Eagle (Eds.), *Psychopathology and social prejudice* (pp. 169–184). Cape Town: University of Cape Town Press.

Matabele People. Retrieved May 13, 2014, from http://en.wikipedia.org/wiki/Matabele_people

Migration Debate Takes Centre Stage in SA. (2014, May 10–16). *The Standard*, p.21.

More than 5,400 foreign teachers work in South Africa's public schools. Retrieved May 13, 2014, from https://www.news24.com/southafrica/news/over-5-000-foreign-teachers-in-sa-20110726, News24, 2011.

Minaar, A., & Hough, M. (1996). *Causes, Extent and Impact of Clandestine Migration in Selected Southern African Countries with Specific Reference to South Africa.* Pretoria: Human Sciences Research Council.

Morris, A. (1998). "Our fellow Africans make our lives hell"The lives of Congolese and Nigerians living in Johannesburg. *Ethnic and Racial Studies, 21*(6), 1116–36.

Multiculturalism. Retrieved May 13, 2014, from http://en.wikipedia.org/wiki/Multicultural

Murombedzi, C. (2014). Skin bleaching: Reflection of a deeper problem, feature/stars. (February 16–22) *The Sunday Mail Leisure*, p.10.

Nuttall, S. (2009). *Entanglement.* Johannesburg: Wits University Press.

Simpson, G., Mokwena, S., & Segal, L. (1992). Political violence:1990. In M. Robertson & A. Rycroft (Eds.), *Human rights and labour law handbook 1991*, 1993—219. Cape Town: Oxford University Press.

Smith, D., & Simpson, C. (1981). *Mugabe.* Pioneer Head: Salisbury.

RacismNoway (nd). The importance of culture, language and identity. Retrieved May 13, 2014, from https://www.racismnoway.com.au/about-racism/understanding-racism/the-importance-of-culture-language-and-identity/

South African Languages and Culture. Retrieved May 13, 2014, from http://www.sa-venues.com/sa_languages_and_culture.htm

Tawengwa, T. (2015). Xenophobia not going away anytime soon, opinion &analysis. (April 26) *The Sunday Mail*, p.10.

Veit-Wild, F. (1993). *Preachers, non-believers: A social history of Zimbabwean literature.* London: Hans Zell Publishers.

Wetherell, M., & Potter, J. (1992). *Mapping the language of racism: Discourse and the legitimation of exploration.* Hemel Hampstead: Harvester Wheatsheaf.

# 7 *Survival by Reciprocity: Zimbabwe's Defensive Foreign Policy (2000–2009)*

Lere Amusan[1]

## *Introduction*

Zimbabwe's crisis took an explicitly international turn when it developed into a global concern because of perceived Robert Mugabe's domestic policies that hinged on other states' international relations. From the year 2000, Robert Mugabe's superficial populist government became a serious threat to the stability of imperialism and capitalism when it let land grabs continue unabated (Moyo, 2014). As far as the West was concerned, the invasion of white-owned land threatened the rule of law, challenged food security and could not be tolerated. The regime had to be curbed and, if possible, eventually terminated. A series of changes in international relations was set in motion as developed states from the western world turned to their diplomatic and capitalist arsenals with the view of ostracizing the country and bringing about regime change. In response, the ZANU-PF government manipulated the historical tensions between East and West and embarked on a "Look East Policy" in search of political reaffirmation and economic support. Not to be outmaneuvered, the West turned to South Africa and the African Union (AU), but they too strategically asserted their Pan Africanism and sovereignty by enacting their solidarity with their African counterpart. To better understand what it is that transpired in the foreign policies of the West and Zimbabwe, systemic theoretical perspective is adopted by this chapter where it is detailed that what impact a sub-system affects the whole system because of a high degree of interdependence (Amusan & van Wyk, 2011).

## *A World Divided: Zimbabwe's Crisis and Its Impasse with the West*

Systemic theory is not a new development in international relations. It was popularized in the 1950s and 1960s by Morton Kaplan (1964). In the contemporary international politics, this theory is popularized by Robert Jackson and Georg Sorensen (2013), and Andrew Heywood (2002). They confirm the relevance of the theory in the 21st century. Before this, philosophers such as Emmanuel Kant, Thomas Hobbes, Plato, Fredrick Hegel and Karl Marx had adopted the approach in their contribution to the study of international politics. The infusion of systemic theory to the study of international politics is borrowed from the natural sciences, mostly biology, where organic linkages among different parts make a whole, and the absence of one is tantamount to the inexistence of the rest. Recent developments in technology have enabled it to develop into a web of transnational relations, linkages and the same impact on the roles of non-state actors as the subject of international law that has rendered Westphalia state system less relevant (Fierk, 2013; Ringmar, 2017).

In this chapter, the concept of a "system," as defined by Jordan (1973:61), is "consisting of a set of elements, of parts, that are interconnected with each other by a discriminable, distinguishable principle." It is empirical and "focuses on external factors as tools of analysis in determining political, economic and social life" (Evans & Newnham, 1998:525). The adaptation of the approach to the political sciences has ensured the development of "scientific politics" and an understanding of different types of behavior in the different political structures of the international system (Kaplan, 1964:4).

Richard Little (1978:183) rightly sees the systemic approach as, "an attempt to focus attention on the complex interactions between states." In this respect, it is a state-centric approach that focuses on states as units of analysis. To Little (1978), it is holistic in its analysis of states' interactions in the context of globalization. The holistic nature of this approach is supported by Kant's position as quoted by Richard Little (1978:183, 185) that:

> The state system reflected a deliberate design to make harmony spring from human discord(…) it assumes that the world around us is organized on the basis of rational principles and that nature fits together as do the parts of a machine, each part interacting with another on the basis of invariant laws.

Going by this theory, its usefulness in the 21st century persists as the rationale behind the study of international relations is situated under globalization. As a concept, it derives its explanation mostly from organic linkages in relations among states. The linkages have been captured by the work of many third world scholars such as Bade Onimode (2000), Jagdish Bhagwati (2004) and

Johari (2012) who, albeit critical of globalization, haveagreed that it is systemic by nature. For this reason, this chapter employed Systemic theory to analyze and elucidate the economic and eventual political crisis Zimbabwe found itself in between 2000 and 2017. It is also indispensable to explaining how the country has managed to diplomatically survive it.

Like other behavioral theories of international relations, the Systemic theory is a partial theory. There is a hiatus in it as regards explaining the international system, and by contraction, a state's behavior, what physical scientists term: 'teleological'; the idea that any action and inaction of a state and its actors is based on purpose, which scientists jettison as non-scientific. The import of this, therefore, is that systemic theory cannot and does not capture the whole gamut of developments in Zimbabwe as they affected the international system. Therefore, at the tangential level, the historical analytical approach sometimes cushions whatever lapses the theory fails to address.

Towards Zimbabwe's 2000 elections, land politics remained the only credible weapon available to the ZANU (PF) government for it to continue enjoying the support of the rural electorate (Agyemang, 2013; Amusan, 2015; Meredith, 2005). The formation of the Movement for Democratic Change (MDC) in late 1999 had already eroded whatever support the ruling ZANU-PF government had in the urban areas. It could ill afford to lose the bulk of its support that lay in the rural areas. Therefore, when peasants, war veterans ruling party-sponsored youth militia (Green Bombers), state security agents (armed forces and paramilitary forces) and civil servants in 2000 started occupying private farmland, the state did nothing to deter them.

State action and inaction have reverberating effects on the general system in the form of "penetrative, reactive or emulative" (Rosenau, 1969:45) consequences. The catalytic culmination of the "land grabs" in 2000 was the departure of some white commercial farmers, disturbances in the agricultural sector, unemployment of former farm laborers, shortages of farm inputs and a drastic decrease in agricultural productivity. Much lowered agricultural productivity severely affected food supply in the Southern African region. The allocation of former white farms to mostly inexperienced politically connected Zimbabweans not only brought about food shortages, but it also aggravated unemployment as many farm workers became redundant. Those who were retained by the new farmer owners could not be sustainably paid because of the poor performance of both the new farms and the country's economy.

On an international scale, Zimbabwe, the erstwhile darling of the British became a rogue state and was placed under various sanctions. The European Union (EU), the United States of America (US) and the United Nations Organization (UN) imposed political, diplomatic and economic sanctions on the country. These were put in place with the aim that the government would reconsider its land reform policy that had aggravated political and food insecurity. Partly in response to Tsvangirai's call for sanctions on Zimbabwe, the USA Congress on 4 December 2001:

> passed into law the Zimbabwe Democracy and Economic Recovery Act (ZIDERA) that became the cornerstone of US foreign policy towards Zimbabwe. Under this Act, the US preconditions for aid and financing were the restoration of the rule of law, free and fair elections, a civilian-controlled military and police force, and a commitment to a transparent, equitable and legal land reform programme. The financial sanctions under ZDERA prohibit[ed] any US person from engaging in any financial transactions with any person or entity found to be undermining democratic institutions and processes in Zimbabwe (Badza, 2009:171).

Through the United Nations Security Council (UNSC), America and Britain voiced their concerns over what they saw as the Mugabe government's violation of the rule of law, political stability and economic development.

However, the truth of the matter was that the plight of many of Zimbabwe's white commercial farmers, descendants of EU countries, gravely concerned their kith and kin back in Europe. The existence of their historical links and the possibility of them moving back to England posed a security concern as they would get back to London not as foreign nationals, but a homecoming with negative impacts on the already saturated employment challenges in the whole of Europe at the time. Besides, Mugabe's call that the British government compensate them would put economic pressure on it.

Post-1994, South Africa's ANC government had adhered to a neo-liberal economic and political development system. The apartheid era's human rights abuses and undemocratic system of governance had encouraged the Nelson Mandela–led government to advocate human rights, democracy and reconciliation as cornerstones of the new South Africa's domestic policy. When in 1999 Thabo Mbeki had succeeded Mandela, he too had committed himself and his government to the same non-racial policies of his predecessor. Therefore, when in the year 2000 both Zimbabwean blacks and whites began migrating to neighboring South Africa, the Mbeki-led government had given some of them asylum and citizenship, respectively. In one ingenious diplomatic stroke, Mbeki managed to allay the West's concerns about white farmers and the humanitarian crisis in Zimbabwe on the one hand and corralled the white immigrant farmers' expertise and liquid capital on the other. In the years to come, Mbeki's diplomat maneuver was to yield dividends. Those of Zimbabwe's migrant whites who did not settle in South Africa migrated to Australia, New Zealand, England, Mozambique, Zambia and as far afield as Malawi and Nigeria. Akin to South Africa, the governments of Zambia, Malawi and Nigeria, for example, took advantage of the presence of the migrants' skills capital and particularly harnessed the farmers' farming expertise to increase their food production, resolve rural unemployment and, in the long run, became exporters of agricultural products.

The status of "pariah" was officially attached on the Zimbabwe government when allegations and accusations of economic mismanagement of both the state economy and money meant for land redistribution were levelled against it. These laid the cause of the land invasions squarely on the ZANU (PF) government's doorstep (Fletcher, 2013). In turn, the Mugabe government counter-accused and counter-argued the country's land issue into a diplomatic impasse with the British governments of both Tony Blair and later Gordon Brown. Such were the counter-accusations and counter-arguments that by the end of 2002, Western states spearheaded by the UK and USA and their private media had relegated Zimbabwe to a pariah state. Mugabe, several of his cabinet and party officials were banned from entering the EU.

International solidarity for the opposition MDC and what could be perceived as vulnerable members of the country's citizenry increased. The United Nation's agencies of UNICEF, World Health Organization (WHO) and UN Development Programme (UNDP) reacted to the humanitarian crisis. Western Non-governmental Organizations (NGOs) like USAID, OXFAM, Save the Children (UK) and World Vision also delivered food and other materials as humanitarian assistance due to political instability that enveloped the country coupled with the crop failure in 2001 because of drought, impact of climate that aggravated food scarcity (Amusan, 2008). The EU's position on the crisis corresponded with that of the British government. Some of its member states and US donors were reportedly funding the opposition MDC. Of all the EU countries, however, Germany explicitly remained objective in its view of Zimbabwe.

Since the dismantling of the Iron Curtain and eventual unification of East and West Germany, the federal republic of Germany has become an influential voice in Europe and the EU. At the international level, the country's need to garner support and regain its past glory and create a sphere of influence in Africa has affected Berlin's foreign policy with the rest of the world. The turn of this century has seen Germany intensify its bid to promote its heritage through the Goethe Institute and a series of bilateral relations with African countries.

At different times of Zimbabwe's crisis, Germany's Chancellor Angela Merkel explicitly and implicitly supported the Mugabe government. For instance, in October 2007 when the then Prime Minister of the UK, Gordon

Brown, vowed not to attend the EU-African states summit in Lisbon if Mugabe was invited, an invitation was still extended to the latter despite an EU travel ban imposed on him in 2002. The political support accorded to Harare meant "Germany's alignment with a state not trusted by the rest of the civilisedworld" (Stelzenmuller 2005:42–45). Crucial to Germany was the need to check the fallout of political instability in Zimbabwe such as illegal immigration, and to consolidate German investments in South Africa where multinational companies such as Daimler-Chrysler, Volkswagen and BMW are located and have markets (Osmanovic, 2007:4) in both South Africa and Zimbabwe.

Further to Germany's stance towards Zimbabwe, Russia and China also tacitly supported the Mugabe government. As members of the United Nations Security Council (UNSC), the two countries applied their veto power to make the Zimbabwean question of political relevance at the international level. The post-Cold War international arrangement had reduced Moscow to a mere participant of the UNSC. All former Soviet states had joined the North Atlantic Treaty Organization (NATO) security umbrella and married neoliberal economic development system. Because of Russia's civil war with the Chechnyan separatist movement, lending support to the Mugabe government most likely offered Moscow an opportunity to fight a proxy war against the US and other Western states.

As for China's support, the West's recognition of Taiwan continues to be a source of both political and diplomatic agitation to the Chinese government (Dukule 2006:8–9). Added to this, China's attitude towards Zimbabwe could also have been the result of both countries' external human rights records. Although China's liberalized and fast-growing economy has improved her relationship with the West and earned her membership in the World Trade Organization (WTO), the rapidly developing nation has historically had an infamously poor human rights record. Based on such accusations of human rights violations both China and Russia have traditionally supported other developing states in the UN Security against the West. As such, when the intensification of Zimbabwe's crisis saw the ZANU (PF) government accused of violating human rights China did not condemn them. Besides this, it has always been Beijing's policy never to interfere in the internal politics of other countries.

Over the years, China's demarcation between politics and economics has discredited its engagement with Africa in the rest of the world. Not only has the country's policy of "consultation, co-ordination and co-operation" been perceived as aimed at the economic underdevelopment of African countries through "joint ventures of unequal exchange" (Wu, 2003:23). The political support it accords to countries such as Sudan, Iran, DRC, Papua New Guinea and Zimbabwe that have poor human rights records against their citizens is an affirmation of the degree to which China is willing to go in the name of its economic interests and growth. Also, the need to be recognized as major political powers in the international system and bitter historical pasts with other world powers influenced Beijing, Berlin and Moscow's policies towards Zimbabwe and caused disharmony in the international community's response to the government in Harare. The Chinese government's continued support to and non-interference in the Zimbabwean state's affairs coupled with the effect of the West's targeted sanctions against the political elite in the country culminated in Harare's Look East policy.

## *The ZANU-PF Government's "Look East policy."*

Since the days of slavery and colonialism, Africa's relationship with the West has always been an unequal exchange. This is because despite such initiatives as the Africa Growth and Opportunity Act (AGOA) and the Millennium Challenge Account (MCA) that, among others, permit selected African countries to export to US markets duty-free, economic relations with the West have generally always been accompanied by stringent conditions. This is, however, not so with the Chinese.

China has no traceable colonial history with Africa. Unlike most Western governments, the country is wellknown for its diplomacy. Its financial assistance to the continent often has fewer conditions and bureaucratic bottlenecks. All this has roots in China's ancient traditions and its need to find a ready market for the country's mass-produced products in Africa. On the other hand, China's rapid industrialization has resulted in an insatiable appetite for a consistent supply of raw materials (Hutton, 2006:223–224) from the African continent.

Zimbabwe's pariah status and the divisions the country's crisis caused among the comity of nations resulted in the state's strategically leveraging bilateral and trade relations with the East's Asian Tigers of China, Malaysia, Vietnam, South Korea, Japan, India and Russia over its traditional West trade partners. By calling for and promoting closer bilateral and trade cooperation with the Asian Tigers, particularly China, the Mugabe government sought to both reciprocate and slight Western powers for their policies towards the country. Trade partnerships, bilateral relations, cultural and economic cooperation particularly with China, an emerging economic giant of the East, and other so-called rogue states in international system guaranteed diplomatic cover for the Zimbabwean state.

The relationship between China and Zimbabwe can be traced back to the height of the latter's liberation struggle in 1979. At the time, the then former Soviet Union had trained and supported ZAPU's armed wing, ZIPRA (Zimbabwe People Resistance Army) led by Joshua Nkomo while Communist China had done the same for Mugabe's ZANLA (Zimbabwe African Nationalist Liberation Army) by supplying them with arms and ammunition. After Zimbabwe's independence in 1980, the then Prime Minister Mugabe had sought to establish a one-party state in line with the two communist states' agendas for their nations.

Between 1980 and the 1990s, Zimbabwe's relationship with China had continued but without any extraordinary fervor. However, after the ZANU-PF government's land redistribution program and the country's fallout with the West in the 2000s, it again gained prominence. In 2004, a Chinese firm received a contract to farm 386 square miles of farmland the government had acquired from under the Land Reform Program. At about the same time, the state's air force bought 8 Karakonum trainer jets worth US$200 million. Because of economic and military sanctions against the country, the Karakonum jets, which are replicas of the British Hawk jet, were bought to counteract future shortages of spare parts from the British manufacturer.

As Zimbabwe's economy continued to decline, in July 2005, President Mugabe visited China's President Hu Jintau to discuss, among others, the two countries' bilateral relations. To ensure the forging of greater ties and cooperation between the two countries, Mugabe encouraged the teaching-learning of Mandarin in Zimbabwe. The University of Zimbabwe launched a Mandarin pilot project. Eisenmann (2005) reports that Zimbabwe's national air carrier, Air Zimbabwe even increased its recruitment of Chinese-speaking flight attendants and embarked on training those already in employ.

The latter part of 2005 saw the Zimbabwean government reportedly purchasing six military aircraft from China. In order to facilitate this, the Chinese government extended $58 million (US) loan to the state. Of the loan, $25 million (US) was reportedly used to import farm machinery, including 424 tractors and 50 trucks. According to the bilateral trade agreement, Zimbabwe would in turn also export 110 million kilograms of tobacco to China to cover the loan. (Wines, 2005)

During mid-2006, the Zimbabwe government allegedly exported 30 tons of ivory to China against the International Convention in the Trading of Endangered Species (CITES). In exchange, Zimbabwe received ammunition, 127 trucks and 3military aircraft. The African state's lack of lines of credit and foreign currency due to sanctions by the international monetary organizations and low agricultural productivity forced it to resort to barter trade. Of this, tobacco accounted for about 90% of total exports to China. Other items the state traded are asbestos, chrome, gold and platinum.

In comparison to cash-strapped Zimbabwe, China had as at November 2009 more than $2 trillion (US) awaiting global investment opportunities (Powell, 2009:52–54). This was such that as of the first half of 2007: 'The Zimbabwean trade deficit amounted to $189 million' (*Financial Gazette*, 2007). By the end of 2009, more than 35 Chinese companies had invested an estimated US$600 in Zimbabwe. Hence the sentiment that China is the "only major international supporter of Zimbabwe" (Eisenmann, 2005).

However, the truth of the matter is that Zimbabwe's mineral wealth of gold, coal, diamonds, copper and commercially viable agricultural products had particularly enticed the Chinese government (Hutton 2006:223–224). In February 2008, a 23-man delegation led by the then Chinese Deputy Minister for Commerce, Gao Hucheng, met the Zimbabwean cabinet in Harare and expressed interest in the country's gold and platinum reserves. As China is a fast-industrializing nation, Wines (2005) affirms that the Chinese are especially interested in Zimbabwe's platinum supplies. Partly as a follow-up on the Chinese delegation's visit, a Chinese company, Sino Steel Corporation, bought a stake in Zimasco Consolidated Enterprises Limited, Zimbabwe's largest ferrochrome producer. It produces 210,000 tons of high carbon ferrochrome annually and accounts for about 4% of global ferrochrome production.

Between 2010 and 2011, as Zimbabwe's economy stabilized partly due to an inclusive government and the introduction of a multi-currency tender system, the then President Mugabe reportedly made his twelfth and thirteenth visits to China, respectively. Strange et al. (2013) also report that in January 2010, the Chinese Ambassador to Zimbabwe, Xin Shunkang,"announced plans to award scholarships to 32 students from Zimbabwe to study in Zimbabwe." This reflects both the importance of China to the country's economic recovery and firm and growing ties between the two countries post the crisis.

After the ZANU (PF) government official pronouncement of the country's indigenization path and some western multinational corporations such as Rio Tinto disinvesting from Zimbabwe, China had by 2013 invested substantially in the country's mining, agricultural, manufacturing and, to some extent, retail sectors. Apparently:

> From 2000–2012 128 Chinese official development finance projects identified in Zimbabwe through various media reports (...) range from a loan of $670 million to expand a hydroelectric dam on Lake Kariba to a $500 million deal to finance Zimbabwe's local cotton production. (Strange et al., 2013)

Whether Chinese trade, investment and loans have been beneficial to Zimbabweans is yet to be extensively researched. In November 2007, however, it was reported that "the RBZ (Reserve Bank of Zimbabwe) bought agricultural equipment" from China after "loan agreement for the provision of agricultural machinery to Zimbabwean farmers' and distributed it 'through the Agricultural Mechanization Programme" (Strange et al., 2013). Just how much of the machinery eventually reached ordinary Zimbabweans is yet to be ascertained, but some Zimbabweans "have complained about the low quality of Chinese goods" (Wines, 2005) which they call: "zhing zhong."

Despite allegations of inferior goods exported to Zimbabwe by Chinese companies, however, Mugabe's relationship with Beijing waxed stronger in a situation where an alternative to this was nonexistence at the time. What is certain though is thatboth during and after the country's crisis, the Chinese have and continue to assist the Zimbabwe government's survival. Considered, however, the survival of the ZANU-PF government during the country's crisis cannot be solely attributed to its Look East Policy and relations with China. The Pan-Africanist spirit of some of Africa's regional and sub-regional member states and the diplomatic interventions of others on behalf of the crisis-stricken country also contributed.

*Regional and sub-regional responses to Zimbabwe's crisis* On the African continent, despite implicit calls by most members of the EU for regime change in Zimbabwe and even an EU travel ban on Zimbabwe's political leaders, in March 2003, President Mugabe was invited to attend the 22nd Franco-Africa summit. Pressure from Africa's most populous nation, Nigeria and largest economy, South Africa was among the reasons why Mugabe had eventually been invited. Albeit contemptible to the western establishment, the elderly statesman's credentials as an African freedom fighter and Pan-Africanist still held sway:

> They regard Mugabe as a real African hero, fighting an African cause, and regard Tsvangirai as a puppet of the West. To them the Zimbabwe crisis is part of a grand imperialist conspiracy to forcibly reform or, if it fails, dislodge, all African 'revolutionary' liberation movements, leaders and rulers, with Zimbabwe just being the pilot project. (Badza, 2009:153)

As part of Mugabe's strategies to avoid EU sanctions, he moved towards France as many other Africans do when they have a political crisis with other European states. The French invitation to Mugabe was finally issued to prevent a likely boycott of the summit by other African heads of state.[2]

However, both Nigeria and South Africa advocated constructive dialoguewith the Zimbabwe government as the best way to proceed. In March

2007, the arrest and torture of Morgan Tsvangirai by Zimbabwe's state agents resulted in the US, the EU and the then Australian Prime Minister, John Howard calling for more sanctions against Zimbabwe. At the UN, South Africa joined Russia and China in blocking the imposition of sanctions on Zimbabwe. When Australia as a member of the Commonwealth of Nations' troika committee tasked with looking into Zimbabwe's crisis further called for the expulsion of the country from the body of England's former colonies, Nigeria and South Africa objected and voted against Zimbabwe's expulsion. The impasse was only resolved when President Mugabe voluntarily pulled the country from the grouping.

On a continental level, the African Union (AU) continued to harbor the West's "authoritarian regime" due to the existence of a solidarity clause among member states. The rebirth of the organization in 2002 came with some innovations geared towards the challenges of globalization and the non-polarity of the international system (Haass, 2008:45). Amongst these, the non-interference clause in the internal affairs of the AU member states (Ar. 4(g)) was no longer sacrosanct (Zakaria, 2008:11). As maintained by David Stephen Krasner (1999, 2004) and Mario Blaser (2001), the Constitutive Act of the AU (Ar. 4(h&J)) and the emergence of the New Partnership for Africa's Development (NEPAD) set up to create sustainable development and eradicate poverty on the African continent made the need to interfere in the internal affairs of the member states a reality. Before, member states' self-assessment on human rights and good governance had been universally disparaged. After 2002, a common position with regards to such issues was in place. The setting up of the African Peer Review Mechanism (APRM) in Addis Ababa, Ethiopia actualized the objectives and principles of the AU as stated in Articles 3 and 4 and vastly improved the continent's governance image. As per these articles, AU member states agree to monitor each other's progress in democracy and political governance, economic development and management, corporate governance and socioeconomic development (Adedeji, 2008:241). The APRM and some clauses of the AU's Constitutive Act thus challenge the organization's notion of solidarity, member states' sovereignty and non-interference. Together with the APRM, the AU's economic organ, NEPAD necessitated an interdependent political economy both on and off the continent as regards how African and extra-Africa states could relate to each other. The implication of this was that the Mugabe government could not consider Zimbabwe's political and economic developments as its internal affairs.

The AU's high degree of political and economic interdependence caused some of the continental body's African leaders to call for urgent intervention in Zimbabwe. The late President Levy Mwanawasa of Zambia and Kenya's then Prime Minister Raila Odinga led this charge. They were to some extent, joined by Senegal's Maitre Abdoulaye Wade. Relatively new to state leadership, Mwanawasa and Odinga explicitly reflected the emergence of a new breed of African leaders who viewed the once sacrosanct concepts of African solidarity and sovereignty as myths that should be probed.

Both Odinga and the late Mwanawasa's views were, however, not homogenous to all on the continent's regional and sub-regional bodies. Their condemnations of the developments in Zimbabwe were not well received by some African leaders and adherents to Pan-Africanist solidarity. The late Mwanawasa's criticism of the Mugabe-led government resulted in Harare accusing Zambia of providing launch pads for British forces to attack and overthrow Zimbabwe's sovereign government. The pro-democracy position of the Zambian government also led to accusations by the Mugabe government that Zambia was collaborating with Botswana to invade Zimbabwe from the state' 2nd Battalion Tug Argan Barracks in Ndola, Zambia. (*The Zimbabwean* 1 December 2008).

On Zimbabwe's domestic scene, the ever-unfolding crisis entrenched what Hutchful (1998:2) describes as a "ruler's security dilemma". In response, the ZANU (PF) government and its state's security agents militarized the state. After the 2008 March elections and in anticipation of the June presidential run-off election, the Mugabe government splurged money on the country's security forces in a bid to maintain its fragile political condition and entrench itself in power. Enriching the military elite promoted security challenges for ordinary Zimbabweans and opposition parties. Before the March 2008 elections, the country's military chiefs had given their support to the Mugabe government and vowed not to recognize an MDC-ledgovernment. The security chiefs were allegedly personally afraid of retribution in a post-Mugabe government, and so truncated any appreciable political solution to the state's crises. Towards the June 2008 presidential run-off elections, the military, militias (Green Bombers) and some members of the Zimbabwean National Liberation War Veterans Association (ZNLWVA) clamped down on opposition parties. NGOs and Private Voluntary Organizations (PVOs) were barred from the country for interfering in the country's politics. As political violence escalated, the opposition MDC-T's Morgan Tsvangirai pulled out of the run-off election. The election proceeded all the same and Mugabe was given another presidential mandate. So controversial was President Mugabe's reelection that his leadership and government were in some circles considered legitimate.

The results of Zimbabwe's sham run-off plunged the country further into retributive economic meltdown. Food and fuel shortages intensified. When cholera broke out in the country's major centers, it could no longer be viewed as an internal affair because of the likelihood of it spreading to other SADC states and beyond. Two opposing positions on Zimbabwe's economic and political logjam emerged. In July 2008, at an AU Summit in Cairo, the Botswana Vice-President, Mompati Merafhe, maintained that "In our considered view... the representatives of the current government in Zimbabwe should be excluded from attending SADC and AU meetings."

To prevent a possible influx of Zimbabwean refugees, added pressure on Botswana's social and infrastructural amenities, terrorism and organized criminal groups, in December 2008 that country's foreign affairs minister, Phandu Skelemani, and Prime Minister Odinga of Kenya made calls for the forced removal of the Mugabe government. This led to the suspicion and accusation by Zimbabwe that Gaborone had set up a base for the MDC to train Zimbabwean youths with the aim of fomenting political instability in Zimbabwe. The accusation was taken up by the Organ, which was then chaired by Swaziland, a moderate pro-South Africa and by extension, an equally pro-Mugabe government ally. The Organ sent a delegation to Zimbabwe and Botswana to ascertain the veracity of the rumors. The allegation could not be confirmed by the delegation.

However, while Botswana and Kenya openly came out against the perceived illegal government of President Mugabe and advocated strict, comprehensive action against it, Angola, the Democratic Republic of Congo (DRC), Mozambique, South Africa, Swaziland, Tanzania and, to some extent, Namibia maintained their non-desultory relations with Harare. The relationship between the DRC and Zimbabwe governments can be traced to 1998 when Laurent Kabila, the father of current DRC president, Joseph Kabila, received military assistance from Zimbabwe after Rwanda, Burundi and Uganda invaded the country. It was rumored that DRC was militarily supporting the Mugabe government. It was rumored that in light of sanctions against Zimbabwe, the DRC was receiving arms and ammunition from China on Zimbabwe's behalf. This was refuted by both China and the DRC. The UN that had earlier accused the DRC of supporting securitocracy in Zimbabwe later denied the same.

As a close ally of South Africa, Swaziland for geographical, political and economic reasons could not act alone on Mugabe without South Africa's support. For its part, the South African government of Thabo Mbeki did not wish to play power politics and spree diplomacy in the matter. Instead, the Mbeki leadership embarked on behind-the-scene, "quiet" diplomacy in dealing with Harare for various reasons. Firstly, the ideology Mbeki sought is one of African solutions to African problems (*The Sunday Independent* 2008:4). Secondly, Pretoria wished to maintain friendly relations as traditionally, economic relations between the two states have been in South Africa's favor. Equally paramount was perhaps the need to check against the hatching of terrorist' cells in relative proximity to South Africa's own relatively stable economy and social order. The SADC region could ill-afford to Zimbabwe's crisis reverberate into member states. So, although South Africa had in the past intervened in Lesotho, Uganda, Burundi, Rwanda, Angola and the DRC, the same was not done in Zimbabwe.

Inside South Africa, Zimbabwe's crisis once again proved divisive. The ruling ANC party and its head of government seemed to have different ideas about how best to solve Zimbabwe's crisis. While the then President Mbeki wanted to tow a conservative, quiet and gradual engagement between the MDC and the ZANU-PF, the Jacob Zuma–led party wanted to sever relations with the ZANU-PF–led government. President Mbeki and the SADC troika of Angola, Swaziland and Tanzania's desire for political stability in Zimbabwe first before elections could be held eventually triumphed.

The AU adopted a similar position to that of SADC. In December 2008, the then British Minister for Africa, Mark Mallock Brown, came to Pretoria to solicit African states' support in imposing comprehensive sanctions on Harare. He was followed by Jendai Frazer, US Assistant Secretary of State for Africa who also visited Zimbabwe to find a catholicon to the crisis bedeviling the African state. Around the same time, the then French President, Nicolas Sarkozy, British Prime Minister, Gordon Brown, UK Liberal Democrat Party leader, Nick Clegg, current British Prime Minister, David Cameron and then US Secretary of State Condoleezza Rice called for the imposition of various other sanctions on Zimbabwe. At the G8 Japan Summit, however, Jakaya Kikwete, then Chairperson of the AU instead called for cooperation with. rather than sanctions on Zimbabwe.

Although the imposition of economic sanctions on Zimbabwe had long proved counter-productive as they mostly affected the masses and not Mugabe and his lieutenants, in December 2008, the UNSC instituted further sanctions on the country. These encompassed military, oil, trade and diplomatic isolation. The additional sanctions accentuated the country's crisis. Many watching thought Zimbabweans would finally stage an uprising and topple the ZANU-PF government. That did not however happen. If anything, it only led to the people's further aggravation and internal displacement as more of them bore their discontent or legally and illegally crossed into neighboring countries and beyond. No Arab Spring scenario broke out and other than falling into a state of disrepair; no infrastructure was destroyed.

Eventually, the culmination of Western sanctions, hyperinflation, Mbeki's "quiet" diplomacy and the AU-SADC's mediation was a Kenyan-style power-sharing agreement between the country's principal political parties of ZANU-PF, MDC-T and MDC-M. Signed on 15 September 2008 and known as the Global Political Agreement (GPA), its signatories undertook to form an Inclusive Government (IG) or what later popularly became known as a Government of National Unity (GNU). This was finally done and 11 February 2009 saw Tsvangirai sworn in as Prime Minister by his political opponent, President Mugabe.

Although under the GPA, SADC had strongly advised that ZANU-PF and MDC-T co-minister the Department of Home Affairs; however, in a move that suspiciously looked to be a bid for self-preservation, Zimbabwe's security service chiefs chose to remain under Mugabe's control as opposed to Tsvangirai. Thus,their jobswere secured, and they avoided prosecution for the human rights abuses they had perpetrated under the guise of state security during *Operation Makavhotera Papi?* (Whom did you vote for?) after the March 2008 elections. Albeit scathed, President Mugabe and his cabinet ZANU (PF) government too had survived. The principals to the power-sharing agreement settled down to governing Zimbabwe.

## Conclusion

Zimbabwe's crisis was not only about the internal affairs of the African state, which calls for Africa solution to Africa problems. Instead, Mugabe's draconian laws in a bid to win electorates favor turned through nationalization of land without due and prompt compensation wore a global outlook. This explains why this chapter adopted the Systemic theory in analyzing the problems that the country faced due to the poor public policy of the government in power till 2017. The result was the internationalization of Zimbabwe's internal affairs and dispute with the West as the EU and UN contended with China, Russia and the AU when it came to the African country.

As the world tangled over it, the Mugabe government capitalized on the situation and went into diplomatic survival mode. It embarked on a "Look East" policy. For historical, economic and political reasons, the Chinese responded to the Zimbabwe government's overture. This rendered the UNSC divided over the government in Harare and proved one of its lifelines. The other stemmed from some African countries' pan-Africanist stance and the need to find "African solutions to African problems" when it came to Zimbabwe. However, the democratization of the AU at the beginning of the millennium meant other less subjective African states could interfere in the internal affairs of the beleaguered country. Two opposing positions thus emerged over Zimbabwe on the continent.

To break both internal and external deadlocks over the future of Zimbabwe, the organs of both the AU and SADC facilitated mediation and negotiation between the political parties concerned. ZANU-PF and opposition MDCs assented with SADC and the only credible power in the sub-region; South Africa's Mbeki and formed a Government of National Unity. Between 2009 and 2013, it was to prove a palliative yet painful solution for the two strange bed-fellows. The coalition government formed could not resolve the crisis in the country. This was evident as the junior partner in the government, MDC, could not come up with its agenda in the government of national unity. The crisis could not receive a permanent solution until 2017 when Emmerson Mnangagwa staged a palace coup with support from the military to oust Mugabe administration after thirty-seven years in government.

## *Notes*

1. Affiliation: Department of Politics & International Relations, North-West University, South Africa.
2. The Guardian, "Several EU Nations Protest Mugabe Plans", 27/01/2003, BBC, "EU to decide on Mugabe trip", 27/01/2003, Reuters, "Four EU nations object to Mugabe's Paris visit", 27/01/2003, Afrol, "EU fails to renew Zimbabwe sanctions", 27/01/2003, Mail and Guardian, "France scuppers EU Zimbabwe sanctions", 28/01/2003. Retrieved on 6 June 2018 from http://paperroom.ipsa.org/papers/paper_26325.pdf.

## *References*

Adedeji, A. (2008). NEPAD's African peer review mechanism: Progress and prospects. In J. Akokpari, A. Ndinga-Muyumba, & T. Murithi (Eds.), *The African Union and its Institutions*. Johannesburg: Fanele.

Amusan, L. (2008). Politics of congruity in international relations: South Africa–Zimbabwe in Perspective. *Nigerian Journal of International Affairs*, *34*(2), 119–146.

Amusan, L. (2015). Working away from a Pariah status: Zimbabwe's defensive foreign policy option. In O. Abegunde (Ed.), *Public policy and development in developing nations: Selected cases* (pp. 227–248). Bloomington, IN: Xlibris Publishing.

Amusan, L., & van Wyk, J. (2011). The complexities of bilateral relations: The Nigeria-South Africa relationships (2000–2006). *Politeia*, *30*(1), 38–55.

Agymang, R. (2013). Mugabe: Villain or hero? *New African*. February, 20–23.

Badza, S. (2009). Zimbabwe's 2008 harmonized elections regional &international reaction. Retrieved June 6, 2018, from http://www.kas.de/upload/dokumente/2010/05/Defying_9.pdf.

Bhagwati, J. (2004). *In defense of globalization.* Oxford: Oxford University Press.

Blaser, M. (2001). Development and changing sovereignties: An analysis of structures in motion. *International Relations, XV*(5), 65–77.

Dukule, A. W. (2006). Between China and the West: The new war of influence. *Corporate Africa, 1*(888), 6–9.

Eisenmann, J. (2005). 'Zimbabwe: China's African ally' 5:15. Retrieved June 6, 2018 from *China Brief (The Jamestown Foundation).*

Evans, G., & Newnham, J. (1998). *Dictionary of international relations.* London: Penguin Books.

Fierk, K. M. (2013). *Political self-sacrifice: Agency, body and emotion in international relations.* Cambridge: Cambridge University Press.

Fletcher, P. (2013). Insight: In the shadow of Mandela, Zimbabwe's Mugabe fights on. Retrieved June 6, 2018, from https://www.reuters.com/article/us-zimbabwe-mugabe-insight/insight-in-the-shadow-of-mandela-zimbabwes-mugabe-fights-on-idUSBRE96T0DM20130730.

Haass, R. (2008). The age of nonpolarity: What will follow U.S. dominance. *Foreign Affairs,* 87(3), 44–56.

Heywood, A. (2002). *Politics.* New York: Palgrave Macmillan.

Hutton, W. (2006). *The writing on the wall China and the west in the 21st century.* London: Little, Brown.

Hutchful, E. (1998). Africa—rethinking security. *African Journal of Political Science, 3*(1), 1–19.

Jackson, R., & Sorensen, G. (2013). *Introduction to international relations: Theories and approaches.* Oxford: Oxford University Press.

Johari, J. C. (2012). *Contemporary political theory: New dimensions, basic concepts and major trends.* New Delhi: Sterling Publishers.

Jordan, N. (1973). Some thinking about "systems". In S. L. Optner (Ed.), *Systems analysis.* Harmondsworth: Penguin Books.

Kaplan, M. A. (1964). *System and process in international politics.* New York: Wiley.

Krasner, D.S. (1999). *Sovereignty: Organized hypocrisy.* Princeton, NJ: Princeton University Press.

Krasner, D. S. (2004). *Sharing sovereignty: New institutions for collapsed and failing states. Quarterly Journal: International Security, 29*(2), 85–120.

Little, R. (1978). A system approach. In T. Taylor (Ed.), *Approaches and theory in international relations.* London & New York: Longman.

Meredith, M. (2005). *The state of Africa: A history of fifty years of independence.* Johannesburg: Jonathan Ball Publishers.

Moyo, S. (2014). Regime survival trategies in Zimbabwe after independence. *Journal of International Relations and Foreign Policy, 2*(1), 103–114.

Onimode, B. (2000). *Africa in the world of the 21st century.* Ibadan: Ibadan University Press.

Osmanovic, A. (2007). Germany's new policy toward Africa. *Corporate Africa,* 30, 1(888).

Powell, B. (2009). China buys the world. *Fortune Magazine.* 160 (8), Coverpage.

Ringmar, E. (2017). The Making of the Modern World. In S. McGlinchey (Ed.), *International Relations: A Beginner's Guide*. E–International Relations Publishing.

Rosenau, J. N. (1969). Toward the study of national-international linkages. In J. W. Rosenau (Ed.), *Linkage politics*. New York: Free Press.

Stelzenmuller, C. (2005). How the Germans see the world. *InternationalePolitik*. Winter: *6*(4). *The Sunday Independent* (2008), December 29. Johannesburg.

Strange, A., Parks, B. C.,Tierney, M. J., Fuchs, A., Dreher, A., & Ramachadran, V. (2013). China's development finance to Africa: A media-based approach to data collection CGD working paper 323. Washington DC: Centre for Global Development. http:china.aiddata.org

*The Zimbabwean*. (2008). 11–17 December. Louis Trichardt, South Africa *Financial Gazette* (2007). *Zimbabwe: Look East or Look Chinese?*, 10–25.

Wines, M. (2005). From shoes to aircraft to investment, Zimbabwe pursues a Made-in-China-Future. Retrieved April 01, 2010 from https://www.nytimes.com/2005/07/24/world/africa/from-shoes-to-aircraft-to-investment-zimbabwe-pursues-a.html

Wu, G. (2003). Enter the dragon? *Business in Africa*. February.

Zakaria, F. (2008). Writing the rules for a new world. *Newsweek* (special edition issues December-February).

# 8 A "Marriage Of (In)Convenience": The Government of National Unity (2009–2013)

FORTUNE SIBANDA AND DENNIS MASAKA[1]

## Introduction

The signing of Zimbabwe's power-sharing Global Political Agreement (GPA) on 15 September 2008 at the country's Rainbow Towers Hotel in Harare lessened some socioeconomic and political challenges that Zimbabwe had been facing since 1999. Although the multi-layered economic challenges were partly caused by the government's preferred political and economic policies (Africa Briefing Report 2008:1), Western sanctions contributed significantly to these challenges.

This chapter argues that although the signing of the GPA was taken as an excellent solution to the crisis' challenges, we seek to argue that it also laid the foundation of an uncertain political future for the country for some reasons. One, the power-sharing deal conferred significant control of the government of Zimbabwe to ZANU-PF via mediation and negotiation and not electoral victory. In this respect, the GPA legitimatized a political process that somehow negated democratic processes of electing governments into power. Two, given the outcome of 29 March 2008, perhaps the leader that was preferred to lead Zimbabwe was Morgan Tsvangirai who had marginally garnered more votes than Robert Mugabe had. The eventual leader of the Inclusive Government (IG) turned out to be Mugabe. However, the Government of National Unity (GNU) had its significant successes much as it had its challenges.

## *Miscalculations, Sanctions, Hyperinflation and Voters' March 2008 Responses*

The Zimbabwean economy experienced a rapid fall from the turn of the new millennium (Clemens and Moss, 2005). The reason for this was primarily due to an array of economic and political miscalculations by the country's incumbent government. These included the granting of unbudgeted gratuities to the country's war veterans in November 1997; an economically costly involvement in the Democratic Republic of Congo's complex war[2]; price controls and eventually, an unplanned land reform program. In 2001, the US State Department's chief African official Walter Kansteiner summarized the country's situation thus:

> The current crisis in Zimbabwe has its roots in many areas.
>
> Broadly speaking, poor fiscal policies and rampant government spending—including the cost of Zimbabwe's military involvement in the Congo—set the stage for the present economic meltdown. Due in large part to an illegal and chaotic 'fast-track' land reform program pursued by the government, the agricultural sector has been severely disrupted. (Bond 2007, p.1–2)

After that, Zimbabwe's economic situation worsened when the European Union (EU) and the United States of America (USA) imposed sanctions on Zimbabwe. The USA and EU's sanctions positions on Zimbabwe are outlined in the Zimbabwe Democracy and Economic Recovery Act of 2001 (115 STAT. 963; 115 STAT. 965), also known as "ZIDERA," and the Council Common Position (2002/145/CFSP) of 2002, respectively. These sanctions' documents clearly stated their intent to exert economic pressure on Zimbabwe so that it could return to democracy, the rule of law, to respect human and property rights, and hold non-violent, free, and free and fair elections. When the world recession hit in 2008, it fomented the country's already worsening socioeconomic and political (Coltart, 2008) problems. The result was a hyperinflationary environment that saw the country achieve the world's highest inflation rates outside of a war zone (Makochekanwa and Kwaramba, 2009:3). Table 8.1 aptly captures the severity of Zimbabwe's economic situation vis-a-vis other countries that have experienced the same during their course of history.

The already poor state of the economy had further deteriorated, and it influenced the voting patterns during the March 2008 harmonized Parliamentary, Presidential Elections. This economic situation confirmed the EU's Council Common Position 2002/145/CFSP of 18 February 2002 and ZIDERA's expectations. As Tarisayi (2009, p.11) noted:

Table 8.1: Highest Inflation Rates in World History. *Source: Adapted from E Tarisayi (2009:13) Voting in Despair: The Economic & Social Context, in E V Masunungure (ed) Defying the Winds of Change: Zimbabwe's 2008 Elections, Harare: Weaver Press.*

| Country | Month with highest inflation rate | Highest monthly inflation rate | Equivalent daily inflation rate | Time required for prices to double |
|---|---|---|---|---|
| Hungary | July 1946 | 1.30 x 1016% | 195% | 15.6 hours |
| Zimbabwe | Mid-November 2008 (latest Measurable) | 79,600,000,000% | 98.0% | 24.7 hours |
| Yugoslavia | January 1994 | 313,000,000% | 64.6% | 1.4 days |
| Germany | October 1923 | 29,500% | 20.9% | 3.7 days |
| Greece | November1944 | 11,300% | 17.1% | 4.5 days |
| China | May 1949 | 4,210% | 13.4% | 5.6 days |

> the declining economy, a collapse of the democratic process, failure of the rule of law, land seizures and the way inflation was manipulated to make the very rich even richer shaped the manner in which the people of Zimbabwe voted, particularly in the March polls.

Zimbabwe's socioeconomic and political crisis favored the opposition. The impact of the EU's Council Common Position 2002/145/CFSP of 18 February 2002 and ZIDERA on creating a situation that favored the opposition parties ought not to be downplayed. The voting public doubted the ZANU-PF government's capacity to resuscitate the economy. On the other hand, some thought that the MDC could correct the economic mistakes that the incumbent government had made.

There was relative peace during the campaign for the March 2008 elections. Contesting parties were allowed some freedom to campaign and sell their manifestos to the electorate. Such a scenario was in contrast to the country's, "chequered electoral history" (Masunungure, 2009:3) when elections had allegedly been manipulated to the advantage of the incumbent and by and large, predetermined.

On 29 March 2008, the day of the election, Robert Mugabe of ZANU-PF, Morgan Tsvangirai of MDC-T, Simba Makoni, of the hastily assembled Mavambo independent political project and the little known independent candidate, Langton Towungana, were on the ballot paper as presidential candidates. In essence, however, "it was a triangular fight between Robert Mugabe of ZANU (PF), Morgan Tsvangirai of the MDC-T" (Masunungure 2009:64). By the end of voting, the country and the international community were primarily satisfied by the course the process had taken. Problems only began afterwards.

In a bizarre twist of events, though parliamentary results were relatively timeously announced, it took five weeks before the announcement of the presidential election results. When they were eventually released, Tsvangirai had garnered 47.9% of the total presidential vote and Robert Mugabe, 43.2%. As Table 8.2 below shows, while the two formations of the MDC combined had defeated ZANU-PF, the MDC-T presidential candidate failed to garner more than the 50% required by law for him to be declared the outright winner.

Morgan Tsvangirai had fallen short of the mandatory fifty plus outright majority required to ascend to the presidency as per the amended Electoral Act of 2007agreed upon by both parties before the elections. (Makumbe, 2009, p.131) Accordingly, neither party could claim victory. In this respect, the Zimbabwe Electoral Commission (ZEC) called for a run-off presidential election between the two principal candidates, that is, Morgan Tsvangirai and Robert Mugabe that was to be held on 27 June 2008.

To overturn the probable eventual victory of the opposition MDC, towards the 27 June 2008 re-run of the presidential elections, ZANU-PF embarked on an intricate and well-calculated strategy of acts of violence, displacement of voters, arbitrary arrests, muzzling of media space and hate speech (Moyse, 2009). Mainly opposition party supporters were brutalized into submission or forced to flee their homes and wards so that they could not vote for their preferred candidate, Morgan Tsvangirai. The use of violence was particularly contrary to the SADC guidelines on the conduct of free and

Table 8.2: The 29 March 2008 Harmonized Elections Presidential Poll Results. *Source: Adapted from Eldred V Masunungure (2009:76) Voting for Change: The 29 March Harmonized Elections, in E V Masunungure (ed) Defying the Winds of Change: Zimbabwe's 2008 Elections, Harare: Weaver Press.*

| Candidate | Number of Votes | Actual percentage |
|---|---|---|
| Makoni, Herbert Stanely Simba | 207,470 | 8.3% |
| Mugabe, Robert Gabriel | 1,079,730 | 43.2% |
| Towungana, Langton | 14,503 | 0.6% |
| Tsvangirai, Morgan | 1,195,562 | 47.9% |
| Spoiled ballots | 39,975 | |
| Total votes cast | 2,537,240 | |
| Percentage poll | | 42.7% |

fair elections that categorically state that "contestants ought to create a fair playing field to ensure that the outcome of an electoral exercise retains a semblance of credibility" (Moyse 2009, p.54–56). As the *World Report 2009—Zimbabwe (2009)* affirms, in contrast to the pre-March 2008 elections:

> [T]he months afterwards were marked by a well-planned and systematic campaign of violence by ZANU-PF and its allies. In an attempt to overturn the vote in the presidential run-off, government-backed militia and war veterans, ZANU-PF officials and supporters, and senior military officers waged a vicious campaign of intimidation against MDC activists and suspected supporters.

The alleged establishment of ZANU (PF) terror camps across the country rekindled the history of organized violence in Zimbabwe's politics. Between April and June 2008, the ruling party allegedly organized its political structures with the intention of victimizing members of the opposition and the general electorate. ZANU (PF) did not want its poor electoral showing of the 29 March 2008 harmonized election to be repeated. According to Matyszak (2009, p.146), in order to accomplish the desired electoral victory, come 27 June, "ZANU (PF) adopted a strategy of seeking to have a maximum intimidatory effect locally, to cause widespread fear and terror, and simultaneously to conceal the campaign from the international community." As a result, the run-up to the June 2008 Presidential run-off election created an unnecessary humanitarian crisis in the country and an uneven electoral playing field that favored the ruling party's candidate. The violence seemed to have worked because MDC-T pulled out of the election re-run citing widespread violence and intimidation of its supporters.

Tsvangirai's withdrawal from 27 June 2008 run-off election effectively made it a one-person race. Despite this, and significant voter apathy, Mugabe proceeded with the run-off election. The election proceeded and Mugabe "won." As shown in Table 8.3 below, the results of the 27 June 2008

Table 8.3: The 27 June 2008 Presidential Run-off Election Results. *Source: Adapted from Eldred V Masunungure (2009:96) A Militarized Election: The 27 June Presidential Run-off, in E V Masunungure (ed) Defying the Winds of Change: Zimbabwe's 2008 Elections, Harare: Weaver Press.*

| Votes | Robert Mugabe | Morgan Tsvangirai | Simba Makoni | Langton Towungana | Total valid |
|---|---|---|---|---|---|
| Popular vote | 2,150,269 | 233,000 | | | 2,383,269 |
| Percentage | 85.5 | 9.3 | | | 100 |
| Spoilt | | | | | 131,481 |

presidential re-run elections are somewhat the complete opposite of what had transpired on the 29 March 2008 election.

Mugabe was declared the winner of the one-person election and installed as president of Zimbabwe until 2013. However, despite this, he faced a crisis of legitimacy. “The election results lacked credibility and broader acceptance both at home and abroad. Mugabe’s presidency became contestable thereby leading to ‘political, legal and moral ramifications” (Linington, 2009, p.98). Within both Africa and outside, his legitimacy was openly contested and disputed. Botswana, one of Zimbabwe’s neighbors, openly condemned the illegitimacy of the ZANU-PF government. Others such as Burkina Faso and Senegal followed suit. Their condemnation resulted in a shift away from blindingly supporting erring regimes in the name of African solidarity and at the expense of their citizens’ rights. Regional and international pronouncements on the election thus made it difficult for the international community to recognize Mugabe as the legitimate leader of Zimbabwe.

At the conclusion of the June 2008 elections, Western sanctions on Zimbabwe intensified in what seemed a bid to effect regime change in Zimbabwe (Clemens and Moss, 2005, p.2). This accelerated Zimbabwe’s slide into more political and economic challenges. For instance, store shelves ran out of food, hospitals out of medicine and cholera spread across the country. At the behest of Southern African Development Community, the then South African President Thabo Mbeki engaged and mediated ZANU-PF and the two MDC factions of Tsvangirai and Professor Arthur Mutambara in talks to end Zimbabwe’s economic and political challenges that culminated in the GPA. We now turn to a consideration of Zimbabwe’s GPA.

## *Understanding the GPA*

The SADC brokered talks between ZANU (PF), and the two formations of MDC-T and MDC-M were meant to resolve the multiplicity of challenges that faced Zimbabwe in 2008. To facilitate the talks, the SADC Extraordinary Summit in Dar-es-Salaam, Tanzania in July 2008 endorsed President Mbeki of South Africa to mediate dialogue between Zimbabwe’s three main political parties (*Herald*, 16 September 2008). The bloc’s Commission chairperson Jean Ping and the United Nations Secretary-General, Ban Ki-Moon’s representative Ambassador Haile Menkerios (*Herald*, 16 September 2008) joined Mbeki in a consultative capacity. A Memorandum of Understanding outlining a framework for talks was signed between the parties on 21 July 2008. On 15 September 2008, the talks culminated in the signing of a historic political settlement by the respective presidents and principals of the parties represented by, Robert Mugabe for ZANU-PF, Morgan Tsvangirai for MDC-T and Professor Arthur Mutambara for the MDC-M. It was witnessed and signed by the then president of South Africa, Thabo Mbeki as SADC's facilitator to the agreement. Officially known as the GPA under it, ZANU (PF) and the two MDC formations resolved to share Zimbabwe's governance with the object to rebuild the country.

According to the Ministry of Constitutional and Parliamentary Affairs of Zimbabwe, the GPA was to be a charter to guide the operations of the transitional GNU. It followed the framework of the SADC Extraordinary Summit held in Dar-es-Salaam, Tanzania, on 29 March 2007 that was subsequently endorsed by SADC in Lusaka, Zambia, on 12 April 2008 and ultimately adopted by the African Union Summit held in Sharm El-Sheikh, Egypt from 30 June to 1 July 2008 (Ministry of Constitutional & Parliamentary Affairs, 2008, pp.1, 3).

Under the GPA, the signatories pledged to formulate a "genuine, viable, permanent, sustainable and nationally acceptable solution to the Zimbabwean situation" (Article 2); to resolve the nagging political and economic crisis and map a new political dispensation. Other pertinent issues constituting the GPA were Sanctions and measures (Article 4), land question (Article 5), Constitution (Article 6) and the promotion of equality, national healing, cohesion and unity (Article 7). On this basis, the signatories dedicated themselves, "to build[ing] a society free of violence, fear, intimidation, hatred, patronage, corruption and founded on justice, fairness, openness, transparency, dignity and equality" (*Herald*, 16 September 2008). As brokers of the deal, SADC and AU were guarantors of the GPA. They were supposed to assist the parties to resolve their differences, challenges and future problems through dialogue.

Zimbabwe's three main political players had put their differences aside for the sake of the nation. The GPA gave hope to the despairing country. It seemed the violence and the economic problems that had gripped the country since the turn of the 21st century would finally be overcome through the brokered power-sharing deal and would see, among others, the drafting of a new constitution within the first eighteen months of the all-inclusive government.

As the years passed, the 2009–2013 Zimbabwean experience of resolving conflict and political impasse turned into a dialectical process amongst the "strange bedfellows." It turned out to be somewhat a marriage of inconvenience yet convenience. The Articles of the GPA formed the basis of the new government's sharing power. The Parties had "declare[d] and agreed to unite whilst creating a genuine, viable, permanent, sustainable and nationally tolerable solution to the Zimbabwean situation" (Ministry of Constitutional & Parliamentary Affairs, 2008, p.3). However, considering the "marriage partners' history," would the marriage last and indeed be fruitful? As matters stood, Mugabe's disdain for Tsvangirai had been evident in his disparaging reference to the opposition leader as a "tea-boy" and the MDC parties as, "...stooges of the West" (Masungure, 2009, p.65). In the president's eyes, Tsvangirai was a puppet of the West who together with his MDC-T party wanted to reverse the gains of independence and the history of struggle that had seen patriotic Zimbabweans fight a protracted struggle to dethrone the white settler government.

To the ZANU-PF party, the opposition MCD-T leader was a "stooge" of the interests and ideals of imperialists and white supremacists. As far as it was concerned and had pronounced throughout Zimbabwe's years of tough economic problems, the situation the country found itself economically and politically was because of Tsvangirai's 2001 "invitation" for sanctions that were imposed on Zimbabwe and isolated it from the international community. This accusation is contestable mainly because the EU and USA that imposed sanctions could have had their reasons to justify the actions that they took.

The result was that both "domestic and foreign supporters and sympathisers (of the) ZANU (PF) government (were) influenced by this perception" (Badza, 2009, p.153). As far as they were concerned, ZANU-PF was a revolutionary party with liberation war credentials and nostalgically obsessed with its past exploits and contribution towards Zimbabwe and Zimbabweans' liberation from colonialism and imperialism. MDC was seen as an imperialist political project intended to reverse the land reform program and the return of white rule to Zimbabwe. This is to the extent that Mugabe on several occasions had vehemently vowed that he would never allow Tsvangirai and his MDC to get into power "come hell come thunder" as "Zimbabwe (would) never ever be a colony again." The MDC was perhaps the last political party ZANU-PF wanted to share power.

On the other hand, the MDC party had from its formation in 1999 accused and believed ZANU-PF to have managed to win previous elections and retained power through violence and vote rigging. As proof of this, it argued that towards the 29 March 2008 plebiscite when the ruling party had abided by the SADC guidelines to a free and fair election it had suffered its first electoral defeat. According to the MDC, this had been despite the ZANU-PF government paradoxically "starving and then helping" the electorate as well as making massive political donations such as farming equipment and food as vote buying antics. To the MDC therefore, it had only been after ZANU-PF again resorted to election intimidation and violence during the 27 June 2008 presidential run-off election that the party had again won resoundingly.

The consensus was that the SADC brokered power-sharing deal that was an agreement between two starkly different parties. In the words of *TheGuardian's* David Smith (2009), the GNU was "Southern Africa's most curious marriage of convenience"because it tied a "Gordianknot" between President Mugabe, "an infamous global dictator and democrats in the form of principals of the two MDC formations." The GPA and its GNU would therefore not have been was it not for the convenience they offered to all concerned.

For ZANU-PF, they legitimized the Mugabe presidency and meant another term in office, albeit sharing power. For the MDC, it was an opportunity to show its capability to govern, an unofficial hand-over-take as it were. This is to the extent that to some observers, the GPA was "historic in that Mugabe fully accepted an irreversible process towards regime change" (Bango 2009, p.2). For the former student leader and youthful president of MDC-M, Arthur G. Mutambara, it was also an opportunity to cut his teeth in governance. For the crisis-weary people of Zimbabwe, it conveniently meant an end to food, fuel and medical supply shortages, a return to normalcy. Brian Kagoro (Gonda, 2009) echoed the sentiments of both Zimbabweans and non-Zimbabweans when he remarked, "for the sake of our beautiful country(…) this marriage of convenience, this polygamous marriage of convenience, the unequal yoking of enemies will prove to be a workable solution."

Despite its various conveniences, however, the coalition remained a fragile one. During the first few months of 2009, the GNU notably reined in the country's hyperinflation through the GNU's official recognition of the multiple currencies of the USA greenback, South African Rand, Botswana Pula, British Pound and, to some extent, Mozambican Metical as legal tender. Inflation abetted and "national temperance and optimism at home and abroad" (Bango, 2009, p.2) returned.

However, after the signing of the GPA, ZANU-PF and MDC-T's irreconcilable differences resurfaced. *World Report 2009—Zimbabwe* (2009) reported that:

> the frailty of the deal was soon apparent as the parties rapidly reached a deadlock on the distribution of ministries, with violence and intimidation against the MDC still taking place. Zimbabwe's political situation remains precarious, and the future looks bleak if the political leadership does not end abuses and address accountability for both past and present abuses.

When it came to the distribution of ministries, President Mugabe and his ZANU-PF party sought to retain control over the country's security key ministries namely defense, police and the judiciary. It is surmised that this was to ensure there would be no retribution against him and members of his party.

Also, although Tsvangirai had on 11 February 2009 been sworn in as Prime Minister, he was reportedly not being left to undertake some of his duties and responsibility as Prime Minister. Mahlangu (2009, p.2) bemoaned the lack of urgency in fully implementing the GPA months after it was signed. Of particular concern was that contrary to the GPA stipulation that Tsvangirai would second Mugabe by controlling and directing cabinet operations, he had been denied the opportunity to chair a single cabinet meeting held in the absence of Mugabe. Put differently, the powers of the Prime Minister were deliberately usurped, thereby drawing the two political parties on a collision course.

As a result, Prime Minister Tsvangirai's MDC-T party "disengaged" from the GNU for a month during the last quarter of 2009, only to again seek accommodation with his coalition partners. The reason for this was partly because, as Global Risks Forecast (2009) highlighted:

> Nor do many citizens wish MDC to leave the government. The uncertainty of the disengagement reportedly prompted an increase in local food prices. The MDC is likely to return to the unity government due to the need to keep it functioning in order to maintain external financial and political support.

This confirmed the GNU as a marriage of convenience. A "divorce" would inevitably have plunged the country deeper into a crisis from buoyancy (Muzondidya, 2009). So, as Africa Confidential, a London-based think-tank envisaged:

> Nor do many citizens wish MDC to leave the government. The uncertainty of the disengagement reportedly prompted an increase in local food prices. The MDC is likely to return to the unity government due to the need to keep it functioning in order to maintain external financial and political support.

However, after Tsvangirai returned to the GNU, he reportedly also developed his counter strategy.

Dzamara (2010:2) reported how:

> The MDC-T leader established his structures and set up operational systems mostly independent of Mugabe or the government's control of funding. Commonly referred to as the 'parallel government' by ZANU PF. Tsvangirai's structures mainly operated away from the Munhumutapa offices, where both the presidential and PM's offices are.

In practice, different partisan agendas continued. In violation of the clauses of the GPA governing the operations of the cabinet, ministries and departments, the "partners" kept the other side at "bay and under check to ensure that it retains political power and control" (Dzamara 2010). There were rifts between the GNU's two significant principals.

In contrast to Mugabe's relations with Tsvangirai, the Deputy Prime Minister, Mutambara and President Mugabe appeared to be getting on well. This was often because of the Deputy Prime Minister's pro-Mugabe stance and what at the time was seen as his detrimental defeatist silence on some matters of national interest. Consequently, despite being a member of the opposition, Mutambara was soon being regarded as an opportunistic "moderate" and Mugabe's aide. Thus, while the coalition remained a fragile compromise between Mugabe and Tsvangirai, it seemed to have reconciled the other two principals.

After Mutambara warming to Mugabe and becoming almost an extension of the ZANU-PF president, in January 2011, he was removed from the position of president of MDC-M party and officially replaced in June 2012 by its secretary-general and the GNU's Minister of Industry and Commerce, Welshman Ncube. As a Principal signatory to the GPA however, Mutambara, with Mugabe's support remained Deputy Prime Minister until after 2013. Until then, the once-promising student leader and academic resolved himself to a ceremonial function in the GNU.

During early 2010, the coalition members began quarrelling over fulfilling the letter and spirit of the GPA. Contentious remained the issue of Western sanctions on the country and travel bans on some members of the ZANU-PF government and politically connected business leaders. ZANU-PF called on MDC to request Western powers that had imposed sanctions on the country to lift them. So tied to the MDC-T were the sanctions that they were often derisively referred to as "*Tsvanctions*" (*Herald*, February 2010), a play on the prime minister's name. ZANU-PF argued that unless the MDC called for the removal of the sanctions it had implored the USA and Western governments to impose, it would also not cooperate in fully implementing the letter and spirit of the GPA.

Western sanctions remained the MDC-T's trump card in its uneasy coalition with ZANU-PF. It was also the MDC's view that Zimbabwe could only pull itself out of its economic situation if it reengaged and reestablished sound relations mainly with Western countries and the USA. These countries had however set steep conditions they wanted fulfilled first, before this could happen. For example, in response to calls to remove the sanctions, both the George W. Bush and Obama administrations argued that the Zimbabwe government had to address, among others, the concerns of the US's ZIDERA and tangibly stop the violation of human rights. USA and other Western sanctions thus remained in place. The retention of the sanctions strained relations between the ZANU (PF) and MDC-T. The MDC was again accused of being unpatriotic and "wining and dining" with Western governments instead of working towards the removal of sanctions.

As 2010 progressed, the GNU became an uneasy marriage of suspicion, fear and mistrust—an inconvenience. To ZANU-PF, the MDC-T's presence in the coalition was not benefiting them and the country as it had earlier anticipated. It wanted the MDC-T to stop Western governments from harboring pirate radio stations such as SW Radio Africa and Nehanda Radio that, it felt, were demonizing its party and president. For its part, the MDC accused ZANU-PF of intransigence over such issues as the president's unilateral re-appointment of the Reserve Bank Governor, Gideon Gono, and the appointment of Attorney-General, Johannes Tomana. It also accused the then president's unilateral swearing in of ZANU-PF provincial governors, the president's use of hate speech and the continuing harassment and imprisonment of MDC supporters, in particular, Roy Bennett. Bennet, a white farmer and the MDC-T's designated Deputy Minister of Agriculture, had been accused of allegedly hoarding arms and plotting to kill Mugabe. (Global Risks Forecast, 2009) He had been arrested in February 2009 just before he was supposed to have been sworn into the GNU cabinet. These and other issues made the GNU a marriage of inconvenience to Zimbabweans.

## *GNU: A Marriage of Inconvenience*

Writing on Christian hope, Denise Ackerman notes that:

> [W]e have to be actively and passionately involved in trying to bring about that for which we hope. This implies hands-on 'doing'. Hope is not an armchair activity. Hope has very little currency if it is just a 'pie in the sky'. (Ackerman 2003:81)

It is paradoxical that it is the same theology of hope by the GNU that eventually co-joined its partners in corruption making the inconvenient alliance convenient for them both. Although by 2010 the GNU had managed to rescue the economy from the brink of collapse and restored some dignity to Zimbabwe and Zimbabweans, the acrimony of its partners continued to retard the country's progress and eventually became an inconvenience. In the hope of finding ways to work togetherbetter, the GNU held some conferences and summits. Despite the belligerents' different personalities and perspectives, such conferences and summits sought to reconcile them. However, it soon became evident this would be at Zimbabwean taxpayers' expense.

The GNU actors were subsequently criticized for procrastinating over the "'outstanding issues whilst they play and fiddle with their endless talks and summits" (*NewsLeader* 2010:8). In 2010, Blessing Vava, the spokesperson of the Zimbabwe National Students Union (ZINASU) also complained about the several summits and conferences held in expensive hotels such as the Rainbow Towers and Crown Plaza as a clear illustration of a "lack of shame among the politicians in the GNU" (2010, p.12). Financial resources were allegedly misdirected and priorities misplaced when a controversial Government Ministerial retreat held at the Elephant Hills Hotel in Victoria Falls ended up being a "whisky retreat" (Vava 2010, p.12) as the ministers allegedly jostled to sip the expensive Chivas Regal whisky at the government's expense. Yet the official position remained that Zimbabwe was sick, broke and bankrupt.

In a demonstration of, "if you cannot beat them join them"; both ZANU-PF and the MDCs politicians were embroiled in scandal and corruption as they prioritized their self-enrichment at the expense of Zimbabwe and Zimbabweans. Vava (2010) exposed and castigated the scramble for luxury vehicles by cabinet ministers and MPs. Some ZANU-PF and MDCs members of parliament had allegedly claimed Isuzu vehicles offered by the Reserve Bank Governor, Gideon Gono as well as collected Mazda BT50s assembled at Willowvale Motor Industries and paid for from the Treasury. They were unwilling to relinquish either. Vava was forced to ask, "Are these leaders interested in improving the livelihoods and aspirations of Zimbabweans or their personal and material benefits?" (2010, p.12) The plight of the masses and the country had become secondary on the GNU's agenda. The GNU's marriage of convenience had turned out to be even more convenient for its politicians and an inconvenience to ordinary Zimbabwean citizens.

Under the GPA, the Parties had been tasked to restore economic stability and growth in Zimbabwe by developing and implementing an economic recovery and strategic plan. This would significantly resuscitate such diverse sectors as agriculture, manufacturing, mining, tourism, commerce, finance, labor and academia, among others. The initiative was to be coordinated by a National Economic Council comprised of representatives of the Parties and answerable to the GNU (Article 3). Such an indispensable council was formed. However, this only stalled the country's economic recovery program.

Between 2010 and 2011, although the economy grew by more than 9% (Hartwell, 2013), it did not come as a surprise when the GNU continued to struggle to entirely turn around the economy and sustainably redress the plight of its citizens. In February 2010, this caused some civil servants who were earning as little as $150 per month to embark on industrial action and demand better salaries and improved working conditions. Given the devastating impact HIV and AIDS had had in Zimbabwe (UNAIDS, 2002, p.8; Chitando, 2007, p.42), many felt the money the GNU was wasting could be better spent caring for the needs of orphans as well as on anti-retroviral drugs. It was not long before some supporters of the GNU parties were calling the principals "sell-outs."

However, contrary to putting their hope into action, in the face of what can be described as "hopelessness and despondency" (Tutu, 1983:26), Zimbabweans remained calm and loyal. Other than hoping that the president would leave and jokingly claim that his initials of "RGM" stood for "Really Go Mugabe," instead of "Robert Gabriel Mugabe," they remained non-violent.

In 2011, President Mugabe declared that the GNU was not working well. The now late second Vice-President, John Nkomo, denounced the coalition as, "a regrettable formation which both wished their party would disengage from" (*ZimbabweWatch*, 2011). For the MDC formations, especially the MDC-T, the GPA was yet to be fully implemented as, "[r]estrictive statutes such as the Access to Information and Protection of Privacy Act (AIPPA) and the Broadcasting Services Act (…) are yet to be repealed despite the GPA's stated commitment to a free and independent media" (*ZimbabweWatch*, 2011).

Political intolerance and the use of violence against political opponents reared when on 29 January 2011 ZANU-PF youth rampaged through the capital city, Harare "injuring dozens of MDC-T supporters" (*ZimbabweWatch*, 2011). On 7 February, they again disrupted business activities in Harare "demanding an immediate take-over of foreign-owned companies" (*ZimbabweWatch*, 2011). Thus, eighteen months after the historic signing of the GPA, cases of politically motivated violence were still being witnessed and reported. Respect for civilian, property, political opponents and the rule of law was yet a long way off.

By 2012, the economic reprieve the GNU had afforded slowed down. Zimbabwe's economy reportedly grew by 5%. (Hartwell, 2013) This was partly due to sanctions that remained in place forcing some factories to close down and partly because of ZANU-PF's Indigenization Program that, among others, required foreign investors to cede 51% of shares to locals. While the MDC-T declared such pronouncements null and void, ZANU-PF insisted on their validity. It was apparent the coalition partners had different economic policies. The fact of this and the Indigenization Program made businesses and potential investors nervous. They headed for other business destinations on the continent.

Another area of concern for Zimbabweans was that of a new constitution for the country. By 2012, the Lancaster House Constitution had been amended some nineteen times. The GPA had emphasized a people-driven constitution that must be inclusive and democratic. The GNU had partly been meant as a transitional arrangement to facilitate such a democratic and credible constitution that would make way for credible, free and fair elections.

However, given the way relations in the GNU were going, the feasibility of it doing so seemed unlikely. This is especially taking into account that it had been the political parties' last attempt at a new constitution that, arguably, had been one of the crisis' many catalysts after it was rejected by a 2000 referendum partly because of "interference of the (people's views) by the ruling elites" (Ndlovu-Gatsheni, 2010). When almost a decade later Zimbabwe once again embarked on a constitution-making process, the same ruling elite was still active in the GNU.

*The path to Zimbabwe's 2013 Constitution* In 2009, a parliamentary committee, the Zimbabwe Constitution Select Committee (COPAC), was set up and tasked with heading the constitution-making process of Zimbabwe's third draft constitution since 1980. However, the First Stakeholders' Conference was allegedly dominated by some ZANU-PF supporters and war veterans. These ZANU-PF stalwarts sought to prevent the constitution-making process and at worst politically manipulate it. This was largely because of the extensive executive powers amendments made to Zimbabwe's 1979 Lancaster House Constitution in 1987 had given to the incumbent president. In addition to other amendments that the *adhoc* Land Reform Program had necessitated, the 1979 constitution had also, over the years, become favorably weighted in ZANU-PF's favor.

Consequently, during mid-2009, the Kariba Draft Constitution, a secretly agreed September 2007 document, "among (the) three political parties' kept being mentioned. ZANU-PF was accused of 'trying to push (it) forward as the blueprint for a new constitution of Zimbabwe" (Ndlovu-Gatsheni, 2010). It would take public participation, civil society organizations and external support before Zimbabwe's constitution came to be. It was only fair that Zimbabweans determine the laws by which they are to be governed.

Public participation is crucial to the process of writing a new constitution. The public must make and own the constitution that governs them. An informed and involved civil society makes it the backbone of such a process. From as early as 2009, the Africa Community Publishing and Development Trust in Zimbabwe had produced a booklet to increase citizen awareness of constitutional issues and participation in the constitution-making debate. Its efforts were augmented by such civil society organizations as the National Constitutional Assembly (NCA), the Zimbabwe Congress of Trade Unions (ZCTU) and ZINASU. Together with COPAC, they participated in constitution outreach community activities to hear and gather Zimbabweans' views on what the constitution should contain.

After four years of the constitution-making process, a draft constitution was published on 18 July 2012. The two MDC factions were quick to endorse it, "but President Mugabe (…) set the process back by rejecting several provisions in it." These included provisions "on devolution, presidential running mates, (…) a constitutional court, a prosecuting authority (…) same-sex marriage, and foreign funding for political parties" (Tinhu, 2013). Instead, ZANU-PF demanded amendments most of which had reportedly not been raised in the COPAC's National Report. Despite this, and although the MDC-T claimed that, "ZANU-PF's proposed draft was (…) a completely rewritten document (…) at variance with what the people said", ZANU-PF's thirty amendments were eventually accepted. The constitution-making process had become conciliatory towards the ruling elite.

By January 2013, the constitution-making process had concluded, and a new final draft constitution was complete. Without too much squabbling, Zimbabweans had managed to come up with a people-driven constitution. Such was the satisfaction with it; the final draft constitution went through both the Senate and National Assembly of Zimbabwe's parliament unopposed. What remained was for it to go to a referendum and thereafter, if accepted by Zimbabweans, gazetted for adoption and enactment into law.

Towards 16–17 March 2013 referendum, all the GNU parties campaigned for its acceptance amongst their various constituencies. The people-driven constitution was resoundingly voted for by 94.5% of those who cast their vote. Never before had the country reached such consensus. The constitution was later signed into law amid jubilation. Although the GNU would be around for a while longer, the coalition parliament disbanded on 29 June 2013, making way for new elections on 31 July .

## *Conclusion*

The chapter has assessed the workability of Zimbabwe's GNU from 2009–2013 in the context of the divergent views of its partners. It has demonstrated how to some extent,the political formation was paradoxically a marriage of both convenience and inconvenience to both those in the government and Zimbabweans. This is especially insofar as the political settlement provided an opportunity to mend Zimbabwe's decade-old economic decline and stagnation on the one hand and fleeced limited resources in a search to be workable on the other hand.

The tragedy of the GNU is that it continued Kenya's bad political precedent following that country's own controversial presidential run-off election vote in December 2007. This strategy as epitomized by both Kenyan and Zimbabwean experience entrenched a system of governance brought on by the defeated candidate's refusal to relinquish power and eventually insinuating himself into the new government by way of a "negotiated settlement." Thus, even in the event of a credible electoral process, all the losing candidate has to do is to refuse to relinquish power and threaten violence until a government of national unity is tabled. In this respect, a government of national unity is often an embodiment of one party's antics in defiance to the winds of change (Ndapadzwa & Muchena, 2009).

Unfortunately, such a government that more often than not is a product of negotiation between and among political gladiators lacks the people's legitimate mandate. This chapter has testified such an arrangement that does not usher in a genuinely democratic and peaceful political dispensation. Such a government of national unity makes the full democratization of African institutions difficult. Some of the hurdles faced by Zimbabwe's GNU are proof of the redundancy of a government that is a product of negotiations rather than a credible election.

## Notes

1. Affiliation: Department of Philosophy and Religious Studies Great Zimbabwe University
2. Though the war in DRC started as a civil war, other African countries subsequently intervened with some supporting the incumbent government while others supported rebel groups (Williams, 2013, p.81).

## References

Ackerman, D. (2003). *After the locusts: Letters from the landscapes of faith.* Glosderry: David Phillip.

Africa Briefing Report. (2009). *Zimbabwe after the elections: Africa briefing report, 8 July 2008–September 2008.* Brussels: Egmont Palace.

Badza, S. (2009). Zimbabwe's 2008 harmonized elections: Regional &international reaction. In E. V. Masunungure (Ed.), *Defying the winds of change: Zimbabwe's 2008 elections.* Harare: Weaver Press.

Bango, T. W. (2009). Ceaseless abuse of our president: A major outstanding issue. In *The changing times*. Issue 9. Harare: MDC Information & Publicity Department.

Bond, P. (2007). *What today's looting of Africa tells us about tomorrow's looting of Zimbabwe* (pp. 1–10). Harare: A New Zimbabwe Lecture for the Zimbabwe Research Foundation, 31 July.

Chitando, E. (2007). *Living with hope: African churches and HIV/AIDS 1*. Geneva: WCC Publications.

Clemens, M., & Moss, T. (2005). *Costs and causes of Zimbabwe's crisis* (pp. 1–4). Washington: Center for Global Development.

StockhölmInternational Peace Research Institute (SIPRI). (n.d.). EU Arms Embargo on Zimbabwe. Retrieved August 26, 2016 from https://www.sipri.org/databases/embargoes/eu_arms_embargoes/zimbabwe

Dzamara, I. (2010). Mugabe, Tsvangirai's tense relationship revealed. *The News Leader, 1*(13), 22–28.

Global Risks Forecast. (2009). PM 'disengages' from national unity government following the arrest of aide, calls for regional support. Retrieved: 23 January 2010 from http://www.maplecroft.com/portfolio/forecast/issues/90/articles/1/.

Gonda, V. (2009). Transcript of interview by Violet Gonda of SW Radio Africa with Priscilla Misihairabwi Mushonga and Brian Kagoro. Broadcast January 30.

Hartwell, L. Reflecting on positive Zimbabwe GNU moments.OPINION *Zimbabwe Independent* 11 July 2013. www.theindependent.co.zw/2013/07/11reflecting-on-positive-zimbabwe-gnu-moments/. Date retrieved: May2, 2014.

Linington, G. (2009). Illegality & Zimbabwe's 2008 presidential elections. In E. V. Masunungure (Ed.), *Defying the winds of change: Zimbabwe's 2008 elections*. Harare: Weaver Press.

Mahlangu, M. (2009). Presentation as presented for delivery: 26th annual Robert F. Kennedy human rights award. November 13, 2009, The White House, Washington, DC in *The Journal of Pan African Studies*, vol. 3, no. 5, e-Document.

Makochekanwa, A., & Kwaramba, M. (2009). State fragility: Zimbabwe's horrific journey in the new millennium. Accra: A Research Paper Presented at the European Report on Development's (ERD), pp. 1–36.

Makumbe, J. (2009). Theft by numbers: ZEC's role in the 2008 elections. In E. V. Masunungure (Ed.), *Defying the winds of change: Zimbabwe's 2008 elections*. Harare: Weaver Press.

Masunungure, E. V. (2009). Introduction.In E. V. Masunungure (Ed.), *Defying the winds of change: Zimbabwe's 2008 elections*. Harare: Weaver Press.

Matyszak, D. (2009). Civil society &the long election. In E. V. Masunungure (Ed.), *Defying the winds of change: Zimbabwe's 2008 elections*. Harare: Weaver Press.

Ministry of Constitutional & Parliamentary Affairs. (2008). Press Statement.

Moyse, A. (2009). The media environment leading up to Zimbabwe's 2008 elections. In E. V. Masunungure (Ed.), *Defying the winds of change: Zimbabwe's 2008 elections*. Harare: Weaver Press.

Muzondidya, J. (2009). From buoyancy to crisis, 1980–1997. In B. Raftopoulos & A. S. Mlambo (Eds.), Becoming Zimbabwe: a history from the pre-colonial period to 2008. Harare:Weaver Press

Ndapadzwa, A. C., & Muchena, E. (2009). The quest for change: Public opinion & the harmonized marched elections. In E. V. Masunungure (Ed.), *Defying the winds of change: Zimbabwe's 2008 elections.* Harare: Weaver Press.

Ndlovu-Gatsheni. (2010). 'The constitution and the constitutional process in Zimbabwe', Solidarity Peace Trust, 18 May www.solidaritypeacetrust.org/703/the-constitution-and-the -constitutional-process-in-zimbabwe/. Accessed: May2, 2014.

Ntoni-Nzinga, D. (Ed.). (n.d.). *Democracy and the ethics of good governance: Reflection on African politics and the role of religion today.*Ecumenical study serie No 1, Unit III. Geneva: World Council of Churches.

Smith, D. (2009). Inside Zimbabwe's marriage of convenience. http://www.theage.com.au/world/inside-zimbabwes-marriage-of-convenience-20090821-etum.html. 22 August. Date Retrieved: January 23, 2010.

Tarisayi, E. (2009).Voting in despair: The economic &social context. In E. V. Masunungure (Ed.), *Defying the winds of change: Zimbabwe's 2008 elections.* Harare: Weaver Press.

The Africa Community Publishing and Development Trust. (2009). *A people's guide to constitutional debate.* Harare: The Africa Community Publishing and Development Trust.

Tinhu, S. (2013). Zimbabwe's draft constitution: By the politicians, for the politicians? Retrieved November 11 2016 from https://allafrica.com/stories/201303130092.html

Tutu, D. M. (1983). *Hope and suffering: Sermons and speeches.* Johannesburg: Skotaville Publishers.

UNAIDS. (2002, July). Report on the global HIV?AIDS epidemic. Retrieved July 9 2017, from http://data.unaids.org/pub/report/2002/brglobal_aids_report_en_pdf_red_en.pdf

Vava, B. (2010). GNU, Hope, constitution. In *The News Leader, 1*(13), January 22–28.

Williams, C. (2013). Explaining the great war in Africa: How conflict in the Congo became a continental crisis. *The Fletcher Forum of World Affairs, 37*(2), 81–100.

World Report. (2009). Zimbabwe Events of 2008. Retrieved December 21 from 2009. https://www.hrw.org/world-report/2009/country-chapters/zimbabwe

Zimbabwe Democracy and Economic Recovery Act (ZIDERA). (2001). Public Law 107–99—DEC. 21, [S. 494].

ZimWatch. 'Two years of GNU—Stormy weather ahead…' www.zimbabwewatch.org/eng/News/2011/Two-years-of-GNU-Stormy-weather-ahead Date retrieved: May 2, 2014.

# *Part 3: Crisis Watershed—Retreat or Surrender*

# 9 *"Killing Zimbabwe Softly, Slowly and Quickly": How Factionalism and Financial Liquidity Fueled the Crisis to a Watershed*

C. Luthuli Mhlahlo[1]

Factionalism has been synonymous with Zimbabwe's political parties since the formation of its first black nationalist party in the late 1950s. During the country's Second *Chimurenga*, factionalism amongst the country's liberation war political parties continued and at times almost derailed the struggle as it led to some members' imprisonment, suspected assassinations and the emergence of splinter political groups. Post-independence, factionalism, especially within the ruling ZANU-PF party, again emerged, albeit intermittently. The years 2002–2012 then saw it abet within the ruling ZANU-PF party but rise in the opposition Movement for Democratic Change (MDC) camp, only to again resurface in the ZANU-PF party at the end of the country's Government of National Unity (GNU) in 2013. This time, however, it was not in the ruling party alone; it persisted in the main opposition party, the Movement of Democratic Change–Tsvangirai (MDC–T). This chapter traces factionalism in Zimbabwe's body politics from the country's pre-independence into mostly its post-independence era. It argues that factional fighting, particularly in the years 2008 and 2013–2017 coupled with the country's liquidity crunch eventually became the fuel at the epicenter of Zimbabwe's terminal socioeconomic and political decline. It concludes that unless checked, the two remain the country's biggest challenges and threats to its recovery and survival.

## *The Rise of Black Nationalist Parties and Factionalism*

In September 1957, Southern Rhodesia's black nationalist movement, the African National Congress (ANC) was launched. It brought together Salisbury's (present–day Harare) City Youth League (CYL) and Bulawayo's ANC "started in the 1930s but (which) had since lapsed into inactivity" (Smith & Simpson, 1981, p.33). The new movement was however promptly banned less than two years later in February 1959 by the then colonial government (Meredith, 2002, pp.22–23). In response, the party renamed itself the National Democratic Party (NDP) in January of 1960. When in July 1960 Leopold Takawira and two of the party's members were arrested, 7000 of NDP's members who now included Robert Mugabe embarked on a protest march to the then Salisbury (Smith & Simpson, 1981, p.37). However, before the demonstration could get to the city center, it was halted by riot police outside then Harare's (now Mbare) Stoddart Hall (Norman, 2008, p.43). Defiant, the demonstrating crowd would return the following day.

By noon of the following day, the demonstrators had grown to 40 000. A makeshift platform was erected, and members of the party were invited to speak. Amongst those invited to speak to the crowd was 36-year old Robert Mugabe, impressively already a holder of three degrees and at the time teaching in newly independent Ghana. With the help of the then colony's first black lawyer, Herbert Chitepo, Mugabe would in October 1960 chair the party's first congress and be elected its publicity secretary (Smith & Simpson, 1981, p.37). From then on, the newly appointed publicity secretary set about broadening the party's support base.

In 1961, the British government called for a conference to be held in Salisbury to determine the colony's future. Joshua Nkomo led the NDP's delegation to the talks. When during the talks Nkomo agreed to a proposal to give the country's black majority 15 seats in the country's 65 seat parliament, Mugabe and other NDP members were not impressed by Nkomo's willingness to make such a concession (Meredith, 2002, p.28). Consequently, by the conference's end, the NDP was a divided party. However, a few of the party's rallies followed before it was banned in December 1961 (Norman, 2008, p.44).

Barely days later, the party had rebranded itself the Zimbabwe African People's Union (ZAPU). Mugabe was elected its publicity as well as general secretary, while Nkomo retained the presidency. The new but old political party soon found itself divided on matters of strategy. Into the 1960s, racial tension and violence against the minority white population by the black majority was on the increase in the then Southern Rhodesia (Meredith, 2002, p.29). To the almost stoic Mugabe, such a state of affairs was a necessary tactic if British imperialism and white minority rule were to be overthrown. Nkomo, on the other hand, was of the view that the party should diplomatically engage the international community to urge the British to accede to black majority rule. In September 1962, ZAPU too was banned. Its leadership was arrested and restricted to their home districts until December (Norman, 2008, p.44).

In the December 1962 general elections, the newly formed right-wing Rhodesian Front (RF) led by Winston Field, Clifford Dupont and Ian Douglas Smith won them on the promise it would safeguard white minority rule by reinforcing security and seeking independence from Britain (Meredith, 2002, p.31). Conversely, divisions again arose among the nationalists when at a meeting of some members of the banned ZAPU, Mugabe again suggested that given their failed or banned demonstrations, it was perhaps time to launch an armed resistance.

The Merriam-Webster dictionary lexically defines a "faction" as "a party or group (as within a government) that is often contentious or self-seeking, a party spirit especially when marked by dissension." Similarly, to The Sage VII English Dictionary a faction is a group of people, usually, a "dissenting clique (often secret) that seeks power usually through intrigue." Lewellen explicates the term further when he writes that: "Groups classed as factions engage in conflict with the official power structures by means of verbal contention and often physical action and violence" (1983, pp.104–105). Also, for a faction to be so called, it "must contain certain elements and act in certain capacities. That includes the organizational structure of the group, their leadership style, and their recruitment and members" Forte, 2013, para, 4). In the ambit of this chapter, however, factionalism is not only understood as in political anthropology when it describes the term as "groups of people formed around a leader who reject the status quo and actively work against established authority within a (…) political party" (Forte, 2013, para, 1). This chapter instead also demonstrates how in the Zimbabwean context, factionalism at times emanated not necessarily from the actions of a group but rather a dissident individual, hence leading to infighting and the division of the political party into identifiable factions.

Mugabe's view of the trajectory the nationalist struggle should take went contrary to Nkomo's—that they leave the country for Dar–es–Salaam and establish a government-in-exile there (Smith & Simpson, 1981, pp. 44–45). His suggestion that they wage an armed struggle from within the country was, however, supported by Julius Nyerere of the then Tanganyika (now Tanzania). With Nyerere's support and some of those in ZANU, Mugabe immediately set about "painstakingly (…) winning friends for the movement (nationalist) in Dar–es–Salaam (…) ambassadors and OAU officials who would be needed in future" (Smith & Simpson, 1981, p. 48). Sensing that his leadership might be in jeopardy, Nkomo "moved quickly to consolidate his position and quell the rebellion before it gathered any momentum. He called for a conference of the party for 10 August" (Smith & Simpson, 1981, pp. 48–49).

On 8 August 1963 however, two days before the conference, those opposed to Nkomo's leadership instead called a meeting at the home of ZAPU militant, Enos Nkala, in Salisbury's high density of Highfields. After the meeting, the then acclaimed nationalist and author, Ndabaningi Sithole, "was presented as the leader of the breakaway party, the Zimbabwe African National Union (ZANU)" (Smith & Simpson, 1981, p.49). As the years passed, this first split from ZAPU was to be the first of several more internal factional fights, squabbles and personality clashes within the newly formed ZANU—during its leadership's imprisonment, the party's armed struggle and after it. Most significant are those which occurred within the ruling party post-independence.

## *Post-independence Factionalism: ZUM, ZUD, ZAPU and MDC*

In April 1980, the newly renamed and elected ZANU-PF came to power reasonably intact. Edgar Zivanai Tekere, a founding member of the party and its high command (*Dare reChimurenga*), was appointed Minister of Manpower Planning in the then Prime Minister RG Mugabe's first government. At the party's first post-independence congress, Tekere was elected its general secretary. A longtime friend and comrade of Mugabe's, Tekere had in 1960 been amongst those who had persuaded him not to return to teach in Ghana, but rather to commit himself to the nationalist movement (Smith & Simpson, 1981, p.26). During Mugabe's detention from 1964 to 1974 first in Salisbury Maximum Security Prison, then Wha Wha and lastly Sikombela detention centers, Tekere had been one of three[2] who had shared a cell with Mugabe. It is he who, when Sithole's leadership waivered and he had renounced violence, who had supported the replacement of Sithole with Mugabe (Smith & Simpson, 1981, pp.72–73). It had also been Tekere who, after their release from prison in late 1974, had escaped with Mugabe to Mozambique to lead the armed struggle. It had been while they were in Mozambique, that "Tekere had crushed a dissident movement among members of his faction in Mozambique in 1978 when the party leader (Mugabe) was in Malta for peace negotiations" (Ross, 1980, para, 44). Understandably,

Mugabe owed Tekere a great debt of gratitude as "Tekere's commitment to (him) was unstinting" (Smith & Simpson, 1981, pp.79). And it was equally unsurprising when post-independence, Tekere seemed to be taking advantage of his friendship with the then prime minister.

Once described as "gunpowder which hasn't exploded yet" (Ross, 1980, para1) soon after his ministerial appointment, Tekere had sometime made an inflammatory statement that went contrary to the new government's policy of reconciliation when he had reportedly said: "There must be no more talk of gradualism" (Ross, 1980, para, 39). Tekere was calling for rapid transformation at a time when Mugabe was calling for a moderate approach. Despite this, on 4 August 1980, clad in military gear, the potential successor to Mugabe and third most powerful man in ZANU-PF had come to meet the then Prime Minister Mugabe and his visiting counterpart, the now late President Samora Machel of Mozambique who was then on a week-long visit to Zimbabwe.

Tekere's wearing of military fatigue "was taken either as an act of defiance or as a silent statement of (what he had done during) the struggle'" (Ross, 1980, para, 36). Obviously spoiling for a fight, it is reported that Tekere and his bodyguards had then gone into the outskirts of western Salisbury in search of ZAPU supporters. However, on finding none, Tekere had allegedly murdered a white farmer, Gerald W. Adams "during what appears to have been a revenge attack on some soldiers over an altercation at a party the previous night" (Ross, 1980, para, 9). At a time when the fledgling nation was still trying to find favor with the international community as well as secure donor funding, Mugabe "stood aside and let the judicial system take its course when his party chieftain was arrested" (Ross, 1980, para, 15) As one diplomat reportedly commented, "By not doing anything, Mugabe sent a message" (Ross, 1980, para, 16).He was not about to jeopardize country for friendship, at least not for Tekere anyway.[3] Tekere, however, retained his ministerial post throughout the trial that ensued. On 8 December 1980, the High Court found Tekere and his bodyguards not guilty as he had acted in the "utter conviction that State Security was at risk" (Zimbabwe Law Reports, 1980, p. 489) when the farmer had confronted one of his bodyguards. There was no evidence to the contrary.

Just over a month after Tekere's exoneration, he was on 11 January 1981 dismissed from his ministerial post. He, however, retained his post of secretary general of the ruling party. Despite his ministerial dismissal, Tekere was however not done. Once described as "an intense, determined man who says what he thinks and doesn't care if people agree with him or not" (Ross, 1980, para, 43) in July 1981, Tekere allegedly "referred to some ZANU representatives as having 'inherited the colonial mentality,' which was straining relations between them and the party's supporters." Tongue in cheek, Mugabe supposedly also retorted that: "Those who are complaining that the revolution is not continuing... are the most immoral and laziest in the party" (Ross, 1980, para, 43). The proverbial gloves were off. As the years passed, relations between the erstwhile comrades became increasingly strained. Tekere progressively came to be considered as leading a rival faction to Mugabe within the ZANU-PF. He was on 9 August 1981 promptly dismissed as the party's Secretary-General and the vacant post was pointedly filled by Mugabe himself.

Despite Tekere's dismissal, however, his stature both within ZANU-PF and the country continued to increase. Indeed such was his popularity; he became provincial ZANU-PF chairman of Mutare, the capital of his home province, Manicaland. His criticism of corruption amongst the party's bigwigs saw him popularly elected to the party's central committee, while his opposition to sporadic farm squatting by ZANU-PF supporters earned him favor with white farmers. To some within ZANU-PF however, Tekere was increasingly becoming a nuisance.

On 22 December 1987, Nkomo's PF ZAPU and Mugabe's ZANU-PF signed the Unity Accord that effectively ended the infamous *Gukurahundi* skirmishes in most parts of Matabeleland and Midlands provinces. In addition to finally bringing peace to the two provinces, the Unity Accord also incorporated PF ZAPU into ZANU-PF and virtually made Zimbabwe a one-party state. However, when the now Excutive President[4] Mugabe began mooting the idea of the country becoming such a one-party state, Tekere vehemently protested. Already a sort of self-appointed "voice of the voiceless," when in October 1988 Tekere's criticism of corruption and one-party state politics persisted, he was finally expelled from the party. Tekere would, however, not go quietly—he proceeded to form his political party.

The Zimbabwe Unity Movement (ZUM) was formed towards the 1990 presidential elections. By the time of the elections, the party and Tekere were ready to take on Mugabe in the presidential race. In contrast to ZANU-PF's socialist-communist style promises, ZUM had as its platform the development of a free market economy. On 23 March 1990, Zimbabweans went to the polls to elect a president and parliament. When the results were announced, Mugabe had emerged the winner with 83.05 percent of the vote to Tekere's 16.95 percent. In parliament, the newly formed opposition party had won two seats out of a possible 120—ZANU-PF garnered 117 of them. In the aftermath of the elections, ZUM supporters were allegedly targeted by ZANU-PF party supporters resulting in the death of five. In the years that followed, ZUM and Tekere's popularity fizzled out. Apart from occasional political commentary, Tekere would intermittently appear at the launch of opposition parties to ZANU-PF. One such party was the Zimbabwe Union of Democrats (ZUD)

In 1995, Margaret Dongo one of a few then young influential female war veterans in ZANU-PF was expelled from the party for being too outspoken and criticizing Mugabe and his government over, among others, the deplorable welfare of war veterans[5] record. After her expulsion, she ran against ZANU-PF's Vivian Mwashita as an independent candidate and when she lost, successfully challenged the election results in court (Sheldon, 2005, pp.203–204). She subsequently won the rerun election for the Harare South constituency seat on 25 November 1995 and proceeded to parliament to champion human rights and democracy (Sheldon, 2005, pp.203–204).

After failing to run against Mugabe in the 1996 presidential elections for being too young, Dongo on 19 December 1998 founded ZUD with the intention of it contesting in the 2000 parliamentary elections. Somewhat akin to Tekere's party manifesto, that of ZUD also promised "a free market economy, job creation through support for small and medium-size enterprises, devolution of power through the creation of provincial assemblies, a reduction in the number of national ministries, human rights and a free and independent media" (EISA, 2002, para, 2). In the 2000 elections that followed, Dongo this time ran as her party's candidate for Harare South but lost to the candidate of an also newly formed opposition party—the Movement for Democratic Change (MDC). New political formations were not only emerging from ZANU-PF. As the country waded into crisis, start-up opposition political parties had also risen from Zimbabwe's civil society and trade union movement.

The end of the last millennium and the ushering in of the new brought with it a myriad of socioeconomic and political problems for Zimbabwe. The implementation of the ill-advised Economic Structural Adjustment Program in 1995 had already led to the massive worker retrenchments and massive unemployment. The awarding of unbudgeted gratuities to war veterans of the liberation struggle and the country's military involvement in the Democratic Republic of Congo (DRC) ignited a sharp rise in inflation and a decline in the standard of living. In response, the Zimbabwe Congress of Trade Unions (ZCTU) and other civil society groups called on workers to stay away from work and demonstrated in the streets. When the Mugabe-led government arrogantly challenged the nation's trade union movement and civic groups to form a political party since they were behaving like one, they ironically did precisely that.

Inspired by the political trajectory of its Zambian namesake, the Zambian Congress of Trade Unions (ZCTU) that on 2 November 1991 had come to power in Zambia as the Movement for Multi-Party Democracy (MMD) with, Frederick Chiluba as president, Zimbabwe's ZCTU and diverse civil society groupings in August 1999 united to form the MDC.The new political formation was led by the ZCTU's former secretary-general, Morgan Tsvangirai. Since the MDC was an opposition political party without any links to the ruling party, it was not long before the party was getting unprecedented support from the public, especially white commercial farmers. Ever since the end of the Lancaster House Agreement's "sun-set" clauses, white farmers had been apprehensive about their security of tenure on the farms. Twentyyears after the Lancaster House Agreement and barely a year before another round of Zimbabwe's general elections, how would a ZANU-PF government finally settle the country's land question? The less militant and moderate MDC seemed their answer.

Unknown to the commercial farmers, however, much as they saw the MDC as a means to securing their tenure of the land, the ZANU-PF government saw their land as a means to securing its political dominance and survival. When in early 2000 therefore, some war veterans of Zimbabwe's liberation struggle led peasants onto some commercial farms in the vicinity of their villages, the Mugabe-led government's response was *laissez-faire* at best. Eventually, it granted its approval to the so-called "land grabs by black squatters"[6]. Support for the ZANU-PF government amongst the war veterans was once again rejuvenated and restored with the peasantry—its traditional electorate. Symbolically, on 12 September[7] 2005, a constitutional amendment legalizing the reviled "land invasions by black squatters" was signed into law. It nationalized farmland acquired through the now Fast Track Land Reform Programme (LRP) process. The only constituents who remained largely landless and dissatisfied were the country's urbanites. They pinned their hopes and votes on the MDC.

Consequently, when the 2000 Parliamentary elections were held from 24June to 25 June, the results almost proportionally mirrored Zimbabwe's polarized population. The MDC won 57 seats of the 120 parliamentary seats, 47 percent of the popular vote. (Lamb, 2009, p.221) That constituted almost all the country's urban seats. Conversely, ZANU-PF garnered 63 seats and 48 percent of popular vote comprising almost all rural and peri-urban constituencies. This voting pattern would remain the same for close to two decades.

*Deadly Factionalism and Financial Liquidity Fuelling Crisis* From 2001 as inflation gripped the nation and prices skyrocketed, the cash in circulation and its denominations quickly became inadequate for the citizenry purchasing needs. In response, the Mugabe government embarked on printing higher denominations of the Zimbabwe dollar. A $500 Zimbabwe Dollar

(ZWD) note denomination was issued as legal tender by the then Reserve Bank of Zimbabwe (RBZ) governor, Leonard Tsumba. The new denomination however only provided temporary relief as it instead drove food prices up and with it, inflation. By 2003, the country's banknote denomination had to be doubled to $1000 (ZWD). In a bid to curtail inflation, in 2003 the RBZ introduced travelers' checks with denominations between ZW$1000 and ZW$100 000. As with its predecessor, the travelers' checks' impact was equally inflationary. In addition, these soon proved unpopular with the public as they were cumbersome and required bureaucratic processing. However, instead of finding other innovative strategies of curtailing the money supply, the RBZ paradoxically flooded the market with other forms of it.

A liquidity crisis is sometimes "referred to as a credit crunch/financial crisis or meltdown." Characterizations of it are a "shortage of physical cash, lending funds, banks (…) running out of cash, defaults, layoffs, bankruptcies and failing financial institutions" (Dlamini & Mbira, 2017, p.212). In the light of the cash shortages Zimbabwe was experiencing and the eroding purchasing power of the Zimbabwe Dollar, on 15 September 2003, Charles Chikaura[8] the then acting RBZ governor introduced Bearer checks [9] and Agro checks in denominations of ZW$5000, ZW$10 000 and ZW$20 000 as emergency currency to ease liquidity. At the same time, the RBZ also authorized Zimbabwe's division of Standard Chartered Bank and Cargill Cotton Group to issue their own special bearer checks of ZW$5000 and ZW$20 000 denominations. Then, at the beginning of October 2005, the new governor of the RBZ, Gideon Gono, added ZW$50 000 and ZW$100 000 denominations to the ones introduced earlier by Chikaura. Ironically and suggestively, these portrayed the country's Victoria Falls—was the country heading to the bottom of a bottomless precipice? In the words of one Zimbabwean interviewee who I met in a bank queue, "these guys are killing Zimbabwe and me slowly and quickly." As far as he could see, the RBZ was using something as insidious as cash to paradoxically destroy the country slowly and the people's lives quickly.

By mid-2006, hyperinflation fueled by the now perennial printing of ever-rising banknote denominations and the so-called bearer checks had reached gargantuan levels. Those who went through the experience report that "foodstuffs were flying off the shelves faster than the store staff could replace them." Shelves went empty as businesses, shop owners and black–marketers moved goods to sell them on black-market at exorbitant prices. As too much money proverbially chased too few goods, severe food shortages resulted and added to the strain of daily survival for the ordinary citizen. Depositors queued from before dawn until the closure of banks only for a lucky few to be able to withdraw in heaps of bearer checks, little more than their transport fares back home. The cash crisis was undoubtedly inconveniencing the population. Given Zimbabwe's renowned highly literate and innovative population, printing money was arguably by far the laziest, most unoriginal, most irresponsible and destructive response to the country's liquidity crunch by those running the RBZ. Not only was it complicit with the crisis, it systematically and simultaneously seemingly enriched and yet paradoxically impoverished both the country and its citizenry.

However, the RBZ was not through. In the face of the cash crisis gripping the country, some companies in collaboration with the RBZ and some petroleum companies, in the year 2005, introduced fuel ration coupons instead of cash for the purchasing of fuel. Their denominations started from one liter and after that in multiples of five up to 50 liters of petrol (gasoline), paraffin (kerosene) and diesel (Smith, 2008, np) and purchasable with foreign currency from fuel stations. In order to retain skilled staff, some companies, universities and power utilities began paying such staff a percentage of their salaries in petrol coupons. McGreal (2008), for instance, revealed that some "businesses, including Western Union, have been reported paying employees with these coupons (while) auctions transacted in this 'currency.'" Employees paid with such fuel coupons would in turn then use them to barter for goods and services of equivalent value.

Eventually, desperate to limit and downsize the denominations and quantity of legal tender in circulation, in 2006 the RBZ redenominated the denominations of the bearer checks then in circulation. Codenamed Operation Sunrise, the redenomination comprised of "slashing" the last three zeros of the bearer checks in the system. Under this currency reform, ZW$5 000 became ZW$5, ZW$10 000, ZW$10 and ZW$20 000, ZW$20. "New style bearer cheques consisting of 14 denominations of 1¢ to ZW$100 000" (Cuhaj, 2009, p.1108) were issued at the beginning of August. All other legal tender issued before 1 August 2006 was demonetized and was declared worthless on 21 August 2006. Due to poor communication about the currency reform and the short notice given, however, many Zimbabweans were still in possession of the pre-1 August 2006 issues on 21 August 2006.

The seven months that followed the August 2006 redenomination seemed to be holding inflationary forces at bay. To buttress the redenominated bearer checks issued in August, on 2 March, the RBZ issued ZW$500 and ZW$50 000 bearer checks "as intermediary denominations between the $1000, $10 000 and ZW$100 000 cheques" (Zulu, 2007, np). Inflation was once again stroked into life—the zeros resurrected. As inflation climbed, a ZW$200 000 denomination was issued on 1 August 2007. The resultant inflationary pressures that followed, combined with the festive season demands for added purchasing power and the payment of end of year bonuses resulted in more printing—ZW$50 000 and ZW$750 000 denomination notes had to be issued on 20 December 2007 (Cuhaj, 2009, p.1109). The issuances brought very temporary reprieve, if at all.

The year 2008 opened with the issuing into circulation of three new denomination notes, the ZW$1 million, ZW$5 million and ZW$10 million. As hyperinflation this time raged uncontrollably, and Zimbabwe's crisis deepened, some "Zimbabweans voted with their feet before the March 2008 elections"—millions left the country for "greener pastures" in western and neighboring climes. Among the country's earlier migrants had even been MDC and Zimbabwe's then youngest Member of Parliament, Tafadzwa Musekiwa, of Harare's Zengeza constituency. Fearing for his life, he left the country for the United Kingdom in 2002 and applied for asylum in that country. The National Council of the MDC gave him until 26 February 2003 to return or lose his parliamentary seat. He opted to remain in the United Kingdom and was reportedly encouraged to do so by the party's leader, Morgan Tsvangirai. It was not long before other members of the opposition were also either being expelled or walking out of the party—factionalism had finally come to the MDC.

In 2002, Munyaradzi Gwisai, MDC's then Member of Parliament for Highfield and the country general coordinator of the International Socialist Organisation (Zimbabwe chapter)[10] was expelled from the party over differences with the MDC's leadership. Perceptions that Gwisai's expulsion was dictatorial and a demonstration of the leadership's intolerance of divergent views almost tore the opposition party. More so when "changes in its National Executive favored those associated with the labor movement while sidelining academics" (The Insider, 2002, np) like Gwisai, within the party. It would, however, take another three years before the opposition party's split.

The MDC's first major factious split finally came over on the 26 November 2005 senatorial elections. Although officially, the disagreement is that it arose over whether the MDC should contest the senatorial elections or not; the fissure had been caused earlier in 2002 when Tsvangirai lost the 2002 presidential elections[11] (Dzamara, 2007, np). Apparently, after those elections, the MDC's secretary general, Welshman Ncube, and some of his colleagues had embarked on "plans to denounce Tsvangirai in the party especially aimed at portraying him as an incapable leader (…) Welshman and company were making steps towards taking over the party" (Dzamara, 2007, np). In this vein, it was alleged that Tsvangirai was not transparent and had clandestinely created a "kitchen cabinet' of his advisors and not the 'Top 6'" (Dzamara,

2007, np) of the National Executive. Criticism was however not only leveled against Tsvangirai. The anti-Senate Tsvangirai faction also leveled allegations of "sexual scandals as well as allegiances."[12] Besides, Tsvangirai and Ncube reportedly also had differing political strategies as to the way forward for the MDC.

In October 2005, the party finally split into two camps—the pro-Senate faction led by Ncube and Vice President Gibson Sibanda on the one hand, and the anti-Senate faction of the then Party President Morgan Tsvangirai and Deputy Secretary General, Gift Chimanikire on the other. Although the popular decision within the party and its National Council was pro-senatorial election participation, Tsvangirai was however against this popular decision and hence seen as "subverting the MDC constitution" (ZimOnline, 2009). Eventually, the pro-senatorial elections faction participated, while the anti-senatorial did not.

In an unexpected but strategic move, after the elections, rather than lead the pro-Senate MDC faction themselves, Ncube and Sibanda who are from Zimbabwe's minority ethnic Ndebele–speaking group instead sought a prominent Shona who would be able to attract the country's majority ethnic Shona-speaking groups to lead the faction. They found him in former University of Zimbabwe (UZ) student activist, Rhodes Scholar, and professor of Robotics, Professor Arthur Mutambara. The result was such that when the MDC formally split into two factions at the beginning of 2006, Mutambara was on 25 February elected president of the MDC-Mutambara (MDC-M) at a congress of the breakaway pro-Senate splinter group. Ncube, Sibanda, Priscilla Misihairambwi-Mushonga and Job Sikhala were amongst the more prominent politicians who joined (MDC-M). Tsvangirai's anti-Senate became known as the MDC-Tsvangirai (MDC-T). Opposition politics in Zimbabwe was once again, steadily weakening.

For some years after that, a few defections of both high- and low-profile members occurred between the two factions and even to the ruling ZANU-PF. Mugabe gleefully mocked the split opposition, calling it the "two head snake" (Mutambara Arrested During Campaign, 2006, p.np). That is perhaps because the factional fighting within, and the fragmentation of the MDC, was happening at a time the party was heading for the March 2008 harmonized elections which, given Zimbabwe's dire socioeconomic state then, the MDC was poised to win—but possibly, only if it was united.

When the long-awaited March 2008 harmonized elections finally arrived however, the opposition MDC was, unfortunately, still fractured and factious. Consequently, towards the 27 March 2008 elections, instead of merging for the good of Zimbabwe and her people, the MDC formations opted to contest the elections separately. Only at the eleventh hour did Mutambara withdraw his presidential candidature in support of erstwhile ZANU-PF MP and Mugabe government minister, Simba Makoni (Mapala, 2008). Aside from this however, the MDC-T and MDC-M, proceeded to contest both the presidency and parliamentary seats as a breakaway factions.

Astoundingly and inexplicably, the announcement of Zimbabwe's long-awaited March 2008 harmonized election results were incredulously delayed. They were all slowly released over a period of more than a month from the day of voting. When they were finally all released, as expected, the opposition's dominant faction, MDC-T had won 99 parliamentary seats, the MDC-M 10 and ZANU-PF 97. Both the MDC-T and MDC-M had won a combined majority in Zimbabwe's House of Assembly. Unexpectedly though, the presidential election results were inconclusive, Tsvangirai had won 47.8 percent, and Mugabe 43.2 percent—both had failed to win 51 percent of the presidential vote as required by the country's constitution. The defeaning effects of factionalism were loud and clear. There would have to be a rerun of the presidential poll. The effects of factionalism were not over.

Horror characterized the two months leading to the June 2008 Presidential run-off election. Some opposition supporters (or those suspected to be) were arrested, detained, beaten and even killed. Opposition activist, Tonderai Ndira, was on 5 May 2008 found murdered having been earlier abducted[13]. Some elements of the military had reportedly gone on a reign of terror in the rural and some high-density areas of the country[14] Fear gripped the electorate. Although some observers argued that the violence was on both sides, MDC-T's Tsvangirai on 22 June 2008 eventually pulled out of the "violent sham" (Shaw, 2008) the June 27 scheduled presidential run-off election had deteriorated. Despite Tsvangirai's withdrawal from the run-off, however, it still went ahead as planned.

Despite winning an overwhelming "a landslide victory," the Mugabe-led government, the country, and its inhabitants were by July 2008 in the direst of straits. Towards the June presidential run-off, the RBZ had on 15 May 2008 issued Special Agro checks. By July; hyperinflation was wreaking havoc. Prices were soaring by the hour. On 1 July 2008, due to a request by the German government and calls for sanctions imposition on the Mugabe government, the Munich-based security printer Giesecke and Devrient discontinued the provision of paper on which to print money. Almost at its wit's end, the RBZ released the now infamous and record contending ZW$100 billion Agro check[15] However, when the ZW$100 billion Agro check failed to reign in the liquidity and hyperinflation crunch, the RBZ once again turned to its tried and trusted redenomination strategy.

At the beginning of August 2008, this time redenomination banknotes and not bearer checks were put into circulation. Known as the 2008 banknote series of the third dollar, Zimbabwe's endemic hyperinflation did not in this round give them a fighting chance—some of them became worthless before they could even be issued for circulation to the public. Hyperinflation had just turned stratospheric. Denominated from ZW$20, ZW$1000 to ZW$50 000 and then ZW$10 million, the notes' newsprint quality was an indication of their worthlessness. The suspended provision of paper on which to print money had forced the Mugabe government to print them on "non-watermarked paper" (Guma, 2008, np). Not that quality paper could have helped, as matters stood there was hardly anything to buy on store shelves. Whatever of value was available was so exorbitantly priced that one needed several hundred million to purchase it. Some shops and businesses which until then had resiliently soldiered on finally closed down. Essential commodities became a luxury, and most citizens emaciated by hunger and, in the absence of medicines, disease. They and the country had become victims of the opposition's factionalism and tragically themselves.

In hindsight, one can only fathom what would have happened in March 2008 had the MDC factions reunited and fielded one presidential candidate. Ncube would later in January 2011confess that "a united MDC would have beaten ZANU-PF 'hands down' in the harmonized elections" of March 2008. Speaking just after assuming the helm of his then recently formed MDC-N, a splinter faction from MDC-M, a regretful and hurt Ncube expressed that "were it not for the split, ZANU-PF would have been history" (Ncube Regrets MDC Split, 2011). However, considering the manipulative circumstances under which the election's results were finally released, it might not have made any difference.

Three quarters into 2008, Zimbabwe faced an imminent humanitarian crisis of catastrophic proportions when the Southern African Development Community (SADC) intervened. It tasked then South African President, Thabo Mbeki, to mediate talks between Zimbabwe's main political players of ZANU-PF, MDC–T and MDC-M. The culmination of the talks was a power-sharing agreement signed on 15 September 2008 in Harare. Under this Global Political Agreement (GPA) ZANU-PF and MDC-T would form a Government of National Unity (GNU) to be presided over by Mugabe, with Tsvangirai as prime minister and Mutambara his deputy. A patriotic unity of purpose had saved Zimbabweans just before the stroke of midnight. Relief would, however, not be as swift in coming as intraparty factionalism of yesteryear now became inter-party political wrangles.

The ink on the GPA had hardly dried and the inclusive government not even constituted, when the belligerents were again at each other. Mugabe speaking live on national television described the GPA as a humiliation and that the only consolation was that "ZANU-PF was still in the driver's seat (and would) not tolerate nonsense" from the MDCs. Unsurprisingly therefore, when on 18 September 2008 the parties to the GNU held talks to discuss and allocate ministerial portfolios, they could not agree on which party would control which ministries. The MDC-T's youthful spokesman, Nelson Chamisa complained that if the portfolios were allocated following ZANU-PF dictates, the militant ruling party would ultimately be in the control of government while the MDC-T would be reduced to "a mere cosmetic accessory and mere lipstick." That to Chamisa was "completely unacceptable as 'the MDC–T was not so desperate to be in the government'" (The Star, Independent, 2008, p. 5). Most contentious between the two parties was which between them would run the ministries of finance and home affairs? The MDC-T particularly wanted control of the finance portfolio after the disastrous way the ZANU-PF party had run it, but the latter was refusing to cede it (Dugger, 2008).

Much like a referee, former South African President Mbeki was again tasked to mediate. In the meantime, some of the country's taps ran dry while cholera in the company of cash shortages ravaged the country. It is estimated that Zimbabwe's hyperinflation finally reached 500 billion percent when in December 2008, a ZWD50 million denomination bill was amazingly issued. Purportedly "printed on pure cotton" (Guma, 2008, np), it was issued to augment the denominated issue of August 2008. When hyperinflation, however, proved more resilient, a ZW$100 trillion banknote, the highest denomination note ever issued on the African continent was put into circulation in January 2009. By all appearances, the country's legal tender of ever-escalating astronomical denominations had finally and undeniably reached the "manure and toilet paper" status many in and outside the country had been calling it. Incredulously, the RBZ once again reformed the country's currency.

On 2 February 2009, the Zimbabwe Dollar was again redenominated by shedding 12 zeros. A new series of banknote denominations between ZW$1 and ZW$500 were issued as the fourth dollar to replace the third dollar of 2008 banknotes. Meanwhile, although not yet permitted by law, some shops had already started selling foodstuff and other goods priced in United States Dollars (USD)[16]. As early as 2007, those with relatives abroad had been accessing foreign currency via bureaux de change such as Western Union and MoneyGram located in either Botswana or South Africa. For such, purchasing goods and services both in neighboring countries and locally was relatively easy. However, some of those unable to do so literally died of hunger and illness.

In the meantime, amidst the record-breaking hyperinflation, cash shortages, dry taps, hours and sometimes days without electricity, ZANU-PF and the MDC-T had from mid-September 2008 into early 2009 had been holding various mediated negotiations with Mbeki and SADC. After what Mbeki later described as negotiations that were "the same as ever, forward and backward, sideways and around (...) the usual "Mugabe on 18 January 2009 called on Tsvangirai to uphold the GPA and form an inclusive government or else withdraw from it. Another marathon SADC meeting followed on 26 January whose outcome was conflicting. SADC and ZANU-PF reported that an agreement had been reached over the adoption of the Constitutional Amendments and the swearing-in of an inclusive government in early February. Conversely, the MDC-T denied there had been any such agreement on those critical issues (Clayton, 2009). Three days later, however, the MDC-T altered its earlier statement and consented there had been an agreement and that they would be joining the inclusive government depending on the outcome of its National Council meeting outcome.

The MDC National Council endorsed the deal on 30 January 2009, and a week later, both houses of Zimbabwe's parliament unanimously passed the Unity Government Bill on 5 February 2009 (Kandemiri, 2009, np). On 10 February 2009, the MDC-T's Tsvangirai and Thokozani Khupe, together with the MDC-M's Mutambara were sworn in by Mugabe as prime minister and deputy prime ministers, respectively. The swearing in of the GNU's ministers and deputies followed on 13 February. Zimbabwe's inclusive government was finally constituted. Yesterday's intraparty and interparty factionalism would in the following years become intergovernmental infighting. For now, however, the GNU set aside political differences and concentrated on resuscitating the Zimbabwean economy.

Because of the state of the nation and the critical condition of the economy, the GNU sworn into office in February 2009 had to hit the road running. Then newly appointed finance minister and MDC-T cadre, Tendai Biti and then RBZ governor Gono, set about trying to reign in hyperinflation and the Zimbabwe Dollar currency challenge. By April 2009, however, it became glaringly apparent that the Zimbabwe Dollar was unrecoverable as legal tender. Although it had unofficially seized to be so months before, it was officially suspended on 12 April 2009 as the country's *dejure* (by law) legal tender. In its place was announced that a multi-currency system would instead serve as legal tender. Initially dominated by the South African Rand when that proved volatile, the new multi-currency regime became led by the U.S. dollar—the country's reserve currency incredulously became the national currency.

This alarmingly fragrant dollarization of the economy temporarily witnessed the return of some normalcy to the country. As Chakravati (2017, p. Business 5) reported, the monetary system became "flush with US dollars, and there were practically no restrictions on the amount of US dollars one could legally take out of the country. The RBZ considered money in individual accounts as 'free funds' and remittances could be legally made without stringent documentation." Given such lax monetary policy and fundamentals, scarce essential commodities like sugar, bread, salt and cornmeal reappeared in stores and on shelves. Long fuel queues which had become a common sight in Zimbabwe disappeared as if overnight. Socioeconomic and to some extent political stability and sanity returned to the country. Inflation lowered to single digit figures. Zimbabweans and the world breathed a sigh of relief.

Amidst it all however, "unfortunately the Finance Ministry and monetary authorities did not properly review the experience of economies that had dollarized in the past[17]." (Chakravati, 2017, p. Business 5) So, for instance, instead of importing spare parts, inputs and machinery vital to restoring the country's manufacturing and industrial productivity, imports tended to be luxury goods and consumerist. Both the GNU and some of the citizenry failed to take advantage of the importation potential of the greenback fully. For a while, they both forgot the situation they had come from and the fact that because the "dollar is an international currency in great demand. It is therefore impossible for a developing country to maintain a dollarized economy (…) surrounded by a non–dollarized region and world" (Chakravati, 2017, p. Business 5). The country's foreign currency reserves were thus literally squandered or externalized out of its economy to others. Zimbabwe's newfound euphoria would last almost four years, however, not without the occasional political turbulence and near capitulations on the GPA.

Not long after the GNU became operational, less than a month into the GNU, Tsvangirai was threatening to pull the MDC-T out of it. According to Tsvangirai, he and his ministers were not being invited by ZANU-PF to Cabinet meetings while some of his duties as premier were either being usurped by ZANU-PF ministers or by President Mugabe himself. On their part, ZANU-PF accused MDC-T of among others, lacking statecraft. On 20 February 2012, Mugabe speaking on state radio called on the police to investigate Tsvangirai for fraudulent activities in the manner he had built his official residence. Other than such bickering, however, the three intermittent belligerents were throughout the existence of the GNU able to productively work together and even score some joint successes. By the time the GNU term came to an end, its most significant successes were undoubtedly socioeconomic stability for Zimbabweans and a new democratic constitution for the country.

With the end of the GNU, however, factionalism once again reared—this time simultaneously in both MDC-T and ZANU-PF. On 31 July 2013, ZANU-PF, and the MDC-T once again faced off in the 2013 harmonized elections. The worst of Zimbabwe's socioeconomic crisis having ameliorated—ironically due to the GNU, the opposition's chances at the polls were this time around not as promising as back in March 2008. As matters stood, Mutambara's had since been expelled from his faction for the alleged hero-worshipping Robert Mugabe whom he had called "Father Africa and the best leader Africa has produced" (ZimOnline, 2009, np). Consequently, Ncube had taken the reins of the MDC-M and renamed it MDC-Ncube (MDC-N). Later, Sikhala had also left the (MDC-N) claiming that Ncube had dictatorial tendencies. He had then formed his own splinter MDC faction, the MDC-99 poignantly so named after 1999—the year the original MDC had been formed.

As for the MDC-T, Tsvangirai had during his tenure as premiere revealed himself to be something of a philanderer who could not concentrate on matters of leadership and state and had been portrayed as such by both national and international media. Consequently, when the 2013 harmonized election results were released, ZANU-PF had won more a two-thirds majority in the House of Assembly and the MDC-T. The ZANU-PF party was once again in sole control of both government and parliament with Mugabe as president. Aside from its parliamentary seats, the MDC-T once again found itself in the doldrums. All blame for the significant opposition faction's post-2013 election condition was squarely directed at and placed on Tsvangirai's shoulders. In April 2014, Tsvangirai and six other senior leaders were suspended by the MDC-T's National Council. Tsvangirai was according to Thornycroft (2014) and the BBC News of 26 April 2014 apparently "kicked out (for) remarkable failure of leadership and creating a divisive atmosphere" (p.90). It was however not the MDC-T alone that was expelling leading members of its party—so too was the ZANU-PF party.

At the end of the GNU, ZANU-PF's two-thirds majority victory and Mugabe's reelection as president, the thenoctogenarian leader of Zimbabwe was only months away to becoming a nonagenarian. He was almost 25 years past retirement, and this showed when on occasion, both the national and international media caught him on camera either dozing in parliament or at some meetings of heads of state and government. By December 2013, illiquidity had returned. After just over four years of sufficient cash flow, headlines were once again screaming: "Mayhem: Cash shortage riots (…) Banking crisis: Causes, consequences, remedies (…) Turmoil in banking sector scares businesses." Despite all this, fighting ever-waning urban popularity, old age and reported ill-health Mugabe did not show nor share any plans of retiring. If anything, he was, God-willing, already poised to stand as ZANU-PF's presidential candidate in 2018 harmonized elections. Evidently, like the famous Zulu king Shaka, Mugabe was not thinking of a future without him. He was not thinking of going anywhere anytime soon, and neither was he planning of relinquishing his presidential seat to anyone in particular. Whenever asked about grooming a successor, choosing one or whom he wished to succeed him, Mugabe would perfunctorily and evasively respond: "Let the people choose." Talk of succession within ZANU-PF became taboo—driving it dangerously underground.

By 2013, Mugabe's intransigent refusal to put both a succession and exit plan in place had given rise to the existence of three factions within the ZANU-PF party—the Gamatox faction of then Vice President Joice Mujuru, the Lacoste or Team Lacoste faction of then Minister of Defense, Emmerson Mnangagwa and the Generation 40 or G-40 faction, and the creation of then Minister of Information and Publicity, Jonathan Moyo, but seemingly led by the then First Lady, Grace Mugabe. Because of the secretive nature of factionalism, however, the history and composition of these blocs within ZANU-PF have been more or less conjecture.

The Gamatox faction derived its name from the brand name of a potent weevil pesticide that is quite common in Zimbabwe. The faction only began to be so called by the ZANU-PF party in 2014 to refer to Joice Mujuru loyalists. It was widely believed to be composed of mostly liberal moderates from Zimbabwe's Manicaland province who had joined the country's liberation struggle quite young and had grownup in it. Most had either/or held a high-ranking military or administrative post during the war and wished Mugabe to be succeeded by one of their own "homeboy of homegirl" from Manicaland. The faction had officially first made its presence felt in September 2004. At the time, the then first Vice President Simon Muzenda had just died, and the first vice president position was vacant when the ZANU-PF Women's League agitated that the post be filled by the then Minister of Rural Resources and Water Development, Joice Mujuru.

Joice Mujuru's nomination was supported by her now late husband, Retired General Solomon Mujuru and other high ranking cadres within the ZANU-PF party. These included the likes of Didymus Mutasa, Ray Kaukonde and Themba Mliswa, all of whom are from Manicaland. On her part, towards the party's congress in December, Joice Mujuru had lobbied other politburo and central committee members. At the ZANU–PF 2004 December congress, in the light of Joice Mujuru's overwhelming popularity over Mugabe's perceived protégé and preferred choice, Emmerson Mnangagwa, the then

President and First Secretary of ZANU-PF assented to the will of the majority and appointed Joice Mujuru first vice president on 6 December 2004. The Solomon Mujuru–led Gamatox faction had just scored a significant victory against Team Lacoste or Lacoste faction.

During the liberation war, Mnangagwa had from 1964 to 1965 led a band of combatants known as the Crocodile Gang. Comprised mainly of war veterans of Zimbabwe's liberation war, Lacoste had been so-called possibly because of its covert support of Mnangagwa whose nickname is *gwena* (Shona for crocodile) and the logo of the French fashion brand, Lacoste. Conversely, it had possibly been so-called in order to identify it as an extension of Mnangagwa's wartime "Crocodile Gang." Whatever the reason, this eclectic bloc believed Mugabe's successor should have strong liberation war credentials, an established track record within party structures and possibly from the Midlands province of the country. It thus had within its ranks war veterans, high ranking officers of the Zimbabwe Defence Forces, some senior members of the party's politburo and a few senior women of the ZANU-PF Women's League.

Like the Gamatox faction, Team Lacoste also first came into the limelight and prominence in November 2004 on the occasion of what became infamously known as the Tsholotsho Declaration. At the time, Zimbabwe's first vice president Simon Muzenda had just passed away and the vice presidency post vacant. It is reported that some Members of Parliament, six provincial chairmen, some high profile war veterans, members of the ZANU-PF Central Committee and Politburo and, most notably Jonathan Moyo, the then Minister of Information had met at Tsholotsho's Dingane Secondary School to deliberate how they would ensure Mnangagwa ascended into the presidium (Magaisa, 2014). When the plot came to light, Mugabe amended the ZANU-PF party's constitution to stipulate that one of the party's vice presidents be a woman. All those involved in the Tsholotsho Declaration, except Mnangagwa, were suspended from the ZANU-PF party for allegedly trying to topple Mugabe (Mbiba, 2014). Mnangagwa was in 2005 reappointed from his position as Speaker of the House of Assembly to Minister of Rural Housing. Although Mnangagwa's ministry was never implicated, it was while he was in this position that the infamous Operation *Murambatsvina* (no to rubbish) occurred. Operation *Murambatsvina* sought to rid Zimbabwe of illegally built urban structures and slum-dwellers living in urban centers by forcing them back to their home in the rural areas. The operation saw the displacement of an estimated 700 000 people[18].

From early 2009 to 2014, Zimbabwe experienced relative political peace. After taking the ZANU-PF party to court over the outcome of the 2013 polls and losing the case, the MDC-T appeared to have conceded defeat and returned to infighting over whether Tsvangirai should continue to lead the opposition MDC-T faction. In 2014 Job Sikhala who had left to join the MDC-M in 2006 and then had left when it became the MDC-N to form his MDC99, returned to the MDC-T's National Council. In the same year, the then First Lady, Grace Mugabe controversially obtained a doctorate from the University of Zimbabwe and suddenly seemed intent on following in her husband's footsteps by launching on a political career.

Until June 2014, the most prominent factions within the ZANU-PF party were Gamatox and Lacoste. However when Mugabe whilst addressing a crowd of mourners at the national shrine, Heroes Acre accused his then Minister of Information of being like a *chipfukuto* (weevil) that destroys good grain (ZANU-PF) and therefore needed to be gotten rid of, the Lacoste faction had acquired the nickname "Zvipfukuto" (weevils). It did not, therefore, escape anyone who Didymus Mutasa, then minister of state for presidential affairs as well as ZANU-PF secretary for administration and in the Joice Mujuru faction, was talking about when a week after Mugabe had called Moyo a weevil, Mutasa addressing a youth rally reportedly said: "You were talking about the issue of weevils here. Way back we used to treat weevils by spraying Gamatox, and they will all die" (Manayiti, 2014). The battle lines were drawn. However, the subsequent volley came from an unexpected source.

From mid-2014, Dr. Amai Grace Mugabe, as the then-first lady was increasingly being called, embarked on what she termed "Meet the People" rallies at which sought to meet ZANU-PF supporters. It was at such gatherings that Dr. Amai systematically embarked on vitriolic verbal attacks against the thenVice President, Mujuru. She accused her of, amongst other things, factionalism, corruption and plotting to overthrow the head of state, by assassination. Mugabe's silence meant his acquiescence with Grace's allegations. To onlookers, it looked as though Grace had overnight become a member of the Lacoste faction that had recently been nicknamed "*Zvipfukuto.*" When therefore towards the November 2014 ZANU-PF party congress, some Zimbabweans took to social media to satirically comment on the political goings-on, they jocularly counted Dr. Amai among Team *Zvipfukuto*[19] members, wherein she was the goalkeeper. The match between Gamatox and Lacoste "Zvipfukuto" would be referred by Mugabe, assisted by two well-known war veterans, Jabulani Sibanda and Joseph Chinotimba.

Dr. Amai Grace's allegations against Dr. Amai Joice Mujuru who incidentally had credibly also graduated with a Ph.D. at the same graduation as Grace was left exposed to a barrage of criticism and allegations. Interestingly, it seemed the attacks were receiving full coverage from the State broadcaster, the Zimbabwe Broadcasting Corporation (ZBC) with the permission of the then minister of information. From 2014 to 2017, both the State's print and electronic media carried disparaging reports and pieces about Joice Mujuru. The effect was such that by the time of the ZANU-PF party's sixth congress in December 2014, Joice Mujuru had fallen out of favor with the public, sections of the ZANU-PF party and most importantly, with Mugabe. So tarnished was Mujuru's image she did not even attempt to seek reelection to the politburo and the central committee.

In response to the first lady's allegations, Mugabe on 8 December 2014 dismissed Mujuru as the second vice president of Zimbabwe along with some ministers classified as of the Gamatox faction. As Mujuru descended, Grace meteorically ascended. She was nominated to lead ZANU-PF's Women League and unanimously elected by the congress' provincial delegates' show of hands and cheers. The position of leader of ZANU-PF's Women League comes with it a seat in the politburo-the party's executive political committee responsible for policy formulation. That seat was now Dr. Amai Grace Mugabe's. In the light of the 2004 party constitutional provision that one of the two vice presidents in the Presidium must be a woman, Dr. Amai's leadership and place in the politburo positioned her barely a step from the vice presidency and two from the presidency. As the vice presidency was vacant at the time of the thenfirst lady's election to the Politburo, many speculated what would happen next.

The then minister of justice Mnangagwa was eventually appointed Zimbabwe's first vice president. Mujuru was expelled from ZANU-PF in early April[20]. To some onlookers, it appeared Grace had all along been paving the way for Mnangagwa. Had she? The answer soon came. After "tearing former Vice President Dr. Joice Mujuru's succession machinations to smithereens (and) earning herself the nickname Mai Stop It, some thought the First Lady was going to slow down" (Lazarus, 2015, p.10). Instead, Grace's rallies continued, she again fell back on to her tried and trusted strategy of vitriolic accusations. This time they were targeted at the thennew Vice President, Emmerson Mnangagwa who she at times chided even in his presence. By all appearances, Grace was not after all of Team Lacoste. It was either she was on a one-woman mission or part of Generation 40 or G40 clandestine faction-that had been formed by Jonathan Moyo.

Unlike either Gamatox or Lacoste, Generation 40 or G40 comprised relatively younger party bigwigs. Still, in their 30s and early 60s, their history with ZANU-PF was quite recent. Some were still in the party's Youth League, while others had joined and risen in the party as technocrats, praise-singers or relatives of Mugabe. They had no liberation war credentials to them and believed that in the event of Mugabe's incapacitation someone of their generation and Mugabe's academic standing should succeed him. It is perhaps because of the latter requirement that Grace had accelerated her acquisition of a Ph.D.

From 2016 to 2017, Dr. Amai Grace's confrontational attention and verbal attacks at her rallies explicitly turned on Mnangagwa. A new power struggle between G40 and Lacoste began. Like Mujuru before him, Mnangagwa now faced Grace's verbal onslaughts. Some of those loyal to him or merely sympathetic towards him booed the then first lady. The masses were getting tired and resentful of Grace. Adding to their agitation was the fact that "despite stabilizing a hyperinflationary pre–dollarization crisis emanating from economic mismanagement, (the use of foreign currency) triggered liquidity challenges" (Kararach *et al.*, 2010 as cited by Dlamini & Mbira, 2017, p.213). Worsening Zimbabwe's liquidity challenges was also that by 2016, the strengthening of the U.S. Dollar had "led to a decline in commodity prices, a development that undermined export receipts" (Dlamini & Mbira, 2017, p.213) from the country's agro and mineral export.

Moreover, in January 2016, the RBZ reported that some companies operating within the country were "externalizing the United States dollar in offshore accounts for speculative purposes and fear of the return of the Zimbabwean dollar" (Dlamini & Mbira, 2017, p.213). When in March 2016 the RBZ finally abolished the system of free funds and easy remittance, it was already too late; most of the cash had already flown out of the system. As externalization and "limited external inflows fuelled the already tight liquidity conditions in Zimbabwe" (Dlamini & Mbira, 2017, p.213), the RBZ in November 2016 introduced Zimbabwean Bond Notes as a kind of surrogate legal tender. In addition to specie, Bond Notes come in two and five dollars that are atpar with U.S. Dollars. Fearful however that the Zimbabwean Bond Notes were a prelude to the reintroduction of the old Zimbabwe Dollar (ZWD) and given that there is a shortage of Zimbabwean Bond Notes, by 2017 millions of Zimbabweans were transacting via EcoCash than any other *dejure* tender. Bond Notes are for internal circulation only and were initially meant to circulate with eight other multi–currencies. These have since varnished from normal circulation and have instead been replaced by EcoCash—"a mobile phone-based money transfer, financing, and micro–financing service launched in 2011 by Econet Wireless for its customers in Zimbabwe" (Sengere, np).

Despite the availability of cashless services, Zimbabweans had until 2013 mostly favored the use of cash. However, when in 2013 illiquidity once again reared and banks promoted such e-platforms as Point of Sale (POS) machines, internet banking, and Real Time Gross Settlements (RTGS) this left Zimbabweans with little option but to resort to such transactional facilities. In a Golden Age of technology, Zimbabwean banks and other service providers are moving towards the latest innovative advancements to reach their client base. To add to financial inclusivity[21], the mobile payments[22] frenzy that first hit the Zimbabwean market around 2011 with the birth of products such as Skwana and Textacash marked the birth a mobile banking revolution. It later took a considerable leap forward with the introduction of Econet Wireless's Ecocash. Similar to Kenya's MPesa, EcoCash provides subscribers with a Personal Identification Number (PIN) that enables them to virtually deposit, withdraw, transfer and pay for goods and services from any handset.

In the absence of a lasting solution to Zimbabwe's cash challenges, in addition to Econet's Ecocash, other mobile banking products had by 2017 also ascended on the market. These include NetOne's OneWallet, Telecel's Telecash, CABS' Textacash, CBZ's Mobile Banking, GetCash's Getcash Wallet, FBC's Mobile Moola and ZIPIT mobile banking. An estimated "45 percent of the adult population (3,25 million) was registered with mobile money platforms in 2014 (…) The increase in the mobile telephone subscribers from three million in 2009 to 12,6 million as of September 30, 2016, has created a growing market for mobile financial services" (Gwanyanya, 2017, p.8). The cash crunch has thus paradoxically turned Zimbabwe into a first-world cashless society. However, while such moves have positively impacted formal and informal trading, they have also added to the country's illiquidity. According to a 2015 Finscope survey, such is the popularity of mobile products among low-income workers that they prefer payment through mobile payment platforms (Mangudhla 2015, p.5). Aside from the convenience mobile payment platforms offer, their use and that of plastic money over conventional banking services have also become a measure of how little Zimbabweans trust their financial institutions and each other.

Sometime in August 2017, Mnangagwa claimed his ice-cream from Gushungo Dairy owned by Grace Mugabe had been poisoned during Grace's Bulawayo Youth Interface Rally that he had attended. Although he later refuted it, when in September 2017 Mnangagwa again reiterated the same claim, he was in October 2017 shuffled out of his secondary post as Minister of Justice and Parliamentary Affairs. In November various accusations that Mnangagwa had discharged "his duties in a manner inconsistent with his official duties, disloyalty, disrespect, deceitfulness and unreliability and a lack of probity in the execution of his duties" (The Herald, np) were leveled against him. On 6 November Mugabe promptly dismissed him as vice president. In fear for his life, Mnangagwa escaped to South Africa. Two days later, he was expelled from the ruling party.

However aware of the threat those heading Zimbabwe's state security forces could pose, in the meantime, Mugabe ordered the arrest of the then head of the Joint Operations Command, General Constantine Chiwenga. In defense of their commander, however, some members of the military thwarted the move. A fourth faction in the military, aligned to Lacoste but probably the most powerful, emerged. An exchange of threats and counter-threats between the Chiwenga and the Mugabes via the State's media followed. The culmination of which was the launch on 14–15 November 2017 of what the military later dubbed Operation Restore Legacy. During the operation, the Mugabes were placed under house arrest and some key members of the G40 faction detained.

With the military's encouragement, on 17 November 2017 thousands of Zimbabweans black and white, young and old urbanites who for years had electorally sought to remove Mugabe from power now took to the streets "to send a message to President Mugabe that he 'must go'" (Protestors March to Mugabe's, p. np). The once feared army now paradoxically turned ally. In response to the people's calls, on 19 November 2017, ZANU-PF dismissed Mugabe as their party's leader. On its part, Zimbabwe's parliament set in motion processes to impeach Mugabe and gave him an ultimatum to either resign or be impeached. Mugabe finally chose to resign. He tendered his resignation on 21 November 2017 marking the end of an era and bringing the country's crisis to a watershed—one from which the country could either move forward and eventually out of crisis or drag it back further into the abyss of crisis.

## *Conclusion*

An analysis of the black nationalist movement in Zimbabwe suggests that it and the history of the country have revolved around factionalism brought about by conflicts in personality clashes and leadership styles. In the early 1960s, Mugabe had risen through the ranks of the NDP, ZANU and lastly ZANU-PF by questioning these formations personalities and leadership. By so doing; he had fueled factionalism and dissent within the parties. Paradoxically, in the 1980s and 1990s, Tekere, Dongo, Mujuru and ironically his wife would use the same strategy in an attempt to divide and lead the ruling ZANU-PF.

Similarly, so too would those in the opposition. As a master of factionalism, Mugabe in his last years in power fanned factionalism among his sycophantic secessionists as a way of keeping them divided and too weak to collectively challenge him. All the while, it is the people of Zimbabwe who bore the socioeconomic and political brunt of both the ruling and opposition parties' factionalism. Ultimately, it would take the emergence of a fourth insidious faction in the military, which aligned to Lacoste but probably the most powerful, to bring Mugabe down and Zimbabwe's crisis to its watershed.

## *Notes*

1. Affiliation: Department of Culture, Communication & Media, University College London & Comecinc Communications and Strategic Solutions Services Incorporated.
2. The other two being the then President of ZANU Dabaningi Sithole and Simon Muzenda.
3. In later years, as some ZANU-PF cadres found themselves on the wrong side of the law, Mugabe would intervene on their behalf.
4. The Unity Accord of 1987 had, amongst others, brought about an amended Constitution of 1987 that had created the post of Executive President, a single voters' roll of both blacks and whites, and abolished the Senate.
5. Its human rights, and bad electoral record, Dongo had in 1989 co-founded the Zimbabwe National Liberation War Veterans Association (ZNLWVA) with Chenjerai Hunzwi.
6. This is how CNN often described what was happening in Zimbabwe at the time.
7. This is the same day when the British South Africa Company's Pioneer Column arrived in what would be Zimbabwe and had until independence been celebrated as Founders Day.
8. Ironically *chikaura* in Shona means now suffer.
9. Bank checks used in lieu of bank notes.
10. This chapter had been in the MDC's broad coalition at the party's inception in 1999.
11. These were in 2014 declared to have been not free and fair by the Khampepe Report.
12. The Ncube faction was also accused of being in league with the then South Africa's president Mbeki and plotting to oust Tsvangirai (Dzamara, 2007).
13. Voice of America (VOA) 21/5/2008 "Another Zimbabwean Opposition Activist Found Dead After Abduction."
14. Sunday Mail 8/6/2008 "The grip of fear: Military reign of terror as Zimbabwe prepares for elections."
15. Were it a banknote, this check apparently would have shared with the Yugoslav 500 billion dinar note of 1993 the record for the most number of zeros on a banknote.
16. As Chakravati (2017, p. Business 5) explains, such market forces finally resulted in the multi-currency solution in late 2008. The government officially adopted the concept through the 2009 Budget.
17. Chakravati, (2017, p. Business 5) explains that "the only countries which have managed to maintain a dollarized economy successfully are those that have a special relationship with the United States banking system, such as Panama and Ecuador. Zimbabwe is not in that situation." Hence his advice the country adopt the South African Rand.

18. See UN Special Envoy Anna Tibaijuka's Report of the Fact-finding Mission to Zimbabwe to Assess the Scope and Impact of Operation Murambatsvina of 18 July 2005.
19. Visit http://www.dailynews.co.zw/articles/2014/10/24team-gamatox-versus-team-zvipfukuto
20. On 3 April 2015, she formed her own political party—Zimbabwe People First (ZPF) with Margaret Dongo. In 2017, she expelled seven senior members, among them Dongo. She had to relinquish the name Zimbabwe People First for National People's Party (NPP). It was again later changed to the National Rainbow People's Party (NRPP).
21. A measure of the proportion of the banked population—from 60 percent in 2011 to 77 percent in 2014.
22. Generally payment services operated under financial regulation and performed via a mobile device, also referred to as mobile money, mobile money transfer and mobile wallet.

## References

Chakravati, A. (2017). Liquidity crunch, adoption of SA rand. (2 April) *The Sunday Mail*, Opinion.

Clayton, J. (2009). Zimbabwe power–sharing talks end in confusion after marathon session. The Times, London.

Cuhaj, G. S. (2009). *Standard catalogue of world paper money. Modern issues:1961–present.* 3:15 Lola. Wisconsin: Krause Publications.

Dlamini, B., & Mbira, L. (2017). The current Zimbabwean liquidity crisis: A review of its precipitates. *Journal of Economics and Behavioural Studies*, *9*(3), 212–219. July.

Dugger, C. W. (2008). Zimbabwe power–sharing deal eludes Mugabe and rival. Retrieved July 3, 2018, fromhttps://www.nytimes.com/2008/08/18/world/africa/18zimbabwe.html?mtrref=www.google.com&gwh=B30A3AA35CBF67FB699498B-603D4EBBC&gwt=pay&assetType=REGIWALL

Dzamara, I. (2007). The untold story of the MDC split. Retrieved June 16, 2018, from www.zimbabwean.co.zw/2007/08/theuntold–story–of the MDC split/

EISA. (2002). Africa democracy encyclopedia project. Retrieved June 16, 2018, from https://www.eisa.org.za/wep/zimparties4.htm

Forte, M. (2013). Factionalism. *Politicalanthropology*. Lincoln Hill: Concordia University. Retrieved June 16, 2018, from http://politicalanthro.wordpress.com/factionalism

Giesecke & Devrient halts deliveries to the Reserve Bank of Zimbabwe. Giesecke & Devrient GmbH, Munich, July 14, 2008.

Guma, L. (2008). Zimbabwe: New Z$50 million cotton bill introduced, Retrieved June 16, 2018, from SW Radio Africa.

Gwanyanya, P. (2017). Mobile money will transform Zim banking (19 March). *The Sunday Mail*, Analysis, p. 8.

IOL. (2006). Mutambara arrested during campaign, Retrieved June 24 from www.iol.co.za/news/africa/mutambara–arrested–during–campaign–march–

Kandemiri, J. (2009). Zimbabwe's Tsvangirai cultivates civic support for planned unity government. Retrieved July 5, 2018, fromhttps://www.voanews.com/archive/zimbabwes-tsvangirai-cultivates-civic-support-planned-unity-government

Lamb, C. (2009). *House of stone: The true story of a family divided in war–torn Zimbabwe.* Chicago: Chicago Review Press.

Lazarus, B. (2015). Dr. Amai is what ZANU-PF needs (30 August). *The Sunday Mail,* Analysis, p. 6.

Lewellen, T. C. (1983). *Political anthropology, an introduction.* South Hardley, MA: Bergin & Garvey.

Manayiti, O. (2014). Mutasa reads Grace's speech. Retrieved July 4, 2018, from https://www.thestandard.co.zw/2014/10/26/mutasa-reads-graces-speech/

Mangudhla, T. (2015). POSB sticks to traditional banking (10–16 December). *Zimbabwe Independent Business Digest,* Company News, p. 5.

Mbiba, L. (2014). They want to topple Mugabe. Retrieved July 5, 2018, from https://www.dailynews.co.zw/articles/2014/11/01/they-want-to-topple-mugabe

Mapala, F. (2008). Mutambara withdraws from race, backs Makoni. Retrieved June 16, 2018, from NewZimbabwe.com February15, 2008.

Meredith, M. (2002). *Mugabe, power, plunder and the struggle for Zimbabwe.* New York: Public Affairs.

News24. (2012). Mugabe threatens to arrest Tsvangirai. Retrieved June 16, 2018, from https://www.news24.com/Africa/Zimbabwe/Fraud-Mugabe-threatens-to-arrest-Tsvangirai-20120221

Newsday. (2011). Ncube regrets MDC split daily. Retrieved June 14, 2018, from https://www.newsday.co.zw/2011/01/2011-01-12-ncube-regrets-mdc-split-daily/

Norman. (2008). *MugabetTeacher, revolutionary, tyrant.* Dublin: History Press.

Protestors march to Mugabe's official residence, 'want to see him out.' (2017, November 18). Retrieved July 20, 2018, from https://www.news24.com/Africa/Zimbabwe/protesters-march-to-mugabes-official-residence-want-to-see-him-out-20171118

Ross. (1980). Case against volatile aide to Mugabe becomes test for premier, Zimbabwe. Retrieved June 16, 2018, from https://www.washingtonpost.com/archive/politics/1980/08/11/case-against-volatile-aide-to-mugabe-becomes-test-for-premier-zimbabwe/61bad227-72a0-4cad-8f09-0ae59cb8a59e/?noredirect=on&utm_term=.05d261ca2669

Shaw, A. (2008). Zimbabwe opposition leader pulling out of election. Associated Press 22/6/2008 Retrieved June 16, 2018, from https://www.deseretnews.com/article/700236997/Zimbabwe-opposition-leader-pulling-out-of-election.html

Sheldon, K. E. (2005). *Historical dictionary of women in sub–Saharan Africa.* Lanham, MD: Scarecrow Press.

Smith, D., & Simpson, C. (1981). *Mugabe.* Salisbury: Pioneer Head.

Smith, E. (2008). Now petrol coupons are the new currency in Zimbabwe. Retrieved June 17, 2018, fromhttp://www.dailymail.co.uk/news/article-1042358/Now-petrol-coupons-new-currency-Zimbabwe.html

Staff Writer. (2008). Zim. deal looks dead in the water. (October 1).The Star, p. 5.

The Insider. (2002). The sacking of Gwisai. Retrieved June 17, 2018, from http://www.insiderzim.com/the-sacking-of-gwisai/

Thornycroft, P. (2014). Morgan Tsvangirai kicked out of MDC party. Retrieved July 4, 2018, fromhttps://www.telegraph.co.uk/news/worldnews/africaandindianocean/zimbabwe/10790207/Morgan-Tsvangirai-kicked-out-of-MDC-party.html

ZimOnline. (2009). Mutambara calls Mugabe father Africa says Sikhala. Retrieved June 16, 2017, from http://www.zimbabweonlinepress.com/mutambara-calls-mugabe-father-africa-says-sikhala

Zulu, B. (2007). Zimbabwe Central Bank lightens purses by issuing Z$ 50,000 note. Retrieved June 16, 2018, from http://webarchive.loc.gov/all/20100723025238/http%3A//www1.voanews.com/zimbabwe/news/a-13-56-74-2007-03-01-voa47-68957637.html

# 10 ZForwards from Zimbabwe (2007–2009): Email as Sociological Imagination and Satire

C. Luthuli Mhlahlo[1]

## Introduction

Crisis of any sort has a sociological impact that, more often than not, culminates in some form of human response. Since the turn of the millennium, the people of Zimbabwe have experienced a tumultuous period. In this chapter, I argue that due to the catalytic effects of the country's Land Reform Programme (LRP) and the numerous political and socioeconomic challenges that emanated from it, the events of the period 2007–2009 provoked the sociological imaginations of some Zimbabweans, both within and without the country's borders. I demonstrate how using electronic and digital media; they creatively produced images that satirically expressed their perceptions, emotions and attitudes towards some of the events that were happening in the country. These creative but critical images were often then emailed as attachments to family, friends, relatives and fellow countrymen who in turn also shared them by forwarding them to others far removed from their initial recipients and beyond different borders. The forwarding of satirical emails ensured that they had a wider audience and so electronically spread what I have here called: "ZForwards" from and about crisis-ridden Zimbabwe. In the chapter, I analyze 28 such ZForwards that were shared among some Zimbabweans as cyber-mediated exchanges at the height of the crisis. The ZForwards selected satirically reflect and comment on some of Zimbabweans' everyday socioeconomic and political experiences during the years 2007–2009.

## *ZForwards and the Sociohistorical Lens: Zimbabwe 2007–2009*

A sociohistorical lens is inalienable to understanding both the country and her people. As Stuart Hall explains, "the black subject and black experience [have been] constructed historically, culturally, politically" (1996, p.1). In the case of contemporary Zimbabwe during the years 2007–2009, "it is certainly true that it would be difficult [...] to meaningfully understand personal lives in abstraction from their social and historical contexts" (Kaarsholm, 2005, p.3). The ZForwards I received between 2007 and 2009 bore truth to this. Most ZForwards from Zimbabwe's period of crisis coherently reflected their creators' experience of lives lived. Indeed it is because of their likeness to, among others African literature, my own ability and that of other Zimbabweans to identify with what they depicted, that in the absence of a critical frame to critically analyze and evaluate ZForwards, I have here deployed Irele's (1971) sociohistorical perspective to analyze the ZForwards I have selected to discuss here.

Irele's sociohistorical perspective dictates that:

> Some inner experience or some inner knowledge, either immediate or acquired of the relations outside the work is necessary for this kind of understanding [...] This approach, in its fullest and most comprehensive meaning, implies that our criticism should take into account everything that has gone into the work, and specifically for our literature, everything within our society which has informed the work. (Irele, 1971:19)

Secondly, a sociohistorical perspective to a study of African Literature approaches literary "work with an insight into, and a feeling for, those aspects of life which stand beyond the text itself, its extensions into the African experience, and its foundations in the very substance of African existence" (Irele, 1971, p.15). In addition, it was also Irele's (1971) view that: "The integrity and specificity of an African work can only be brought to light if the work itself is situated within its perspective and related to African references [...] the concrete and the local" (15–16). It is against this sociohistorical-critical apparatus, that I consider the ZForwards I received from 2007 to 2009 depicting varying aspects of the country's crisis as also a form of "digital sociological imagination"—however, one residing outside of conventional literature, yet "growing with modern African Literature" (Irele, 1971, p.15). Consequently, much like literature, I treat the ZForwards explored here not only as a kind of exploration of the life lived but also a postmodernist Zimbabwean literary expression of various imaginations as derived from Zimbabweans' experiences of crisis.

Approximating relatively neophyte but ever -evolving African literature, the creation of digital ZForwards and their accompanying communication was at the height of Zimbabwe's crisis "new in every sense of the word: in the obvious sense, it (was) by and large a recent development and still growing—to borrow Wole Soyinka's term–something of a half-child" (Irele, 1971, p.11). Reminiscent of the development of the early days of the continent's literature, when African writers had mainly mimicked the writing styles of western authors to tell African stories, creators of ZForwards also borrowed and tailored digital graphics to portray the Zimbabwean crisis. So, albeit western in origin, the tailored graphics could comprehensively convey the message or comment on it as it was intended to.

Although different from conventional literary genres, ZForwards I received aroused the thoughts of their mostly Zimbabwean creators and elicited the same emotional responses associated with written literature. In this vein, therefore, just as "we must see the (literary) critic (…) as the active and intelligent mediator between (his/her) consciousness and the responses of [the ZForwards'] larger audiences" (Irele, 1971, p.14) so too must we also, arguably see creators of ZForwards. Like their literary predecessors and their products, creators of ZForwards similarly offered "seemingly endless possibilities for the discrimination of values, the sharing of insights" (Irving Howe, 1956, p.37 cited in Irele, 1971, p.11) that Zimbabwe's crisis provided. The situation in Zimbabwe from 2007 to 2009 and the ZForwards it produced all bore witness to this.

At the beginning of the last year of the twentieth century, Zimbabwe was virtually a one-party state. Joshua Nkomo's Zimbabwe African People's Union (ZAPU) had after the 1987 Unity Accord become part and parcel of the ruling ZANU-PF party. The now late Edgar Tekere's political formation, the Zimbabwe Unity Movement (ZUM) had all but disappeared from the political landscape. Margaret Ndongo's fledgling ZimbabweUnion of Democrats (ZUD) was by and large in a quagmire. The ruling ZANU-PF party faced no formidable political opposition—that is until September 1999.

On 11 September 1999, the Zimbabwe Congress of Trade Unions (ZCTU) under the leadership ofits then Secretary-General Morgan Tsvangirai, together with other civil society formations, amalgamated to form a political party. Judging by media accounts, they were allegedly being bankrolled by some of Zimbabwe's white commercial farmers. The latter's association with the newly formed opposition party was seen as an ultimate betrayal of the ruling ZANU-PF party's reconciliation policy. For close to two decades, the then Mugabe-led government had let white farmers peacefully continue owning and farming the same land that had been at the center of the liberation struggle. Despite this, they were now supporting a new opposition party bent on unseating the ruling party. The policy of reconciliation and integration with the white commercial farmers had apparently failed. When therefore, in early 2000 peasants and war veterans began reclaiming the country's farmland by invading farms, they received the ruling party's explicit blessing to do so. Sometimes referred to as the fast-track Land Reform Program, the occupations were at times marked by violence against both white farmers and their black farm laborers. As the years progressed, political violence, mass migration, socioeconomic instability, and general decline followed. Between 2007 and 2009, it reached its zenith and inspired the first batch of satirical ZForwards.

On 11 March 2007, the MDC organized a prayer rally. Police violently quashed it. The bashing that ensued necessitated the hospitalization of the political party's Morgan Tsvangirai, Grace Kwinjeh, Thokozani Khupe and Lovemore Madhuku, among others. It is against this background, that to borrow Mbembe's words writing in a different context, "the task of critique (became) to bear witness to scenes of mourning, in those spaces of loss and destruction where" (Mbembe, 2012, p.23) new forms of behavior replaced lamentations of old. The events unfolding in the country provoked both the ire and the imaginations of some in the country. Such responses were, however, unconventionally not put on paper but rather digital graphics and attached to electronic mail for onward sharing and broadcasting. They were encouraged and displayed the media and correspondence of the age.

In an age of rapid advancement in digital and communication technology, "new forms of behavior" innovatively manifested themselves in graphic and digital representations and critiques of some of the country's sinister goings-on. Access to the internet and computer technology is essential to create digital images and send them as electronic mail (Email). Towards the mid-2000s, the availability of dial-up internet modems, internet cafes and, later, mobile smartphones in Zimbabwe made internet accessibility and connectivity possible for many living in the country's urban centers. As such, it can, therefore, be assumed that the creation and forwarding of ZForwards during the period was substantially attributable to white and black urbanite Zimbabweans and possibly others from without the country's borders.

Undoubtedly spurred by the sociological imagination the crisis provoked, some Zimbabweans and those interested in developments in the country resorted to digital and inventive ways of graphically critiquing, reimagining, representing, communicating and satirizing Zimbabwe's unfolding drama. Aided by editing software such as Photoshop, digitalized images caricaturing political personalities at the center of satirized events in Zimbabwe were emailed to various destinations and relations both within the country and abroad. However, because they were autonomous of the reality in the country, this often made them identifiable, comprehensive and appealing for their recipients to forward them. As such, they often were further launched into cyberspace as ZForwards where like chain messages, they exchanged inboxes among both Zimbabwean and non-Zimbabwean nationals and circulated even further. In this regard, ZForwards usually relied on their recipients for their audience and life-span.

Much like art, writing or theater, some ZForwards were aesthetically very appealing, making them the more emotive and affective. In some instances, they carried satirically, thought-provoking political commentary embedded with both implicit and explicit political statements and positions that solicited responses from those who eventually encountered them in cyberspace. An analysis of ZForwards from the period 2007 to 2009 testifies not only to an "obliquity of the relationship between (ZForwards) and politics" (Mbembe, 2001:181) but also to the intimacy between the two.

Post President Robert Mugabe's forced resignation in November 2017, debatably his status as a revered nationalist leader remains intact. In most parts of Zimbabwe, the continent and indeed the world, he continues to enjoy widespread support for his stance against colonialism and imperialism. Arguably, like Abraham Lincoln and John F. Kennedy, his presidency and legacy of educating Zimbabweans and land reappropriation or expropriation without compensation will cast a shadow over his successors and other African leaders for generations to come. However, between 2000 and 2009 his tenure as president and popularity as a leader was viewed in the most unfavorable hues and lowest ebb.

Of the several ZForwards, I received in 2007, notable was one forwarded to me in mid-March. The result of the 11 March 2007 violence and perhaps those which had gone before, it was a photoshopped poster of the perceived main antagonist in the country's growing political crisis—Robert Mugabe. Merely entitled *B.O.B*, the colloquial form for Robert, it had a photoshopped picture of a stern-looking Mugabe brandishing a huge, menacing and glistening knife, ready to strike. On his face, is a murderously cold and yet, almost sad scowl. The caption below it read: "Zimbabwean Psycho." Most probably inspired by the blockbuster *AmericanPsycho*, accompanying the picture was a chilling, tragicomic poem written mostly in English but with a mixture of Shona colloquialism.

> I am the *bhoza* (boss) of Zimbabwe.
> I am the bomb
> Born of Bona

I am Bob, the boss
My people love me
Whether they like it or know it
I am the first and best secretary
Unbeaten in eight major elections (Anonymous)

In most pieces of literary writing, "It is not the work itself which in the last resort is of value (…) but the human beings behind the writing" (Irele, 1971:22–23). It is from their lives and situations that they draw inspiration and imagination. In light of the violence that had happened in the country, and was happening at the time, the knife-brandishing Mugabe represented how many perceived the country's leader. Of course, while some such perceptions had been created and spread by the western media's references to Mugabe as a murderous tyrant and dictator, his claims that he had "degrees in violence" fueled the views.

The photoshopped image of Mugabe brandishing a butcher knife had apparently been inspired by the mindless political bloodletting in Zimbabwe since the beginning of the crisis. To express this, its creator had digitally altered the poster to the American motion picture: *AmericanPsycho*. Coincidentally, the movie was released in 2000, the same year as the unleashing of the first wave of political violence in the country. In the ZForward, the menacing knife-wielding picture of the movie's star, Christian Bale, who plays the psychotic Patrick Bateman in the film had been edited out, and that of President Mugabe photoshopped and superimposed in its place. Moreover, the movie's title had also been changed from *American Psycho* and retitled: *ZimbabweanPsycho*. Below the digitally altered picture, its anonymous creator had written an accompanying poem, supposedly composed by the persona in the poster.

For Irele, in order to be able to interpret African Literature, "The most worthy and enduring appreciation of the writer's work is that which partakes in the imaginative process in which the senses are alive to the verbal signposts which the writer has planted along the path to his profound intentions" (1971:14). However, in order to arrive at the creators' intentions necessitates going beyond a piece of literature, and seeking to understand how "each captures a moment of historical consciousness of society" (Irele, 1971:16). In my critique of the ZForwards selected and explored here, I have as much as possible, tried to partake "in the [ZForwards creators'] imaginative process" by putting them in their socio-economic and political context as well as, where possible, kept my own senses "alive to the verbal sign-posts […] planted along the path to [their] profound intentions". Given the socioeconomic and political state Zimbabwe had deteriorated into, analogous to literature, the

ZForwards I received betrayed "the feelings of the people whom it represents" (Irele, pp.22–23). The digital visual artistry and snide creativity tended to rancorously center on President Robert "Bob" Mugabe as the epicenter of the country's crisis. Inherent in such ZForwards were their creators' odious emotions and perceptions about the situation in the country and those whom they perceived as the principal antagonists in Zimbabwe's unfolding production.

Recalling that *American Psycho* is mostly about a highly educated psychotic killer's irrational, heinous and serial acts of bloodletting, the change of the film's title to *Zimbabwean Psycho* explicitly changed the context and attributed the movie's antagonist's psychotic acts to the Zimbabwean leader. By extension, the mental state of the then president of Zimbabwe was not only likened to that of the *American Psycho* antagonist, Patrick Bateman; its stability was also questioned.

Irele (1971) alerts that: "At the heart of the African frame of reference stands the very use of language" (p.19). In the BOB ZForward, the picture and poem used had been deliberately created to convey their creator's "frame of experience." The poem's title: "bhoza," its diction, as well as its photoshopped picture, gave it a distinct Zimbabwean background. The language of the poem had been deliberately chosen. It had a distinctly Zimbabwean structure and was not far removed from its frame of origin and experience. The poem's simple rhyme, code-switching from English to Shona diction, the combination of colloquialism and metaphor, "I am the bomb" also betrayed its origins, that of its creator and its intended audience.

By the end of 2007, the ZANU-PF had been in power for twenty-seven years, President Mugabe was eight-three years old and one of Africa's longest serving presidents. In addition to this, as the president and first secretary, or as the poem puts it,"the first and best secretary," of the ruling ZANU-PF party, he had led the party since the departure of Ndabaningi Sithole during the country's liberation struggle. It is, therefore, not surprising that in the poem accompanying the BOB ZForward, the persona refers to himself as: "the 'bhoza' (boss) of Zimbabwe/I am Bob, the boss" and believes himself, "the bomb," colloquially the best.

On the contrary, with the country's command economy near collapse, it was widely thought that "the boss" should retire. So, while in the poem the persona refers to himself as: "the bomb," the best, the phrase can also be metaphorically understood to mean that "the bhoza" had become the country's ticking bomb. Despite this, "[u]nbeaten in eight major elections," in March 2008, he again stood for reelection. In a way, the March 2008 harmonized Parliamentary and Presidential elections in a way sought to test the veracity of whether "My people love me."

Ironically, however, indicative of the state of fear and suspicion Zimbabwean society had become under Mugabe's rule, most probably afraid of possible reprisals, its creator had put merely put bob.co.za[2] As matters stood, rumor had it that some of those supporting opposition to the ruling party and its leadership had been "disappeared" by the Central Intelligence Organisation (CIO), the country's secret service. Consequently, none of the ZForwards' creators ever laid claim to their work. Instead, they censored themselves or assumed pseudonyms for fear of how their creations might be understood and so cause offense. Judging by the spurious website at the bottom of the picture, the anonymity that ZForwards' creators assumed made it difficult to easily identify them[3].

After almost a decade of socioeconomic decline, the 2008 harmonized elections served as a measure of the ruling party and its leaderships' popularity. Towards them, the mood in the country was such that a joke doing the rounds at the time went that even if the MDC fielded a baboon against a ZANU-PF candidate, the baboon would win. Many in the country anticipated a protest vote and therefore regime change. Held in an atmosphere of relative peace and transparency, Zimbabwe's March 2008 elections were seen by some as an ideal opportunity to usher in a new socioeconomic and political dispensation. Consequently, ZForwards exchanging inboxes towards the country's harmonized Presidential and Parliamentary elections expressed and digitally imagined a transition to a post-Mugabe era.

In a ZForward I received, that had as its reference: "Independence Day 30 March 2008", two photoshopped photographs were juxtaposed. The first one featured a surly and shabbily dressed man with the touched up face of Robert Mugabe photoshopped onto it. In the picture, "Mugabe" is pulling a cart (popularly known as a scania in Zimbabwe), apparently either at his "impending job" of a carter or moving his belongings using such a cart. In contrast, the second photograph that originally had been of President Mugabe had been digitally altered such that instead of him coming out of the presidential limousine and being saluted as head of state, it was now Morgan Tsvangirai, the leader of the opposition. In the body of the ZForward were the hopeful words: "Already enjoying Independence 30 March 2008, *Pakadii apo* (how about that)!!!"

The humor of the images aside, apparent in the ZForward was the desire among some of the country's populace for a post-Mugabe era. Also pathetically evident was that as far as they were concerned, 18 April 1980 was no longer the country's day of independence. Instead, they pathetically hoped that with the opposition's victory, 30 March 2008 would usher in a new political dispensation and a new day of independence.

However, when the Zimbabwe Electoral Commission (ZEC) took almost over a month to announce the final results of the March 2008 harmonized elections, whatever hopes some had for a new political order were deferred and depression set. This was manifested in a satirical ZForward that had as its reference: "I have just one question" on top of the digital photograph. It featured a white baby with a dejected scowl on its face whose initial demeanor and context of production was not the March 2008 aftermath. The dejected white baby was wearing what seemed the opposition's color which is mainly red. Below the image was the caption: "*Tinoluma here kana kuti dzimwe 5 years futi*" (Are we going to celebrate or is it going to be another 5 years?) The dejected baby was expressing the thoughts, dejection and fears of many at the delayed results. The fear of most was that akin to the 2000 and 2002 elections whose victory had allegedly been stolen from the opposition by nefarious means; another election victory was going to be stolen. After which the opposition would have to wait another five years before the next election.

Judging by the colloquial Shona in the caption, the ZForwards creators' language of choice depended on their target audience. In this regard, the languages that often accompanied ZForwards ranged from simple English to Shona to Zimbabwean slang and, in a few cases, Ndebele to communicate a ZForward's main message. By so doing, the artistic burden English at times imposes on "the writer who is implied by an incomplete mastery of the linguistic medium" was done away with by communicating some Zimbabweans' crisis experiences "in their very 'speech'" (Irele, p.19). The use of recognizable languages made each ZForward readily understandable, humorous and some of their accompanying utterances thought-provoking and memorable.

As the nation was still awaiting the results, I received yet another ZForward related to the wait. Attached was a photograph of the First lady, Grace Mugabe, and her husband, Robert Mugabe, both tittering and laughing almost hysterically. The photograph had been taken in a different context but was now being deployed as concerning the March 2008 delayed election results. Below it was the caption: *MaResults munoadii? Tanga watora ako kuNew Start Centre* (What do you want the results for? First go and get your (AIDS) results from the New Start Centre). Interpreted, the then First couple was asking why anyone who wanted the election results and if they did, they must first go and get their own AIDS results from the New Start Centre, the HIV AIDS testing clinic. To the creator of the ZForward, after the delayed election results, the Mugabes were having the proverbial last laugh.

Aside from satirizing the country's socioeconomic and political crisis, the creators of ZForwards also helped recipients of their ZForwards; their audiences laugh at themselves and the crisis they found themselves. Instead of being merely disappointed and dejected, they also sought to bring out the humorous side of the Zimbabwean crisis. Indeed, so crisis-weary had some citizens become they need some comic relief from the everyday drudgery of crisis. When eventually all the results were released, MDC's Tsvangirai had narrowly beaten the incumbent; neither he nor Mugabe had attained the necessary 51 percent of the vote to ascend the presidency. This necessitated a rerun or runoff of the presidential election in June 2008.

To ensure that the majority of the country's people voted for the ruling party's candidate, the ZANU-PF party embarked on a gruesome and disturbingly violent election runoff presidential campaign. The violent presidential election rerun campaign that ensued saw some Zimbabweans beaten, tortured, maimed or killed. The homes of some opposition party members were torched. Given the violence and intimidation, some Zimbabweans questioned why they should even vote. The result was a ZForward that was circulated towards the election rerun. The idea contained in this particular ZForward had been adapted from the American television program, *Cheaters* that investigates couples' infidelity. Attached to the ZForward was a digital poster that had been especially created for electronic circulation. On top of it, in bold capital red letters was the question: "WHY VOTE?" In the middle of the poster was a picture of a burning file marked: "ZANU PF Confidential" and the caption: "Cheaters: Voters prepare to be fooled."

Of all the ZForwards I received during the period, this one required the most visual literacy. As far as I could comprehend, the use of capital letters and the color red, the universal symbol of danger, indicated that the poster served as a warning. The burning confidential file seemed to be an allegation that the poster's creator had discovered that a plot was afoot to rig the June election by "A–plus cheaters"—most probably the ruling party. To some extent, it could be said the poster decried the infidelity, the betrayal of what had once been a people's party. Voters were, therefore, being warned to: "prepare to be fooled" and discouraged from voting. Inescapable was that the ZForward's creator was urging the electorate to no longer trust the country's electoral process.

When towards the rerun of the June 2008 Presidential election campaign violence escalated, Tsvangirai withdrew from the race. However, in yet another disturbing and tragicomic turn of events, ZANU-PF's candidate, Robert Mugabe, contested the election alone and against himself. As expected, he "won" the rerun by a landslide and was duly declared president. Despite this, some voters had adamantly still voted for the opposition or gone merely to vote but heartrendingly spoilt their ballot papers.

Zimbabwe's deepening political crisis and its primary antagonists were once again caricatured and satirized then shared via ZForwards that jumped from one inbox to another amongst Zimbabwe's nationals both within the country and abroad. The contents of ZForwards I received during early July reflected the disappointment some Zimbabwean felt at the state of the country's politics and its players. Thus, for instance, although infancy is associated with vulnerability and innocence, after the June 2008 rerun elections, I received a ZForward that had as its reference: "Lost Child." To it was attached a digitally altered photograph. Given the disturbing tragicomic events of June 2008, the photograph bore the then State President Mugabe's calm, almost whistling nonchalant face photoshopped onto what looked like a fiendish dwarf or child's body. On closer inspection and judging by the amulet and wristlets, it could be that its creator had intended to be a fiendish dwarf's body.

However, because of what at best can be described as the ruling party and its leader's violent temper tantrums and childish behavior during the run-up to, and after the runoff election, the ZForward's attachment was supposed to be that of a child. More so since at the bottom was the caption: "If anyone has seen this child, please call 10111 urgently, his parents are looking for him!!!" The ZForward was thus poking fun at the shenanigans of the June 2008. Due to what had transpired towards and during the June 2008 presidential election rerun, the creator of the ZForward perceived that Robert Mugabe—one of Africa's most educated statesmen had reduced himself to a troublesome "lost" child only whose parents could possibly want. So, although Mugabe was undeniably a giant of African politics, the insinuation was that he had by his evil actions virtually belittled himself into a fiendish dwarf.

Besides, by declaring himself the winner of a one-man race, it was perceived by some that President Mugabe had in June 2008 effectively refused to hand over the baton stick, the presidency of Zimbabwe to MDC's Tsvangirai and as such, despite his age had opted to continue running the whole race himself selfishly. That was aptly portrayed in the infallible humor of the creator of a ZForward I received around the same time. Entitled "Zim Relay," it had attached to it satirical cartoon caricatures of Mugabe and Tsvangirai. Visible on the face of an aged Mugabe is his exhausted but sheer determination to keep the baton stick-cum-Zimbabwe from the younger Tsvangirai's outstretched hand. The result of which is the piteous face of the MDCT's Tsvangirai. Victim of Mugabe and the ZANU-PF party would become the hallmark of Tsvangirai's political career until his death from colon cancer in early 2018.

Africa has often been criticized for its "woeful reluctance … to chastise, ostracize or help to oust villainous leaders" (Mathuthu, 2010, np). However, after the fiasco of the June 2008 Presidential rerun elections and the acceleration of Zimbabwe's decline that followed, the African Union (AU) and the Southern African Development Community (SADC) were both finally cajoled to reign in Zimbabwe's socioeconomic and political crisis. South Africa's Mbeki was tasked to facilitate and mediate talks between the ruling ZANU-PF and opposition parties of MDC-T and MDC-M.

From August 2008 till early February 2009, the views and opinions of the ZForwards I received concerned themselves with South Africa's former president Thabo Mbeki. To some, President Mbeki's facilitation and mediation reflected Zimbabweans' failure to achieve its own political transition and was sympathetically described as tantamount to the country's political leaders cunningly hurling explosives at "other Africans to detonate" (Mathuthu, 2010). Others were, however, less sympathetic. In their view, Mbeki's adoption of a *laissez-faire* approach or what he termed: "Quiet Diplomacy" towards his facilitation role was ineffective and suspicious.

Subsequently, there soon arose those both inside and outside Zimbabwe who felt former President Mbeki was not undertaking his mandate seriously. These questioned his impartiality on the basis that the African National Congress (ANC) of South Africa had historical links to ZANU (PF). Against this background, it was the view in some circles that because of their "Quiet Diplomacy" and apparent inaction, it was African leaders such as Mbeki who were "complicit in the 'genocide' and demise of Zimbabwe" (Mathuthu, 2010). As Zimbabwe's sociopolitical and economic situation worsened, this view of Mbeki as a passive mediator who was not in a hurry to resolve Zimbabwe's crisis was evident in a ZForward that I received in August 2008.

Cynically entitled "Crisis? What crisis?" the ZForward had attached to it, a touched-up photograph. It featured both the then presidents Mbeki and Mugabe with their heads thrown back laughing hysterically. In the photograph, speech bubbles had been added in which the two leaders were asking: "what crisis?" while in the background, riotous Afrophobia against Zimbabweans who had ironically fled the crisis was being perpetrated against some of them. This was an apparent reference to so–called xenophobic attacks against some African immigrants that had taken place in May 2008. In front of the armed and rampaging xenophobic attackers was the burning body of Irmao Ernesto, a victim of the May attacks. Among those killed and injured, the majority were some Zimbabweans who had immigrated to South Africa as economic or political refugees. For Mbeki and Mugabe to be questioning whether there was a crisis in Zimbabwe was by some viewed as callous and absurd.

So, while it has been said that "in discussions of the imagination, politics is usually not the first matter to arise," (Gaylard, 2005, p.181) for those creatively responding to crisis-ridden Zimbabwe, however, that was not the case. ZForwards on aspects of the Zimbabwean crisis as the ones discussed above served to demonstrate the topicality of the country's politics and how it continually occupied imaginations. That as it may be, however, it is not the country's politics alone which inspired the sociological imagination, insofar as the 2007–2009 political impasse severely impacted and mangled the already crippled economy, they are those, both in and outside the country, who sought to represent by way of ZForwards, Zimbabwe's socioeconomic crisis.

## *From Hero to Zero: Zimbabwe's Socioeconomic Crisis 2007–2009*

At Zimbabwe's independence in 1980, the Zimbabwean dollar had traded at par with, if not stronger than the British pound. However, by the end of 2007, it was no longer worth the paper on which it was printed. Neither could it continue to be traded against the world's major currencies. Chief amongst the reasons for the worthlessness of the Zimbabwe dollar was what can at best be described as the ZANU-PF government's unplanned land redistribution exercise and economic, political and international fundamentals' responses to it. The resultant disruptions to agriculture subsequently led to a reduction in foreign currency inflows from the country's agro-economy. Arguably, punitive economic sanctions from both the European (EU) and the United States (US) resulted in few lines of credit and markets for Zimbabwe's exports. The loss of hard currency and lines of credit vital to the importation of some vital inputs and spare parts necessary for industrial production ultimately culminated in the closure of many of the country's industries. Zimbabwe's production base narrowed, and the demand for manufactured goods escalated. The resultant inflationary pressures on the country's currency had by 2008 reached stratospheric levels.

The cause of this was mainly because in response to inflationary pressures in the country's economy, although unsupported by foreign currency reserves, the Reserve Bank of Zimbabwe (RBZ) resorted to printing higher denominations of the country's currency. The Zimbabwe dollar lost ground against most major currencies, and hyperinflation abounded. Hanke (2008, p.1) affirms that the RBZ was the chief cause of hyperinflation as "it financed government projects and other quasi-fiscal activities by printing money."

Thus, despite experiencing growth in the 1980s and 1990s, from the early 2000s, the country's economy found itself on a downward spiral.

By 2007, Zimbabwe's economy was hurtling towards meltdown. Some of the ZForwards I received between 2007 and 2009 on Zimbabwe's economy once again constituted what Irele (1971) writing on African literature described as, "the most original among them do so with the conscious purpose of presenting" (p.15) Zimbabweans' economic experience of the crisis. In view of the country's economic tragedy, in late 2007 I received a ZForward to which attached was the photograph of a toothy and dirty Zimbabwean boy of not more than ten years old, presumably a "street-kid" or street urchin stood in what was obviously one of the country's streets carrying a pile of money. He was dwarfed by wads of 200 000 Zimbabwe dollar notes tied into bundles with elastic. Despite his "mountain of money" and toothy smile, the boy was visibly hungry and judging by his hair and skin, somewhat malnourished. So, aside from lamenting Zimbabwe's socioeconomic situation, the ZForward revealed the country's children as amongst the crisis' most vulnerable victims[4]. Despite the boy's heap of money, the paper currency in his possession was worthless. Besides, whatever it was worth was immaterial since the country's stores and supermarkets were empty of commodities.

Due to Zimbabwe's volatile currency and lack of foreign currency manufacturers and importers of consumer goods had respectively stopped their production and importation. The closure of some manufacturing factories had resulted in most retailers running out of supplies. Others simply removed existent goods from the shelves and put them back in storage. Consequently, the shelves were bare but goods were available either in storages or on the country's black market.

As Zimbabwe's economic downturn intensified, heads of households bore the brunt. Zimbabwean households' incomes paradoxically skyrocketed and plummeted rapidly due to the country's crippling hyperinflationary environment. This is because while salaries rapidly rose, their purchasing power simultaneously fell. So while on paper Zimbabweans were figuratively "the richest people in the world"; their currency could buy little if anything at all. As such, families increasingly required much money to sustain them. The extent and impact of Zimbabwe's hyperinflationary and illiquid environment on householders was satirically expressed in a ZForward I received at the beginning of 2008. Attached to it was the self-explanatory cartoon in Figure 10.1.

The cartoon depicted what presumably was supposed to be a Zimbabwean family man crying for help from beneath the debilitating weight of country's hyperinflationary cost of living. What was heartrending was that while the bill

*Figure 10.1:* A cry for help

for his basic daily requirements totaled over a trillion Zimbabwe dollars, he could only withdraw 100 billion from the Automated Teller Machine (ATM). What the cartoon portrayed had become the daily experience of the majority of Zimbabweans during the crisis.

When ATMs could no longer dispense the trillions of Zimbabwe dollars that survival in the country's hyperinflationary environment required, the then RBZ governor, Gideon Gono, revalued the country's currency by removing the last three zeros from denominations of ten thousand and above. The revaluation was done in a bid to bring down Zimbabwe's inflation and some sanity to its monetary system as well as the lives of Zimbabweans. However, doing so was only a temporary and populist solution to a more severe economic problem. Moreover, so, as a ZForward, I received towards the 2008 harmonized elections depicting the zeros Gono had "slashed off" threatened, as they marched out from the dustbin in which they had been thrown, they would "be back in time for Christmas."

The cartoon attached to the ZForward featured then RBZ governor announcing to a packed and jubilant stadium the slashing and disposal of "the zeros." However, as had happened in the past, "the zeros" were threatening "to be back in time for Christmas." And sure enough, true to their promise they always returned with a vengeance and managed to worsen the country's already hyperinflation. Such ZForwards informed and updated those outside the country of economic developments in Zimbabwe and at the same time questioned the RBZ's recycling of failed strategies to rein in the country's inflation. To those inside the country, depressing as it was, the ZForwards helped them reflect on their experiences by satirizing tried and ineffective ways of taming a currency gone extremely wild.

By late 2008, true to "the zeros" threat that they would have returned by Christmas, they had. Their return was testified to by a ZForward that I received at the end of 2008. Titled: "Figures Zimbos will need to learn"; in it, a man held up what was supposed to be an RBZ issued bank note for "five so many trillions (Zimbabwe) dollars." At the bottom was a list of numbers ranging from one trillion (12 zeros) to one nonillion (30 zeros) which given the country's stratospheric hyperinflation, Zimbabweans or "Zimbos[5]" were being urged to learn. Implicit in the ZForward was that the country's bank notes were to surpass the trillion denomination.

The intensification of Western "smart sanctions" after the June 2008 Presidential runoff elections, low agricultural productivity and an outbreak of cholera accompanied by limited but very expensive to no stock at all in the country's retail outlets, saw Zimbabwe's socioeconomic crisis reach its zenith by the end of 2008. Most of the populace almost starved. Such was the severity of the country's food crisis that in the hope of stretching household food supplies that much further, a ZForward I received towards the beginning of 2009 and which implied that Zimbabwean men had had to assume non-traditional roles in order for their families to survive.

Culturally, the role of most Zimbabwean men has been that of breadwinner and that of women, nurturer whose responsibility includes preparing, cooking and dishing food for the family. However, implicit in the photograph was that during the 2008 crisis food had become so scarce and of such importance that Zimbabwean men had had to assume the non-traditional role of "food monitors." In a photograph sent with the ZForward, a man, presumably Zimbabwean, could be seen directing his wife what to dish for each member of the family. Embedded in the photograph was that he was doing so in as a way of avoiding wastage and thus prolonging his family's food supplies.

At the end of 2008, Zimbabwe's unemployment reportedly stood at above 80% and poverty ran very deep. In a bid to at least earn some form of income and alleviate their suffering, there had since emerged among some Zimbabweans, "a pronounced trend towards the informalization of the economy" (Sachikonye, 2005) as they turned to informal trading. This general informalization of the country's economy was caricatured in a ZForward I received in early 2009 that had yet another photograph attached.

The photoshopped photograph showed what were meant to be young Zimbabweans presumably at the country's airport, trying to sell food and fruit to travelers alighting from the country's national carrier, Air Zimbabwe. The reason they were portrayed as vending at the airport was perhaps because those coming from outside the country often brought with them much sought after foreign currency which exchanged for much more local currency on the country's thriving foreign currency black market. The result was such that as Raftopoulos points out, "as the informal economy became the dominant form of production, the ruling party created a state-based less on formal bureaucratic procedures than on the politics of coercion and the politics of patronage" (2009:231). After which Zimbabwe's already unstable socioeconomic and political environment became even more so.

In response to Zimbabwe's ever deteriorating socioeconomic situation, some of those not involved in the country's informal economy strove to migrate beyond the country's borders in search of survival and a better life. Between 2000 and 2009, an estimated three million Zimbabweans left the country. Emigrants ranged from skilled to unskilled labor, and their destinations varied from South Africa to Canada to China. The result was a large emigrant Zimbabwean population both in neighboring countries and overseas as some left the country temporarily while others did so permanently.

The goal of most Zimbabwean emigrants whatever their destination was to find some form of work and then remit foreign currency to relatives they had left back home. However, some emigrants' desperation to remit money at times led to their severe exploitation in various host countries. The desperation and exploitation of some Zimbabwean migrants living abroad was captured in a ZForward simply titled: "Diaspora" that had a photograph attached to it.

In the photograph, what looks like a staged or photoshopped photograph, an amorous white couple in an unnamed country is sitting on horseback some distance from the beach. A black man, apparently a Zimbabwean, was between the couple's two horses, literally struggling to keep his head above water. Aside from almost drowning, the man has inexplicably missing teeth and is evidently in pain. While at first glance, the photograph's humor is evident, closer examination elicits pathos. Suggested was that desperation and hardship had led some Zimbabweans living abroad to take on precariously dangerous jobs in order to sustain themselves and those back home.

Whoever the man was and whatever his story, he represented the suffering, humiliation and indignity that some Zimbabwean migrants endured and continue to endure outside the country. Hence, the ZForward's in-text declaration that: *Kana iriyo diaspora yacho ngazvigare* (If this is what it is like abroad then I am not going.)." The ZForward in the tragicomic vein of some of its predecessors sought to discourage emigration which instead of respite was for some proving worse than life back home.

Their host countries' labor laws exacerbated the desperation and exploitation of some Zimbabweans laws. In some cases, the requirement that local qualifications authorities first evaluate academic qualifications before they are recognized or the lengthy duration it took from the job interview to work permit and final appointment often meant some Zimbabwean professionals were left with few options but to work menial jobs in order to survive. Back in Zimbabwe, menial jobs done by those in the diaspora or neighboring countries such as Botswana and South Africa were known as *rese rese* (any odd job). However, this as it may, in the majority of cases, it is such jobs done out of desperation and in order to survive, which helped many emigrants earn money and save some for remittance home for the maintenance and education of relatives in Zimbabwe.

Desperation for survival was, however, not only the Zimbabwean people's, but it was also the then ZANU-PF government's. As a result of hyperinflation, an almost worthless currency and lack of creditworthiness, smart sanctions and critically depleted foreign currency reserves, the country found itself in a virtual trade embargo. Particularly affected were the country's fuel reserves. Most industries and modes of transport which required a constant fuel supply either virtually ground to a halt purchased fuel on the black-market, proactively imported fuel or joined the country's long and winding fuel queues. In major cities, queues of several kilometers long could be seen waiting for fuel deliveries which sporadically materialized, if ever.

Belief in ancestral spirits is prevalent among some Zimbabweans. This is to the extent that when misfortune strikes, such traditionalists will resort to traditional healers and even witchdoctors. Similar to some African Literature, ZForwards which I received towards the end of 2008 concerning Zimbabwe's fuel situation, therefore, "help[ed] not only in rendering a true account of (…) developments (within the country) but also of giving them meaning and relevance within the context of a contemporary African situation" (Irele, 12). Thus, in what appeared to be a sign of desperation and the toll the crisis was having on the then ZANU-PF government, it was seen turning to the ancestral spirits for succor.

At the height of Zimbabwe's fuel shortages a self-proclaimed witchdoctor/spirit medium, Nomatter Tagarira, the ZANU-PF government with claims that the ancestors had directed her to a diesel-producing rock. Since such a rock would inevitably end the country's fuel woes; some senior government officials were promptly dispatched to confirm the authenticity of Tagarira's find. On their return, the officials confirmed the existence of the witchdoctor/spirit medium's diesel-producing rock, and she reportedly was handsomely rewarded for her find.

Unfortunately, however, when time and further investigation later revealed Tagarira had duped the ZANU-PF government, the Zimbabwean public's discovery of such gullibility on the part of the then leadership was munificently shared in a ZForward that had, what by all appearances, a genuine photograph attached.

In the photograph, Tagarira the witchdoctor is dressed in traditional garb and is surrounded by some senior ZANU-PF politburo members and government officials. Identifiable in the picture are senior government officials, Sidney Sekeramayi and Didymus Mutasa, who are seen gleefully looking at the liquid gushing from a pipe that is in Tagarira's hand. To the discerning eye, Tagarira is holding the pipe like a phallus, and the expressions on the two ministers' faces are gleeful of two satiated men who are almost envious of the creamish-green liquid coming out of Tagarira's pipe. All the while, Tagarira disinterestedly wields the pipe, a symbol of her power and, unknown to the two enchanted and outwitted government ministers, her emasculation of them.

Insofar as "[o]ur appreciation of what an African writer does cannot be complete unless that African dimension is considered and consequently brought to light [and …] related to a specific cultural framework" (Irele, pp. 17–18), as required by tradition on such occasions as the one Tagarira had engineered, the ZForward's photograph also revealed both Mutasa and Sekeramayi markedly barefoot. To further add to the traditional flair, both are holding carved walking sticks. Not only was tradition being caricatured, but it was also being presented as provident to both. Tagarira was manipulating it for fraudulent gain, while the ministers and the government they represented hoped it could provide a quick and easy solution to the economic quagmire the country found itself. On another level, the photograph also bore testimony to just how desperate the country's fuel crisis had made those in power.

Post the June 2008 runoff Presidential election; the Zimbabwean crisis generally was revealed to be taking its toll on the country's political leaders. This was poignantly and effectively satirized in a ZForward which I received sometime in late July 2008 that had Figure 10.2 as one of two attachments.

*Figure 10.2:* Wrestling for Zimbabwe

The ZForward had attached two juxtaposed cartoons. The first showed the then President Mugabe and the opposition's Tsvangirai arm wrestling each other. Mugabe, who is arm wrestling while sitting on a woman representing the country Zimbabwe, suddenly asks Tsvangirai if they can take a break as his (Mugabe's) "back is killing him." The woman-cum-Zimbabwe that Mugabe is sitting on cynically acquiesces by saying, "Tell me about it."

Albeit humorous, the cartoons were aptly and creatively allegorizing what had been happening on Zimbabwe's political scene since the formation of the MDC. Indeed it could be said that since 1999, the ZANU-PF and the MDC leaders had been "arm wrestling" each other over Zimbabwe. As Figure 19 indicated, the political wrangling had caused much distress to both the wrestlers and the country as symbolized by the kneeling groaning woman, the motherland, Zimbabwe. To those who received the ZForward, inescapable was that after almost a decade of crisis, both the country's leadership and the citizenry over whom they had been playing their power games were by 2008 physically and emotionally tired of and sore from it. The country had virtually ground to a halt, and the break in the arm wrestling match was understandably required and also a reference to "the quiet diplomacy" mediated by President Mbeki of South Africa.

In an animated satirical attack on what it boldly captions as "SADC JUSTICE," the other cartoon depicted Tsvangirai standing next to Mugabe and complaining to Mbeki about how he (Tsvangirai) had "won the Lotto" (a reference to the March 2008 elections) only to have Mugabe steal the winning ticket. In response, the officious pipe smoking caricature of Mbeki advises the two that they will "have to share the winnings!!" The cartoon was unmistakably a reference to talks that the two main antagonists of Mugabe and Tsvangirai were said to be undertaking with the then President Mbeki of South Africa as the SADC mediator. The culmination of the mediation was initially the signing of a Memorandum of Understanding (MoU) and later the Global Political Agreement (GPA).

Signed at Harare's Rainbow Towers on 15 September 2008 by three political principals of Zimbabwe's March 2008 elections, namely: Robert Mugabe, Morgan Tsvangirai and the then leader of MDC-M, Arthur Mutambara, the GPA committed its signatories to the sharing of political power as a resolution to the country's political impasse. As a ZForward that I received soon after the signing of the GPA and that had attached to it what looked like a genuine photograph of the GPA's jovial signatories and a photoshopped one of an equally celebratory old man attached testified, Zimbabweans from all walks of life were elated by the GPA.

The ZForward had as its subject: "Names to consider for your next child." Attached to it is a heart-warming photograph of the then Zimbabwe's erstwhile adversaries of Robert Mugabe, Morgan Tsvangirai, and the then leader of MDC-M, Arthur Mutambara, smiling and holding hands after signing the GPA. The second was an equally beaming face and toothy grin of a man, supposedly Zimbabwean[6]. All seemed ecstatic at the signing of the GPA. Behind the man was an equally happy white woman. Explicit in the ZForward's photographs was the genuine and extreme joy the GPA had brought to all the country's stakeholders, both political and private citizens of all races. It had been a while since the country witnessed such euphoria. President Mbeki's "quiet diplomacy" had been vindicated and hope for the people of Zimbabwe restored. The acknowledgment of its success and the people's elation was also evidence of the objectivity of the ZForwards' creators.

As at times happens in Zimbabwean culture, when a child's birth coincides with an auspicious or joyous occasion, it is named or given a name related to or derived from the occasion. In this regard, the informational text of both photographs had name suggestions for future children born to the ZForward's recipients. Its comedic streak was in the humorous names it suggested its recipients give any future children they might have. To the observant eye, the names suggested had all been derived from jargon and venues synonymous with the mediation process that had led to the GPA.

The ZForward's photographs ended with the caption: "Let's celebrate, Zimbabwe has a deal now! Tea inemukaka (*tea with milk*)." Drinking tea with milk in black Zimbabwean society is seen as a sign of affluence. As such, touching was the optimism of the ZForward's closing line. Expectations were that, with the signing of the power-sharing deal, Zimbabweans would finally be able to drink "tea with milk." Because of the austerity and scarcity that the crisis had plunged the country, drinking tea with milk had become something few could enjoy, a luxury. Putting the "tea with milk" in capital letters was thus, not only an expression of the hope that with the signing of the GPA basic consumer goods would return to shop shelves, but it was also an expression that Zimbabweans' standard of living would now normalize.

However, because of the acrimonious history between the GPA's principal players, observers both within and without the country were skeptical that the Inclusive Government (IG) would survive let alone last long enough to normalize Zimbabwe's socioeconomic environment. So, when barely a few weeks after the GPA its two principal signatories were again at loggerheads and bickering over a few critical ministerial posts, onlookers' skepticism seemed credible. Despite this, however, the finale was commendably the country's IG or Government of National Unity (GNU) as it became popularly known.

Since under the GPA, the leaders of Zimbabwe's three main opposition parties had amicably agreed to share administrative power and jointly govern the country, it comprised mainly of ZANU-PF and MDC-T cabinet members, with the then President Mugabe at the helm, Joyce Mujuru and the late Joseph Msika, as his deputies. On 11 February 2009, MDC-T's leader Morgan Tsvangirai was sworn in as Prime Minister, and Arthur Mutambara, the then leader of the MDC-M faction, assumed the position of Deputy Prime Minister. A ZForward I received in early 2009 and that had a seemingly genuine photograph of the GPA's signatories entourage attached, more or less represented both the structure and feelings of the main principals of the country's GNU.

The ZForward's photograph shows an entourage headed by a radiantly smiling, visibly confident then President Mugabe accompanied by two bodyguards. However, behind the bodyguards is an unsure looking Prime Minister Tsvangirai and directly behind him, Deputy Prime Minister Mutambara wearing what looks like a self-satisfied smile. By all appearances, then President Mugabe was more than happy to have retained power with the MDC-T's support. Then Prime Minister Tsvangirai was unsure if he and his party had the right decision, while Deputy Prime Minister Mutambara was more than satisfied with the personal political gains his short stint in Zimbabwean politics had yielded. As the photograph pointedly suggested, the country's GNU was united and on the move. Or was it?

A ZForward I received at around the same time as the one above and that had a cartoon attached suggested that behind the scenes, Zimbabwean politics was not as united and its actors as happy-go as they appeared. The ZForward that was titled: "By the balls" had attached to it a cartoon of then President Mugabe sourly shaking hands with then Prime Minister Tsvangirai whose face is visibly in pain. This is because unknown to onlookers, crouching behind the then president is one of the country's police service chiefs with his left hand running between the then president's legs and squeezing the Prime Minister's private parts. After which the Prime Ministeris gritting his teeth, visibly in much pain. The cartoon seemed to be suggestively representing the reality of Zimbabwe's political dispensation. However, there was more to it than which met the eye. Implicit was that there were senior members of the service forces manipulating events and possibly the political players within the GNU.

That as it may have been, however, on the socioeconomic front, the dawn of the GNU mercifully saw the materialization of Zimbabweans' hopes for a better standard of living. This was primarily achieved through the new unity government's introduction of a multicurrency system to replace the Zimbabwe dollar as local tender. At the beginning, depending on a Zimbabwean province's proximity to the borders of a neighboring country, some Zimbabweans were using different currencies from the rest of the country. A ZForward that I received in 2009 had a map of Zimbabwe informatively attested.

Titled: "Zimbabwe Monetary Areas," the ZForward had attached the country's map demarcated along its tribal regions as identified by their inhabitants' colloquial names. The regions had been color-coded and a key provided as to which foreign currencies were accepted in each. In a country that had gradually become one of unreliable or restricted media coverage, the ZForward was most informative about Zimbabwe's new multi-currency system and which currency was being accepted where. Judging from the map, the United States dollar and South African rand seemed to have become the country's main "new currency." Other than the humorous use of inhabitants' nicknames to denote the country's provinces notable was the absence of previous ZForwards' stinging satire. By all appearances, Zimbabwe's new multi-currency system had the approval of the country's satirists.

From mid-2009 onwards, indicative that Zimbabwe's crisis was abating, ZForwards not only lost their satire and humor, they also gradually became fewer. Instead, they became less critical and more informative about socioeconomic developments in the country. This was reflected in one of the last ZForwards on the situation in Zimbabwe that I received mid-2009. Attached to it were what looked like genuine photographs of what was then happening in the country's retail sector.

At the height of the crisis, Zimbabwe had become synonymous with hyperinflation and food shortages. In this regard, the first photograph that featured a bare supermarket and its equally empty refrigerators served to remind recipients how previously, when the country had used its own currency store shelves and fridges had run and remained empty. To this effect, the empty fridges had nothing in them except a sign written "Local Currency." However, post the GNU, after the introduction of a multi-currency system, the second photograph affirmed that the result had been improvements in the availability of food. Consequently, the second photograph showed fridges full of consumer goods available for sale, albeit in foreign currency. As such, a sign written "US Dollar Products" hung over the refrigerators which had consumer goods in them. By the end of 2009, Zimbabwe's once infamous inflation had more than exponentially lowered and the country well on its way to normalcy. Evidently, with the introduction of a multi-currency system, the country's food shortages which had for so long captured the imaginations, social commentary and been represented in so many ZForwards as sociological imagination was finally over. At the back of many people's minds, however, was the question of how long the socioeconomic stability brought by Zimbabwe's multi-currency system would last. It would last more or less past 2017.

## *Conclusion*

From 2007 to 2009, the rapid development and rise in the popularity of electronic mail, digital technology and media within the context of Zimbabwe's socioeconomic and political crisis gave impetus to new forms of sociological imagination that were shared as ZForwards. Rich in creativity and reflective of the country's experience of crisis, ZForwards captured some significant moments of Zimbabweans' lives. This is such that akin to most postcolonial literary, sociological imagination, some of these ZForwards enabled the "mutual imbrication of the imagination and the political" (Gaylard, 2005:182) to give a sociohistorical perspective, analysis, understanding and explanation to what was happening in the country. In most cases, the result of this was running satirical commentary and humor in the context of crisis. Subsequently, ZForwards served to not only reflect some Zimbabweans' sentiments about the goings-on in their country; they also brought out the comic in the tragic, helped their recipients empathize, stay informed and arguably alleviated their pain. Recipients of ZForwards were thus left both weeping and laughing at the country's state of tragicomedy. However, for ZForwards to be able to do so they called for some visual literacy and knowledge of what was happening in Zimbabwe. As the crisis fermented ZForwards, when from 2009 the socioeconomic crisis began abating, so too did the sociological imagination that had been so pivotal to their emergence. The number of ZForwards equally dwindled and then ceased.

## Notes

1. Affiliation: Department of Culture, Communication & Media, University College London, Email: corwin.mhlahlo.16@ucl.ac.uk & Comecinc Communications and Strategic Solutions Services Incorporated, Email: tenderinfo@comecincs.com
2. As the source. This could have been done to throw off those who might have wanted to trace the poster's origins.
3. This had made tracing and obtaining copyright permission from ZForwards' creators most difficult.
4. Many children reportedly dropped out of school to become, among others, informal traders or alluvial gold-panners.
5. Short form for Zimbabweans, while the country's currency was referred to as the "Zimdollar."
6. Although the Portuguese wording in the background, however, indicated the photograph had its origins possibly in Mozambique and not Zimbabwe.

## References

Gaylard, G. (2005). *After colonialism: African postmodernism and magical realism.* Johannesburg: Wits University Press.

Hall, S. (1996). Who needs identity? In S. Hall & P. Du Gay (Eds.), *Questions of cultural identity* (pp. 1–17). London, Thousand Oaks & New Delhi: Sage.

Hall, S., & Du Gay, P. (Eds.). (1996). *Questions of cultural identity.* London, Thousand Oaks & New Delhi: Sage.

Hanke, S. H. (2008). *Zimbabwe: Hyperinflation to growth.* Harare, Zimbabwe: New Zanj Publishing House.

Heywood, C. (1971). *Perspectives on African literature: Selections from the proceedings of the conference on African literature held at the University of Ife 1968.* London: Heinemann.

Irele, A. (1971). The criticism of modern African literature. In C. Heywood (Ed.), *Perspectives of African literature:Selections from the proceedings of the conference on African literature held at the University of Ife 1968* (pp. 9–24). London: Heinemann.

Kaarsholm, P. (2005). Coming to terms with violence: Literature and the development of a public sphere in Zimbabwe. In R. Muponde & R. Primorac (Eds.), *Versions of Zimbabwe: New approaches to literature and culture* (pp. 3–23). Harare: Weaver Press.

Mamdani, M. (2008). Lessons of Zimbabwe. *London Review of Books*, *30*, 23, December.
Mathuthu, M. (2010). The real villains in Zimbabwe crisis (April12, 2010). NewZimbabwe.com.
Mbembe, A. (2001). *On the postcolony*. Berkeley: University of California Press.
Mbembe, A. (2012). Metamorphic thought: The *works* of Frantz Fanon. *African Studies*, *71*(1), 19–28, DOI: 10.1080/00020184.2012.668291.
Muponde, R., & Primorac, R. (Eds.). (2005). *Versions of Zimbabwe: New approaches to literature and culture*. Harare: Weaver Press.
Raftopoulos, B. (2009). The crisis in Zimbabwe 1998–2008. In B. Raftopoulos & A. Mlambo (Eds.), *Becoming Zimbabwe: A history from the pre-colonial period to 2008*. (pp. 201–232). Harare: Weaver Press.
Sachikonye, L. (2005). *Political parties and the democratization process in Zimbabwe: EISA research report1*. Johannesburg: EISA

# 11 From Grace to Disgrace: The Paradoxical Role of Women, Africanization, Age and African Modernity in the Rise and Demise of R. G. Mugabe

C. LUTHULI MHLAHLO[1]

On 17 November 2017, over thirty-seven years since becoming Zimbabwe's first democratically elected ruler, Robert Gabriel Mugabe submitted his long-awaited resignation as president. For many within the country and indeed around the world, Mugabe's resignation marked the end of an administrative era that at its advent had once held so much promise. Now, most Zimbabweans, especially urbanites and those whom Mugabe's rule had driven out of the country, diasporans of all races, could hardly wait to see his departure from office. What had made such a once revered statesman become so reviled? To the spectator world and some within the country, the reason primarily lay in Mugabe's socioeconomic and political policies and their controversial legacy. To others like me who for years had followed Mugabe's rule, the people's ire went far beyond. It also lay in the paradoxical role that women, Africanization, age and African modernity had played throughout his life.

## The Formative Years: Mbuya Bona and Amai Sally Mugabe

Having both a mother and father is vital to a child's formative years. For young Robert Mugabe, mother was Bona Mugabe, "a formidable woman imbued with a Christianity that mixed intensity with piety" (Smith & Simpson, 1981, p.11). In 1934, when young Mugabe was ten years old, his father left "his family for a jobbing carpenter's position in Bulawayo, and then the mines in South Africa. He did not return" (Smith & Simpson, 1981, p.11). It was left to the mother of four to raise her children on her own.

Bona's "only income came from teaching the village girls their catechism" (Smith & Simpson, 1981, p.14). Under her care, young Mugabe grew into what the priest Father O'Hea of Kutama Mission[2] would in 1970 describe as " 'an exceptional mind and an exceptional heart' " (Smith & Simpson, 1981, p.11). Years later, the priest would also recall Mugabe's "hunger to learn in class (and) his devotion to his mother, with whom he always came to church" (Smith & Simpson, 1981, p.13). It is perhaps because of this attachment to his mother, that young Mugabe was "taunted by many of the other children, who regarded him as a coward and a mother's boy" (Holland, 2008, pp.6–7).

Such was Bona's faith in God and young Robert that, despite the family's meager resources, "when Father O'Hea told her just how much he wanted Robert to go ahead and train as a teacher, Bona agreed immediately. Whatever the cost to the family, Robert would go" (Smith & Simpson, 1981, p.14). And go he did. "Before long he was teaching his classmates how to teach" (Smith & Simpson, 1981, p.14). In 1945, aged 21, Mugabe graduated with a teaching diploma and "left Kutama—a serious young man, something of a loner, diligent, hard-working, a voracious reader who used every minute if his time, not much given to laughter: but, above all, single-minded" (Smith & Simpson, 1981, pp.15–16). The world lay before him.

Armed with what Bona and Kutama Mission had taught him, Mugabe ventured forth. Teaching stints at Dadaya Mission among others and eventually a scholarship to South Africa's Fort Hare University to study for a Bachelor of Arts followed. In 1955, Mugabe found himself first in Zambia "to teach and study, this time for his third degree" (Smith & Simpson, 1981, pp.20–21). Then in the autumn of 1957, he moved to Ghana: "Kwame Nkrumah, the leader of the country's nationalists and shortly to be the first president, was inviting literate Africans from other countries to work, study and teach in his country" (Smith & Simpson, 1981, p.21). It was while in Ghana that Mugabe met Sally Heyfron, his future wife.

The adage goes that: "Behind every successful man is a woman." According to Smith and Simpson (1981) while in Ghana that Mugabe burnt himself and was admitted into hospital. It was then that Sally, whose family "went out of their way to entertain and take care of the Africans Nkrumah had invited to teach in Ghana (…) visited him regularly" (p.22). Described as strong and unselfish, Sally had "a toughness and serenity which is rare and which (…) Mugabe recognized that he needed." Over the years, it would be she who "honed his political instincts into the politician Mugabe" (Smith & Simpson, 1981, p.22) he was in the early 1960s and 1980s.

When asked how the Mugabes felt about each other, Sally said: "that she loves him for his kindness and his integrity as a man" (Smith & Simpson, 1981, p.22). While Mugabe coyly would say, "I married a Ghanaian because Ghanaian women don't leave men to do all the work" (Smith & Simpson, 1981, p.22). The couple was married in Harare on 21 February 1961. Sally's positive influence on Mugabe as his helpmeet would over the years be obvious. Several times, "She, like him, was to be imprisoned for her political activities" (Smith & Simpson, 1981, p.39).

After the death of their son Nhamodzenyika "from encephalitis—cerebral malaria—at the home of Sally's parents in Ghana" (Smith & Simpson, 1981, p.58), Sally returned to the then Salisbury (present-day Harare) to be close to her husband who was then in prison. After that, with the help of the Ariel Foundation, she received a scholarship to study Home Economics "concentrating on diet and nutrition: areas of neglect in Rhodesia's colonial society" (Smith & Simpson, 1981, p.59). Although Zimbabwe's independence was not yet in sight, Sally was already preparing herself for a constructive role to the people of her adopted country.

During her time in London, Sally also used the opportunity to attend many receptions "where she met British members of parliament, whom she lobbied fervently (…) for Mugabe's release and the future of her adopted country" (Smith & Simpson, 1981, p.59–60). When Sally was not studying or lobbying, her time was poignantly "spent in London libraries summarizing, and sometimes copying out in full, books for Mugabe's studies in jail" (Smith & Simpson, 1981, 60) then sending them as letters.[3] Elizabeth Walston, the wife of a Labor peer in the House of Lords, remembers how Sally " 'wrote out Robert's law books by hand (…) line by line. All the time she was so terribly concerned about Robert in detention" (Smith & Simpson, 1981, p.61). Although physically apart for the greater part of their marriage, when in 1975 the couple was eventually reunited in Mozambique, Sally quickly set about turning their Portuguese-style villa into a home (Smith & Simpson, 1981, p.88). Sally was however to prove more than just a homemaker.

After the mid-1970s, Mugabe's leadership of the Zimbabwe African National Union (ZANU) in Mozambique faced opposition from some within the party. These included, among others, Rex Nhongo and Dzinashe Machingura whose influence over the freedom fighters was strong (Smith & Simpson, 1981, p.99). To consolidate her husband's position, Sally "traveled to the guerrilla and refugee camps in northern Mozambique and Tanzania, spending days listening to the problems they had" (Smith & Simpson, 1981, p.99) such as those of food shortages, clothing and medicine. In response, she was soon visiting "the Scandinavian countries regularly, especially Sweden, giving emotional and moving accounts of the refugees' plight based on her own first–hand experience" (Smith & Simpson, 1981, p.99). It was not long before she "proved to be an accomplished fund–raiser as well as an articulate advocate of the Zanu cause" (Smith & Simpson, 1981, p.99). Aside from doing it all for the refugees and the freedom fighters, Sally was doing it to elevate her husband's name.

During the war for Zimbabwe's liberation, Mugabe and the country's struggle was also Sally's. In a letter to Lady Walston, she wrote: "Regarding our struggle, we are still at it (…) This year we congratulate ourselves for many achievements, but we continue to be cautious and guard against complacency" (Smith & Simpson, 1981, p.115). Albeit of Ghanaian descendant, Sally had adopted her husband's country and country folk. As such, their enemies and that of her husband were her enemies too. Post-Zimbabwe's independence, Sally's close relationship with the country and its people would endear her to them. However, before this could happen, support for Mugabe and Zimbabwe's liberation effort arose from one other woman neither he nor the world would have fathomed.

On 3 May 1979, Margaret Thatcher was elected as British Prime in the Conservatives' landslide election victory. It was widely anticipated that she would support the Ian Smith and Bishop Abel Muzorewa regime that had recently won Zimbabwe's first but largely boycotted election for an internal settlement. Nonetheless, at the Commonwealth conference in August 1979, Prime Minister Thatcher astonished the world and indeed the nationalists fighting for Zimbabwe's liberation when she announced that her "government was prepared to decolonize Rhodesia and bring it to independence just like they had Kenya and Tanganyika[4]. She knew Britain's responsibilities, and she was determined to fulfill them" (Smith & Simpson, 1981, p.119).

On the ground though, the tide of the country's civil war had also changed. The freedom fighters were in control of most of the countryside and winning against the Rhodesian forces. All that now remained was to take it closer to the urban areas. Despite this however, in response to Thatcher's pro-black-majority rule in Rhodesia Commonwealth speech, representatives from "Tanzania, Zambia, Nigeria, Jamaica, Australia—sat down with Mrs Thatcher and Lord Carrington, her foreign–secretary to hammer out the details (…) step by step, they built a working agreement for an all-party conference" (Smith & Simpson, 1981, p.120) at Lancaster House, in London.

In September 1979, the Mugabes and some central committee members of both ZANLA and ZAPU forces arrived in London for what is now known as the Lancaster House Conference—interparty talks with Rhodesia's internal settlement government of Ian Smith and Bishop Abel Muzorewa. It would take until 18 October 1979 before all the parties concerned agreed to the British-brokered Lancaster House Constitution. Among its concessions, whites were "guaranteed 20 percent of the seats in the new parliament. Also, on land, the Constitution protected property rights to the degree that made Zanu's longtime promise to redistribute the white farmlands to the people look hollow, if not downright false" (Smith & Simpson, 1981, p.127). What now remained was an accord on the transition period to democracy and the ceasefire terms.

Regarding the transitional period leading to elections and ceasefire, it was proposed that Abel Muzorewa would relinquish power to a British governor who "would keep law and order during the campaign through the existing Rhodesian police force" (Smith & Simpson, 1981, p.129). Mugabe would however not acquiescence to such a transitional arrangement. Instead, he wanted either a United Nations (U.N.) or Commonwealth peacekeeping force of several thousand present during the transitional period and legal recognition of the Patriotic Front's armies. Furthermore, he wanted Lord Peter Carrington, the Conference's chairperson to guarantee that there would be no external involvement in Rhodesia, mainly from South Africa, once a ceasefire and British governor were in place. After much ado about operational bases and assembly points, the Lancaster House Agreement was finally signed on 21 December 1979 paving the way for the formation and recognition of a Republic of Zimbabwe.

On 27 January 1980, Robert and Sally Mugabe returned to the then Salisbury and set about campaigning for the Zimbabwe African National Union (Patriotic Front) ZANU (PF) in preparation for the country's first democratic general elections.

When the results of Zimbabwe's first democratic elections were announced on 4 March 1980, ZANU (PF) had won a landslide victory. Sally officially became the wife of Zimbabwe's new Prime Minister. Her support for Mugabe when necessary and her political skill had contributed to the victory.

Post-independence, *Amai*[5] (Mother) Sally Mugabe as Sally reverently and affectionately became known for years tirelessly worked or lent her name to various charities, orphanages, and nursing homes. Most memorably, in 1983 she established the Zimbabwe Child Survival and Development Foundation to cater for orphaned and vulnerable children. She did not, however, confine her humanitarian work to Zimbabwe alone. Abroad, she was involved and supported the then London-based *AkinaMamawaAfrika* (Swahili for African Women)—a small community organization that has since grown into a Pan-African non-governmental organization that is headquartered in Kampala Uganda and focuses on development and women's issues in both Africa and the UK. In 1986, she launched the Zimbabwe Women's Cooperative in the UK. Sally's charitable works earned her approval both at home and abroad. As for Mugabe himself, albeit once labeled a bloodthirsty terrorist or "terr" of Rhodesia's bush war, he too set about endearing himself to both the local and international community.

## *Mugabe's Age and African Modernity: Embellished in Shona Tradition*

At the end of Zimbabwe's war of liberation, Mugabe was 55 years old—relatively young then in comparison with his compatriots both on and off the continent. Already reputed for being "intellectually and academically a man of strong moral fiber and a disciplined sense of purpose" (Smith & Simpson, 1981, 68), his leader identity[6] then, his age and academic stature identified him a kind of African modernist.

African "modernity" assumes lenses and thought-lines along both modern and postmodernist perspectives in a modernizing African context. It is a perspective that for many spatially has its roots in an urbanizing African environment. Thus to James Ferguson for instance, "an urbanizing Africa was a modernizing one" (Ferguson, 1999, p.5). Geschiere (1997, p.213) sees African modernity as emerging from a linear unfolding of "urbanization and the emergence of new inequalities (accompanied by) an increase in the scale of human relations" (in Ferguson, 1999, p.281). To Cooper, "The liberal affirmation that the African was becoming an urbanite was an affirmation of modernity" (Cooper, 1983, p.12 in Ferguson, 1999, p.5). To Geschiere (1997) Copper (1983) and Ferguson (1999) therefore, urbanization is "a teleological process, a movement toward a known point that would be nothing less than Western-style industrial modernity" (Ferguson, 1999, p.24) for both the African and his context.

While this chapter to some extent assimilates a few of the ideas spelt out above about African "modernity," for it, the idea has its origins beyond just urbanization and is not necessarily tied to westernization. That is since I am of the view that African "modernity" in the context of post-independence Zimbabwe, like that of Zambia, was not only "guaranteed by its urban industrial core" (Ferguson, 1999, p.38) but also its citizens' uptake of education and the consequences thereof. In this respect, to me, African modernity also hinges on the education received leading to the adoption of a unique African style of modernizing without necessarily westernizing.

During his years in exile, Mugabe had learned from the late President Machel of Mozambique that armed struggle was about defeating colonialism, rather than the whites. In its 1980 Election Manifesto, therefore, ZANU (PF) had declared that: "Zimbabwe cannot just be a country of blacks. It is and should remain our country all of us together. Let us thus work together and build a nation, united and strong" (Smith & Simpson, 1981, p.169). Mugabe and his party were seemingly moving with the times. After all: "The Rhodesian whites, whatever their failings, had much to offer the new Zimbabwe in (terms of) building the economy after independence" (Smith & Simpson, 1981, p.168). So, post-1980, when some of Mugabe's Central Committee Marxist hardliners had pushed for "large–scale nationalization, the immediate transfer of land from the whites to the Africans, even the breaking of ties with South Africa" (Smith & Simpson, 1981, p.167). Mugabe had decided to follow Machel's advice and embarked on a reconciliatory path, a "politics of pragmatism" (Smith & Simpson, 1981, p.167). It was one that would realistically, rather than ideologically, ensure the continued socioeconomic stability of the young nation. The economic future of Zimbabwe somewhat secured, Mugabe turned to another pillar of the country's survival—education.

Zimbabwe's new prime minister had once been described as a man "of that African rarity, of both intellect and principle" (Smith & Simpson, 1981, p.113). He held a reputed seven academic degrees, and many honorary doctoral degrees would follow. Yet, despite this, he was unbelievably articulate and fluent in both Shona and English. To the young and not so old, there was a leader who could academically inspire them to emulate both his academic prowess and form of African modernity. Spurred on by Mugabe's own love for Western education and first-hand experience in Mozambique of what an uneducated and professionally bereft black population could spell for a postcolonial economy[7], the growth of African modernity in Zimbabwe was enabled by the new black government's building of schools in the previously disadvantaged rural and most black high-density areas of Zimbabwe.

Though in Zimbabwe the former white Rhodesian government had not deprived the country's black population of education and training as much as in neighboring Mozambique, it had not been too liberal about providing it either. Consequently, although churches and missionaries in the country had over the years tried as best as they could to compliment the former government's provision of education and training, when Mugabe's first government came to power, they found "a system of education that was racially biased and unequal in both governance and quality" (Shizha & Kariwo, 2011, p.2). Not to mention quantity.

To ameliorate the new state's disparate education levels among its citizens, in 1980 the new prime minister declared education a fundamental human right and had this enshrined in the country's constitution. Primary and secondary education was made free and compulsory for every Zimbabwean child of school-going age. Primary schools increased from "2,401 in 1979 to 4,530 in 1990. Secondary schools increased from 177 to 1,512 in 1990" (Ndlovu, 2013, p.3). Edwards and Tisdell (1990) report that between 1979 and 1984 "primary education saw the greatest increase in enrolments and secondary education the greatest proportional increase" (p.307). The newly set up Ministry of Education and Culture set about introducing reforms aimed at providing "a more scientific and technical bias to curricula, particularly within secondary schools" (p.298). In 1987, the Education Secretary's Policy Circular No. 12 declared that "the minimum expected educational outcome for all students is functional literacy and numeracy by the end of primary school." (Mutepfa et al. 2007, p.343). Zimbabweans were to all acquire as sound education as possible.

To complement the changes in curricula and exponential increase in enrolment and the number of schools, enrolment in teacher training colleges "increased by 2,4 times over the period, while enrolments in tertiary education went up by 2,8 times and 2,9 times in vocational education" (Edwards & Tisdell, 1990, p.307). Due to the Mugabe governments' post-independence efforts in developing both educational infrastructure and Zimbabwe's education system, Zimbabweans are today amongst the most literate in Africa and most educated people in the world.

Since the arrival of such missionaries as John and Robert Moffat and their London Missionary Society that paved the way for white settlement of parts of modern-Zimbabwe, blacks in the country had been discouraged from following the traditions and customs of their forefathers. By the 1960s therefore, generations of black "Africans had been taught to scoff at traditional religion, dancing, food, dress, customs, even names" (Smith & Simpson, 1981, p.37). At Kutama Mission close to Mugabe's traditional home area of Zvimba, the founder of the mission, Father Loubiere, and his black assistant, Joseph Dambaza,had ensured that: "There was little room for African customs, let alone tribal religion" (Smith & Simpson, 1981, p.10). Despite this, however, once at home from school, young Mugabe "had a traditional, active African upbringing" (Smith & Simpson, 1981, p.11). It is perhaps because of this that some 40 years later, Mugabe as both prime minister and later president of Zimbabwe respectively would be able to juggle both modernity and tradition. For now, however, the young Mugabe sought to restore African identity and traditions through an Africanization program.

The Merriam-Webster dictionary defines to Africanize as firstly "to cause to acquire a distinctly African trait" and secondly as "to bring under the influence, control or cultural or civil supremacy of Africans, especially black Africans" (Merriam-Webster, n.p). This chapter subscribes to both these definitions of the word. However, it also understands it to mean that while African "modernity" is largely about the urbanized educated African's bid to align his/her identity with the urbanizing globalizing milieu, Africanization is, among others, the imposition of one's African identity and values on an African context so that it is representative of not only one's African identity but also that of its majority African inhabitants.In 2008, the then President Mugabe would define his increasingly radical brand of Africanization thus: "independence means power has come to the indigenous people of the country. In every area, we should show that we can exercise that power" (CEN, np).

On becoming the National Democratic Party (NDP) publicity secretary in October 1960, Mugabe having witnessed his tribe's "African way of life so effectively wiped out at the mission (…) appealed to their (black people's) emotions and their spiritual and cultural values. He encouraged them, through party publicity, to value their heritage" (Smith & Simpson, 1981, pp.10, 37). Thus "drawing on his experience from Nkrumah's youth league, Mugabe began organizing the NDP Youth Wing (…) to search for what he called 'cultural roots'" (Smith & Simpson, 1981, p.37). The late Dr. Nathan Shamuyarira[8] recalls how during Mugabe's tenure as the NDP's publicity secretary, "Thudding drums, ululation by women dressed in national costumes and ancestral prayers began to feature at meetings more prominently than before" (Smith & Simpson, 1981, p.38). At the nationalist party's meetings, "Youth Leaguers ordered attendants to remove their shoes, ties, and jackets as one of the first signs in rejecting European civilization. Water served in traditional water–pots replaced Coca-Cola kiosks" (Smith & Simpson, 1981, p.38). In later years, Mugabe as prime minister of independent Zimbabwe would "insist on the 'Africanisation' of his people" (Smith & Simpson, 1981, pp.10). In this Mugabe had a close ally—*Amai* Sally Mugabe.

From the time Mugabe became prime minister to the time of her death in 1992, rarely was *Amai* Sally Mugabe ever seen in public not wearing African attire. Her simple African attire often comprised an ankle length sarong of African print, a blouse and a *dhuku/doek* (headgear) of the same material. Despite their simplicity, she wore these with pride and dignity. As for the then Prime Minister and later President Mugabe, in African modernist fashion, he alternated between safari suits and formal western two- and three-piece suits. Only when on the campaign trail or attending his party's political rallies would Mugabe be seen in African attire bearing the ZANU (PF) insignia of a cockerel and a picture of himself.

Before independence, black African schools had primarily taught in Shona and rarely in English. Post-independence, a formal language policy was instituted whereby rural and urban high-density primary schools would teach their charges in "their native local language, typically in Shona or Ndebele and then transition to English by Grade 3." That was not only done to ensure that pupils effectively grasped foundational concepts delivered in their mothertongues; it also promoted and edified the importance of local languages. Shona, Ndebele, and English were declared Zimbabwe's national languages. To ensure that pupils took local languages as seriously as other subjects, "At the end of Grade 7, students take a national examination in Mathematics, English, Shona or Ndebele and General Paper" (Kanyongo, 2005, p.65).

For his part, Mugabe's fluency in Shona[9] enabled him to promote the importance of indigenous languages. So, when speaking to a largely Shona crowd, he always ensured he spoke in a language he knew and felt they could best understand—Shona. To those who ever met him, "his deep and genuine pride in Shona culture and customs was evident, and, thought, was to his credit" (Roberts, 2017, np). His reverence of the legendary Mbuya Nehanda and for traditional chiefs as custodians of Zimbabwe's customs and traditions is wellknown. However, whether his respect of both was genuine or a means of ingratiating himself with the traditional leaders of his mainly rural electorates is debatable. Whatever the reason, it won Mugabe favor with traditional leaders and in turn, their rural subjects.

On coming to power, Mugabe had set about Africanizing Zimbabwe's then mostly white-controlled civil service. Perhaps conscious that Africanization should uphold "the pursuit of excellence with a clear sensitivity to locatedness, relevance and impact" (Maluleke 2013:97) white civil servants from the old Rhodesian order who voluntarily resigned or retired were replaced with qualified black Zimbabweans. In this way,Mugabe was able to please educated black urbanites and responsibly Africanize Zimbabwe's civil service. As the years passed, however, Mugabe's Africanization program would no longer confine itself only to dress, language, education, and the civil service. Nor would it and he always please everyone, both within and without Zimbabwe.

*The demise—Grace Mugabe* Towards the end of the 1980s, *Amai* Sally Mugabe was diagnosed with kidney failure. Years of hemodialysis and eventual hospitalization followed. She finally succumbed to the illness on 27 January 1992, exactly 12 years after her return from exile. As recognition of her contribution to the founding of Zimbabwe, *Amai* Sally Mugabe was buried at the country's National Heroes Acre.

Mugabe's loss of two children in infancy had strengthened his "enormous affection for children and the delight he takes in being with them is apparent to this day" (Smith & Simpson, 1981, p.48). It was therefore not surprising when in April 1995, the monthly magazine Horizon "after interviewing Grace's father and other family members, reported that Mugabe had fathered two children (with Grace Marufu, a secretary in the Office of the President) and subsequently married (her) in a traditional African ceremony paying the customary *lobola*, or bride price" (Meredith, 2009). In May of the same year, the weekly Financial Gazette, acting on information provided by, "powerful political figures in the ruling party who feared that the emergence of a Mugabe dynasty might one day eclipse their chances of preferment" (Wetherall, 1995) further claimed that "Mugabe had in fact already married Grace (…) at a wedding ceremony witnessed by a High Court judge and a cabinet minister" (Meredith, 2009). What surprised most, however, was that Mugabe had married, but rather that the eldest of the two children, a daughter, poignantly named Bona Mugabe, was already aged 7 and her brother Robert Peter Jnr 5. The two children had undoubtedly been conceived and born sometime before the death of *Amai* Sally Mugabe.

In Shona tradition, when an aging or elderly wife can no longer undertake her wifely duties or bear children, her elderly husband can request or merely be given a "substitute wife" from his wife's family. That is especially so if he has a good relationship with his in-laws, has paid all the *roora* (bride price) for, and has been living well with his first wife. Such a substitute wife or young girl given to a man in his old age by his wife's relatives is called a *bondwe/chitsaramvi* (Gombe, 1986, p.43, Chigidi, 2009:180). As with his first wife, the elderly man is expected to pay a reasonable bride price for the much younger substitute wife. According to Gombe (1986) customarily, a young woman given to such an elderly man would be expected to pluck the old man's gray hairs out of embarrassment that she is married to a graying old man. In other words, she is expected to uphold her and the old man's public standing and image.

Depending on the part of the country, Gomwe (1986) explains that the substitute wife could also be considered a *chigadzamapfiwa/chimutsamapfihwa* (substitute wife). However, the circumstances surrounding such a substitute wife tend to differ. In the latter case, the young woman or girl is given where the man's wife is deceased or has failed to bear him children. Both customs are today rarely practiced as postmodernist Zimbabwean society severely frowns upon what they perceive to be an outdated, unfair, and criminal treatment of the girlchild.

Despite most Zimbabwean urbanites unfavorable sentiments towards the customary practices of *bondwe/ chitsaramvi* and *chigadzamapfiwa/chimutsamapfihwa* however, in what can be seen as an attempt to portray Grace as a kind of *bondwe/ chitsaramvi*, Mugabe on a few occasions in both the 1990s and 2000s publicly put it on public record that Sally had before her death consented to his relationship with Marufu and having children out of wedlock with her. Speaking in 2013 to Dali Tambo, presenter of the South African Broadcasting Corporation (SABC) television program People of the South, Mugabe claimed that he had revealed his affair with Grace to Sally who "accepted the new relationship before she died of kidney failure in 1992" (Nehanda Radio.com). According to Mugabe, towards Sally's last few days, "although it might have appeared to some as cruel, I said to myself well, it's not just myself needing children, my mother has all the time said, ah, am I going to die without seeing grandchildren?" And "so it was. We got our first child when my mother was still alive" (Nehanda Radio.com). To the enquiring mind, why had it taken him until Sally's last few days to inform her of the relationship? By all appearances, Mugabe seemed to be laying blame for his infidelity on the two women who perhaps loved him the most—*Mbuya* Bona and *Amai* Sally Mugabe

Besides this, from a Shona traditional perspective, however, Marufu could not have been described as a *bondwe/ chitsaramvi*. That is because although Grace Mugabe is 41 years Mugabe's junior, she is not even remotely related to Sally in any way or form. As such, in postmodern-day Zimbabwean culture, she would at best be crudely described as Mugabe's "small-house" rather than a *bondwe/ chitsaramvi*. A "small-house" is the term given to a kept woman with whom a married man secretly has a second family. More often than not, this occurs without the consent or knowledge of his wife or immediate family. Such a small-house at times begins when the married man in question is the much younger woman's "sugar-daddy" or material provider. In such cases, the sugar-daddy provides materially for the much younger woman and she, in turn, reciprocates sexually. In the event of the younger woman at times falling pregnant and starting a family with her sugar-daddy, the said family then becomes a small-house provided for by the erstwhile sugar-daddy.

Conversely, further considering that Grace had curiously had Mugabe's two children while still legally married to her then-husband, Zimbabwe Air Force officer Stanley Goreraza, hers and Mugabe's relationship had then been at worst an adulterous affair and at best a kind of surrogacy. Andrew Norman (2004, p.91) calls the relationship adulterous. Whatever the nature of the relationship, Mugabe was furious that his relationship and the existence of his two children with Marufu had been made public by the independent press.

Trevor Ncube, the then Executive Editor of the Financial Gazette, and his deputy editor, Simbarashe Makunike, were detained and brought before the courts on criminal defamation charges. Mugabe would never again be the same admirable, rational and instructive 1980s leader. In hindsight and all fairness to Grace, however, Mugabe had long stopped being the admirable, rational, and instructive leader of the 1980s much earlier.

Mugabe's very macabre side had revealed itself as early as January 1983 when he was still married to Sally. Then, he had unleashed the country's "North Korean-trained Fifth Brigade—under the jurisdiction of Emmerson Mnangagwa, who was (then) Security Minister in charge of the Central Intelligence Organisation at the time and—was pacifying (parts of) Matabeleland" (Roberts, 2017, np). Inhabited mostly by Ndebele-speaking people, some of whom are of Zulu descent, the Fifth Brigade's "pacification" military campaign now infamously known as *Gukurahundi* (Shona for the early Spring rains that sweep away the chaff) had been triggered when the veteran nationalist and one time ally of Mugabe's, Joshua Nkomo and his disgruntled Patriotic Front-Zimbabwe African People's Union PF-ZAPU were accused of hiding arms caches on some of their party's farms with the intention of overthrowing the Mugabe government. The military "campaign against these 'dissidents' (resulted in the killing of an) estimated 20,000 people" (Roberts, 2017, np) in parts of Matabeleland and the Midlands provinces for cavorting with the dissidents. The skirmishes and killings which followed between the dissidents and sections of the Zimbabwe National Army would only end in 1987 with the signing of the Unity Accord between ZANU-PF and PF-ZAPU that integrated the latter political party into the former and made Mugabe executive president.

In 1996, Mugabe and Grace officially tied the knot at a wedding controversially presided over by the Catholic Church. Despite a massive public attendance at what the State-controlled press billed the "wedding of the century" Meredith (2009), Grace Mugabe would however never find the same genuine endearment in the hearts of Zimbabweans as *Amai* Sally Mugabe had won. The fact that she and Mugabe had started their liaison while both of them were married and had consummated it and conceived twice when Sally was still alive and suffering from a chronic kidney ailment did not help matters. That is especially also taking into consideration that what the Horizon magazine and Financial Gazette newspaper had earlier reported was after all correct. If they had not before, the urban public began to see Mugabe in a new light. In the coming years, as Mugabe became older and yet still hung on to power, he and his wife would come under increased independent and international media scrutiny. Both Mugabe's public and political images would increasingly be tarnished and his much younger wife Grace directly or indirectly held responsible for it.

When from the year 2000 onwards, the electorate through the ballot voiced its displeasure with the now 76-year-old Mugabe and his revolutionary ZANU-PF party, From the leader identity perspective, "Mugabe transitioned from the revolutionary democrat that he (had) wanted people to see of him, to the obtuse demagogue" (Kumbuka, 2018, para, 6). Having earlier authorized the payment of unbudgeted hefty gratuities to veterans of Zimbabwe's liberation war in 1997, a year after officially marrying Grace, Mugabe now sanctioned unplanned land reform via land invasions of commercial white–occupied farmland which had sporadically started in 1999—Africanization had moved to land. The resultant disruption of the country's economic mainstay—agriculture and the response of the western international community to the land reform horrendously impacted Zimbabwe's economy. The country catapulted into socioeconomic instability. Hyperinflation reared and scarcity set in. Government's economic measures in the form of price controls and monetary policies to curtail the situation only served to further fan inflation and black-market activity. Corruption and self-aggrandizement in emulation of those in the echelons of power intensified.

Into the 2000s, as Mugabe's grip on power firmed and took on ever despotic hues, his popularity in the urban areas waned. In response, he extended his increasingly radical Africanization program not only to land, but also the country's mineral resources and even religion. In 2000, the mining sector contributed "8% of Zimbabwe's GDP (and) generated about 40% of annual export earnings. A record 28 tonnes of gold exported in 1999 (had raised) nearly $450 million or 30% of the value of exports" (news.bbc.co.uk, np). That same year, Mugabe announced his intention to Africanize Zimbabwe's mines: "After land, we must look at the mining sector; there must be Africans as owners, not just as workers" (news.bbc.co.uk). However, since it was "not entirely clear what Mr. Mugabe has in mind by the Africanisation of the mines—nationalization or transfer to favor black owners" (news.bbc.co.uk), the lack of clarification triggered disinvestment by those already invested in the country. Some companies' operations hurriedly moved to neighboring countries, mainly to South Africa. Most feared Mugabe's next round of radical Africanization would target the banking and other commercial sectors.

As the Indigenization program, the next phase of Mugabe's radically transforming Africanization program slowly began to take shape; the opposition MDC accused "Mr. Mugabe of trying to buy the votes of Zimbabwe's elite with a plan that could lead to economic disaster" (news.bbc.co.uk). Political analysts and observers asserted that it was "characteristic of the irrationality of a desperate government (ready) to do anything to stay in power." As with the Africanization of Zimbabwe's land, the pending one of the mining sector paradoxically brought Mugabe both approval and disapproval. To those who understood it and saw its empowering possibilities, it met with approval. However, to those Zimbabweans who were out of work as a result of company and marginal mine closures or their relocations, the proposed Indigenization program met with mortification. The uncertainty the Indigenization program and Mugabe's utterances about it into the 2000s left the country a pariah investment destination.

By 2007, Zimbabwe had virtually been reduced to a banana republic and a failed kleptocratic state where only individualism ruled supreme. In spite of the deprivation of the majority of the population, the lifestyles of those linked to ZANU-PF and its government becamemore sumptuous and opulent. So while Mugabe called for patriotism and sacrificial austerity in the face of the opposition Movement for Democratic Change (MDC) western sanctions, he and those close to him lived apparently without any. One such financially unrestricted person close to Mugabe was none other than his wife, Grace.

As Zimbabwe cascaded into hyperinflation and financial ruin, The Daily Telegraph in 2003 revealed that the Mugabes were completing the president's "new £6 million residence, the largest ever built in either Rhodesia or Zimbabwe. With 25 bedrooms, spas and a swimming pool, its roof clad with blue glazed tiles from Shanghai" (Thornycroft, 2010, np). Known as Gracelands, it was apparently being "built using various government funds that were intended to help low-income Zimbabweans" (Meldrum, 2005, 86). Confronted about the mansion however, one-time secretary Grace claimed she was building the sprawling mansion from her own personal savings. Many wondered how Grace had been able to "save" so much money in such a short space of time.

Sometime after the beginning of the Land Reform Program, it was alleged that: "Mr. Mugabe had quietly taken control of four of Zimbabwe's most profitable white-owned farms. They were secretly managed by state employees with all the profits going to him, his second wife, Grace, and their close relatives" (Thornycroft, 2010, np). As the years passed, allegations arose claiming the Mugabes owned a total of 21 farms in Zimbabwe, real estate in Scotland, Hong Kong, Malaysia, and South Africa. Most believed that Grace Mugabe's "shopping addiction has contributed to his (Mugabe) increasingly greedy rule." Over the years Grace's penchant for extravagant shopping abroad became legendary, earning her the nickname "Gucci Grace."

In March 2007, the Catholic bishops in Zimbabwe published the pastoral statement: "God Hears the Cry of the Oppressed." In it, they bravely criticized Mugabe and the Zanu PF government that: “As the suffering population becomes more insistent, generating more and more pressure through boycotts, strikes, demonstrations, and uprisings, the State responds with ever harsher oppression through arrests, detentions, banning orders, beatings, and torture.” Mugabe instead boasted of possessing “degrees in violence” and called for even the Africanization of religion. Speaking in Bulawayo on the eve of the March 29 General Elections, Mugabe, “called for the ‘Africanisation’ of Christianity in Zimbabwe, calling upon the nation’s churches to break free from foreign overlords.” (CEN, np) From then on, Mugabe fell out of complete favor with the broader international Catholic Church.

It was, however, not only with the broader international Catholic Church that Mugabe had fallen out with—most Zimbabwean urbanites could not wait for an end to his rule. For the average man, “hyperinflation had soared so high that prices doubled and redoubled over a single day. Life expectancy for women had fallen to 34—half that of 1980—and of men to 37” (Thorncroft, 2010, np). The continuous printing of ever-increasing banknote denominations betrayed an insolvent national treasury, the Reserve Bank of Zimbabwe. Apart maybe from among those within Mugabe’s own ruling ZANU-PF party, notably its loyal Women’s League and arguably some of those in the rural areas and military, his popularity was in 2008 at its very lowest ebb.

In the now much disputed March 2008 elections which followed and whose results took almost a month to be announced entirely, it is widely suspected that the opposition MDC and its then leader Morgan Tsvangirai won that harmonized plebiscite outright. However, when all the results were finally officially announced, Mugabe and his ruling ZANU-PF had conveniently polled 43% and Tsvangirayi the MDC 47 of the vote. Neither Mugabe nor Tsvangirayi had clinched the requisite 51% of the votes for either to rule Zimbabwe as stipulated by the country’s Constitution. The Presidential election would have to be rerun[10].

Towards the much publicized 27 June 2008 Presidential election rerun violent anti–imperialist rhetoric, electoral intimidation and atrocious violence purportedly by both sides marred the process. Subsequently, the opposition MDC’s Morgan Tsvangirai was forced to withdraw from the rerun of the presidential race in order to save his supporters from further violence. Despite his withdrawal, however, the now sham elections went ahead, and Mugabe and the ZANU-PF party returned to power with an overwhelming majority of over 85% of the voter turnout. Zimbabwe’s socioeconomic situation accelerated its descent.

Zimbabwe was on the brink of a possible humanitarian catastrophe and the Southern African region a refugee crisis when the African Union (AU) and the Southern African Development Community (SADC) "recommended third–party mediation" (Ndlovu–Gatsheni, 2013, p.44) in Zimbabwe. Then South African President Thabo Mbeki was elected to mediate. The culmination of the Mbeki mediated power-sharing negotiations with the ZANU-PF party and main MDC opposition faction of MDC-Tsvangirai (MDC-T) was initially the signing of a Memorandum of Understanding (MOU). It was followed in September 2008 by a Global Political Agreement that in February of 2009 paved the way to an Inclusive Government (IG) also popularly known as the Government of National Unity (GNU).

Although the GNU of the ZANU-PF party and opposition MDC-T was more a coalition of convenience than mutual respect, its tenure from 2009 to 2013 markedly stabilized Zimbabwe's economy. The implementation of a multi-currency system that saw the economy using different foreign currencies notably the United States Dollar (USD) vastly improved the country's macroeconomic situation, albeit at the expense of the nation's foreign currency reserves and future industrial development. Consequently, by the end of the GNU, although the economy was steadier than in 2008, little infrastructural and sustainable development had taken place and this time a foreign currency liquidity crisis was threatening.

On 31 July 2013, Zimbabwe again held another harmonized poll of presidential, parliamentary, and local government candidates. As with the March 2008 poll disgruntlement with the voters' roll, lack of electoral reforms, claims of vote-rigging, and voter intimidation in some parts of the country persisted. In all fairness, however, the main opposition party, the MDC was in disarray. That party had since 2008 fragmented into MDC-T, MDC-Mutambara (MDC-M) and most recently MDC-Ncube (MDC-N) as a result of a conflict of personalities and leadership styles. Towards the elections, the leader of the most popular of the splinter parties, Morgan Tsvangirai, was depicted in both local and international media as a philanderer. Unsurprisingly, therefore, when the election results were this time timeously announced, Mugabe had won a seventh presidential term and a two-thirds majority in the parliament.

For some Zimbabwean urbanites, the election results were nothing to celebrate. However, afraid of the consequences toopenly voice their displeasure in the repressive environment Zimbabwe had become, most turned to various social media to do so. Paradoxically, as beneficiaries of post-independence Mugabe instituted education reforms, as far as they were concerned, Mugabe was a tired octogenarian stuck in time warp whose liberation war credentials were holding the country at ransom. Images of him dozing at both local and international meetings became the butt of many jokes. Those of him leaning on Grace or one of his bodyguards for support proved his dotage.

To unemployed millennials born 20 years after Zimbabwe's independence, Mugabe was insufficiently in touch with their plight and that of the country. This was reflected by his regular appointment of mainly aged ministers oblivious of international trends and developments and if youthful appointees, they were his extended family members. It seemed that as his aged advanced, Mugabe had become not only nepotistic but also "aloof and indifferent to the country's mounting problems and seemed only interested in spending his time aboard aircraft hopping from one international conference to the next stopping only briefly in Zimbabwe" Kumbuka (2018, para.9). As far as they were concerned, Mugabe had nothing more or new to offer the country and if he and ZANU-PF wanted to continue ruling,it was thought that they should at best elect a successor and groom him/her. Such sentiments were vindicated when in February of 2015, the now nonagenarian president tripped, stumbled and fell on his return from Ethiopia. It was at the same airport where for years it had become customary for "hordes of ululating women and sloganeering ZANU-PF youth bussed to the airport to see the president off on a foreign trip or welcome him home" (Kumbuka, 2018, para, 4). They were again present to witness the evidence of an aged president.

Nevertheless, when it came to calls to elect a successor, "characteristically, Mugabe (would always) let the debate run its course inside his own Central Committee (…) collegiate style leadership, rather than making his own independent choice and pushing it through" (Smith & Simpson, 1981, p.157). It was precisely what he had done back in Mozambique during the armed struggle. By the end of 2013, various hypotheses had emerged as to why Mugabe was not electing a successor. The first posited a monarchical perspective of the presidency and so wanted one of his children, most likely the more academicallyinclined Bona, to succeed him.

The second argued that Mugabe had already elected and was grooming Joice Mujuru then his Vice President since 2010 and wife of retired ZANLA and Zimbabwe Defense Forces (ZDF) commander, General Solomon "Rex Nhongo"[11] Mujuru. Akin to the second school, a third hypothesized that although then Vice President Mujuru was the most likely candidate to succeed Mugabe, his preferred choice was his wartime *chef de cabinet* (chief of the cabinet) bodyguard and early 1980s post-independence Minister of State Security, Emmerson Mnangagwa. Unfortunately, however, Mnangagwa was not as popular in some of the party's provinces and leadership as Mujuru was. The last speculated that because of Mugabe's involvement in the Gukurahundi atrocities, he wished to be life president so he could remain diplomatically immune to prosecution, whether national or international. By the end of

2014, some of these hypotheses were to prove to some extent wrong and yet right.

The years 2014–2016 were relatively good years for the Mugabes. In early March of 2014, their daughter Bona got married to Simba Chikore, an airline pilot at a lavish wedding attended by local and international dignitaries. In September of the same year, Grace controversially graduated with a Doctor of Philosophy in Sociology from the University of Zimbabwe (UZ)—barely two months after registering for it. Armed with her newly acquired Ph.D., the now Dr. Amai Grace Mugabe who until then had hardly shown a serious interest in politics now launched herself onto the national political platform.

From 2014, Dr. Amai embarked on self-styled "Meet the People" rallies at which she sought to meet ZANU-PF supporters. It was at such meetings that fashionably clad in ZANU-PF party regalia; Grace gradually embarked on vitriolic verbal attacks against the thenVice President Joice Mujuru. She accused her of, amongst other things, factionalism, corruption and plotting to overthrow the head of state, by assassination. Mugabe's silence meant his acquiescence with Grace's allegations. Dr. Amai Mujuru who incidentally had credibly also graduated with a Ph.D. at the same graduation as Grace was left exposed to further criticism and allegations. It was such that by the time of the ZANU-PF party's sixth congress in December 2014, Mujuru had mainly been ostracized within the party.

Already referred to as "Dis–Grace" by some nationally and internationally, Grace had over the years already shown she was unafraid of confrontation—physical or otherwise. In 2009, while shopping in Hong Kong, she had joined her bodyguard in the beating, at her behest, of Sunday Times photographer, Richard Jones. Then in August 2017 while on a medical trip to Johannesburg, South Africa, she assaulted and brutally wounded Gabriella Engels after finding her in the hotel room of her sons Robert Jr. and Chatunga Bellarmine. Being Mugabe's wife, however, Grace had on both occasions been given diplomatic immunity from prosecution.

In response to Grace's allegations, Mugabe on 8 December 2014 dismissed Mujuru as the second vice president of Zimbabwe. As Mujuru descended, Grace's ascension became meteoric. She was nominated to lead ZANU-PF's Women League and unanimously elected by the Congress' provincial delegates' show of hands and cheers. The position of leader of ZANU-PF's Women League comes with it a seat in the Politburo—the party's executive political committee responsible for policy formulation. That seat was now Grace's. Within the short space of one year, Grace had positioned herself barely a step from the vice presidency and two from the presidency. As the vice presidency was vacant at the time of Grace's election to the Politburo, many uneasily marveled at what would happen next.

Two days after Mujuru's dismissal, Mnangagwa was on 10 December 2014 eventually appointed Zimbabwe's first vice president and sworn in two days later. To some onlookers, it appeared Grace had all along been paving the way for Mnangagwa. Or had she? The answer came in 2016 when, as Grace's rallies continued, she again fell back on to her tried and trusted strategy of vitriolic accusations. This time they were targeted at the then-new Vice President, Emmerson Mnangagwa, who she at times chided even in his presence. By all appearances, Grace was not after all of Team Lacoste but instead of Generation 40 or G40 clandestine factions in ZANU-PF.

By the end of the GNU in 2013, Mugabe's refusal to formally select a successor had led to the formation of three factions within the ZANU-PF party—Gamatox, Lacoste or Team Lacoste and later Generation 40 or G40. The former, Gamatox faction, derived its name from the brand name of a potent weevil pesticide that is quite common in Zimbabwe. The faction only began to be called such by the ZANU-PF party in 2014 to refer to Joice Mujuru loyalists. It is widely believed to have been composed of mostly liberal moderates from Zimbabwe's Manicaland province who had joined the country's liberation struggle quite young and had grownup in it. Most had either/or held a high ranking military or administrative post during the war and wished Mugabe to be succeeded by one of their own from Manicaland. The faction had officially first made its presence felt in September 2004. At the time, the then first Vice President Simon Muzenda had just died, and the first vice president's position was vacant when the ZANU-PF Women's League agitated that the post be filled by the then Minister of Rural Resources and Water Development, Joice Mujuru.

Lacoste comprising mainly war veterans of Zimbabwe's liberation war well into their late 60s and over had been socalled for its covert support of Mnangagwa whose nickname is *gwena* or crocodile, the logo of the Lacoste brand. This bloc believed Mugabe's successor should have liberation war credentials and an established track record within party structures. It thus had within its ranks war veterans, high ranking officers of the ZDF, some senior members of the party's politburo and senior women of the Women's League.

Generation 40, on the other hand, consisted of fairly younger party bigwigs. Still, in their 30s and early 60s, their history with ZANU-PF was relatively recent. Some were still in the party's Youth League, while others had joined and risen in the party as technocrats, praise-singers or relatives of Mugabe. They had no liberation war credentials to them and believed that in the event of Mugabe's incapacitation someone of their generation and

Mugabe's academic standing should succeed him. It is perhaps because of the latter requirement that Grace had accelerated her acquisition of a Ph.D.

In Shona custom, *murume akadyiswa* is what the English would call a man "under petticoat government," a man so under his wife's power that he is willing to go to any length to do her bidding. "The main reason for such behavior is sometimes attributed to a concoction or love portion that the man will have been given." (Nhemachena, 2015, p.13, 21) Nehemachena (2015) proffers other interesting reasons for such behavior. At other times, however, such a situation pertains because the husband is afraid of his wife, has perhaps been possibly assaulted by her once before or is just much older than her and so largely depends on her for tender loving care.

From 2016 to 2017 Grace's confrontational attention and verbal attacks at her rallies turned on Mnangagwa. A new power struggle between G40 and Lacoste began. Like Mujuru before him, Mnangagwa now faced Grace's verbal onslaughts. Some of those loyal to him or merely sympathetic booed the First Lady. In August 2017, Mnangagwa claimed his ice-cream from Gushungo Dairy owned by Grace Mugabe had been poisoned during Grace's Bulawayo Youth Interface Rally that he had attended. Although he later refuted it, when in September 2017 Mnangagwa again reiterated the same claim, he was in October 2017 shuffled out of his secondary post as Minister of Justice and Parliamentary Affairs. In November various accusations that Mnangagwa had discharged "his duties in a manner inconsistent with his official duties, disloyalty, disrespect, deceitfulness and unreliability and a lack of probity in the execution of his duties" (The Herald, np) were leveled against him. When at one of his rallies Mugabe "complained about how his wife sometimes nagged him at home, many took it as an innocent presidential joke" (Kumbuka, 2018, para.14). The possibility of Grace's nagging, however, came to light when on 6 November Mugabe promptly dismissed Mnangagwa as vice president. In fear for his life, Mnangagwa escaped to South Africa. Two days later, he was expelled from the ruling party—a decades-long camaraderie with Mugabe was over, and many suspected that Grace had most probably instigated it.

Meanwhile, Grace set about courting key ZANU-PF members and structures to support her for the presidency. However aware of the threat those heading Zimbabwe's state security forces could pose, in the meantime then President Mugabe ordered the arrest of the then Head of the Joint Operations Command, General Constantino Chiwenga. In defense of their commander, however, some members of the military thwarted the move. An exchange of threats and counter-threats between the Chiwenga and the Mugabes via the State's media followed. The culmination was the launch on 14–15 November

2017 of what the military later dubbed Operation Restore Legacy. During the operation, the Mugabes were placed under house arrest and some key members of the G40 faction detained.

With the military's encouragement, on 17 November 2017 thousands of Zimbabweans black and white, young and old urbanites who for years had electorally sought to remove Mugabe from power finally had the courage to march on the streets of Harare "to send a message to President Mugabe that he 'must go'" (News24, 18/11/2016). The once feared army now paradoxically turned ally. In response to the people's calls, on 19 November 2017, ZANU-PF dismissed Mugabe as their party's leader. On its part, Zimbabwe's parliament set in motion processes to impeach Mugabe and gave him an ultimatum to either resign or be impeached. The same man who for decades had polarized Zimbabweans black and white, young and old, ruling and opposition parties was now paradoxically uniting them against himself. With few options left, Mugabe finally chose to resign. He tendered his resignation on 21 November 2017 marking the end of an era.

To some, however, even though Mugabe had fallen from their good graces, he remained revered as a "nationalist hero, a symbol of the struggle to throw off the legacy of colonial rule" (Moyo, 2017, para. 6). As one war veteran of Zimbabwe's liberation war put it, "Mugabe was my leader; in fact, he is still my leader, but that wife of his!" The war veteran's sentiments about Grace were also echoed by Shadrack Gutto, director of the Center for African Renaissance Studies at the University of South Africa when he is reported to have said: "She (Grace) overreached herself. She has done a lot to accelerate her husband's removal from power" (News24.com.27/11/2016). After the departure of her husband, nothing more was heard from Grace Mugabe as her erstwhile arch-enemy, "be replaced by the same person (she and Mugabe) had sought to humiliate" (Kumbuka, 2018, para. 21). Mnangagwa returned from his brief self-imposed exile to assume the presidency that had so eluded him for so long.

## *Conclusion*

The women in Mugabe's life, his mother, Bona, his first wife, Sally and lastly his second wife, Grace paradoxically contributed to the promising man, leader and later authoritarian he later became. However, as this chapter has demonstrated, it was also Mugabe's paradoxical relationship with African modernity and his increasingly radical Africanization agenda that coupled with his advanced years, finally added to his demise and eventual removal from power.

## *Notes*

1. Affiliation: Department of Culture, Communication & Media, University College London, Email: corwin.mhlahlo.16@ucl.ac.uk& Comecinc Communications and Strategic Solutions Services Incorporated, Email: tenderinfo@comecincs.com
2. The Jesuit mission located in Zvimba, Mugabe's village.
3. That was due to restrictions imposed by Rhodesian prison authorities during the 1970 son study materials prisoners could access (Smith & Simpson, 1981, p.60).
4. Modern day Tanzania.
5. Sally earned the title "Amai" while still in Mozambique where it was given her for her motherly role and care of Zimbabwean refugees in the camps.
6. See Introduction for definition.
7. At the dawn of Mozambique's independence on 25 July 1975, the country's then President, Samora Machel "inherited a country bankrupt of educated, skilled labour because the Portuguese had carefully ensured that only the whites were trained to any professional level" (Smith & Simpson, 1981, p.165). Besides, as the former colonizers withdrew, they had destroyed, most if not all the country's infrastructure.
8. Princeton-educated political scientist, nationalist member of ZANU (PF) Central Committee, ZANU (PF) Information Secretary and Minister of Information in Mugabe's subsequent governments.
9. About 80% of Zimbabwe's population is Shona-speaking.
10. The then Constitution's Electoral Act (Chapter 2:13 as amended, 110) stipulated that when no candidate wins an absolute majority, a run-off must be held between the two candidates who obtained the most votes.
11. His *nom de guerre*

## *References*

Africanize. (n.d.). Retrieved July 20, 2018, from https://www.merriam-webster.com/dictionary/Africanize

Chan, S., & Primorac, R. (2013). *Zimbabwe since the unity government.* New York: Routledge.

Chigidi, L. T. (2009). *The Journal of Pan African Studies*, *3*(1), September2009.

Cooper, F. (1983). Introduction: Urban space, industrial time and wage labour in Africa. In F. Cooper (Ed.), *Struggle for the city: Migrant labor, capital, and the state in urban Africa* (pp. 7–500). London: SAGE Publishers.

Ferguson, J. (1999). *Expectations of modernity: Myths and meanings of urban life on the Zambian Copperbelt (Perspectives on Southern Africa)* (1st ed.).Berkley, Los Angeles, London: University of California Press.

Edwards, G., &Tisdell, C. (1990). *Post–independence trends in education. Kanyongo, Gibbs. South African Journal of Economics*, *58*(4).

Geschiere, P. (1997). The Modernity of Witchcraft: politics and the occult in postcolonial Africa. Charlottesville,VAand Londen: University Press of Virginia.

Gombe, J. M. (1986). Tsika Dzavashona *(Tradition of the Shona)*. Harare: College Press Publishers Pvt Ltd.

Holland, H. (2008). *Dinner with Mugabe: The untold story of a freedom fighter who became a tyrant*. Johannesburg: Penguin Books.

Kanyongo, G. Y. (2005). Zimbabwe's public education system reforms: Successes and challenges. *International Education Journal, 6*(1), 65–74.

Kumbuka, D. (2018). Robert Mugabe—a sad tale of hero to zero. Retrieved May 13, 2018, from https://

Maluleke, T. S. (2013). Africanization is about more than playing Aida at graduation ceremonies. In M. Anderson (Ed.), The University of South Africa: memories, transformation and Africanization (pp. 90–7). Johannesburg: Real African Publishers.

Meldrum, A. (2005). *Where we have hope: A memoir of Zimbabwe*. New York: Atlantic Monthly Press.

Meredith, M. (2002). *Mugabe: Power and plunder in Zimbabwe*. Oxford: Public Affairs Press.

Meredith, M. (2009). *Mugabe: Power, plunder, and the struggle for Zimbabwe's future*. Oxford: Public Affairs Press.

Moyo, J. (2017). "Mugabe Must Go" thousands in Zimbabwe rally against leader. Retrieved April 28, 2018https://www.nytimes.com/2017/11/18/world/africa/zimbabwe-mugabe-march.html.

Mutepfa, M., Mpofu, E., & Chataika, T. (2007). Inclusive education in Zimbabwe: Policy, curriculum, practice, family and teacher education issues. *Childhood Education, 83*(6), 342–346.

Ndlovu, M. E. (2013). Zimbabwe's Educational Legacy from the 1980s: Was it all so rosy? Retrieved April 28, 2018 http://archive.kubatana.net/html/archive/demgg/130521sok.asp?sector=edutra&year=2013&range_start=61.

Ndlovu-Gatsheni. (2013). Angola–Zimbabwe relations astudy in the search for regional alliances. In S. Chan & R. Primorac (Eds.), *Zimbabwe since the unity government*. New York: Routledge.

Nehanda Radio. (2013). Mugabe claims he told Sally about affair. Retrieved May 13, 2018 http://nehandaradio.com/2013/05/25/mugabe-claims-he-told-sally-about-affair-with-grace/.

Nhemachena, A. (2015). Sensing presences: Health, illness, and resilience in contemporary rural Zimbabwe. *The Journal of Pan African Studies, 8*(8), 7–35.

Norman, A. (2004). *Robert Mugabe and the Betrayal of Zimbabwe*. London: McFarland.

Roberts, J. (2017). Mugabe Resigns–has god heard the cry of the oppressed. Retrieved May23,2018http://www.thetablet.co.uk/blogs/5/1091/mugabe-resigns-has-god-heard-the-cry-of-the-oppressed.

Shizha, E., & Kamuriwo, M. T. (2011). *Education and development in Zimbabwe: A social, political and economic analysis*. Rotterdam/Boston/Taipei: Sense Publishers.

Smith, D., & Simpson, C. (1981). Mugabe.Pioneer head: Salisbury the Church of England Newspaper (2008) "Mugabe calls for 'Africanisation' of churches in Zimbabwe" 27 March, Religious Intelligence Section.

Thornycroft, P. (2010).

Wetherall, I. (1995) "Mugabe cracks down on press" Mail & Guardian, 19 May https://mg.co.za/article/1995-05-19-mugabe-cracks-down-on-press.

# 12 *Operation Restore Legacy: The Coup d'état That Was but Was Not*

C. LUTHULI MHLAHLO

Political events in Zimbabwe from 13th to 21st November 2017 left many questioning whether what had transpired from the early hours of Wednesday 15th November 2017 was a coup d'état, a military mission, a popular demonstration or a legitimate constitutional change in power. Based on some eyewitness, print and electronic media accounts of the political events of Zimbabwe's most memorable eight days, this chapter traces, juxtaposes,and examines some features of those fateful days to what, over the years, have been considered coup d'états, particularly in other parts of Africa and generally the world. After which examination, it evaluates whether what unraveled in Zimbabwe was, as the world seemed to witness, a popular public demonstration that had necessitated military "intervention," followed by a constitutional change in power or more directly, an old-fashioned coup d'état in 21st-century Southern Africa. The chapter's evaluation paradoxically concludes that what transpired over those eight days in November 2017 was initially a coup d'état, that eventually became a constitutional change of power.

## *Trends of Some African Coup d'états*

On 21st November 2017, much to most of the world's amazement and other's relief, President Robert Mugabe's long-awaited resignation and retirement from power finally happened. It had been seven days in the making, and to many, bittersweet. Reasons for this oxymoronic effect of Mugabe's departure were varied. For some, it marked the end of an era of, arguably, one of Africa's greatest statesmen—albeit one who had brought both pride and pain to many. For others, it was a departure long overdue, but one that, when it eventually came, was reminiscent of some of the continent's coup d'états of yesteryear.

Often defined as the "sudden, violent overthrow of an existing government by a small group," coup d'états in Africa, although intermittent in more recent years, are not alien to the continent. According to Kazeem (2017, p.np.), "since the 1960s, Africa has seen at least 200 successful and failed coups." Of these, Burkina Faso holds the record of having had a total of 10 coups. Nigeria follows it on eight and Burundi, Chad, Ghana, Comoros, and Mauritania with six each. They are, however, "extremely rare in southern Africa's post-independence history" (Kazeem, 1917, p.np). Until November 2017, Lesotho had been the only country to have had a coup, with a total of two.

Over the last 60 odd years, the different coups which have occurred across the African continent often have been the result of "a cocktail of ingredients" and have been characterized by a "sequence of events" (Kazeem, 1917, p.np). Among some of the causes behind both Africa's violent and bloodless coups have been fractious political power struggles involving the military, claims of the country's lack of economic growth, increased inflation, corruption, and unemployment. Of these, fractious political struggles involving the military seem to hold sway. For example, in July 1960, when a power struggle developed in the newly independent government of Democratic Republic of Congo[1] between President Joseph Kasavubu and Premier Patrice Lumumba, that country's secretary of state for national defense, Joseph Désire-Mobutu "covertly supported Kasavubu's attempt to dismiss Lumumba" (The Editors of Encyclopedia Britannica, 2018, p.np). However, when Lumumba then "rallied his forces to oust Kasabuvu in September 1960, Mobutu seized control of the government and announced that he was 'neutralizing' all politicians" (The Editors of Encyclopedia Britannica, 2018, p.np). Mobutu later "turned over the government to Kasavubu, who made Mobutu commander–in–chief of the armed forces" (The Editors of Encyclopedia Britannica, 2018, p.np). Mobutu would again depose Kasavubu in a 1965 military coup "after a power struggle developed between President Kasavubu and his premier, Moise Tshombe" (The Editors of Encyclopedia Britannica, 2018, p.np) and, this time, install himself as president.

In 1982, Blaise Compaore, leader of the then Upper Volta[2] national commando training center at Po "became deeply embroiled in national politics when his friend and colleague, Captain Thomas Sankara, resigned from his government post to protest policy decisions" (McKenna, 2019, p.np). When a year later, the power struggle between the government and Sankara resulted in the latter's imprisonment, "Compaore mustered the support of the commando unit at Po and, with Ghananian and Libyan help, led a coup on August 4, 1983, that installed Sankara as head of state" (McKenna, 2019, p.np). Commandant Jean–Baptiste Lingani and Captain Henri Zongo who had assisted Compaore and Sankara organized the coupand joined the latter two in the country's leadership.

From 1985–1987, "Compaore served as minister of state at the presidency (1983–1987), essentially making him second–in–command in the regime, and also as minister of state for justice" (McKenna, 2019, p.np). However, in the years that followed, Compaore, Lingani, and Zongo would eventually overthrow Sankara in a military coup of their own. The cause and aftermath of the coups in Zaire and Burkina Faso are, to some extent, reminiscent of the trajectory of the November 2017 military "intervention" in Zimbabwe.

Since the beginning of Zimbabwe's crisis in the late 1990s, some political pundits, fundis, and even ordinary Zimbabweans had speculated that the only way Mugabe could be dislodged from power would have to be from within his inner circle. One speculation was that either some members of ZANU-PF or the military's rank and file would eventually topple the de facto life president. It is perhaps for this reason that, to prevent the ever-present threat of a coup, President Mugabe had since 2000 ensured that the top brass of the country's defense forces was financially and materially comfortable. To this end, amidst Zimbabwe's economic decline, the army's leadership was placated with extremely high salaries, farmland, luxury vehicles, sprawling mansions, and even mineral concessions. Consequently, the thought that Mugabe would likely be deposed by members of the military's upper echelon had gradually been shelved. That is until the race to succeed Mugabe pitted Emmerson Mnangagwa's Lacoste ZANU-PF faction against Grace Mugabe's Generation/G–40.

## *Mugabe Dynasty Building: Lacoste Versus G40 and the Road to Coup d'état*

By early 2014, nonagenarian Mugabe's intransigent refusal to identify and name a successor, announce his retirement, or discourage then First Lady Grace Mugabe's powerplay for political positions had both the rumor mill and the private media ablaze. As long suspected, it whispered that Mugabe sought to create a dynasty. Speculation had it that, with his purge of the ZANU-PF party's Gamatox faction leader and former firstvice president, Joice Mujuru, and the ascension of his wife to the ZANU-PF party's powerful politburo, Mugabe was positioning Grace to not only become the country's first vicepresident, but eventually its president. A position in which she could serve as a kind of regent while Mugabe's progeny, daughter Bona or son Robert Junior, matured enough to be inducted into ZANU-PF's structures. Then, meteorically rise to influential positions within the party—as their mother had done—and eventually ascend to the presidency. Such conjecture continued to be bolstered by Grace's political activities since 2014, as well as other suggestive reports concerning younger members of the Mugabe family.

From mid-2014, Dr. Amai Grace Mugabe, as the then first lady was increasingly becoming known, had embarked on what she termed "Meet the People" rallies aimed at meeting and addressing ZANU-PF supporters. It was at such gatherings that Dr. Amai had systematically embarked on vitriolic verbal attacks against then Vice President Mujuru whom she accused of, amongst other things, factionalism, corruption, and plotting to overthrow the head of state, by assassination. To most, Mugabe's silence over such accusations and Grace's untethered authority to organize and address such rallies meant they had his tacit support and approval. Towards the end of 2014, Grace's vitriolic attacks and allegations against Joice Mujuru would eventually lead to the latter's dismissal as first vice president and a member of the ZANU-PF party.

Before Joice Mujuru's purging in December 2014 however, in August, the UK-based *SW Radio Africa* had announced that Robert Mugabe junior was set to enter the political arena. This was apparently after the weekly *Zimbabwe Standard* had reported that ZANU-PF youths from Mashonaland West—Mugabe's home province—were agitating for the young Mugabe to enter politics in the hope that this would "stabilize the party which is torn by factional fights as the race to succeed Mugabe gains momentum" (Sibanda, 2014, p.np). However, as a political observer, Mutsa Murenje commented, the elevation of Dr. Amai and her son into ZANU-PF structures would only raise tensions in "a party that is already divided right down the middle(…) having Grace and her son take up influential positions in ZANU PF might create the impression that Mugabe is building a dynasty that will take over the reins once he's out of the picture" (Sibanda, 2014, p.np). As the year progressed, with Mugabe visibly frail, and young Robert Junior concentrating more on becoming a socialite than a politician, it seems it was left to Grace to fuel and fulfil the ailing president's dynasty-building ambitions.

The last quarter of 2014 saw both the State's print and electronic media carry disparaging reports and pieces on then Vice President Mujuru. Such was their intensity that by the time of the ZANU-PF party's sixth congress in December 2014, Vice President Mujuru had fallen out of favor with both some sections of the party and the public. Most importantly, President

Mugabe no longer supported her. Mujuru's image became so tarnished she did not even attempt to seek reelection to the party's politburo and the central committee. On December 8, 2014, Mugabe finally dismissed Mujuru[3] with immediate effect for conduct "inconsistent with the expected standard"[4] and in response to her fallout with the public consequent to the damning allegations leveled against her.

As Mujuru descended[5], Grace Mugabe meteorically ascended. She was nominated to lead ZANU-PF's Women League and unanimously elected—by the congress' provincial delegates' show of hands and cheers. The position of leader of ZANU-PF's Women League automatically guaranteed her a seat in the politburo—the party's executive political committee responsible for policy formulation. That seat was by 2015 Dr. Amai Grace Mugabe's, and in the light of the 2004 party constitutional provision that one of the two vice presidents in the Presidium must be a woman, her place in the politburo placed her barely a step from one of the vice presidencies and two from the presidency.

The Mugabes' dynasty building seemed on course, and as the first vice presidency was vacant at the time, many speculated what would happen next and most anticipated Grace to fill it. That is, until then minister of justice Emmerson Dambudzo Mnangagwa was on December 12, 2014, eventually appointed Zimbabwe's first vice president and Phelekezela Mphoko his second. To some onlookers, it appeared Grace had after all been paving the way, not for herself, but rather Mnangagwa—one of Mugabe's long-serving aides, lieutenants, rumored to be his perceived protégé, and the preferred choice to succeed him. Such rumors, however, would eventually prove untrue.

Grace's early opposition to Mnangagwa's ascendancy soon made it clear she was mistress of her destiny. After "tearing former Vice President Dr. Joice Mujuru's succession machinations to smithereens (and) earning herself the nickname Mai Stop It, some thought the First Lady was going to slow down," (Lazarus, 2015, p.10) but she did not. Instead, Grace's infamous rallies continued. She again got back to her tried and trusted strategy of vitriolic accusations, only this time against the new first vice president and the leader of ZANU-PF's Lacoste faction, Emmerson Mnangagwa who she at times ridiculed and chided even in his presence. A new power struggle between Grace Mugabe's G40 and Mnangagwa's Lacoste ZANU-PF faction began.

Judging by Grace's vitriol which she, from 2015 onwards, specifically aimed at Mnangagwa, she was after all not a part of Team Lacoste[6] that until Mujuru's dismissal had been her Gamatox faction's main rival. So, if Grace belonged to neither Team Lacoste nor Gamatox factions, which faction was she working to advance? Was she on a one-woman mission or possibly part of Generation 40 or G40[7]—a clandestine faction suspected to have been formed by then controversial minister of information and publicity, Jonathan Moyo—but now seemingly led by the First Lady? Time would eventually tell.

From February 2016 to November 2017 most of Dr. Amai Grace's confrontational attention and relentless verbal attacks at her Meet the People rallies targeted and intensified against Mnangagwa. Like Mujuru before him, it was now his turn to face the onslaught of Grace's venom. While some loyal Mnangagwa loyalists and sympathizers booed the brazen first lady for what many saw as "a campaign for Generation 40 (G40) faction, which (had) vowed to derail Vice–President Emmerson Mnangagwa's presidential bid" (Zhangazha, 2016, p. np), others praised her for speaking truth to the corrupt and influential individuals in her husband's cabinet. Generally, however, the masses were getting tired and resentful of Grace. Her husband, on the other hand, was not, and lent her a sympathetic ear.

The largely covert power struggle between Grace Mugabe and her husband's first vice president was steadily bubbling, when in August 2017, Mnangagwa claimed his ice-cream from Gushungo Dairy (owned by Grace Mugabe) had been poisoned when he had attended Grace's Bulawayo Youth Interface Rally. Although Mnangagwa later refuted the accusation, when in September 2017 he again reiterated the same claim, October 2017 saw him shuffled out of his secondary post as minister of justice and parliamentary affairs. In early November 2017, various accusations were leveled against Mnangagwa. Among them were that he had discharged "his duties in a manner inconsistent with his official duties" and had shown "disloyalty, disrespect, deceitfulness and unreliability and a lack of probity in the execution of his duties" (Machivenyika, 2017, p.1). Thereafter, on November 6, 2017, President Mugabe promptly dismissed Mnangagwa as first vice president of the republic. In fear for his life, Mnangagwa escaped to South Africa. Two days later, he was expelled from the ruling party.

Subsequent to Mnangagwa's self-imposed exile, President Mugabe possibly aware of the threat those heading Zimbabwe's state security forces could pose and plan in cohorts with external assistance had, after Mnangagwa's flight, reportedly ordered that then Commander of the Zimbabwe Defence Forces (ZDF) and head of the Joint Operations Command (JOC) General Constantine Chiwenga be arrested at the Harare International Airport upon his return from a trip to China[8]. However, in defense of their commander, some members of the military had dramatically thwarted the move when dressed as airport ground crew, they had by force of arms prevented Chiwenga's arrest when then police commissioner Augustine Chihuri and several of his police officers had tried to do so. To most, it is Mugabe's abrupt dismissal of Mnangagwa as vice president and the failed attempt to arrest Chiwenga that ultimately forced high-ranking elements of the army to reveal where their loyalty lay in the factious fighting within ZANU-PF.

After the sacking of Mnangagwa and Chiwenga's attempted arrest, a salient power struggle ensued between Chiwenga and Mugabe. On Monday November 13, 2017, then Commander of the ZDF Chiwenga called a media conference at Army Headquarters in Harare. At the conference "attended by about 90 senior army officers" (Thornycroft, 2017, p. np), the army commander issued a press statement castigating and warning those behind "the current treacherous shenanigans that when it comes to matters of protecting our revolution, the military will not hesitate to step in" (Dzirutwe, 2017, p.1). Chiwenga's statement constituted the first public military threat to Mugabe's 37-year administration. The army commander's overt support for the Lacoste faction was unsurprising. Not only was Chiwenga a war veteran like most Lacoste members, he had also served under Mnangagwa when the now-former vice president had held the portfolios of minister of state security and later defense.

Direct and indirect threats and counterthreats via the State's media between Chiwenga and the Mugabe administration followed. In response to Chiwenga's media statement, ZANU-PF Youth League secretary, Kudzai Chipanga vowed that the Youth League was "prepared to die for Mugabe" "We're Prepared To Die" (2017) and pledged the league's support for Mugabe and his family. The following day, as the world anxiously awaited the leadership's response to Chiwenga's statement, then president and command-in-chief of the country's uniformed forces, Robert Mugabe responded via ZANU-PF's spokesperson Simon Khaya Moyo. The press statement released by S.K Moyo vehemently reprimanded Chiwenga for making a statement that was "an outrageous vitiation of soldiership" and one that suggested, "treasonable conduct on his part as it was meant to incite insurrection and violent challenge to the Constitutional Order."[9] Chiwenga's warning that the ZDF would "step in" had been rightly "interpreted in its most extreme form to suggest that the Zimbabwe National Army could overthrow the Mugabe–led government or at least the pro–Mugabe ZANU-PF faction" (Waddington, 2017, p.np). A standoff between the ZDF's commander and the country's executive followed. It was one that could only be resolved by a show of strength by either's side. For Chiwenga's side, the culmination was the launch on November 14–15, 2017, of what those involved in the military maneuver dubbed Operation Restore Legacy.

Modern-day coup d'états are characterized by certain explicit and implicit features and sequences. As an explicit first step to a coup, its leaders will often, as both a show of strength and force, mobilize forces and armored vehicles to secure military barracks and surround key installations and state institutions. More frequently than not, in order to ensure control of channels of communication, a military overthrowing a sitting head of state will overrun and secure the country's television and radio stations. After that, the spokesperson of those leading the coup will then proceed to address the nation and give reasons for the military takeover. During such an address, the spokesperson will usually inform the nation of the ousting, arrest of the incumbent head of state and those loyal to him as well as their pending fate. Moreover, depending on whether they would like to impose military rule or not, the coup leaders' spokesperson will, "for the good of the country," assure the public and the international community when elections will be held and who the interim rulers will until then be. For a coup to have reached this ultimate stage, however, it is to be assumed that the coup leaders will have undertaken the initial implicit requirements for a successful coup.

Firstly, these include the indispensable and guaranteed cooperation of all heads of the country's security forces and their subordinates. Secondly, as Pakistan (2016, p.np.) writing in a different context advises, in undertaking a coup, "Never underestimate the power of the common man." In this vein, coup leaders must ensure the unpopularity of the targeted leadership and its main actors first, before finally staging a coup. This is essential if both the coup leaders specifically and military generally will have public support in the coup's aftermath. Just to what extent both these implicit and explicit characteristics of the course of a coup were present or absent in what happened in Zimbabwe from November 14–21, 2017, is critical to evaluating whether what transpired was indeed a coup or not.

*The Coup That Was but Was Not: Return to Constitutionality.* Many eyewitness accounts and media versions of what transpired in Zimbabwe from November 14–21, 2017, abound. Nevertheless, amid these varied tales regarding the chain of events, individual threads are consistent with what has become the official tapestry. Eyewitness accounts supported by reliable media report sources claim that on the afternoon of November 14, 2017, *Twitter* became abuzz with reports "that a coup to oust President Robert Mugabe was underway in Zimbabwe. The rumors stemmed from a collection of photographs and video clips showing armored vehicles[10] on some of the city's roads, purportedly headed towards the capital, Harare" (Waddington, 2017, p.np). In one of the online videos, a motorist described how military police and several tanks had blocked Kirkman Road—the road that leads to Two Presidential Guard barracks in the Harare high-density suburb of Dzivarasekwa. By all appearances, it looked as if elements of the ZDF were putting into effect the first explicit step to executing a coup. Was a coup in progress or was the army simply conducting a military exercise? Only time would tell.

What followed during the evening of Tuesday 14 November is mostly a mix of conjecture and some sketchy media and eyewitness accounts. According to these, that evening, Mugabe and his motorcade left his Munhumutapa offices after a cabinet meeting for his "Blue Roof" mansion in Borrowdale Brook. It is still unclear whether Mugabe was at the time already aware of the armored vehicles that had been seen that afternoon and were now blocking roads to Two Presidential Guard barracks. Or that the Zimbabwe Republic Police's Support Unit had been disarmed and keys to its armory taken by army personnel. Whatever President Mugabe might or might not have known, the narrative goes that when he had arrived at his "Blue Roof" mansion, his presidential guard was promptly and bloodlessly disarmed[11], and he and his family placed under house arrest. While it is also still unclear whether Mugabe had arrived to find his family already under house arrest and then joined them on arrival, what is, however, public knowledge is that, as happens during some coups, the incumbent leader and his family were put under house arrest.

That same night, other explicit coup-like events escalated elsewhere in the capital city. Some of the ZDF personnel and armored vehicles seen earlier that evening stationed themselves around the city of Harare and, without taking any hostile action, blockaded some roads. These included those leading to the Mugabes' private residence and that heading to the state broadcaster, the Zimbabwe Broadcasting Corporation (ZBC) at Pockets Hill. In the early hours of Wednesday 15 November 2017, coup-like events intensified. At about 1 a.m., there were reports of periodic "gunfire or explosions or both, at unknown locations in Harare" (Waddington, 2017, p.np). Towards 4 a.m., ZDF personnel then reportedly took control of the ZBC's Pockets Hill studios.

Sometimes during a coup, loyalists of the incumbent are rounded up by the military and summarily executed. Although it has still to be ascertained and officially corroborated, it is rumored that some Central Intelligence Officers (CIOs) loyal to Mugabe and Grace Mugabe's G40 were allegedly rounded up, tortured, and eventually "disappeared." The "bloodless" military takeover was apparently not so bloodless after all. What, however, has been publicly verified is that some members of the G40 faction such as Mugabe's nephew Ignatius Chombo, then minister of finance, had their houses attacked and ransacked while they were allegedly beaten and detained[12]. Others like Saviour Kasukuwere, then minister of local government, rural development, and national housing, as well as, then minister of higher education, Jonathan

Moyo escaped with their lives to Mozambique and Kenya, respectively, after an attempt was made on Kasukuwere's life and a warrant of arrest issued for Moyo. Some like Patrick Zhuwao, then minister of public service, labor, and social welfare, and yet another of Mugabe's nephews sought refuge in South Africa—en route to Zimbabwe from Argentina where he had been on an official visit. Those who remained either went underground or fled the country.

After a military takeover, overthrow, or coup d'état, those who have stage publicly broadcast their seizure of power. At 4 a.m., then Major–General Sibusiso Moyo of the ZDF appeared on Zimbabwe's only national television. However, to his audience's surprise, it was to announce and stress that the military had not "carried out a coup but instead was acting to quell tensions following the sacking of the vice president" (Kazeem, 2017, p.np). Perhaps unsure as to how the public would react and the extent of their sentiment towards a deposed Mugabe, Moyo then went on to inform his audience that President Mugabe was "safe and sound" and that the military operation was "only targeting criminals around him" who had been "causing social and economic suffering in the country in order to bring them to justice." ("Timeline: How Zimbabwe's 'coup'", 2017). Despite the coup-like sequence of events and signs thereof, the leaders of the "military operation," most likely because of the stigma and consequences[13] of staging a coup d'état, were extremely reluctant to call it one.

As day broke and morning progressed, the military's televised statement, coupled with its trucks "stationed menacingly on the streets of Harare" (Kazeem, 2017, np) and uniformed soldiers "controlling access to parliament, ruling party headquarters and the Supreme Court" ("Timeline: How Zimbabwe's 'coup'", 2017) made it "clear that at least some part of the military had taken control of, if not the government, then at least Harare" (Waddington, 2017b, p.np). In the meantime, members of the ZDF disarmed members of the Zimbabwe Republic Police (ZRP) guarding parliament and patrolled the streets of Harare searching vehicles for G40 members or supporters.

Reaction to what had happened then began. Reminiscent of the Hans Christian Andersen story about the emperor's new clothes[14], the head of the African Union Alpha Conde of Guinea reportedly said, "the situation seems like a coup" ("Timeline: How Zimbabwe's 'coup'", 2017). As usually happens after a coup, by midday, the embassy of the United Kingdom was urging its nationals in Zimbabwe to "to remain safely at home or in their accommodation until the situation becomes clearer" (Zimbabwe crisis: Army takes over, 2017, p.np). Similarly, the United States advised its citizens in the country to "shelter in place until further notice" "Zimbabwe crisis: Army takes over" (2017). The South African presidency's official website confirmed that South African President Jacob Zuma had been in contact with President Mugabe who had "indicated that he was confined to his home" ("Update on the Zimbabwean", 2017).

Most importantly, however, President Zuma voiced his concern over the constitutionality of what had happened and "hoped events in Zimbabwe would not lead to 'unconstitutional changes of government.'" "Zimbabwe crisis: Army takes over" (2017). Similarly, the news agency, AFP Africa correspondingly reported that the African Union was urging that the constitution be respected[15]. As it has so often done in world affairs, the constitutionality of what had transpired gradually began to take center stage.

Constitutionalism and constitutionality formed the bedrock and were pivotal to both the creation and establishment of what is Zimbabwe today. It was by means of an October 1923 constitution that then crown colony of Southern Rhodesia achieved responsible government from the imperialist British South Africa Company (BSAC). Forty-two years later, it was through an unconstitutional unilateral declaration of independence by Ian Douglas Smith that then Southern Rhodesia independent broke from British imperial control and entrenched white supremacist rule over the country's black majority. It would take a protracted civil war and the signing of the 1979 Lancaster House Constitution to finally bring black majority rule and establish what is now the nation-state of Zimbabwe.

Soon after Zimbabwe's independence, then Prime Minister Robert Mugabe had in September 1987 amended the constitution in order to abolish the premiership and entrench himself in power as the country's first executive president. Over the years, other constitutional amendments such as Access to Information and Protection of Privacy Act (AIPPA) and Public Order Security Act of 2002 that had paradoxically trammeled Zimbabweans' freedoms and human rights had also followed.

As a measure of the importance of constitutionality in Zimbabwe, then ZDF Commander Chiwenga's media briefing on November 13, 2017, had "began by quoting the preamble of Zimbabwe's Constitution" ("Timeline: How Zimbabwe's 'coup'", 2017). However, when during the same media statement Chiwenga had then unequivocally proceeded to threaten military intervention in the governance of the country should the purges in the ruling party continue, ZANU-PF Youth League secretary, Chipanga, had rightly castigated Chiwenga for making threats that were in "violation of the country's constitution" ("We're Prepared to die", 2017). Chipanga had remonstrated that Chiwenga's utterances were "an assault on our freedom as we now have a new (2013) constitution which places soldiers in barracks and civilian authority in power (…) The guns will follow the politics and not the politics following the guns" ("We're Prepared to die", 2017).

Akin to Chipanga's remonstrations, the press statement issued by the ZANU-PF national secretary for information and publicity, SK Moyo, in response to Chiwenga's, had also alluded to the country's Constitution when it had described the general's statement as a "violent challenge to the Constitutional Order(…)what happens when the gun seeks to overreach by dictating to politics the norms of Constitutionality." To both the informed and uninformed, these various references to the country's constitution were a pointed reminder of the need for constitutionality if a constitutionally elected leader is to be removed from office. Failure to which constitutional adherence those illegally replacing the incumbent would be ostracized regionally, continentally, and, indeed, internationally.

At the turn of the millennium, then Organization of African Unity (OAU) and current African Union (AU) had "adopted the Lomé Declaration, replacing its long-standing tolerance of military seizure of power with a blanket rejection of coups" (Nathan, 2016, p.1). Since succeeding the OAU, the AU "has strengthened the OAU position through several legal instruments, chiefly the AU Constitutive Act of 2000, the 2002 protocol establishing the AU Peace and Security Council (PSC) and the 2007 African Charter on Democracy, Elections, and Governance" (Nathan, 2016, p.1). Of these instruments, the African Charter on Democracy, Elections, and Governance specifically "includes a ban on coup legitimation, which bars the perpetrators of unconstitutional action from contesting elections held to restore democracy and from holding any position of responsibility in the political institutions of their state" (Nathan, 2016, p.1). Just to what extent this has been adhered to by the AU since 2000 or was upheld in Zimbabwe's case is hugely debatable.[16]

It is perhaps in the light of the stance of the AU on coups as spelled out in the instruments outlined above that, aside from a coup being treasonous and cause for both continental and international ostracization, the leaders of the ZDF's military takeover had been careful to call the events of November 15, 2017, an "operation" or a "mission" at best, and an "intervention" at worst. Not once did they term it a coup. Doing so would only "irreparably tarnish the administration aiming to take over" "Treacherous Shenanigans" (2017). Unsurprisingly, therefore, as the aftermath of the ZDF's intervention ticked away, the constitutionality of what had happened became central to the interventionists' "mission" moving forward. From that point onwards, the constitutionality of all the events which would follow thereafter became paramount. To ensure this, those who had spearheaded "Operation Restore

Legacy" realized that for their "mission" to be rendered constitutional, some events of the last few days had to be reordered, some key actors who had initially been omitted had to be included, and, generally, at least a sense of normalcy needed to be restored. This they set about doing from November 16, 2017.

On November 16, 2017, General Chiwenga, Sidney Sekeramayi, then minister of defense, and Kembo Mohadi, then minister of state security in the president's office, accompanied by Father Fidelis Munokori SJ and some envoys of the Southern African Development Community (SADC) met with the beleaguered President Mugabe at his Blue Roof mansion. The objective of the meeting was primarily to engage Mugabe and persuade him to resign constitutionally. However, after the reportedly very tense meeting, Mugabe, who holds, among several other postgraduate degrees, a Master of Laws degree from the University of London, reportedly "remained defiant" ("Treacherous Shenanigans", 2017). He would not accede to relinquishing power.

Despite Mugabe's largely ruinous 37-year rule and calls by his ailing arch-rival opposition MDC–T leader, Morgan Tsvangirai, the 93-year-old statesman still would not constitutionally stepdown. Instead, it is reported that: "the world's oldest head of state put his foot down: "Bring me the constitution and tell me what it says, he ordered military chief Constantino Chiwenga, according to two sources present." ("Treacherous Shenanigans", 2017). If a kind of coup-cum-constitutional resignation was what those who had deposed Mugabe from power were hoping for, then they needed to rethink their strategy. The constitutionality of had transpired on the morning of November 15 was Mugabe's last resort, and he was not going to budge but rather draw it out for as long as possible.

Some coups in the past, on and off the African continent, have at times been kindled by widespread protests against an unpopular incumbent leader leading to the military seizing power. This could be because "Protests aggregate citizen information and provide elites with a public signal which helps them coordinate a coup" (Casper and Tyson, 2014, p.548). The most memorable of such protests-cum-coups are those that brought then Captain Muammar Gaddafi and his Free Officers Movement to power in Libya in 1979 and most recently, General Abdel Fattah el–Sisi of Egypt in 2013. According to Casper and Tyson (2014, p.548), "Other examples of protests preceding coup attempts include Dahomey (1963), Greece (1973), Burma (1988), Thailand (2006)." All these events, they note "are suggestive of a general phenomenon—popular protests with the intent to secure political reform tend to be accompanied by coup attempts" (Casper and Tyson, 2014, p.548). Until November 16 2017, aside from Major–General Sibusiso Moyo's televised address to the nation, the ZDF had not involved the Zimbabwean populace in its military operation. However, after Mugabe's refusal to constitutionally leave office, this changed. Those in-charge of the military and the unfolding events coopted into Operation Restore Legacy, if not the Zimbabwean people, then at least some of the people of Harare.

In what can be read as attempts to return to some appearance of constitutional normalcy, a bid to test Mugabe's popularity as well as involve the general public in the resignation of their embattled leader, on November 17, 2017, President Mugabe made his first public appearance. Despite earlier confirmation that he was under house arrest, he officiated at the Zimbabwe Open University (ZOU) graduation ceremony in his capacity as Chancellor of all State Universities and president of Zimbabwe, where he capped that university's 2017 graduands. To the Operation leaders' chagrin, members of the media present reported "that his(Mugabe's)appearance received cheers from the crowd" (Waddington, 2017, p.np). By all appearances, the president remained popular among some members of the public.

In view of this, as if to challenge these lingering pockets of Mugabe's popularity, Christopher Mutsvangwa, "the leader of the influential war veterans' association, once loyal to Mr. Mugabe—said he should step down at once. He called for a huge turnout in street protests on Saturday." ("Zimbabwe Latest: Embattled Mugabe", 2017). Interestingly, Mutsvangwa was quoted as saying, "we can finish the job which the army started (…) There's no going back about Mugabe. He must leave" ("Zimbabwe Latest: Embattled Mugabe", 2017). Amid calls for Mugabe to stepdown and others for him to stay, Mutsvangwa's demand for Mugabe's departure was paradoxically echoed by a more likely public civil society pro-democracy group, though unlikely ally.

Empirical analysis of protests and coups conducted by Casper and Tyson (2014, p.548) revealed that "the effect of protests on coups is exacerbated in countries where media is free." In early 2016, the youthful founder and pastor of His Generation Church, Evan Mawarire, came to public attention when, draped with the Zimbabwean flag, he began a protest movement on social media platforms. Called #ThisFlag, Mawarire's pro-democracy crusade had, among other things, decried the escalating cost of living, the Mugabe regime's abominable human rights record, and the bad governance in Zimbabwe. It had not been long before Mawarire caught the attention of the country's security services.

Due to Mawarire's pro-democracy activism, he soon found himself the target of police attention. His house was summarily searched, and he was in 2016 arrested "on charges of inciting violence" and allegations of "stealing a baton stick and police helmet with the intention to incite violence" "Developing: Cops seize Mawarire's" (2016). Three other arrests followed: one in February 2017 for "trying to overthrow President Mugabe's government after calling for protests," "Pastor Mawarire arrested on" (2017). Another in June of the same year "for 'praying with students' at the protest" (#ThisFlag leader Mawarire, 2017, p.np) at the University of Zimbabwe. Before the events of November 2017, Mawarire was arrested in September for "criticizing Zimbabwe's economic crisis" "Evan Mawarire arrested after criticizing Zim's" (2017). Given Mawarire's pro-democracy activism, it came as no surprise when he and his #ThisFlag movement rallied behind Mutsvangwa's call for a mass demonstration against Mugabe.

Amid the euphoria of the impending mass demonstration, however, more skeptical and analytical observers like Magwenzi Nzou took to their *Twitter* accounts to warn that: "Zimbabwe has been hijacked by the military and 37–years of suffering has blinded Zimbabweans into foolishly believing that a coup by Lacoste will rescue them" "Tomorrow Zimbabweans stand together" (2017). From a constitutional point of view, others like then US Secretary of State Rex Tillerson reminded the "people of Zimbabwe that they must choose their own government through elections" "Timeline: How Zim's coup" (2017). Despite such explicit and subtle urgings not to be manipulated, however, on November 18, 2017, thousands of Zimbabweans, black and white, young and old urbanites, the end of years of frustrated hope and stagnation seemingly in sight, took to the streets with the military's tacit blessing.

Once feared and hated by the general populace, the army ostensibly turned ally. The protestors who for years had electorally sought to retire Mugabe from power freely demonstrated in order "to send a message to President Mugabe that he 'must go'" "Protestors March to Mugabe's" (2017). Mawarire's #ThisFlag "anti-government group, appeared to play a prominent organizational role" (Waddington, 2017b, p.np). Similar protests, albeit with fewer numbers were also held in Zimbabwe's second largest city, Bulawayo. For their part, Mutsvangwa's war veterans staged peaceful demonstrations which included "a sit–down protest" ("Timeline: How Zim's coup", 2017) at the ruling party's headquarters. In all evidence, it appeared Mugabe had overstayed and become extremely unpopular—at least among some urbanites in the critical city centers of Harare and Bulawayo.

On November 19, 2017, in a demonstration of the caprice of loyalty, the ZANU-PF Youth League that barely a few days earlier had pledged its allegiance to Mugabe and vowed to die for him was now also calling for the First couple of Robert and Grace Mugabe to go. The ruling party's central committee summarily dismissed Mugabe as leader of the party and gave him an ultimatum to either resign "as president by Monday (20 November 2017) or face impeachment" ("Timeline: How Zim's coup", 2017). The G40 cabal of "Grace Mugabe, then Vice President Mpoko, cabinet ministers Jonathan Moyo, Savior Kasukuwere, Patrick Zhuwao, Ignatius Chombo, Samuel Udenge, Walter Mzembi, and Mandi Chimene" (Waddington, 2017a, p.np) were conversely expelled from the ruling party. Emmerson Mnangagwa's ZANU-PF membership was reinstated, and he was elected interim party president.

For its part, Zimbabwe's parliament set in motion impeachment processes aimed at removing Mugabe as state president. To many onlookers, the writing seemed visibly on the proverbial wall for the embattled geriatric leader. In the ominous words of the war veterans' association leader, Chris Mutsvangwa, "the game was up" for Mugabe and the "army (would) finish with him today" "Timeline: How Zim's coup" (2017). By all appearances, Mugabe's presidency was about to come to abrupt and long-awaited halt. Unknown to most, however, the grand old man of African politics still had an ace up his sleeve—the Constitution of Zimbabwe. If he was to relinquish power legitimately, it would have to be nothing else but, constitutionally.

So, when on the evening of November 19 Mugabe, flanked by the country's service chiefs, appeared on State television to give his long-anticipated resignation speech—at the end of which—he awkwardly and amazingly defied all expectations and did not. To those watching the broadcast, even more mystifying was when at the end of the televised address, President Mugabe stood up and all the country's service chiefs took turns to shake his hand and salute him. To the discerning eye, not all was well. Most notably, during the address, Mugabe had made uncharacteristic reading errors. Moreover, the conclusion of the address had looked staged to give the impression that Mugabe was still in control of the armed forces' command. To possibly legitimize the perception that Operation Restore Legacy had simply been a military mission and not a coup, it was imperative that both Mugabe and the armed forces' chiefs give the semblance that the chain of command still prevailed—that Mugabe was still president and commander-in-chief of the armed forces.

The following day, November 20, 2017, the notion that President Mugabe might still be in control, after all, was again given when a more constitutional foundation when a conciliatory and apparently more constitution-conscious General Chiwenga issued a press statement. In it, he seemed keen to ingratiate the army with the general public, show the armed forces' continued respect for President Mugabe, absolve the military from any accusations that it had staged a coup, and chart a leadership course for the country. The statement read:

> As your Defence and Security Services, we are heartened by your display of composure, order, and discipline during various matches. Meetings with His Excellency, the President, and Commander-in-Chief of the Zimbabwe Defence Forces, Cde RG Mugabe have gone on in an atmosphere of mutual respect and several guarantees have been made. As your Defence and Security Services, we remain seized with the operation code-named 'Operation Restore Legacy.' Following the address to the Nation by His Excellency the President of the Republic of Zimbabwe, and Commander-in-Chief of the Zimbabwe Defence Forces last night, we have made further consultations with the President to agree to a Roadmap on the prevailing situation in the country. The Zimbabwe Defence Forces and Security Services are encouraged by new developments which include contact between the President and former Vice President, Cde ED Mnangagwa, who is expected in the country shortly. 'Chiwenga Issues New Statement' (2017)

Most notably, Chiwenga referred to the military intervention as "Operation Restore Legacy" and was twice emphatic about addressing Mugabe as the "His Excellency, the President, and Commander-in-Chief of the Zimbabwe Defence Forces." The notion that Mugabe was still "His Excellency, the President, and Commander-in-Chief of the Zimbabwe Defence Forces" was at noon reinforced when he significantly defied the ultimatum to resign or face impeachment. To onlookers, it seemed that, if Mugabe was to "go," as "the general public was demanding", it would only be on his own terms or those of Zimbabwe's constitution.

However, desperate to rid themselves of Mugabe, in response to his apparent refusal to loosen his grip on the presidency, thousands of University of Zimbabwe students boycotted classes and demonstrated at their main campus calling for the sitting president to step down. This was reinforced by, the Zimbabwe National Liberation War Veterans Association (ZNLWVA) chairman, Chris Mutsvangwa's call for "immediate protests outside Mugabe's private residence," ("Timeline: How Zim's coup", 2017). Interestingly, on its part however, the ZNLWVA filed a court application "seeking an order declaring the interventions of the Zimbabwe Defence Forces(…)as a lawful and justified action meant to defend constitutionalism (…) and the nation at large in terms of Section 212[17] of the Constitution of Zimbabwe." ("War Vets Seek Court", 2017). In addition, the war veterans' organization "also filed a separate urgent chamber application requesting the court to treat the declaration matter with urgency" ("War Vets Seek Court" , 2017). The ZNLWVA's chairman, Chris Mutsvangwa, spearheaded the organization's court application.

As a measure of their own resolve to unseat Mugabe as president, the ZANU-PF party issued a press statement in which it announced that: "the Party has instructed the Chief Whip to proceed with impeachment processes against Cde RG Mugabe as it has not received the anticipated confirmation of his resignation from the Speaker of Parliament (...) The motion of proceedings is expected to be tabled before parliament when it seats on Tuesday, 21 November 2017" (Press Statement By The ZANU-PF Secretary, para.2 and 3). At last, a constitutional process aimed at correcting the military's intervention finally looked underway.

Concerted efforts of both the ZNLWVA and the ZANU-PF party to constitutionally oust Mugabe were further buttressed, when ZANU-PF turned to "the main opposition, Movement for Democratic Change (MDC) seeking their cooperation to pass the necessary parliamentary votes" ("Timeline: How Zim's coup", 2017) to impeach the president and the MDC-T agreed. In the afternoon of November 21, 2017, therefore, a jointsitting of the Senate and National Assembly of the Fifth Session of the Eighth Parliament issued a communiqué accepting a motion by Senator Mutsvangwa of ZANU-PF and Honorable Maridadi of MDC-T under Section 97(1) of the Constitution of Zimbabwe Amendment (No.20) to impeach the State President on the grounds of "(a) serious misconduct (b) failure to obey, uphold or defend the Constitution, (d) inability to perform the function of the Office because of physical and mental incapacity"[18]. Mnangagwa, in exile since his dismissal issued a statement calling "for Mugabe to stand down." ("Timeline: How Zim's coup", 2017, np). Amid protests for Mugabe to resign, an impeachment process in motion and calls for him to step down, his time in office was clearly and constitutionally finally up.

After 37 tumultuous years as Zimbabwe's head of State and government, Robert Gabriel Mugabe undramatically and constitutionally resigned on November 21, 2017. He submitted his resignation to the Speaker of Parliament, Joseph Mudenda, by courier to be read out to parliamentarians and the nation at large. In his resignation letter, Mugabe poignantly "said the decision was voluntary, and he had made it to allow a smooth transfer of power" ("Zimbabwe's Robert Mugabe Resigns", 2017). The announcement of his resignation was met with jubilant celebration both in parliament and on some of the country's streets.

While Mugabe's resignation marked the end of an era, his resignation was, however, not the only one tendered. It was interestingly and tellingly followed by those of some of the ZDF's most high-ranking officers. Among them were General Chiwenga and Major–General Sibusiso Moyo, the most visible forerunners of Operation Restore Legacy. Their resignations constitutionally made them civilians eligible, under the African Charter on Democracy, Elections, and Governance to hold "any position of responsibility in the political institutions of their state" albeit having been possible "perpetrators of unconstitutional action." They would both later assume the influential governance roles of first vice president and minister of foreign affairs, respectively.

After November 21, the country busied itself with the prospects and challenges of a post-Mugabe era. Although constitutionally Mugabe's successor should have been then Vice President Phelekezela Mpokho, "a supporter of Grace Mugabe" ("Zimbabwe's Robert Mugabe Resigns", 2017), the ruling ZANU-PF party chief whip, Lovemore Matuke, informed Reuters news agency that: "Mr. Mnangagwa 'would be in office within 48 hours'" ("Zimbabwe's Robert Mugabe Resigns", 2017). The days which followed ensured just that.

The ruling party promptly dismissed Phelekezela Mpokho as vice president, making way for Emmerson Mnangagwa's return on November 22, 2017, from self-imposed exile in South Africa. He interestingly first assumed his old position of vice president and that of interim ZANU-PF leader. As the only vice president in office, he "would serve the remainder of Mr. Mugabe's term until elections that are due to be held by September 2019" "Zimbabwe's Mnangagwa promises jobs" (2017). Notably, speaking at the ZANU-PF headquarters after his return, Mnangagwa "thanked the army for running the 'process' of removing Mr. Mugabe peacefully" ("Zimbabwe's Mnangagwa promises jobs", 2017). On November 23, 2017, president-elect Mnangagwa would interestingly again claim "to have been in contact with military authorities since the moment he was fired by Robert Mugabe" ("Zimbabwe's Mnangagwa promises jobs", 2017). The coup that was, but was not, was increasingly raising eyebrows.

Any constitutional gray areas surrounding what had transpired in the afternoon of November 14 and morning of November 15, 2017, were however finally and constitutionally put to rest when on November 24, 2017, the High Court of Zimbabwe responded to the ZNLWVA's application for a declaratory order requesting that "the court should correctly interpret the law and proclaim the legitimacy of the military intervention to the dire situation since Tuesday last week" ("War Vets Seek Court", 2017). In its judgment, the Court affirmed the legality of the ZDF's actions and "ordered by consent that the actions of the Zimbabwe Defence Forces (ZDF) in intervening to stop takeover of first respondent's [Robert Mugabe] constitutional functions by those around him are constitutionally permissible and lawful" (Waddington, 2019, p.np). It left the path to the presidency constitutionally open for Emmerson Mnangagwa's inauguration as Zimbabwe's third president.

With Mugabe's departure, Mnangagwa's return and eventual assumption of the presidency on November 24, 2017, on the one hand, and Zimbabwe's pending 2018 general election on the other, the country's crisis was in November 2017 brought to a watershed. It is one encapsulated in the comments made by two Zimbabweans from totally different walks of life. Speaking to AFP news agency after the announcement of Mugabe's resignation, Togo Mdhlalambi, a hairdresser was quoted as saying, "We are just so happy things are finally going to change" ("Zimbabwe's Robert Mugabe Resigns", 2017). Conversely, David Coltart, a prominent Zimbabwean opposition politician, retorted "We have removed a tyrant, but not a tyranny" ("Zimbabwe's Robert Mugabe Resigns", 2017). The two comments paradoxically mirror the mixed optimism and yet pessimism that most perceived to be Zimbabwe's future, at the end of 2017. After close to two decades of crisis, the country once again found itself in an interregnum, a watershed moment—one from which it could either move forward and return to normalcy or be again dragged down into the abyss and quagmire of decay.

## *Conclusion*

What occurred from November 13–24, 2017, in Harare, Zimbabwe, was the climax of the factional fighting at play in the ZANU-PF party. By all appearances, the Lacoste faction decided to use its last trump card, its support by, and control of the ZDF's top brass to check the Mugabes' perceived dynasty-building ambitions and also oust the rival G40 faction. However, by "stepping in and intervening" to dislodge a rival faction that was intimately supported by the country's president, the officers commanding the defense forces then found themselves inadvertently staging a coup d'état, by any other name. To rid themselves of the stigma of a coup, therefore, the victorious faction and the officers who had staged it attempted to reverse or mask what they could of their takeover or power grab. Firstly, they "reinstated" the incumbent but ensured his position became one of a ceremonial figurehead. Secondly, with a constitutional transition as their endgame, aided by the ZNLWVA and susceptible and patriotic civic groups, they raised the barometer of the incumbent's unpopularity through genuine and fanned urbanite mass protests which ensured the need for a constitutional "roadmap" into the future. Lastly, with the aid of the ZNLWVA, the ruling ZANU-PF party and reminiscent of 2009, the cooperation of the main opposition, the MDC–T, constitutional processes were orchestrated and set in motion, culminating in Robert Mugabe's resignation. Accordingly, turning a coup d'état that initially was, into a constitutional change of power endorsed by the high court.

## *Notes*

1. Later renamed Zaire by Mobutu Sese Seko. Then changed back to Democratic Republic of Congo (DRC) by Laurent–Désire Kabila in 1997 after a popular rebellion against Mobutu.
2. Later renamed Burkina Faso.
3. Mujuru was dismissed along with seven government ministers, among them, then state security minister, Didymus Mutasa, and energy minister, Dzikamai Mavhaire, both from the Gamatox faction.
4. Statement issued by then chief secretary to the cabinet Misheck Sibanda on December 9, 2014.
5. On April 10, 2015, she formed her own political party—Zimbabwe People First (ZPF) with Margaret Dongo. In 2017, she expelled seven senior members, among them Dongo. She had to relinquish the name Zimbabwe People First for National People's Party (NPP). It was again later changed to the National Rainbow People's Party (NRPP).
6. During Zimbabwe's liberation war, Mnangagwa had from 1964–65 led a band of combatants known as the Crocodile Gang. Comprised mainly of war veterans of Zimbabwe's liberation war, Lacoste had been so-called possibly because of its covert support of Mnangagwa whose nickname is *gwena* (Shona for crocodile) and the logo of the French fashion brand, Lacoste. Conversely, it had possibly been so-called to identify it as an extension of Mnangagwa's wartime "Crocodile Gang." Whatever the reason, this eclectic bloc believed Mugabe's successor should have strong liberation war credentials, an established track record within party structures and possibly from the Midlands province of the country. It thus had within its ranks war veterans, high ranking officers of the Zimbabwe Defence Forces, some senior members of the party's politburo, and a few senior women of the ZANU-PF Women's League.
7. Unlike Lacoste, Generation 40 or G40 comprised relatively younger party bigwigs. Still, in their 30s and early 60s, their history with ZANU-PF was quite recent. Some were still in the party's Youth League, while others had joined and risen in the party as technocrats, praise-singers or relatives of Mugabe. They had no liberation war credentials to them and believed that in the event of Mugabe's incapacitation someone of their generation and Mugabe's academic standing should succeed him. It is perhaps because of the latter requirement that Grace had accelerated her acquisition of a Ph.D.
8. According to unconfirmed reports, Chiwenga had gone to China to ask Zimbabwe's largest trading partner whether it would accede to the overthrow of Mugabe.
9. Press Statement by the ZANU-PF National Secretary for Information and Publicity, S.K Moyo issued at 10:19 on November 14, 2017.
10. According to the African Defence Review, "the vehicles appeared to be either Norinco-made Type 63 armored personnel carriers (APCs)."
11. The South African *Mail & Guardian* would later report that heavy gunfire had been heard that evening near Mugabe's residence. While other unnamed sources claim those commanding the Presidential Guards were in cohorts with the coup plotters and so did not resist.
12. See https://allafrica.com/stories/201711240436.html.

13. Watching Sibusiso Moyo https://twitter.com/povonewstv/status/930628396098510848 one cannot help but note his tightly clenched hand.
14. In the story, a fashionable vain emperor is duped into prancing around nude after being fooled by a clever visiting tailor that he is wearing invisible clothes. That is until a boy points out that the emperor is in fact, naked.
15. See AFP Africa's Twitter feed https://twitter.com/AFPAfrica/status/930821285193699329.
16. See Paul Williams, "From Non-Intervention to Non-Indifference: The Origins and Development of the African Union's Security Culture," *African Affairs* 106, no. 423 (2007): 253–79; and Eki Omorogbe, "A Club of Incumbents? The African Union and Coups d'État," *Vanderbilt Journal of Transnational Law* 44, no. 1 (2011): 123–54 for scholarly debate on this issue.
17. Section 212 of Zimbabwe's 2013 Constitution falls under Chapter 11: Security Services, specifically Part 2: Defence Forces and deals with the Function of the Defence Forces. Visit: https://www.wipo.int/edocs/lexdocs/laws/en/zw/zw038en.pdf for more information.
18. Visit http://www.newsdzezimbabwe.co.uk/2017/11/impeachment-charges.html for document.

## References

Associated Press. (2017, November18). Protesters march to Mugabe's official residence, 'want to see him out'. Retrieved January 23, 2019, from https://www.news24.com/Africa/Zimbabwe/protesters-march-to-mugabes-official-residence-want-to-see-him-out-20171118

Casper, B. A., & Tyson, S. A. (2014). Popular protest and elite coordination in a Coup d'état. *The Journal of Politics*, *76*(2) (Mar. 3), 548–564.

Dzirutwe, M. (2017). Zimbabwe's top general ready to "step in" to end purge of ousted VP supporters. Retrieved June 13, 2018, from https://af.reuters.com/article/zimbabweNews/idAFL8N1NJ6E6?feedType=RSS&feedName=zimbabweNews

Evan Mawarire arrested after criticizing Zim's economic crisis. (2017, September24). Eyewitness News, p.np. Retrieved June 5, 2018, from https://ewn.co.za/2017/09/24/evan-mawarire-arrested-after-criticising-zim-s-economic-crisis

Kazeem, Y. (2017). What is a coup? These 40 African Countries could help explain. Retrieved May 2, 2018, from https://qz.com/africa/1130009/what-is-coup-zimbabwe-joins-40-african-countries-that-have-had-coups/

Machivenyika, F. ZANU-PF Expels Mnangagwa. (2017, November9). *The Herald*, p1

McKenna, A. (2019). Blaise compaore. Retrieved May 17, 2019, from https://www.britannica.com/biography/Blaise–Compaore

Mushava, E. (2016, July 12). Developing: Cops seize Mawarire's phone. Retrieved from https://www.newsday.co.zw/2016/07/developing-police-arrest-mawarire-want-phone/

Nathan, L. (2016). Trends in mediating in Africa Coups, 2000–2015. In *International studies association 2016 annual convention*, Atlanta, March 16–19.

Pakistani, S. K. (2016). How to execute asuccessful military coup–key lessons from a Pakistani. Retrieved June 13, 2018, from https://www.parhlo.com/how-to-execute-a-successful-military-coup-key-tips-from-a-pakistani/

Pastor Mawarire arrested on return to Zimbabwe from US. (2017, February2). Retrieved August 23, 2018, from https://www.enca.com/africa/pastor-mawarire-arrested-on-return-to-zimbabwe-from-us

Sibanda, T. (2014). Zimbabwe: Robert Mugabe junior to enter politics. Retrieved May 3, 2019, from https://allafrica.com/stories/201408050205.html

The Editors of Encyclopedia Britannica. (2018). Mobuto Sese Seko. Retrieved May 7, 2019, from https://www.britannica.com/biography/Mobutu-Sese-Seko

THE PRESIDENCY Republic of South Africa. (2017). Update on the Zimbabwean situation. Retrieved May 10, 2018, from http://www.thepresidency.gov.za/press-statements/update-zimbabwean-situation

#ThisFlag leader Mawarire arrested for 'praying with students' at protest. (2017, June26). Retrieved May 10, 2018, from https://mg.co.za/article/2017-06-26-evan-mawarire-arrested-at-university-of-zimbabwe-protest

Thornycroft, P. (2017). Zimbabwe's army chief warns Mugabe's party that military may intervene after sackings. Retrieved June 12, 2018, from https://www.telegraph.co.uk/news/2017/11/13/zimbabwe-army-chief-warns-mugabes-party-military-may-intervene/

Timeline: How Zimbabwe's 'coup' unfolded. (2017, November 21). Retrieved May 10, 2018, from https://mg.co.za/article/2017-11-21-timeline-how-zimbabwes-coup-unfolded

Tomorrow Zimbabweans stand together for a #fresh start. (2017). Retrieved June 13, 2018, from https://twitter.com/PastorEvanLive/status/931537765170335745

Treacherous Shenanigans: The inside story of Mugabe's downfall. (2017). Retrieved June 3, 2018, from https://ewn.co.za/2017/11/26/treacherous-shenanigans-the-inside-story-of-mugabe-s-downfall?wp=true

Waddington, C. (2017a). Something is happening in Zimbabwe. It might be a coup. It might not. (UPDATED: It now appears more likely that it is). Retrieved May 4, 2018, from http:www.africandefence.net/something-is-happening-in-zimbabwe-it-might-be-a-coup-it-might-not-it-probably-is-not/

Waddington, C. (2017b). A timeline of the coup in Zimbabwe. Retrieved May 19, 2018, from https://www.africandefence.net/a-timeline-of-the-coup-in-zimbabwe/

War Vets Seek Court Order Over ZDF intervention. (2017, November 21). Retrieved May 12, 2018, from http://www.newsdzezimbabwe.co.uk/2017/11/war-vets-seek-court-order-over-zdf.html

We're Prepared To Die For Mugabe. (2017, June 17). *Daily Sun*. p.np. Retrieved June 18, 2018 from https://www.dailysun.co.za/News/International/were-prepared-to-die-for-mugabe-20171114

Zhangzha,V. (2016). Grace resumés 'meet the people tours'. Retrieved September 19, 2018,fromhttps://www.theindependent.co.zw/2016/02/12/grace-resumes-meet-the-people-tours/

Zimbabwe crisis: Army takes over, says Mugabe is safe. (2017). Retrieved June 3, 2018, from https://www.bbc.com/news/world-africa-41992351?ocid=socialflow_twitter
Zimbabwe Latest: Embattled Mugabe in first public appearance. (2017, November 17). Retrieved May 23, 2018, from https://www.bbc.com/news/world-africa-42024920
Zimbabwe's Mnangagwa promises jobs in 'new democracy'. (2017, November 22). Retrieved May 25, 2018, from https://www.bbc.com/news/world-africa-42077233
Zimbabwe's Robert Mugabe Resigns, ending 37–year rule. (2017, November 21). Retrieved May 25, 2018, from https://www.bbc.com/news/world-africa-42071488

# *Part 4: Beyond Crisis: Walking and Working Away from a Pariah Status*

# 13 Non-party Consensual Democracy: An Alternative to "Democrazy" for Zimbabwe and Africa

Munamato Chemhuru[12]

## *Introduction*

Elections held in Zimbabwe between 2000 and 2013 were mired in controversy. It is in light of this that this chapter proposes an alternative to democratic electoral processes and dominantparty of governance in the form of a non-party consensual democracy as generally characterized traditional African societies. It posits that post-Zimbabwe's Government of National Unity (GNU) such a system is the most viable future solution to some of the problems the majority rule of Western electoral democracy has spawned on the African continent and which bedevilled the country's recent past. Indeed, as I have argued elsewhere, a non-party consensual democracy being a "viable adaptation and transformation of the African democratic heritage could help Africa's multi-cultural societies to escape current forms of democracy, which generally are flawed"(Chemhuru 2004, p.1). This chapter still follows that argument and argues that, as Zimbabwe moves forward, rather than continuing to rely on democratic electoral principles and ending up with dictatorial rule, election violence, vote-rigging and militarization of the state, it is time both Zimbabwe and Africa turned to a non-party consensual democracy that also considers the will of minority votes. So, although a non-party consensual democracy is commonly viewed as an anachronism and as such, irrelevant to world's modern social order, the chapter sees it as paradoxically holding the answer to Zimbabwe and Africa's futures.

The chapter begins with a short history and etymology of the Western origins of democracy. It does so in an attempt to arrive at a working understanding of the concept such that the geography and definition of the concept can be mapped out and its feasibility examined vis-à-vis Zimbabwean and African traditional value-systems. After that it juxtaposes and examines liberal democracy, in particular, the electoral majoritarian democratic principle against Zimbabwe's tightly contested presidential elections held between 2000 and 2013. Whereupon, it proffers that in view of some of the problems regarding electoral democratic principles, in particular, the majority rule principle, Zimbabwe and Africa adopt a "consensual democracy in a non-party environment" (Chemhuru 2004, p.2) that is more aligned to what is intrinsically valuable to African societies' traditional experience as an alternative system to Western democracy. In the case of Zimbabwe, only then, will the post-GNU era be able to see sustainable reconstruction, lasting peace and development.

## *Western vis-a-vis African Democracy: A Short History and Etymology*

An appreciation of a short history and etymology of the Western origins of democracy from both a historical and a phenomenological perspective is pivotal before any serious attempt to examine its practical significance to Zimbabwe is undertaken. This is because as McGowan (1991, p.21) once noted, if democracy is not adequately defined and understood, people will "continue to live in an extricable confusion of ideas, much to the advantage of demagogues and despots". The truth of this is indeed evident on the African continent and beyond.

One of the main reasons why democracy has paradoxically been both pleasure and pain the world over is because the concept is highly subjective, making it a heavily contested one. In many so-called democratic countries divergent notions of democracy and how it should be practiced exist among different social, political and other institutions. It is one word that over time and history has changed meaning more than once and in more than one direction. At the same time, it is one form of governance that most politicians, including despots the world over, purport to be governing by or at best aspiring to. It is such that democracy has become "democrazy" because of some of the perceived "craziness" it has come to be associated with and is traceable to the concept's origins.

In ancient Greece, from whence democracy originates, it was a practice through which only male citizens could meet, discuss and deliberate on matters affecting humanity. Pointedly, it excluded women, children, slaves and foreigners. Ironically, the term's Greek etymology*demokratia* means,"rule by the people", the opposite of the Greek word*aristokratia*"rule of an elite"

(Liddell & Scott, 1989), which is what is obtaining in most post-colonial African democracies. According to Grinin (2004), the form of democracy exercised particularly in Athens was a direct democracy which is distinguished by, "the random selection of ordinary citizens to fill the few existing government administrative and judicial offices". Also, eligible Athenian citizens were elected to a legislative assembly from where they were able to participate and control the Athenian political and judicial process actively.

As the idea of democracy spread, it is important to note it took on ideological and nation-specific definitions. In America, for example, J. Arthur Partridge in 1866 wrote, "Democracy is Government by the people" (Partridge, 1866, p.2). Abraham Lincoln's own expansion on what constitutes a representative democracy followed when he defined it in his famous Gettysburg address as merely a government of the people, by the people and for the people. Over time, democracy has developed many other facets and is perceived differently by different people.

Broadly speaking, it has seen the emergence of two forms of democracy. These are direct democracy and representative or indirect democracy in which members of parliament act on behalf of citizens that elected them (Gutmann, 1993). There are various types of representative democracy. Notably, by the end of the last century scholars such as Petre Roman were no longer talking of democracy per se. Instead, he spoke of a "spirit of democracy" by which he meant "above all, liberty of choice of human beings (…) democracy, in both its individual and collective forms, is the main engine of the eternal human striving for justice and prosperity" (Roman, 1996, p.1). It was no longer possible to simplistically refer to democracy and be understood.

In today's modern world, democracy is understood along the same lines as it was defined by Lincoln and the liberal Democrats' definition of the concept. The most widely known and practiced form is liberal democracy. It is a system that protects individual freedoms such as property rights, human rights, freedom of speech and the free distribution of political power via elections. However, this is not to say it is necessarily always practiced as Lincoln and the liberals define it. As Ouwaseyi (2009, p.14) endorses, "it is evident that the most popular form of government today in the world is a democracy, judging by its wide acceptance and pretensions to it by those who in reality are disinclined to its tenets". That is especially so because of the discrepancies that exist between the theory and practice of democracy which has complicated the concept over the years.

To Falaiye (1998, p.97), one of the fundamental problems with Western democracy lies in the elasticity of the term. Adediran (1996, p.47) for instance, notes how, "the promotion, practice and vicissitudes of democracy in different parts of the world have exposed it to some definitional haze and diverse forms of interpretation". Democracy's pretensions have been evident in the so-called democratic Western countries' interactions with "undemocratic" countries and even in their domestic policies. A case in point is when on 1 May 2003, the United States invaded Iraq under the guise of maintaining peace in the free world and later summarily executed Iraq's "dictator" Saddam Hussein. Interestingly, it had taken a judicial process for the invading force's Commander-in-Chief, President George W. Bush, to ascend the presidency after the 2000 presidential election that pitted him against Al Gore. Fareed Zachariah later wrote, "In 1900 not a single country had what we would today consider a democracy: a government created by elections in which every adult citizen could vote" (2003, p.13). It appears what defines democracy continues to diverge and mutate.

More recently, the then Obama administration's drone aircraft allegedly violated sovereign air-space, abducting, imprisoning and killing foreign civilians in the name of democracy and the "war against terror". In 2013, the USA's security agency, the National Security Agency (NSA), was accused of spying on US citizens and those of other nations. The same agency allegedly even went so far as to spy on German chancellor Angela Merkel and Brazil's president Dilma Rousseff. An even more bizarre example of democracy was the impasse between the Republicans and Democrats over the US' debt ceiling and the country's debate over gun control.

To those on the African continent watching the USA's"might is right" tactics and its brand of democracy, the superpowers' is the epitome of inconsistency, indeed a justification of the "craziness" of Western democracy. It appears that in the USA, an illiberal democracy prevails as that country's elected representatives seem to have the freedom to rule as they like. Consequently, in Africa and among some Africans, the sense and compatibility of the concept to the continent is continuously a contentious one. That is mostly because before colonialism's advent, African societies had their systems of governance which, in hindsight, might today be perceived as equally democratic. As Ilinga–Kobongo (1986, p.35) stresses, "democracy is not intrinsically alien to African people or [un]African and i[n] many traditional systems in Africa, it was the political principle around which life evolved". Thus, while externally, an African country's show of Western liberal democracy is considered a precondition for Africa's development, Wamba–dia–Wamba (1994, p.3) asks the question whether democracy per se should in essence viewed as something foreign to Africa.

Despite evidence of the existence of precolonial democratic practices on the African continent however, in the face of a world that only accepts

Western-type democracies, Huntington (1968); Akindes (1996, pp.178–9); Huntington and Nelson (1976, p.114) and Gordon (1997, p.153) are all of the view that Africa's traditional as well as economic factors are obstacles rather than enablers of the democratization process on the continent. It is such perceptions that have resulted in most African countries trying to pursue Western-style democracy and yet, in most cases, remaining undemocratic. In my view, this has been Zimbabweans' experience of postindependence democracy.

## *A Tyranny of the Majority: 2000–2008 Harmonized Elections*

Of particular interest to this chapter are twin types of representative democracy often associated with liberal democracy. These are an electoral democracy and the dominant-party system. Electoral democracy is founded on the electorate voting in elections and the party with the majority votes, the dominant political party, forming a government. Wiredu reports that:

> current forms of democracy are based on the majority principle. The party that wins the majority of votes, if the system in force is one of proportional representation, is then vested with governmental powers. Parties under this scheme of politics are organizations with the sole aim of gaining power for the implementation of their policies. (1996, p.187)

Before and after the year 2000, Zimbabwean politicians often boasted that they had brought liberal democracy and majority rule to the country. That was despite the absence of such fundamental benchmarks of liberal democracy as human rights and freedom of expression. Evidence of this lay in the Gukurahundi massacres in the early 1980s up to 1987, the 2000 post-referendum violence, the country's media laws and the 2008 election violence. If anything, a closer examination of the kind of "democracy" such politicians bragged often revealed that, while they had indeed Zakaria's 2003 democracy of universal suffrage, individual liberties of both the minority and the majority continued to be violated. Despite political independence and the vote, Zimbabweans continued to be summarily arrested, tortured, "disappeared" and gagged by such legislation as Public Order and Security Act (POSA) and the Access to Information and Protection of Privacy Act (AIPPA) of 2002. What Macpherson had observed in a different context is that:

> [D]emocracy used to be a bad word. Everybody who was anybody knew that democracy in its original sense of the rule by the people or government in accordance with the will of the bulk of the people would be a bad thing, fatal to individual freedom and all graces of civilized living. (Macpherson 1966, p.1)

became true in Zimbabwe as the country's 2000–2008 elections witnessed. Particularly when during the 2000s, democracy became "a bad word" and expressing a contrary opinion became tantamount to "selling out". Anyone supporting the opposition Movement for Democratic Change (MDC) became branded a "teaboy", a colonially minded servitudious person who pandered after serving white people and their demands. In this regard, the majority inherently became unfair, unjust and tyrannical to a minority that all things being equal might have been in the majority. Democracy thus entrenched the polarization of an already polarized country.

Between 2000 and 2013, Zimbabwe held six elections. The first was in 2000; the second, a presidential election, was in 2002; the third, a parliamentary election, was in 2005 and the fourth, a harmonized election, was held concurrently with the parliamentary and senatorial elections and took place in March 2008. The fifth and most controversial presidential run-off election followed in June 2008, and the last and most recent was the July 2013 harmonized election. In this section, I critically analyse the loopholes of electoral democracy's majority rule principle. I do so by focusing on presidential elections held between June 2000 and March 2008. The reason for this is because comparative analysis of the first two presidential elections held during these periods reveals what has been problematic for Zimbabweans about the majority rule principle of electoral democracy in particular and liberal democracy generally.

During the classical Platonic-Aristotelian era, democracy was commonly described as a tyranny of the minority by the majority. Between 2000 and 2009, Zimbabwe held three parliamentary and two presidential elections. The 2000 parliamentary election was contested over 120 constituencies. In addition to these 120 seats, twenty more seats were reserved in the constitution for the president to elect people he wanted to be members of parliament. An additional ten seats were reserved for traditional chiefs nominated by the Chiefs' Council and elected by the president to sit *ex officio* in parliament. That brought the total number of parliamentary seats to 150, thirty of which were presidential appointees. Since the country's constitution stipulated this, it was, therefore, constitutionally democratic.

The 2000 parliamentary election was the first time the ZANU–PF party faced formidable political opposition since coming to power in 1980. The ruling party had as its principal rival thus far the newly formed Movement for Democratic Change (MDC) also contesting the election. When the election results were announced, Robert Mugabe of ZANU-PF had won by 1 211 284 votes while Morgan Tsvangirai of the MDC narrowly lost by 1 171 096 votes. In terms of percentage votes, ZANU-PF had 48.6% while MDC had 47% of the total votes[3]. Only 1.6% separated the contenders.

Analytically speaking therefore, both political parties commanded a substantial majority of the votes. However, looked at from a democratic electoral perspective, it is ZANU-PF that had the majority number of votes and the MDC the minority. The minuscule difference between the two parties made what constitutes the majority, and minority is contentious. Indeed, while 48.6% is a higher percentage than 47.0%, both were arguably a reflection of the majority and as such, equal. It is for such reasons that Gutmann writing in a different context argued, "there is also a problem of whether the freedom of a few should be limited for the sake of authorizing the many to shape social policy" (1993:411). That is especially so when one takes into account and considers the percentage of spoilt votes and eligible voters who did not cast their votes. So considered, Macpherson (1966) and Hardin's (1990) view that democracy should not necessarily be limited to majority rule becomes credible. Zimbabwe's very close 2000 election results had shown democracy's cracks.

To further tarnish the already flawed democratic process, some international observers claimed electoral fraud and voter intimidation had occurred during the election. The presidential elections of 2002 held between 9 and 10 March were contested by the ruling party's Robert Mugabe of the Zimbabwe African National Union (Patriotic Front) ZANU (PF), Morgan Tsvangirai of the Movement for Democratic Change (MDC), William Kumbula of Zimbabwe African National Union-Patriotic Front (ZANU) Ndonga, Shakespeare Maya of the National Alliance for Good Governance (NAGG) and Independent Candidate Paul Siwela. The reported allegations of intimidation and violence aside, the results of the two main rivals Mugabe and Tsvangirai indicated that Robert Mugabe's ZANU-PF had won 1 685 215 votes constituting 56% of the total votes, while Morgan Tsvangirai's MDC had polled 1 258 401 votes, 42% of the total votes[4].

In a democracy, it is often acknowledged that the party that wins the majority of votes also wins the election. During the 2002 presidential elections, result differences again showed the high popularity of both candidates. An analysis of the presidential election results above reveals that the leading presidential candidates had substantial portions of the votes cast. So, while the ZANU (PF) candidate had 1 685 215 constituting 56.2% of the percentage poll and Morgan Tsvangirai's MDC had 1 258 401, almost 42.0% of the votes, the substantial support both candidates garnered from the electorate is evident. This state of affairs again substantiated Hardin's assertion that "democracy is sometimes narrowly identified with majority rule" (1990: 185). President Mugabe won the election but the opposition candidate's minority was so significant that democracy as a "rule of the people by the people" should have been taken into account and their voice heard.

Given the numbers who also voted for Tsvangirai, it would be unfair to conclude that the outcome became the rule of the minority by the majority. Somewhat it, in my view, became the rule of the majority by the majority. I, therefore, agree with both Macpherson (1966) and Hardin (1990) that democracy should at times not necessarily be limited to majority rule. That is because as in Zimbabwe's 2000 and 2002 polls, the majority rule principle of electoral democracy has sometimes been unfair to the vast minority whom I am hesitant to refer to as the "minority".

Although the African Union described the 2002 election as "transparent, credible free and fair", the Commonwealth observer strongly condemned the same 2002 presidential election. While on their part, Norwegian observers and other Western governments did not. The right to media freedom as enshrined in a liberal democracy has at times been overstepped by media houses that support opposition political parties. Private media such as the British Broadcasting Corporation (BBC) in its news of 3 November 2003 condemned the election. It instead alleged that the ruling party had used preelection violence, vote-rigging and intimidation in order for it to win. Of equal concern to observers both in and outside the country was the ZANU (PF) party's dominance of state electronic and print media for propaganda and hate speech purposes. In their view, the opposition's failure to access public media had severely challenged the democratic process during Zimbabwe's 2002 election.

Democracy's electoral principle of universal suffrage and majority rule does not always solve a society's problems. At times it worsens them. In the USA, for instance, despite the minority African-American population obtaining the vote in 1965, it took the country over forty years before the country elected its first president of colour. That is mostly because of the "the majority's worldview (was) racist, unfair and unjust" (Mohor 1993, p.36). The flaw and complexity of electoral democracy's majoritarian principle emerged again seen at play in Zimbabwe's first round of harmonized presidential, senatorial and parliamentary elections held towards the end of March 2008. Although the 2008 elections were held concurrently, what is of particular interest here is again the presidential election. This time around, it pitted President Mugabe against his now archrival Tsvangirai of the MDC-T faction. In sharp contrast to the ideals of a democratizing party, the MDC had ironically split over, among others, Tsvangirai's dictatorial tendencies. Simba Makoni, an independent candidate and Mugabe's former finance minister, made up the trio of leading contenders. Such was the assumed popularity of the three contenders, some in Zimbabwe expected a voting paradox of the majority preferring Tsvangirai to Mugabe and another majority preferring Mugabe to Makoni and yet another majority preferring Makoni to Tsvangirai.

In the run-up to the March poll, all contestants campaigned freely and had their fair share of media coverage. Although according to the AFP (*IOL*) Report of 11 March 2008, observers from the European Union and the United States were not admitted into the country to observe the elections. ZANU-PF's reasons for this were that Westerners tended to be partial towards opposition parties and never reciprocated invitations to Zimbabwe to come and, for instance, observe US elections. Zimbabwe did, however, invite 47 observer teams, amongst them observers from the Southern African Development Community (SADC), the African Union (AU), China, Russia and Iran. By all appearances, democratic electoral processes had finally found their way to the country.

At the close of polling, the Zimbabwe Electoral Commission (ZEC) announced the parliamentary election results "as they came in". The parliamentary results for the March 2008 indicate that Morgan Tsvangirai's MDC-T won 100 seats with 1 110 694 votes, 45.95% of the total valid votes cast. Robert Mugabe's ZANU-PF got 99 seats with 1 041 176 votes (42.88%) while Arthur Mutambara's MDC-M had 10 seats with 202 259 votes, 8.39% of the valid votes cast[5]. As the results testify, ZANU (PF) had lost its parliamentary majority for the first time since 1980. In all fairness, however, ZANU-PF had done equally well.

By garnering 3.07% less than the MDC, ZANU-PF could not be said to have lost the elections. Fortunately, unlike in a presidential race, proportional representation ensured that the votes the party had won could translate into an equal number of seats in parliament. It is perhaps for this reason that the ZEC quite comfortably released the parliamentary results before those of the presidential race in which there can be only one winner.

It took a suspicious and unprecedented four weeks and three days before the "meticulously verified" presidential results were on 2 May 2008 finally announced. When they were, the results of the first round of elections held on 29 March 2008 revealed that the MDC-T of Morgan Tsvangirai had won 47.9% of the vote against Mugabe's 43.2%, a difference of 4.7%[6]. Resonant to Tsvangirai's 2002 votes at the poll, Mugabe's March 2008 winnings were equally commendable and also in the range of what can accurately be the majority. However, instead of Tsvangirai being declared the winner, his failure to win an outright majority of 51% majority as agreed by the contesting parties before the March 2008 elections meant a runoff election.

Paradoxically, therefore, by the majoritarian principle of electoral democracy alone, Tsvangirai had democratically won the election, but it would be undemocratic to declare him president because of the contesting parties' pre-election agreement that stipulated victory by an outright majority. Ironically, whereas in 2002, Mugabe's majority had been enough for him to retain the presidency, Tsvangirai's 2008 majority was not "majority enough" to secure him the presidency. For all its good intentions, in 2008 electoral democracy's principle of majority rule was outfoxed by the dominant-party system requirement of victory by an outright majority. So, if the run-up to Zimbabwe's presidential runoff election finally held on 27 June 2008 was marred by violence, electoral democracy was arguably mostly to blame.

*The Minority as the Majority 2002–2013: Lessons from the Past: Non-party Consensual Democracy Elections.* Judging by the above, electoral democracy, in particular, its principle of majority rule, is a problem and shall continue to plague African elections. That is because despite its many virtues, an electoral democracy which is good is also wrong because it does not consider the "majority" of the minority as a mitigating factor. As Eze (1997, p.315) sees it, every party is a government in waiting and as such, "the principle of governance should be the reconciliation of competing social interests. Rather, reconciliation, agreement, consensus and not the rule of the majority should make up the political axiom". Gutmann's view is akin to Eze's in that to him, despite:

> majority decision making a possible measure of democratic rule, (…) it cannot be a sufficient 'democratic' standard. Other standards concerning who rules, by what procedures, over what matters, within what limits and with what degree of deliberation have from the beginning been implicated in the ideal of democracy as a rule by the people, and continue to be entailed by the public aspirations of democratic and democratizing societies. (Guttmann 1993, p.411)

Looked at in this light, democracy must not only be understood simply as a rule by the majority. Other factors should apply in order for a society to be deemed democratic. In the case of Zimbabwe's elections held between 2000 and 2013, the electoral principle of majority rule and the timeous holding of elections continued to be the prescriptive characteristics of the country's "democracy". That is to the extent that despite the socioeconomic and political crisis the country was wallowing in, between 2000 and 2008 five rounds of elections were held. For the sake of democracy, no "other standards concerning who rules, by what procedures, over what matters, within what limits" (Guttmann, 1993, p.411) were considered.

Unfortunately, the reason for this might be because, resonant to the Greek's initial and exclusionary meaning of democracy, instead of all nations being judged equal and having the right to be heard, "being democratic today now signifies being good and admissible into the comity of nations as opposed to the isolation meted out to regimes considered to be despotic" (Ouwaseyi 2009:14). Thus, for instance, ZANU-PF's 2008 harmonized elections defeat at the hands of MDC-T also ought to be looked at in the context of the socioeconomic calamity that was partly authored by the imposition of sanctions by the democratic West. The sanctions had ironically been meted out on the ZANU-PF government for taking land from the white minority and democratically giving it to the black majority.

As a result, in pursuit of ever-elusive democracy, Zimbabwe's main political parties continued to focus on attaining the largest majority win. In so seeking, both parties resorted to all nature of violence. However, with the security forces, the youth militia or so-called Green Bombers and war veterans on the ruling party's side, ZANU (PF) often won the day. It was because of election violence meted on Tsvangirai's supporters that he withdrew from the June 2008 presidential runoff election. In an apparent pursuit of "democracy" for democracy's sake and in order to legitimize his presidency, Mugabe carried on and ran against himself.

Unlike in March, in the June 2008 presidential runoff, ZANU-PF's Robert Mugabe emerged with a "landslide election victory" of an unprecedented 85.5% "outright majority". Incredulously, some of the electorate had still exercised their democratic right to freedom of choice and voted for the opposition MDC-T leader, Morgan Tsvangirai. Thus, despite Tsvangirai officially withdrawing from the race, according to the election results, 9.3% of those who determinedly cast their ballots still voted for him. BBC described the June 27, 2008, presidential election "a sham". Undoubtedly, between 2000 and 2008, such pronouncements on the democratic process were being thwarted. The country's practice of democracy had become "tyranny of the minority".

This tyrannical rule of the "ruling minority" continued into 2009 when ZANU (PF) and the MDC formations of MDC-T and MDC-M as represented by Mugabe, Tsvangirai and Arthur Mutambara, respectively, signed the Global Political Agreement (GPA) that eventually paved the way for Zimbabwe's Government of National Unity (GNU) with Mugabe as president. However, considering that Tsvangirai had in the credited March 2008 poll garnered the most votes, the minority candidate was now somehow president. It is therefore not surprising that after the power-sharing agreement and formation of a GNU, the relationship between ZANU (PF) and the two MDC formations continued to be acrimonious. The situation was such that Kagoro in a 2009 interview on SW Radio Africa's *African Executive* commented how the then GNU was a:

> cohabitation of 'totally uneasy souls' who do not like each other at all, who in fact resent each other. The suggestion when two betrothed lovers abuse each other thoroughly that somehow if you force them into a marriage the abuse will end by virtue of a contract of marriage seems to me as misplaced as the notion

> that people who call each other stooges, sell-outs, idiots almost naturally, will manufacture national consent and consensus simply because SADC has acted like God and directed that there must be by decree a Government of National Unity. (Kagoro, 2009 interview)

The two parties' divergent ideological views on what constitutes democracy haunted the lifespan of the GNU. In 2012 it ironically was the ideological contradictions between the MDC and ZANU-PF over democratic principles such as same-sex marriages that almoststalled Zimbabwe's constitution-making process.

Zimbabwe's most recent and arguably successful attempts at democracy were during 2013. On 16 March 2013, after an extensive and intensive constitution-making outreach program by the Zimbabwe Constitution Select Committee (COPAC), Zimbabweans voted in a national referendum on the final draft of the country's new constitution. In comparison to the country's 2000 referendum, this was peaceful, and voters voted overwhelmingly for the new draft constitution. On 22 May 2013 saw its enactment into law as Zimbabwe's new constitution and paved the way for new elections.

The GNU had been a transitional government to facilitate a return to the rule of law, oversee the writing of the new constitutionandopen up a democratic space by way of electoral reforms leading to free and fair elections. By 2013, however, because of the continuation of targeted restrictive measures against ZANU-PF stalwarts by some democratic Western states, electoral reforms as stipulated in the GPA remained unimplemented. Despite this, however, the leading contenders of the ZANU-PF party, MDC-T and MDC-Ncube, previously MDC-M and the Zimbabwe African People's Union (ZAPU), took to the election trail. After violence-free campaigning, Zimbabweans headed to vote on 31 July 2013.

Although it is perhaps not a realistic possibility to hold a truly fair election, there were some exceptions to Zimbabwe's 31 July 2013 poll that made it unfair. A hardcopy of the voters' roll only was made available a day to polling day. Its validity and reliability were questionable as thousands of some of the voters on the roll were incredulously 120 years old. According to the Zimbabwe Election Support Network (ZESN) up to a million voters from the opposition's urban strongholds were alleged to be missing from the roll. In the absence of electoral reforms, state media bias still pervaded. Only on the day of the election did the location of voting stations become known. Despite such electoral irregularities, the poll proceeded, and Zimbabweans turned out in their thousands to cast their votes. In an unusual turn of events, at some rural polling centres, an unusually high number of those who came out to vote were reportedly assisted to vote.

That is taking into consideration that Zimbabwe has one of the highest literacy levels in the world.

At the end of polling, and even before the election results' official announcement, the leader of MDC-T Morgan Tsvangirai had already pronounced the election a farce and a sham. However, the AU was of the opinion that the poll had been "free, honest and credible" (ENCA, 2013). SADC pronounced the election "free and peaceful" (ibid). The EU voiced its concerns about irregularities and the poll's lack of transparency. When the presidential election results were this time around timeously announced, Mugabe had won 61.09% of the vote, Tsvangirai 33.94% and MDC-N's Welshman Ncube 2.68%. The ZANU (PF) party further secured 197 seats, a two-thirds majority in the country's House of Assembly, the MDC-T 70 seats and MDC-N 2 seats. Most African leaders and Russia's President Vladimir Putin congratulated the incumbent for winning and holding "peaceful and credible elections" (Free & Fair Zimbabwe Election, 2013). On the other hand, the BBC on 3 August 2013 reported that the US administration was of the opinion that the results were not a "credible expression of the will of the Zimbabwean people". Once again, the world was divided over the democratic process in Zimbabwe.

Some Zimbabweans cried foul and claimed the vote had been rigged. They could, however, not clearly explain nor provide proof how the rigging had taken place. There was the suggestion that the many assisted voters had been intimidated into voting for ZANU-PF. Others put forward the conspiracy theories that ZANU-PF had conspired with the Chinese and the Israelis. On 6 November 2013, a UK-based Zimbabwean radio station, *Nehanda* Radio among other accusations, accused the Chinese of providing ZANU-PF "with special watermarked ballot paper designed to give all the votes cast on it to ZANU-PF candidates through sophisticated paper technology". Israel's infamous spy agency Mossad was said to have manipulated the voters' roll through its company Nikuv Projects. If at all accurate, then such machinations had on 31 July 2013 proved that democracy could be circumvented.

However, there were those who admitted that the polls electoral irregularities aside, the voting had been credible and ZANU-PF's win legitimate. For these, the problem lay with the MDC formations and its presidents. Since becoming part of the GNU, both had proved incompetent and corrupt. For example, they cited the leader of the MDC-T's, Morgan Tsvangirai, "democratic" lifestyle of a philanderer. Ever since becoming prime minister, he had become embroiled in some sexual escapades, love affairs, pregnancies and court battles involving different women, both married and unmarried. In a relatively conservative African country such as Zimbabwe that is battling with issues of HIV and AIDS, the premier's behaviour was found to be scandalous and contemptible for someone with presidential aspirations.

Besides, others argued that MDC-T councils could not even run the towns under their control and their councillors were incredibly corrupt. Despite all these flaws within the opposition party, its leaders had taken the electorate for granted and still expected them to vote for it. ZANU-PF's victory had thus been a rude awakening for both the MDC-T and democracy. Claiming to espouse Western democratic principles does not automatically guarantee a political party. Winning elections requires so much more. It requires not taking the electorate for granted, convincing them of a party and its leaders' consistency, practicability and ability to deliver.

It is in view of the agonies that democracy electorally transpired in Zimbabwe between 2000 and 2009 and which other parts of Africa continue to have, that I am of the opinion there is at best the need for some kind intervention and at best, alternatives to Western current liberal democratic principles if Zimbabwe is to have sustainable stability. It is in light of this that I at this juncture propose the system of a non-party consensual democracy as an alternative.

Western democracy is heavily rooted in the politics of liberalism which, in some respects, is alien and eccentric to not only Zimbabwe's politico-existential experiences but also to the conception of the Africanness (Hinden, 1963, p.3; Legum, 1986, p.177–9). That is because, in the African context, being is always seen from a communitarian perspective, rather than from the perspective of an individually existing ontological being with only reason, willanddesire. Most traditional Zimbabwean communities, like many in other African societies, remain communitarian, if not structurally, then mentally. The hallmark of this is that matters of importance to the individual and the community are discussed and then decided on by consensus. Decision-making, so pivotal to modern-day governance, is in this respect by consensus. It is for this reason that a non-party consensual democracy becomes more compatible with the sociopolitical background, culture and history of African societies such as Zimbabwe.

Concisely defined, a non-party consensual democratic system holds periodic general elections by secret ballot without voting for political parties. Governance is after that based on the accord of the elected than on majority rule. A non-party consensual environment is, in essence, not a new phenomenon to Africa. Non-party consensual democracy has in the past been used in African traditional societies with much success. In such societies, decisions regarding the community were based on stakeholder participation and consensual agreement. Lessons from the continent's past such as this are relevant to Africa's present.

So even though the world has entered the space age and the world has become a so-called global village, Zimbabwe's experimentation and experiences with electoral democracy, thus far, are valid grounds for examining and instituting aspects of traditional systems of governance in the modern African state. Primary of these lessons is that of consensus outside the realm of party politics. Indeed, as I see it, precolonial Africa's non-party consensual democracy remains one of the most important political tools that can be deployed to resolve problems some Western democratic principles such as that of majority rule have caused in Zimbabwe over the last ten odd years.Indeed, although the traditional systems of kinship that provided the mainstay for consensus no longer exist, Gyekye and Wiredu (1992) and Wiredu (1996) have also argued and emphasized the importance of consensus for modern African societies.

According to Serge and Doise (1994, p.1) consensus is "when people seek to associate together, act in consent and make decisions". This definition implies that consensus in a non-party consensual democracy needs to be primarily founded on stakeholders agreeing on specific fundamental issues. Ironically, the GNU was perhaps the closest Zimbabwe's political formations ever came to a consensual democracy, albeit not a non-party one. As Morgan Tsvangirai confessed,

> There are indeed many areas where we differ, but we agree to differ. We communicate we talk, we discuss, we don't believe that there's anything insurmountable to discuss (…) I'm very free. I've decided that I will not keep anything to myself. I will express it—and express it forcefully—if it affects my constituency, my party and the general thrust of the inclusive government (…) But let's not miss the goal … We will keep our eye on the ball until such time as we are going to have an election which is free and fair. (Smith, 2009)

From the above, it is clear that, although not always reaching a consensus, the principals to the GPA and the GNU had learnt to accommodate compromise, compete and, when necessary, postpone and avoid specific issues until the 2013 election when, hopefully, one of them would be in total control. Notably, consensus as the basis of non-party consensual democracy comes via the exploration of any conflicting viewpoints and possibilities. After that, it focuses and directs them towards an entente that all parties acknowledge. In this regard, to Wiredu (1996), a consensus is a form of agreement and compromise, whose compromise streamlines individuals' interests in order that something familiar and essential may be agreed. Thus considered, consensus need not be merely a demand for conformity.

According to Datezone (2005) in conflict resolution, accommodation is when one party agrees to a solution that will make the other party happy. On the other hand, compromise is when both parties give up something to solve the problem. When both sides stand their ground until one emerges as the winner, this resolves conflict through competition. Collaboration is when parties negotiate the best solution for both parties. Research has also shown that compromise solves most conflicts whereas avoidance is where the conflicting parties avoid the problem instead of solving it. However, it also notes that conflict is not always solved if one party always gives in to "keep the peace". The reason for this was because as Badza noted:

> [T]he Zimbabwe crisis is just a microcosm of a broader political contest between, at least, two emerging categories of African leadership. The first category comprises the heroic but old-style conservative leadership, the vanguard of the liberation struggle, which brought independence from colonial rule (… and) the second category consists mostly of a new and young generation of modern, pragmatic and forward-looking African leaders who appear to be politically and economically reform-oriented. (Badza, 2009, 153–154)

Badza identifies the reform-oriented group as predominant in opposition politics. To it, ascendance to power and legitimacy of leadership is inevitable if one is "democratically-elected and subservient to the principles of democratic governance" (2009: 153–154). In my view, it is the second group's slavish subservience "to the principles of democracy" that is problematic and the first's dismissal of the fundamental principles of democracy that is a hindrance. What both groups are oblivious to both is their potential to serve the country and its populace when they agree and work together. It cannot be denied that the political shortcomings and personality politics of the GNU aside, it was developmentally positive for Zimbabwe and Zimbabweans.

As the GNU's two breeds of political gladiators, these strange bedfellows take turns to exit Zimbabwe's political arena, and therefore, patriotic non-party consensual democracy is sorely needed. The ultimate goal for the country should be the ability to reach consensus on issues confronting the nation patriotically. Indeed, as reinforced by the Ghanaian philosopher Kwasi Wiredu (1996:182), "where consensus characterizes political decision-making in Africa, it is a manifestation of an approach to social interaction". It is such social interaction that Zimbabweans must build towards going forward.

As was witnessed in Zimbabwe between 2000 and 2013, political parties in some modern African countries today are bent on gaining and maintaining power only. Such a conception of politics has over the last decade produced self-styled Machiavellianswho solely view politics as a power game. Moyo (1992:312) concedes when he writes that, "the political party in Africa is an instrument of power and domination". In a non-party consensual democracy, however, rather than focusing on who ultimately wins the elections and thereafter engaging in bickering for the next five years, such a system can help politicians to immediately turn their attention to the more fundamental issues of development that are crucial to a country's development.

A non-party consensual democracy has the unique ability to stop political party competitiveness and disagreements which often bedevil the winning and losing party. Partly due to democratic electoral process, Zimbabwe was from 2000 torn apart by recurring political conflicts and hatred as a result of liberal democratic principles. The catalytic effect of this was the breakdown of the country's socioeconomic fabric. Instead of the political parties concerned sitting down and dialoguing about the problems bedevilling the country they resorted to name-calling and other forms of hate speech.

Interestingly, though a non-party consensual democracy may on the surface seem and sound outmoded and unviable in a computerized world, its cornerstone is dialogue. The conversational nature of non-party consensual democracy also guarantees the participation of every individual in almost all political decisions as it is discussion oriented. Notably, the Czech democrat politician and philosopher Tomas Garrigue Masaryk (1850–1937) reportedly often said, "democracy is a discussion". Non-party consensual democracy is especially promising in the context of Zimbabwe where divergent political views have resulted in conflict and the parties concerned are in dire need of reconciliation and discussion.

Comparing majority rule with non-party consensual democracy in traditional African societies, Wiredu notes that,

> all decisions of the council were based on consensus. The elders would keep on discussing an issue till a consensus was reached, a method that contrast with the decision by majority vote that prevails in modern democracies. The rationale of a decision by consensus as can be inferred was to forestall the trivialization of the right of the minority to have an effect on the decision. (1996, p.163)

The late Bingu waMutharika of Malawi reaffirmed this when he wrote, "an important aspect of political accountability which the traditional African society has handed down from generation to generation is the sanctity of dialogue" (1995, p.9). In Zimbabwe, the beginning and an example of the power of consensual democracy and decision-making was seen on 21 July 2009 when the MDC formations and ZANU (PF) finally sat down and signed a Memorandum of Understanding (MOU) outlining a framework for the talks.

The parties' negotiations eventually led to the GPA and the formation of a GNU. By putting the country first, the parties were able to discuss and reach a consensual agreement to work together towards solving social, political and economic problems that characterized Zimbabwe in the post-2000 era. Undeniably, consensus solved the problems created by the majoritarian principle of liberal Western democracy. In principle and practice, therefore, non-party consensual democracy has already proved a solution to the problems posed by liberal democratic principles before, and it can do so again. Other than advocating the unperturbed access of both local and international election observers to observe the conduct of periodic free and fair elections, one of globalization's other indices is the enthronement of human rights.Besides participation in national affairs being guaranteed for minorities, non-party consensual democracy also solves the controversial issue of human rights which plagued Zimbabwe between 2000 and 2008. In a non-party consensual democracy, human rights are taken into cognizance, especially those of the minority who in modern liberal democracies continue to be undermined by the majority. Indeed, only when there are such non-party consensual democracies globally can globalization be guaranteed the equal participation of minorities. In the words of Frederikse writing in a different context, "by instituting a non-party consensus democracy, Zimbabwe would be introducing to 'the world a new pattern for democracy" (1990:266).

However, much as a non-party consensual democracy is preferable to Western liberal democracy, there is no denying that people have and will continue to have different and diverging views and ideologies. It is almost inevitable that disagreements, differences and diverging social and political opinions will arise. That is because a non-partisan consensual democracy does not always result in agreement on all issues. However, it is essential to keep in mind that where an agreement cannot be struck, some form of compromise must at least be reached by the different stakeholders. That can be done by taking seriously and considering all contributors' points of view, reconciling them and arriving at a compromise. As Wiredu (1996, p.303) explains, in early African societies, "consensus was taken as a basis of joint action and was taken axiomatically". In this regard, for the sake of nation-building, peace and the prosperity of the Zimbabwean nation-state, a non-party consensual democracy is vital and is the best route to consider and seriously take post the 2018 elections.

## *Conclusion*

An examination of Zimbabwe's experiences of democracy between the years 2000 and 2009 ironically reveals how the majority rule principle of electoral democracy caused rather than solved problems of political violence and disputed elections as political parties pursued the majority of votes. That is especially so when tightly contested presidential elections resulted in two "majorities" due to the small percentage of votes separating the two main rivals of ZANU–PF's Robert Mugabe and MDC-T's Morgan Tsvangirai. More often than not, the aftermath of such electoral battles for the presidency was bruising party political contestation leading to crises instead of developmental progress.

It is in light of this that the chapter has advocated for a non-party consensual democracy that is more compatible with both Zimbabwe and the continent's past. As a new generation of young leaders gets ready to assume leadership in Zimbabwe and their respective African countries, the non-party consensual democracy system of governance needs to be seriously looked into, discussed and implemented if an African-style democracy, good governance, peace and development are to be achieved both in Zimbabwe and indeed, on the continent. Failure to do so will only ensure the perpetuation of political bickering, economic stagnation and unnecessary human suffering that have characterized Zimbabwe and many other African nations since the dawn of the spectre that is the Western democracy.

## *Notes*

1. Affiliation: Department of Philosophy & Religious Studies, School of Arts, Culture and Heritage Studies, Great Zimbabwe University.
2. Research Associate in Philosophy, Faculty of Humanities, University of Johannesburg, South Africa.
3. Visit http://en.wikipedia.org/wiki/Zimbabwe_parliamentary_election_2000 for more details.
4. Visit http://en.wikipedia.org/wiki/Zimbabwean_parliamentary_election,_2002.
5. Visit http://en.wikipedia.org/wiki/Zimbabwean_parliamentary_2008.
6. Visit http://en.wikipedia.org/wiki/Zimbabwean_presidential_election_2008.

## *References*

Adediran, T. (1996). Democracy and the rule of law: History, concepts and contending ideas in Nigeria. In A. Ajomoet al. (Ed.), *Democracy and the rule of law*. Lagos: Obafemi Awolowo.

Akindes, F. (1996). *Les Mirages de la Democratie en Afrique. SubSaharrienne Francophone.* Dakar: CODESRIA.

Badza,S.(2009).*Zimbabwe's2008HarmonizedElections:Regional&InternationalReaction.* Retrieved, December 9, 2013, from https://www.kas.de/c/document_library/get_file?uuid=2e617114-48e2-5a93-758c-2fe42e8b1bba&groupId=252038

Chemhuru, M. (2004). *Democracy in Africa: A defense and justification of Kwasi Wiredu's non-party consensual democracy.* Harare: University of Zimbabwe.

Eze, E. C. (1997). *Post-colonial African philosophy: A critical reader.* Oxford: Blackwell Publishers.

Falaiye, M. (1998). African democracy: Its problems. In M. Dukur (Ed.), *Philosophy and politics.* Lagos: Obaroh & Ogbinaka Publishers Limited.

Gyekye, K., & Wiredu, K. (Eds.). (1992). Person and Community: Ghanaian Philosophical Studies. Washington, DC: Council for Research in Values and Philosophy.

Gordon, D. F. (1997). On promoting democracy in Africa: The international dimension. In M. Ottaway, (Ed.), *Democracy in Africa: The hard road ahead.* London: Lynne Publishers.

Grinin, L. E. (2004). *The early state, its alternatives and analogues.* Moscow: Uchitel Publishing House.

Gutmann, A. (1993). Democracy. In R. E. Goodin & P. Pettit (Eds.), *A companion to contemporary political philosophy.* Oxford: Blackwell Publishing Company.

Hardin, R. (1990). Public choice versus democracy. In J. W. Chapman & A. Wertheimer (Eds.), *Majorities and minorities.* New York: New York University Press.

Hinden, R. (1963). *Africa and democracy* (Vol. 8). London: Encounter Pamphlet Series.

Huntington, S. P. (1968). *Political order in changing societies.* New Haven: Yale University Press.

Huntington, S. P., & Nelson, J. (1976). *No easy choice: Political participation in developing societies.* Cambridge: Harvard University Press.

Ilunga-Kabongo. (1986). Democracy in Africa: Hopes and prospects. In D. Ronen (Ed.), *Democracy and pluralism in Africa.* Boulder: Lynne Rienner Publishers.

Legum, C. (1986). Democracy in Africa: Hope and trends. In D. Ronen (Ed.), *Democracy and pluralism in Africa.* Boulder: Lynne Rienner Publishers.

Liddell, H. G., & Scott, R. (1989). *An intermediate Greek-English lexicon.* Oxford: Claredon Press.

Macpherson, C. B. (1966). *The real world of democracy.* Oxford: OxfordUniversity Press.

McGowan, J. (1991). *Post modernism and its critics.* Ithaca: Cornell University Press.

Mohoh, C. S. (1993). *The funeral of democracy.* Lagos: African Philosophy Projects Publications.

Moyo, J. (1992). State, politics and social domination in Zimbabwe. *The Journal of Modern African Studies, 30,* 2.

Mutharika, B. (1995). *One Africa, one destiny: Towards democracy, good governance and development.* Harare: S.A.P.E.S Trust.

Ottaway, M. (Ed.). (1997). *Democracy in Africa: The hard road ahead.* London: Lynne Publishers.

OuwaseyiO. A. (2009). Democracy and Africa's search for development. *The Journal of Pan African Studies, 3*(1).

Partridge, A. (1866). *On democracy.* London: Trubner & Company.

Roman, P. (1996). *The spirit of democracy and the fabric of NATO—the new European democracies and NATO enlargement.* Retrieved December 9, 2013, fromwww.fas.org/man/nato/natodocs/an246pc.htm.

Serge, M., & Doise, W. (1994). *Conflict and consensus: A general theory of collective decisions.* Oxford: Sage Publishers.

SW Radio Africa Transcript. (2009). Zimbabwe GNU: A Marriage of Convenience? (Interviews with Priscilla Misihairambwi Mushonga and Brian Kagoro)African Executive. Retrieved December 9, 2013, from https://africanexecutive.com/index.php/article/read/4084

Wamba-dia-Wamba, E. (1994). Democracy in Africa and democracy for Africa. *CODESRIA, Bulletin, 2*, 3.

Wiredu, K. (1996). *Cultural universals and particulars: An African perspective.* New York: Indiana University Press.

Zakaria, F. (2003). *The future of freedom: Illiberal democracy at home and abroad.* New York: W. W. Norton & Company.

## *Other Sources*

AFP (IOL). (2008). SADC observers arrive to monitor Zim poll on March 11, 2008.

B.B.C. (2003). Was Zimbabwe's election fair? BBC News, November 3, 2003.

C.N.N. (2008). Mugabe accused of election-rigging plan, CNN, March 23, 2008.

# 14 *Beyond Mugabe: The Pursuit of National Healing and Government Relations*

C. Luthuli Mhlahlo[1]

> We can become stronger and whole if we believe in our own traditions (Vera 1993, p.79)

Zimbabwe's new people-driven democratic constitution enacted on May 22, 2013, the country's harmonized elections held on July 31, 2013, and the November 2017 removal from power of Robert Mugabe marked and arguably closed and yet opened other chapters in the country's history. As the country continues further into the millennium under the presidency of Emmerson Mnangagwa of the ZANU-PF party, what visions light Zimbabwe's path? Is the country to determinedly stagger and grope in the dark on the same trajectory as it has done for most of the 21st century? Or alternatively, will Zimbabwe collectively reinvent itself, reform its institutions, and build socio-economic stability? This chapter looks beyond the Mugabe administration. It argues among others that, if the country is to embark on a sustainable socio-economic and political growth path, its leadership needs to consciously and urgently confront the country's tumultuous past and for the sake of posterity, pursue national restorative healing. In this regard, the chapter advises that Zimbabwe paradoxically draw from both the traditional and the modern. As such, it suggests that this be done firstly from the sagacious fountains of traditional African values and indigenous knowledge systems—some of which resonate with biblical scripture and can also be illuminated by African literature. Then secondly, it advocates instituting modern, innovative developments in governance if the government is to forge mutually beneficial relations with its citizenry and the international community.

## *Restorative Justice as Healing and Restitution*

Very much like human beings, nations are in no small extent free and responsible for what they become. This is because more than anything, the trajectory of nations is entwined with the humans who live in them and the leaders whom they choose to lead them. During the 19th and 20th centuries, Zimbabwe witnessed several particularly bloody episodes. Summing up the country's violent postindependence past, a 2012 pastoral letter by the Zimbabwe Catholic Bishop's Conference asserted that:

> The conflicts which render national healing and reconciliation imperative in Zimbabwe are pre-colonial, colonial, and postcolonial. In postcolonial times there was the Matabeleland crisis of the 1980s, violence unleashed by war veterans and youth militias in the rural and farming areas, and political clashes in communities. (Zimbabwe Catholic Bishops Conference pastoral letter, 2012, np)

Oral tradition carries Zimbabwe's conflicts of the precolonial era, and violent memories of the country's colonial period are well documented. However, it is those of Zimbabwe's postindependence period which still linger on the tongues and minds of many, who experienced, are still living and remain traumatized by them. Of particular note and forever indeliable are the *Gukurahundi* massacres and atrocities that took place in parts of Matabeleland and the Midlands regions of the country and that saw an estimated 20 000 people horrifically lose their lives. Terence O. Ranger writing on these 1980s atrocities and barbarities which were committed by both the Zimbabwe People's Revolutionary Army (ZIPRA) dissidents and the Zimbabwe National Army's 5th Brigade reports the horrified eyewitness account of an administrator in southern Matabeleland thus:

> The number of people killed and maimed in Matabeleland during this period could well equal those killed during the Liberation War(…) Thousands of people were thrown into disused mine shafts either dead or alive. At the roadblocks that were mounted everywhere people of all ages were thoroughly screened. Young men and women were sent to camps where they were tortured and killed. Tortures included 'castrations, forced intake of poison, head-butting trees, rocks, and walls, cutting open pregnant mothers' abdomens, women and children asked to beat their husbands to death, stamping new born-baby boys to death. 'Plastic papers were tied to genitals and set alight' Men and women were tied behind donkeys and set alight so that the donkeys stampeded, smashing them 'against rocks, trees, tree stumps…one would pick up a leg there and a broken head there' Women who had given birth to boys 'were forced to put them in stamping mills where they stamped these newly born baby boys to pulp. (Ranger, 2002, pp.208–209)

Indeed, so violent was the *Gukurahundi* period that the late Zimbabwean novelist Yvonne Vera employed its backdrop for her novel, *The Stone Virgins*

(2002). In this now literary-historical novel, Zimbabwe is newly independent; the setting is Kezi, Matabeleland South. Political instability and internal divisions suddenly split the nation and bring it to the brink of civil war. Although all-out war does not engulf the entire nation, horrific acts of violence and callous murder resume and are perpetrated against some of Kezi's rural-folk. One of the protagonists, Thenjiwe, is beheaded and her young sister, Nonceba, is raped and her lips mutilated by Sibaso, a dissident ex-freedom fighter. Such is the intensity and horror of what both Vera and Ranger capture and try to re-present that it boggles the mind just what was and can ever be done to atone for the suffering, pain, loss, and grief those who were victims went through.

*Gukurahundi* atrocities finally came to an end when in 1987 the then Zimbabwe African National Union (ZANU) Patriotic Front merged with Joshua Nkomo's Patriotic Front Zimbabwe African People's Union PF (ZAPU) and formed the Zimbabwe African National Union (Patriotic Front) ZANU-PF. The *Gukurahundi* atrocities and massacres were merely pronounced by then President Mugabe as "a regrettable, moment of madness" (Marwizi, 2006) and left in the dark vaults of the past. No commission of inquiry nor any explicitly remorseful apology let alone any traditional act of atonement was nor has been made to and for those who perished during *Gukurahundi*. More recently, neither have any been made for those who lost their personal possessions or died as a result of the recent political violence that again revisited sections of the nation between 1999 and 2009.

At the turn of the millennium, Zimbabwe once again witnessed more pain and bloodshed. Starting in 1999, the violence this time took the form of numerous but localized outbreaks on the country's commercial farms when some Zimbabwean peasants and war veterans embarked on a reappropriation exercise of commercial farmland seized from blacks during the colonial period. During this reappropriation exercise, it is my view that some existentialist strategies were employed by some of those involved in the exercise. It is some such strategies which I have argued elsewhere[2] contributed and are perpetuating the crisis and challenges Zimbabwe and Zimbabweans are still plagued with today.

From the year 2000, political electioneering and the ruling party's populism instigated the violence that was witnessed nationwide. The culmination was that from Zimbabwe's 2002 parliamentary elections to the June 2008 presidential rerun elections, a culture of violence steadily entrenched itself and twisted the country's moral compass. Brother turned against brother and neighbor hunted neighbor in the name of either the ZANU-PF party or Movement for Democratic Change (MDC). Most memorably, during the June

2008 presidential rerun elections, scenes of civil unrest and pandemonium reminiscent of those in Stanley Nyamufukudza's *The Non-believer's Journey* were televised globally. The world watched as life imitated art as "burning buildings and bleeding, and screaming men, women and children [...were] plagued once again with violence and intimidation by thugs" (Nyamfukudza, 1980, p.15). In the ensuing political violence, hundreds, if not thousands of Zimbabweans were once again seriously injured, maimed, or killed. Tears and blood drenched the land as hundreds were intimidated, beaten up, displaced, or simply "disappeared." Some of them remain so to this day.

After the June 2008 presidential rerun election that saw the return of the Mugabe administration, Zimbabwe's economy spiraled into stratospheric hyperinflation. The lack of clean drinking water, food, consumer goods, medication, and cash resulted in the death of thousands more Zimbabweans. Cholera, dysentery, and hunger claimed many until the unfolding catastrophic socioeconomic crisis was to some extent finally halted by the signing of the Global Political Agreement (GPA) and its subsequent Inclusive Government (IG) or Government of National Unity (GNU). Close to five years of relative stability, peace, and prosperity followed. This in my view is because with the advent of an IG, the country's violent past, specific existentialist occurrences, issues of Zimbabwe's governance, and the country's economy that for years had and have held back the country's progress and shall continue to do so unless effectively addressed were directly or indirectly beginning to be addressed. Alternatively, at best, political will and the hope of their redress arose.

Christendom believes that vengeance is God's and that He ensures that unrepentant perpetrators of violence "die in a parody of the sufferings of their victims. Insanity, paroxysms of guilt, possession by vengeful spirits, suicide—these are the fates of the guilty" (Ranger, 2002:209). Zimbabwean African traditions, on the other hand, lack the concepts of heaven and hell. Instead, like most African traditions, those of Zimbabwe have their own notions about crime and punishment. While these may differ, there are certain humanistic elements that are homogeneous to them all. Central to this is that evil acts have negative consequences on life in this world.

Consequent to the four periods of violence outlined above, some Zimbabweans who lost their lives or just disappeared today still lie in unmarked graves. Considering the country's profoundly traditional and spiritual foundations, this is especially horrific. In many black Zimbabwean communities, as I surmise is the case in so many others of the world, the decent burial of a deceased is paramount. This is because, in most African traditions, the decent burial of a deceased one is believed to have a bearing on both the departed's spirit and those left behind. It is therefore supreme that the deceased be buried in accordance with the correct funeral rites, especially if they are to make as smooth a transition to the next life possible and not return to trouble their living relatives.

In Zimbabwean Shona and Ndebele traditions, the proper performance of the funeral rites is thought to be of extreme spiritual importance as it facilitates the return and entry of the deceased's spirit into the family home. Given this, the spirits of those indecently buried in mass graves and those who were "disappeared" need to, where possible, be identified and their remains brought back home to their relatives for interment. The failure to do so, some Zimbabwean traditionalists believe, causes the restless spirit to roam the earth angrily and has the potential to bring *ngozi* (curse) on the perpetrator's family.

For the harm, misery, death, and heartache a perpetrator might have caused, Zimbabwean black traditions believe the aggrieved spirits of the dead avenge themselves. The Shona people in particular genuinely believe in the sanctity of human life and to some extent that of personal possessions, especially those of the dead. This reverence stems from the belief that acts such as murder must be avoided lest the spirit world releases harmful effects upon the person or family concerned. The effects are known by the Shona word *ngozi*. *Ngozi* is literally a family curse that causes death. It visits itself not so much on the perpetrator of the crime or act, as on his/her close family members, especially so,on the offspring or immediate family of the perpetrator. *Ngozi* in this respect resonates with Exodus 34 verses 6–7 of the Old Testament under which the Israelites were warned that: "The Lord Jehovah God does not acquit the guilty; visiting the sins of the fathers on their children and on their grandchildren to the third and fourth generation."

Akin to the curse in Exodus 34 verses 6–7, *ngozi* can be administered by the wronged spirit over a period. In the canonical Zimbabwean novels of *On Trial for My Country* (1966), *Waiting for the Rain* (1975), *Bones* (1988), *and Under the Tongue* (1996), for instance:

> The forgotten kinsmen or kinswomen seek justice. The spirits of the dead haunt individuals, families, communities. These are avenging spirits that demand remembrance, recognition, and re-incorporation into cultural memory. (Muchemwa, 2005, p.198)

Over time, a perpetrator thus loses family members to inexplicable illness, insanity, freak accidents, murder, and at time suicides. Such is the retributive justice that is *ngozi* in Zimbabwe. Its primary objective is for the perpetrator to languish from the heartache and mental turmoil of losing loved ones before eventually succumbing to death him/herself.

Retributive justice is aptly defined as punishment that is inflicted in the spirit of moral outrage or personal vengeance and is common to almost all human societies. However, some societies also appreciate that justice need not always be retributive, but somewhat restorative. In restorative justice, the objective is "not so much to punish as to redress or restore a balance that has been knocked askew" (Desmond Tutu, in Rosenberg, 1996, p.86). Examples of restorative justice can be found not only in the Bible but also in African literature as well as Zimbabwean society.

Today, Christianity hinges on the belief that Adam's disobedience that led to sin and death was reversed by the second Adam, Jesus' obedience in the face of temptation and his willingness to be an expiatory ransom sacrifice. By dying on a torture stake, therefore, Jesus is seen as having gracefully restored humans' relationship with God under a new covenant, "so that whoever believes in Him shall not perish, but have everlasting life" (John 3 verse 16). As such, restorative justice is seen as leading not only to a relationship but also to life.

In Chinua Achebe's *Things Fall Apart* (1958) when a clansman from neighboring Mbaino kills a clanswoman from the main protagonist Okonkwo's village of Umuofia, the woman's family is compensated with Ikemefuna and an unnamed virgin girl. Although readers do not get to know the fate of the girl, unfortunately, in an act of restorative-cum-retributive justice, the Umuofia's elders later decide to sacrifice Ikemefuna. Likewise, Christendom believes that those who refuse to accept Jesus' restorative grace will after the Rupture, the apocalyptic battle at Armageddon, face retributive judgment and justice (cf Zephaniah 3 verse 8; Revelations 16:16; Revelations 20 verse 12). Similarly, in Exodus 21 verses 23–24 we further read and learn that: "But if there is further harm, then it is life for life, eye for an eye, tooth for a tooth, hand for a hand, foot for a foot." In this respect, the failure to repent and accept the restoration that has been made leads to retribution and not salvation.

Shona tradition likewise, dictates that when *ngozi* befalls a family, it must somehow be appeased for it to release the family from its curse. This can be done by *kuripa* (to restore/repay) in either cash or kind. In extreme cases, as happens in *Things Fall Apart*, the relatives of the deceased can demand that the life that was lost be replaced or restored by a human life in the form of a young person from the appeasing family. However, if this is not done, then *ngozi* can easily wipe out the perpetrator's whole family, if not clan.

Although the days of compensating a human life with another by deliberately killing are both legally, spiritually and morally over, I firmly believe restorative justice in cash or kind still has a part to play in Zimbabwean society.

Both the victims and families of Zimbabwe's bloody years need, and common decency and tradition dictate that there be some restorative justice if there is to be closure. It is primarily for this reason that I recommend restorative as opposed to retributive justice for victims that are still living and/or their survivors.

When in 2009 an Organ for National Healing, Reconciliation and Integration was set up under three co-ministers from the country's main political parties, many thought that, finally, the cries from beneath the land had been heard. By all appearances, it at long last looked like Zimbabwe's leadership was finally ready to confront its torrid past and cleanse itself of the blood crying beneath the land. However, when one of the three co-ministers of the Organ, Moses Mzila Ndlovu, was arrested as part of the ongoing (and unnecessary) political feud between ZANU-PF and MDC-T, any hopes of past pain being acknowledged and restorative healing applied were once again dashed. This was confirmed when post the GNU no organ or ministry to do with healing, reconciliation, and integration was ever mentioned. At worst, this was a clear indication that post the GNU, the then Mugabe government was still hesitant about confronting the country's violent past. Zimbabwe's current and future governments need to proactively and constructively approach and systemically address the question of those whom the country's violent past has victimized. It is a specter that finally and adequately needs to be laid to rest for the good of both the nation, present, and future generations.

In the light of the loss and pain that often accompanies both retributive and restorative justice, modernity has sometimes opted for the biblical concept of forgiveness or reconciliation. On a political level, Zimbabwe's GPA and its resultant GNU were to some extent reconciliatory, albeit temporarily so. Before it was the reconciliation that was propagated immediately after Zimbabwe's independence in 1980 and then again 14 years later when democracy dawned in neighboring South Africa.

Depending on the different parties' perspectives of reconciliation, neither of them often suffers any tangible loss nor gain. However, in my view, reconciliation should, where possible, paradoxically constitute both tangible and intangible loss and gain, yet resulting in a win-win for all concerned. Intangiably, reconciliation's strength and weakness lie in the fact that it provides all concerned with room for reflection, planning,and strategizing as to what corrective measures to take and accept, respectively. In cases, however, where this does not occur, social injustice, animosity, bitterness, loss and pain continue to fester and at times lead to hostilities intermittently breaking out. This is because, as the Archbishop Emeritus Desmond Tutu[3] rightly points out:

> Peace without justice is an impossibility (…) I hope that the work of the Commission, by opening wounds to cleanse them will thereby stop them from festering. We cannot be facile and say bygones will be bygones because they will not be bygones and will return to haunt us. (Tutu, 1995, np)

Due to the traditions surrounding life and death that exist in the Zimbabwean context, reconciliation is only possible between political parties. It is therefore, not the panacea to appeasing the victims of Zimbabwe's bloody past. If anything, a reconciliatory approach would, in my view, be incommensurate with the justice deserving the sanctity of human life. Taking such a route would only perpetually threaten whatever socioeconomic and political progress the country manages to make in the future.

It is perhaps because of sentiments above that in 2012, then Zimbabwe's information minister and member of ZANU-PF's politburo, Jonathan Moyo rightly cautioned that:

> The Gukurahundi issue is not a closed chapter and ZANU-PF must take the lead in resolving the issue or risk having charlatans and vile opportunists exploit the explosive subject for cheap political advantage. (*Financial Gazette*, 2012, July 19)

Viewed from that Moyo's angle, the Organ for National Healing, Reconciliation and Integration was a prudent development on the part of the IG.

Carefully considered, however, lack of government initiative in the project is perhaps for the best as it actually should not be government's responsibility to take the lead in matters of national healing, but rather tangible compensation. Instead, the onus should be placed upon apolitical civil society to play a mediatory and facilitation role. This is mainly because some atrocities, disappearances, and deaths of the last twenty years need to be revisited and assessed through neutral lenses which are impartial, transparent, and can hold truly accountable.

As such, in striving for national healing, what Zimbabwe needs is more than a South African-style Truth and Reconciliation Commission process. Given the traditionalism of sections of Zimbabwean society and the composition of most victims of the country's bloody past, an eclectic mix of traditional values, indigenous knowledge systems, modern thought, and Christianity must be consulted. Zimbabwe's repositories of traditional values and indigenous knowledge systems such as the Zimbabwe National Traditional Healers Association (ZINATHA) and the Chiefs' Council would be relatively rich and invaluable in this respect. Civil society organizations such as the Zimbabwe Peace Project (ZPP), the Zimbabwe Lawyers for Human Rights (ZLHR), and the Catholic Church Justice Project (CCJP) would add academic, modern, and Christian points of view. Ideally, whatever organ, institution, or organization is finally put in place to steer the healing, reconciliation, and integration of families, parties and the nation must be an independent permanent body of the country's proven sagacious elders, spiritual leaders, members of civil society, and mental health professionals. Its explicit primaru mandate being that of navigating the nation beyond its bloody past to restoration.

In seeking how best Zimbabwe's indigenous knowledge systems can help the country better understand its future, there is also need for thoughtful selection of which indigenous knowledge is best. This is insofar as Wehrs (2003, p.780), writing in a different context, critically observes that in Africa, "the roots of both failures and their remedies lie in indigenous cultures, [and] not solely in Western manipulations." In preparation for a time when such indigenous knowledge will be required, therefore, a possible rule of thumb is to select that indigenous knowledge which best resonates with Christian values and principles.

For instance, both African traditions, as well as Christendom, have sets of spiritual rituals which are performed when individuals or communities feel they have erred in some way and have been struck by misfortune as a result. In Christendom, Luke 24:47 informs us that, "repentance, leading to forgiveness of sins, should be preached in His name to all nations beginning at Jerusalem." Archbishop Tutu endorsed this process when at the TRC he said:

> Forgiveness, in turn, depends on repentance, which must be based on an acknowledgment of what was done wrong and therefore on disclosure of the truth. You cannot forgive what you do not know. (Tutu, 1995, np)

Interestingly, akin to Christendom, in African and particularly Shona tradition, repentance also starts with what is known as *kuteura* (confession) or *kudura* or *kubuda pachena* (to come clean). Where an individual has killed, s/he should confesss to the victim's family as an acknowledgment of the wrong done. And just as in Christendom, "The wages of sin is death" (Romans 6 verse 23) likewise, in some African traditions, it is believed a failure to confess one's sins and repent will equally lead to death and confession to conditional forgiveness.

However, while in Christendom confession and repentance lead to unconditional forhivenesss, in Shona tradition, forgiveness of the perpetrator only comes with their adoption of responsibility and restorative accountability for the pain and loss they would have caused. The performance of these rituals should seek forgiveness and should be followed by a mutually agreed restorative penalty as imposed for wrongdoing. The restoration must be satisfactory to the representative of the wronged party if the penalty is to be removed. Such processes are yet to and desperately need to take place in Zimbabwe as soon as possible.

In addition to the adoption, adaptation, and implementation of Zimbabwe's traditional values and indigenous knowledge systems to the pursuit of victim's compensation and national healing, there is also the need to take into cognizance the psychological state of the nation. According to the aforementioned 2012 pastoral letter by the Zimbabwe Catholic Bishop's Conference, "The net effect of (Zimbabwe's) conflicts have been a polarized, wounded, traumatized and uncertain society." Based on this observation, therefore, there is a need not only for spiritual and compensatory restoration. Treatment and restoration of the mental well-being and health of those who are still surviving but who, on the one hand, experienced and, on the other hand, perpetrated Zimbabwe's postindependence violence is essential. This needs to be urgently done if both these sets of victims are to overcome the deep-seated psychological barriers of their pasts and have both closure and peace.

Consultations of a psychological or psychiatric nature should be voluntary and available to whoever requires them. Carefully chosen individuals outside the structures and authority of the government or any political affiliation. should be available to guide, facilitate and mediate between those who would like to repent of their past deeds, apologize, and make restitution to their victims or their representatives. I believe, only then will some Zimbabweand be able to put the past behind them and begin again. On a governmental level, so too can the country's governing leaders also restore their relations with themselves, their political opponents and citizens.

## *From Politicking to Government Relations and Development*

Zimbabwe's political landscape has during the past seventeen years since the turn of the millennium witnessed vitriolic name-calling and mudslinging mainly between cadres of the ruling ZANU-PF and MDC-T parties. On occasion, the two parties' politicking escalated into open violence that in 2008 "left 200 people dead, 10 000 injured and nearly 30,000 displaced" (Webber, 2013). Consequently, the last seventeen years have "complicated the definition of 'the people' beyond belonging to ZANU-PF or MDC" (Ndlovu-Gatsheni, 2010: np). Partisan conflict in the form of endless, unconstructive bickering in Zimbabwe's political sphere needs to come to an end, and a patriotic reconciliation agreed.

As a nation, Zimbabweans must collectively and determinedly commit themselves to pursue common socioeconomic goals "that cut across gender, class, race, generation, and ethnicity" (Ndlovu-Gatsheni, 2010: np) by setting aside of partisan differences for the constructive good. In the words of Fanon (1963) writing in a different context, as a nation, it is time Zimbabwean political parties took "part, in a sort of *auto-da-fe*, in the destruction of all idols: egoism, recrimination that springs from pride, and the childish stupidity of those who always want the last word" (Fanon, 1963, pp.46–47). What Fanon seems to be suggesting here is that it is time Zimbabwe rediscovered:

> [T]he substance of village assemblies, the cohesion of people's committees, and the extraordinary fruitfulness of local meetings and groupments. Henceforth, the interests of one will be the interests of all. (Fanon, 46–47)

A glimmer of such a united nation was seen in 2012 during the country's second All-Stakeholders Conference.

At the opening of the conference, then President Mugabe and his archrival Prime Minister Tsvangirai set aside their difference and "danced to Oliver Mtukudzi music" (Hartwell, 2013: np). In his address to the conference, President Mugabe renounced political violence and urged their respective political party supporters to see and treat each other as neighbors. This call for a nonviolent political campaign continued throughout the 2013 election campaign. Consequently, Zimbabwe's July 2013 poll was arguably one of the most peaceful the country has ever experienced.

The new draft constitution that emerged from the second All-Stakeholders Conference was rightly called "a product of a collective effort" (Hartwell, 2013: np) by then Minister of Constitutional Affairs Eric Matinenga. Moreover, when it was later signed into law, then minister of industry and commerce and current president of the MDC-N formation Welshman Ncube reportedly remarked:

> We finally have a constitution that we can truly call our own (…) As we move forward to rebuild our Zimbabwe, let the challenge be ensuring that our political and governance practices measure up to the letter and spirit of this supreme law. (Hartwell, 2013: np)

For once, since the turn of the century, Zimbabweans seemed to be sharing a similar patriotic vision for the country. Unfortunately, the camaraderie among both the leadership and their followers would not last beyond the 2013 elections.

As forewarned by Ncube, among Zimbabwe's challenges is the need for the government of the day to always fully adhere and respect the liberties and provisions as enshrined in the country's new constitution. The spirit and letter of such draconian mass media laws such as AIPPA and POSA that during the Mugabe years stifled media freedom and information dissemination must be repealed and civil liberties upheld. The new constitution's Declaration of Rights as contained in its Chapter 4 must see an end to human rights abuses, arbitrary arrests, political interference in the justice system, and unlawful detentions. Zimbabweans' conduct and that of their leaders must always be judged through the lenses of the country's constitution and their contribution towards the development of the nation, both locally and abroad.

Traditionally, leadership in Africa, as in some medieval societies, tended to be hereditary, nepotistic, or at best partisan. Postindependence, this lingering perception of leadership has caused many challenges for many modern-day African countries like Zimbabwe. Often it has meant that no matter a leader's ineptitude, the people under his rule have had to tolerate him or hope for Death's salvation. In other cases, African leadership has so tenaciously held on to power to the point of making it hereditary or become so entrenched as to make it a career. In other cases, it has been the refusal to accept election outcomes by either the incumbent or the opposition candidate that has added to citizens' burdens.

Although Zimbabwe's 2013 constitution limits presidential powers and terms, most African governments have in the past had difficulties delivering on the principles of democracy and constitutionalism unaided. As such, the organs of the AU and SADC should continuously give direction, assist, and, when necessary, intervene if true constitutionalism and democracy are to flourish both in Zimbabwe and on the continent.

The mushrooming of governments of national unity in different parts of Africa over the years has paradoxically helped but also not helped. While Zimbabwe's July 31, 2013, election was by all appearances credible and free, it once again raised the issue of electoral reforms and their implementation. In their absence, it was not long after the poll that the opposition MDC-T's now late leader, Morgan Tsvangirai, was crying foul and making claims of electoral fraud. To some onlookers, it looked like both Tsvangirai and his party wanted the lifespan of the GNU extended and were making claims of electoral fraud to this end. However, judging by the way Tsvangirai had conducted his personal affairs[4] during the time he was the GNU's prime minister and the complacency that seemed to have gripped the MDC-T, it is entirely possible that the 2013 poll was an accurate reflection of voters' sentiments.

The IG indisputably had a positive socioeconomic effect on Zimbabwe. However, much as that may be so, it also set a bad precedent whereby future election results will always be circumvented by politicians in favor of power-sharing deals. The will and views of the Zimbabwean people as protected by the constitution must hold sway always. For this to happen however, transparent electoral processes that can enable the electorate to participate freely and judge the conduct of elections must also be in place and be adhered. For all this to be possible, Zimbabwe requires responsible, responsive, trustworthy, and capable leadership that can share its vision for the country and work in unison with the citizenry for the deliverance of sustainable development, decent and dignified lives for all.

A wise Shona proverb goes, "*Gudo guru peta muswe kuti vadiki vakutshe*" (Big baboon humble yourself so that the little ones can respect you.) What this means is that when one is older or in a position of leadership, s/he must be humble if s/he is to get the respect of those who are younger of following them. Similarly, in the Bible, we read of how Saul was anointed "leader over (God's) people Israel" (1 Samuel verse 16). However, when he later became proud and "did not keep what the Lord commanded (him)" (1 Samuel 13 verse 14), he lost God's favor and was replaced with David. Zimbabwe's crisis experience has shown that what the country needs is a leadership that is forever cognizant that its role is not a right, but a sacred duty to serve the people. This calls for selfless sacrifice, humility, love, and the ability as well as willingness to objectively listen to different views for the good of the collective.

Election into a position leadership does not mean one has become a deity and unanswerable to the same constituency which, ironically, elected one into office. It is when leadership is sensitive and empathetic to the needs and aspirations of the citizenry that like a good father or mother, it can both lead, serve and nurture with both principle and integrity, conscientiously accepting responsibility for its actions and creating an enabling environment for the growth and prosperity of the country's citizens.

Today's globalized environment calls for contemporary African leaders who are consciously futuristic enough to chart the nation's course. However, contemporaneity need not mean westernization and the discarding of spiritual, traditional, and humanistic African values. In this vein, moving forward Zimbabwe needs genuinely God-revering leadership that knows His Word and can lead by Godly principles. For the sake of Zimbabwe's future development, it is such leadership that must be sought, consciously and continuously inculcated in emerging, current, and future leaders of Zimbabwe and indeed the continent.

On their part, Zimbabweans who deem themselves stakeholders need space for constructive engagement and communication with their leadership if they are to be able to cooperate and reinforce government's vision and developmental efforts. In this regard, Zimbabwe's leaders need to foster and imbibe a culture of government relations. However, for this to be possible, coherent Government Relations (GR) and lobbying strategies to facilitate discourse are essential.

Government Relations (GR) is relatively new to African governance. GR as Government Relations is at times popularly referred to has as its primary goal, awareness creation about critical dynamics that might or do arise with transition of any kind. It involves and relates to the planned, deliberate, tactical management of the relationship between the public and either local and/ or national government in ways which facilitate clear and direct channels of communication on matters of mutual interest. GR thus manages and concerns itself with those dynamics which if not timeously attended to or mishandled can have adverse consequences for either party.

Transition is part of any nation's life and is ongoing. However, as observed by Charles Darwin, "It is not the strongest species that survive, nor the most intelligent, but the ones who are most responsive to change." Change, development, and socioeconomic growth are entwined. As such, the government and citizens of Zimbabwe need to be continuously responsive to the daily changes and challenges confronting the nation-state. Years of crisis have seen Zimbabwe undergoing a negative transition that has left the country in dire need of a reversal of the decline. Developing a comprehensive GR strategy at a time of mostly negative socioeconomic transition such as the one Zimbabwe has experienced over the past 20 plus years is pivotal to the successful reversal of the general deterioration.

Putting in place a proactive government relations communications plan which effectively communicates and manages the developmental transition and its aftermath entails various considerations. Firstly, the aim of such a government relations strategy should be to initiate and engage all relevant stakeholders on how best to successfully navigate present and future developments across the spectrum of national life. To facilitate this, a GR department must be set up. To this end, an existing relevant government ministry department can be reassigned to take on a GR function; and if the necessary expertise is available, this can then be reskilled.

Alternatively, and ideally, the government can create a new stand-alone GR ministry and recruit experts and personnel specifically to handle the GR role and functions. Expert personnel that is vital to a successful GR department is relevantly qualified, skilled, and experienced in communication, public relations, marketing, risk management, governance, politics, constitutional law, research, and change management. While communication, public relations, and marketing competencies and skills are essential to GR, knowledge and understanding of change management is equally important.

On both an organizational and national level, change management is a structured approach to transition. It involves careful planning, consultation with, and involvement of the people most likely to be affected by the implementation of changes in either an organization or nation. Change management is a mark of planned and futuristic leadership as its goal is to minimize the negative impact the implementation of change might or will have. In the context of Zimbabwe, GR, particularly its component of change management has been sorely absent over the years. This was evident during the land reform program, Operation *Murambatsvina*, the mercurial introduction and withdrawal of various banknotes, checks, and multicurrency as legal tender. The lack of GR during such crucial transitional periods of both the country and its inhabitants' lives has not only betrayed management by crisis, haphazard planning, and poor communication; it has also demonstrated a callous disregard and utter disrespect for the citizenry. Consequently, mistrust and antagonism have festered among a people who are continuously made to feel ostracized in their own country.

Citizens' participation in the socioeconomic and political life of a country regardless of race, religion, sex, ethnicity, party affiliation, or level of education forms the bedrock of a sustainably developing and progressive nation-state. Since GR adopts and deploys elements of both direct and indirect democracy such as in representative, participatory, popular, deliberative, and anticipatory democracies; it enables citizens' participation in the socioeconomic and political life of a country. Specifically, GR assists in this by encouraging the principles of direct and popular democracy.

Direct democracy is whereby citizens actively participate in the decision-making processes of government. Conversely, in popular democracy, referendums such as those held in 2000 and 2013 would have been continuously used first to determine the will of the people and secondly as the basis to planning how best to empower them. In addition to the principles of popular democracy, GR also adopts those of participatory and deliberative democracies. In this vein, GR seeks and promotes the participation and deliberation of the views of more ordinary citizens. For instance, instead of the president both selecting and appointing the cabinet, under a GR arrangement ordinary randomly selected interested citizens would be invited to participate in the selection, evaluation, and dismissal of cabinet ministers. This would ensure their input is represented in all those who finally serve them and most likely minimize the unimaginative and wasteful recycling of incompetent perennially non-performing ministers who are long past retirement.

For GR to be useful, the government and citizens must work together for the achievement of goals and objectives. Civil society and all interested citizens should be willing to foster relations with the administration of the day. In the words of Henry Ford, "[c]oming together is a beginning, staying together is progress and working together is a success." Lobbying is one strategic way in which citizens as stakeholders can resort to if relations between the government and the people are to work and be mutually beneficial.

Lobbying involves an ordinary individual or group persuading others to their point of view, opinions, and activities. In the context of GR, these stakeholders then lobby either public officials or their member(s) of parliament on the matter(s), or issue(s) they think is of communal and/or national importance to getting it presented and deliberated at appropriate fora. However, for the process to successfully work, such lobbyists need to understand who best to approach and how to lobby effectively.

Effective lobbying requires elements of anticipatory democracy that call for researched and informed knowledge of the past and present and how both are likely to affect the future. In such cases, lobbyists should be able to research and make available researched information about an issue, law, regulation, or development they wish to engage government. If they are unable to do so on their own, research experts and/or consultants from either the private sector or GR department or ministry should be engaged. After that, lobbyists must identify relevant officials and follow the correct protocol and procedure to present their issues, activities, views, or opinions as supported by relevant, ethically valid and factually reliable researched information which can assist or chart a way forward or arrive at a decision. Depending on the scope of the issue at hand, this might require the establishment of coalitions with other interested groups and/or communities for support.

Proactively engaging government by way of GR structures and lobbying is a way Zimbabweans can constructively engage their representatives and contribute towards the country's development, growth, and stability. This is mainly as GR facilitates national discourse and results in what Wehrs (2003) writing in a different context describes as an "expressivist model of legitimacy in which the (ruling) party should not just have contacts with the masses" (p.768) but rather "be the direct expression of the masses" (Fanon, 1963, p.187–188). This is insofar as GR enables citizens to speak for themselves and put forward their views and ideas.

The resultant rapport that is nurtured also ensures that communication between the government and the citizenry is not only via the media but rather that sensationalist distortions of information which in the past have resulted in the government's suppression of the media are curtailed. It is, however, not only the government's relations with Zimbabweans that need to be improved. The country's relations with the international community also need to be reconstructed and built upon, if Zimbabwe's socioeconomic well-being is to be restored and reach its full potential.

Innovations in electronic communication over the past few years have improved democratic processes and at times even overtaken mainstream media. During the last seventeen years, the Zimbabwean government has left the international media to tell the country's story. In response, the government's voice has been miniscule and at times, conspicuously silent. The implementation of a sound GR strategy in Zimbabwe must equally, therefore, be accompanied by a sound communication strategy with the international community. This will require reinventing Zimbabwe's current foreign affairs ministry into one that has an international relations thrust. To do so, the scope of the country's international reach will need to be broadened by, among others, employing the latest and most effective media technologies and platforms. Doing so would, for instance, enable the government of the day to monitor news about the country from around the globe, timeously and adequately respond to it by articulatingand explicating its positions and policies.

For their part, Zimbabwean citizens with access to the internet and are tech-savvy can boost the government's efforts to improve the country's image by taking advantage of innovations in electronic communication to objectively blog on and represent Zimbabwe on various platforms. Such a dialogic and visible international presence of both the government and its citizens would undoubtedly make available transparent and credible information about the country.

## *Conclusion*

Zimbabwe's torrid and violent past calls for restorative justice if the country is to heal its festering wounds and finally move into the future. To do so, this chapter has advised that the country should draw from its indigenous knowledge systems, some of which resonate with biblical scripture and modern understandings of justice. To neglect the country's traditional values, knowledge systems, and biblical principles would be to do so at the country's peril as in some of them are the keys to understanding, resolving, and healing the hurts of yesterday. Secondly, given the government's disconnect with the citizenry and its strained to severed relations with the international community, it has advocated instituting a Government Relations strategy and other innovative governance developments to connect specifically with its citizenry and the international community generally. Going forward, therefore, Zimbabwe's nation-building, development, and growth must rest on a syncretic mix of traditional, humanist values, competent leadership, innovation, open dialogue, and transparency with itself and indeed the world if the country is to solve and move beyond its past.

## Notes

1. Affiliation: Department of Culture, Communication & Media, University College London & Comecinc Communications and Strategic Solutions Services Incorporated.
2. See opening chapter of this volume.
3. From 1995–2003 Tutu chaired South Africa's Truth & Reconciliation Commission (TRC). The 1995 remarked attributed to him are from a November 30 statement he made on his appointment to the TRC. See: http://www.justice.gov.za/trc/media/pr/1995/p951130a.htm
4. Tsvangirai was reportedly involved in multiple scandalous love affairs.

## References


Fanon, F.(1963). *The wretched of the earth*. Trans. Constance Farrington. London: Penguin Books.

Giddens, A. (1981). *A Contemporary Critique of Historical Materialism: Volume One: Power, Property, and the State*. Berkeley, CA: University of California Press.

Giddens, A. (1987). *The nation-state and violence: Volume two of a contemporary critique of historical materialism*. Cambridge: Polity Press.

Harris, A. (2005). Writing home: Inscriptions of whiteness/descriptions of belonging in white Zimbabwean memoir/autobiography. In R. Muponde & R. Primorac (Eds.), *Versions of Zimbabwe: New approaches to literature and culture* (pp. 103–118). Harare: Weaver Press.

Hartwell, L. (2013). Reflecting on positive Zimbabwe GNU moments. Zimbabwe Independent. Retrieved, March 6, 2018, fromhttps://www.theindependent.co.zw/2013/07/11/reflecting-on-positive-zimbabwe-gnu-moments/

Hove, C. (1988). *Bones*. Harare: Baobab Books.

Irele, A. (1971). The criticism of modern African literature. In C. Heywood (Ed.), *Perspectives of African literature:Selections from the proceedings of the conference on African literature held at the University of Ife 1968* (pp. 9–24). London: Heinemann.

Marwizi, W. (2006). *The standard*, 1–7 October. Harare

Masilela, N. (2003). New Negro modernity and new African modernity. Paper for conference *The Black Atlantic: literatures, histories cultures forum*. Zurich: January 17–19.

Muchemwa, K. (2005). Some thoughts on history, memory and writing in Zimbabwe. In R. Muponde & R. Primorac (Eds.), *Versions of Zimbabwe: New approaches to literature and culture* (pp. 195–202). Harare: Weaver Press.

Muponde, R., & Maodzwa-Taruvinga, M. (Eds.). (2002). *Under the tongue* and *without aname. Sign and Taboo perspectives on the poetic fiction of Yvonne Vera*. Harare: Weaver Press.

Muponde, R., & Primorac (Eds.). (2005). *Versions of Zimbabwe: New approaches to literature and culture.* Harare: Weaver Press.

Ndlovu-Gatsheni, S. J. (2010). The constitution and the constitutional process in Zimbabwe. *solidaritypeacetrust.* Retrieved, November 8, 2018, from http://solidaritypeacetrust.org/703/the-constitution-and-the-constitutional-process-in-zimbabwe/

Nyamfukudza, S. (1980). Non-*believer's journey.* Harare: Baobab Books.

Ranger, T. (2002). History has its ceiling. The pressures of the past. In R. Muponde & M. Maodzwa-Taruvinga (Eds.), *Under the tongueandwithout aname. Sign and Taboo perspectives on the poetic fiction of Yvonne Vera* (pp. 203–216). Harare: Weaver Press.

Rosenberg, T. (1996). Recovering from Apartheid. (November 10). *The New Yorker.* p.86. Retrieved, October, 3, 2018, from https://www.newyorker.com/magazine/1996/11/18/recovering-from-apartheid

Samkange, S. (1966). *On trial for my country.* Salisbury: Heinemann.

Tutu, D. M. (1995). Statement by Archbishop Desmond Tutu on his appointment to thetruth and reconciliation commission. November, 30. Retrieved, October, 3, 2018, from http://www.justice.gov.za/trc/media/pr/1995/p951130a.htm

Vera, Y. (1993). *Nehanda.* Harare: Baobab Books.

Vera, Y. (2002). *The stone virgins.* Harare: Baobab Books.

Webber, F. (2013). The arrest of lawyer Beatrice Mtetwa- a new low for lawyers *Zimbabwe' NewStateman*, May 27.

Wehrs, D. R. (2003). Sartre's legacy in postcolonial theory; or who's afraid of non-Western historiography and cultural studies. *New Literary History, 34*(4), *Multicultural Essays*, 761–78.

# 15 *Virtue Ethics as a Panacea to Zimbabwe's Business Malpractices*

DENNIS MASAKA[1]

## *Introduction*

A business' credibility like that of any nation's is predicated on its moral base. In all likelihood when a company is steeped in ethics, then its economic activities will be equally virtuous. More often than not, this leads to goodwill and profitability in both the short to medium terms. This chapter philosophically reflects on the ethical challenges that Zimbabwe's business sectors faced between the years 2000 and 2009 and, to some extent, continue to suffer to the present day. From Aristotle's perspective of virtue theory, it demonstrates how the period was characterized by unethical conduct. It argues that post-2009 and beyond, there is an urgent need to inculcate virtue ethics particularly in the country's general and business sectors if they are to move beyond the unethical profiteering rut they had fallen into during the crisis. It concludes that such an endeavor is central and worthwhile to ensuring the success of the country's economy going forward. For, if Zimbabwe can manage to ameliorate and even eliminate unethical practices in the future, then the business potential for the country is endless.

## *Immoral Beginnings: Virtue and Zimbabwe's Crisis*

Popularized by Aristotle, virtue ethics is a classical Hellenistic tradition that emphasizes the cultivation of a commendable character from which virtuous actions proceed. To Aristotle, the primary function of morality is the cultivation of noble traits in individuals. To him virtue:

> is a state of character concerned with choice, lying in a mean, i.e., the mean relative to us, this being determined by a rational principle and by that principle by which the man of practical wisdom would determine. (Boylan 1995, p.9)

It is the mean between two extremes or the intermediate state of character. As such, virtuous activities are not only voluntary but are also one's choice. In Aristotle's view, if a person acts on impulse or with full knowledge of the consequences of his action, then he is responsible for the outcome of his actions. Maclntyre (1966) extols that virtue entails doing one's best or excelling in what one does. If, however, one has to be forced to do something that sh/e does not want to do, then they will not feel obliged to bear responsibility for what they would have done (Ross, 1964). Virtue ethicists differ from principle-based moral philosophies.

In contrast, principle-based moral philosophies evaluate the morality of business operations based on their consequences (utilitarianism) or the intention of the moral agents (Kantianism) and not necessarily character. Looked at from this angle, as far as Aristotle was concerned, all trade is a kind of exploitation where the active participants are motivated more by greed than a cause to ensure the excellent exchange of commodities. To him, anyone trading solely for profit is therefore devoid of virtue in that their acts are purely selfish and do not accord with sound business practices. It is in this regard that Aristotle can rightly be perceived as "the first economist" (Solomon 1999, p.82) and the first business ethicist genuinely interested not only in the exchange of goods but also ethics in business. Virtue ethicists thus blame a person who performs immoral business practices to some moral deficiency in her/his character. It is such a moral deficiency that in my view has been absent in Zimbabwe since the inception and establishment of colonialism and was further cultivated by the country's postcolonial economic meltdown of 2000–2009.

For many, the economic crisis that afflicted postcolonial Zimbabwe from 2000–2009 was attributable to the inheritance of an economy reeling under United Nations imposed sanctions (Tekere, 2007) and the ZANU–PF government's postindependence flawed economic policies. However, in this section, I argue that the seeds of the crisis can also be better understood by taking a moralistic paradigm of the Zimbabwean nation-state from its colonial inception to the end of the first decade of this millennium. The moral compass of what today is the modern state of Zimbabwe was set when in the late 1880s, the British South Africa Company (BSAC) recruited white settlers to whom it "promised gold claims and 3,000 acres each" of land (Moore, 2005, p.ix). To fulfill its promise, in the years 1893 and 1896–1897, the BSAC's Pioneer Column waged war with the both the Ndebele and Shona.

The defeat of which two tribes saw their violent and forcible removable from all the arable and mineral-rich land that had previously been theirs. The culmination was scandalous and racialized resource disequilibria between the black people of Zimbabwe and the white settlers. It was a scenario that during the twentieth century, was from 1957–1979 to form the impetus of, "a brutal war against 200,000 white settler colonial Rhodesians (with 40,000 black casualties)" (Bond, 2001, p.29) and finally lead to the political independence of the country's black majority on April 18, 1980.

During the first ten years after Zimbabwe's attainment of independence, the country's economy was vibrant and mostly stable. The new black government's policies and programs attracted a steady flow of donor assistance and investor confidence. However, as the country entered the last decade of the previous century, corruption soon manifested itself in the upper echelons of power in such sociopolitical programs as the War Veterans' gratuities, War Victims Compensation Fund, the military intervention in the Congo, and the British-funded land resettlement exercise. In 1997, the quick and unbudgeted payment of gratuities to some 75,000 veterans of the national liberation war marked the beginning of the economic situation that was to evolve into a spectacular crisis between 1999 and 2009.

Starting with the payment of unbudgeted compensation to the country's war veterans, the folly resulted in a "Black Friday" (Moore, 2005, p. x) on the country's stock exchange. The country's currency and industrial indices fell. To add to this, from 1998–2000 Zimbabwe's Commander-in-Chief of the armed forces and President of the Republic Robert Mugabe sent close to 10,000 Zimbabwean troops (Bond, 2001, p.25) to prop up the fragile government of Laurent Kabila and later his son, Joseph Kabila, in the Democratic Republic of Congo (DRC). This further immersed the country into ignominy. The country's military adventurism in the DRC was allegedly in exchange for cash, mines, and mineral rights (Masiwa, 1999).

The country's deathknell finally tolled over the land issue. Despite independence's advent and initial economic stability, the country's reclamation of the land had since 1980 become embroiled in the legalities of the Lancaster House Agreement that had ushered in the country's independence. This is because, among others, the signatories to the agreement had agreed that the future black government would purchase white-owned land on a "willing buyer willing seller." By so doing, the expeditious return of the black people of Zimbabwe was taken away from them.

What subsequently followed was a situation where the land willingly sold by white farmers was more often than not either exhausted or in the country's arid Region 5. In other cases, the more arable land that the postindependence government managed to purchase was either cooperatively settled or corruptively leased to government officials on 99-year leases. The British-funded land resettlement exercise meant to benefit the landless poor partly became a more natural way for government officials' to own farms. In this way, some in political positions of power amassed extreme wealth. The return of Zimbabwe's immorally and colonially expropriated land equally became unethical. It is apparently for this reason that the British Labour Party that was elected into power in 1995 reneged on its earlier agreement to bankroll land redistribution in Zimbabwe (Herbst, 1990). They saw the ill-conceived, ill-fated, and immoral VIP Resettlement Scheme "as an expression of political patronage in which the Head of State sought to reward his loyal ZANU (PF) political supporters with material benefits" (Moyana 2002, p. 188).

Corruption as defined by Transparency International is: "The abuse of entrusted power for private gain" and ranks world countries according to the extent to which corruption is perceived to exist among public officials and politicians "as perceived by business people and country analysts and the index ranges between zero, which is highly corrupt, and 10, which is very clean" (Makochekanwa & Kwaramba 2009, p.12). Towards the end of the last century, Zimbabwe's rating steadily declined. The 99-year leases and the abuse of funds meant for land redistribution perpetuated the historically skewed land distribution. Coupled with the IMF-imposed Economic Structural Adjustment program that led to the streamlining of the civil service and retrenchments, poverty levels among Zimbabwe's black population rose. Primarily due to unethical behavior by political leaders, political independence had by 1999 failed to bring about the socioeconomic reforms that had informed the liberation struggle.

## *Land Reform: An Ethical Program Hijacked and Its Unethical Aftermath*

In 1998, for what can be considered valid moral reasons, the Svosve people "invaded" their former ancestral land from which they had been evicted at the onset of Zimbabwe's colonization. Taking their cue from the people of Svosve, other villagers in places such as Nyamandlovu and around the country followed suit and "invaded" white commercial farms. They were led by war veterans who during the country's Second Chimurenga had promised them the economic resources of independent Zimbabwe, primarily the land. For either true nationalist reasons or political expediency or both, after some initial hesitation, the Zimbabwean government tacitly authorized the "invasion" of white commercial farmers. This occupation of white-owned farms

2000 with "military muscle, police protection, and executive endorsement" (Moore, 2005, p.ix) by war veterans and land-hungry peasants was to later lead to the immoral use of the war veterans and country's security forces for personal rather than public gain.

From 2000, however, after the land-hungry peasants and war veterans initiative, their "land invasions" were formalized under the ZANU–PF government's fast-track land reform program. The redistribution of the country's agricultural land that followed saw most large tracts of the best arable land going to politicians, police,and military personnel affiliated to the ruling party. Although thousands of peasant households benefitted from land reform to many, the exercise was seen as a political ploy by a beleaguered ruling party faced with a watershed national election that was to be tightly contested between itself and the then newly formed Movement for Democratic Change (MDC).

Undertaken during the height of Zimbabwe's agricultural season, the fast-track land redistribution exercise did not make economic sense. The occupation of farmland displaced and stopped farming activities essential to agricultural productivity for the nation's short- and long-term survival. It proved most detrimental to the country's largely agrarian economy. So, although the program's aim of redressing land imbalances in Zimbabwe was morally justified, the means of executing are even today still mired in controversy. It is in light of this, given the chaotic and rushed nature of land reform then member of the Natural Resources Board, Lance Smith prophetically warned that:

> Making political capital out of the land issue [...] without ensuring that sustained agricultural production would be safeguarded could have disastrous consequences [...] condemn[ing] us all to a future of abject poverty. (Moyana, 2002, p. 179)

In the years that followed, the country lost its breadbasket status in Southern Africa partly because of the country'sland reform program (Sachikonye, 2002). The unprecedented decline in agricultural production was to result in Zimbabwe's worst food shortages in recorded history.

Zimbabwe's failure to adhere to the rule of law by embarking on its fast-track land reform program and the abuse of human and property rights during farm occupations was in 2002 met with smart sanctions from the USA and other targeted economic restrictions from the European Union (EU). The assets of the country's ruling elite and some business persons associated with ZANU-PF were frozen (Bond & Manyanya, 2003). This also fomented international lending institutions, investors, and donors to withdraw lines of credit, investment, and stop funding, respectively. The measures heavily impacted on Zimbabwe's economy. Never before had a people and country been so punished for reclaiming their heritage.

Indeed, to the ZANU-PF government and others in Zimbabwe, the restrictions became in essence economic sanctions meant to punish the indigenous people of Zimbabwe for claiming their birthright, the land. On the other hand, to then opposition MDC party, the sanctions were directly politically targeted restrictive measures directed at ZANU (PF) individuals responsible for gross human rights abuses and their business concerns and assets in foreign lands. Whatever the projected impact such targeted economic restrictions were meant to have, in the face of disturbances in agricultural, mining, and manufacturing productivity, the socioeconomic consequences were severe.

Credit lines with international financiers were cut due to Zimbabwe's substantial external debt (Bracking and Sachikonye, 2009, p.15) and trade relations severed; the country's credit rating worsened an already precarious economic situation. Both local and international suppliers demanded cash payments for goods and services before delivery as the country's ability to service meet its debts became doubtful. The steady decline of foreign currency in the country and the cessation of international lines of credit particularly impacted on the importation of raw materials and spare parts for the manufacturing sector. This resulted in a sharp decline in productivity and a widespread shortage of essential commodities as "the manufacturing capacity of major suppliers of commodities slumped to record lows of below 10% by 2008" (Biti, 2009, p.33).The country's micro and macro fundamentals tottered and created the potential for both social and economic crimes. Economic uncertainty made business people anxious, and immoral business practices surfaced.

The manner in which political leaders run a country and chart its destiny can never be divorced from the manner critical sectors of the economy such as business carry out its activities. Therefore, when those who have "a public mandate to enforce laws and acceptable conduct in business dealings are immorally complicit" (Makochekanwa & Kwaramba, 2009, pp.12–13) and largely part of the purveyors of scandalous business practices then unethical practices pervade. In the absence of a "role model character" (Coltart, 2008), the Mugabe government partly contributed to unprecedented moral decay in the conduct of the business sector in Zimbabwe.

Corruption in both the government and the business sector quickly crippled Zimbabwe's economic activities. Among others, it was alleged that because of the shortages of foreign currency in the country, both businesses and the Reserve Bank of Zimbabwe (RBZ) were purchasing foreign currency from the black market. This had forced the RBZ to print more of the country's currency such that there was too much money chasing after too few goods. Some black market foreign currency dealers were found with newly printed and yet to be issued denominations of the Zimbabwe dollar. As Coltart (2008:1) later affirmed, "at the root of Zimbabwe's problems is a corrupt political elite that has, with considerable international support, behaved with utter impunity." Aware of the government's lack of integrity to institute checks and balances in the conduct of business, laxity in monitoring mechanisms occasioned various uncouth activities in the economy that threatened the welfare and well-being of Zimbabwe's citizenry. This is to the extent that according to Transparent International's (TI) Corruption Perception Index (CPI), the country's levels of corruption dramatically increased.

In any capitalist economic system, the most significant measure of success of any given business venture is its ability to make as much profit as possible for its owners. The pursuit of super profits and strict adherence to the classical Aristotelian virtue can at times contradict. In an unusual business environment of scarce commodities as Zimbabwe became between 2000 and 2008, goodness threatened the capitalistic economic principles of demand and supply as well as the profit-making objective of engaging in business. Some business owners took advantage of the drop in productivity and the scarcity of commodities to profiteer by employing scandalous practices. For instance, they resorted to hiking prices of old stock by the hour. This so-called price madness drastically pushed inflation up to hyper levels and left most Zimbabweans living below the Poverty Datum Line (PDL). While prices were perhaps partly related to market forces, they are those in government who saw in businesses price hikes a bid to rile the Zimbabwean populace and bring about regime change.

The result was the government's flawed attempt at managing business activities in the country. In response to the goings-on in the economy, therefore, the ZANU-PF government resorted to price controls in the hope of reigning in ruthless profiteers bent on effecting regime change through what it read as speculative pricing. At the end of June 2007, the government announced a command economy-type price control policy:

> [T]o stem runaway inflation, [...] halving all prices. In the six months that followed, manufacturing output fell by more than 50 percent and, unless they could export their goods, many manufacturing firms had to shut down." (Coltart 2008:1)

Paradoxically, the well-intentioned price controls instituted to both protect the interests of the economically vulnerable members of Zimbabwean society and at the same time win the ruling party political mileage soon led to disastrous consequences. To the business sector, the government's implementation of price controls was a declaration of war. In protest, some members of the business community removed stock from shop shelves and put them on the black market for even higher prices and higher profit margins. Business sector indiscipline rose. Food, fuel, and other essential commodities became acutely scarce only to resurface on the parallel black market where they were sold at exorbitantly very high prices. Business malpractices such as the hoarding of consumer goods soon emerged. All manner of corruption abounded in the distribution of the scarce food and basic needs still in supply. Instead of improving the well-being of ordinary citizens and reducing escalating inflation, the price controls worsened the country's socioeconomic landscape.

Realizing its grave economic miscalculation of price controls, and, at the mercy of the business sector, the government revised the price blitz at the end August 2007 and allowed businesses to peg prices of commodities to market levels. This saw price inflation grow unabated and inflict the most disastrous economic consequences. Consumers were left at the mercy of greedy business operators who sold commodities of mostly scandalously poor quality at the most exorbitant of prices. Ordinary people found themselves at the grim end of pervasive immoral business practices in an economy facing the highest inflation figures (Makochekanwa & Kwaramba, 2009, p.3) in recorded African history. Desperate consumers became mere "cash cows" to be milked for outrageous profits and fortunes.

Nefarious profiteering, the sale of cheap commodities and the parallel marketing of products, among other economic ills, contributed to moral decay in the economy. The total was a plethora of shortages of basic human needs, biting corruption, and other cancerous immoral practices in Zimbabwe's economic sector (Masaka, 2007, p.32) which led to untold suffering. Long winding queues and empty store shelves became the country's significant feature as consumers queued for hours for such staples as bread, milk, and maizemeal. This was such that business sectors previously not involved in the food and beverages market got into it. For instance, clothing stores began stocking foodstuffs imported from neighboring countries. In the face of a weak market, other businesses performance slumped resulting in massive unemployment. Inflation continued to spiral, and Zimbabwe soon found itself at the vortex of a devastating economic crisis.

The socioeconomic problems that Zimbabwe faced in the first decade of the new millennium created fertile ground for immoral practices in the business sector. Business people and companies exploited the economy management crisis that the country found itself in to engage in some unethical business practices. This is to the extent that it warranted a Ministry of Anti-Corruption and Anti-Monopolies to see to it that corruption cases were exposed, investigated, and the culprits punished for their immoral and illegal business practices. However, the ministry's sincerity in curbing corrupt and dishonest business practices was questionable. No meaningful effort in that direction was pursued. If anything, immoral business practices increased as the economic crisis deepened.

The end of Zimbabwe's dubious June 27, 2008, presidential and its equally inconclusive result saw the zenith of Zimbabwe's food and basics shortages. The tightening of sanctions, failure to import fuel for tillage, and erratic rainfall resulted in poor maize harvests. Zimbabwe's agricultural sector failed to maintain or increase production capacity to meet domestic and export markets. The severely devalued Zimbabwe dollar hindered the importation of food to augment the meager tonnage produced by existing and resettled farmers. To maximize their profits and acquire foreign currency, some producers of maize and wheat immorally smuggled their wares to neighboring countries and externalized their foreign currency earnings offshore. The moral deficiency of some business people led them to illicitly sell fuel and other commodities in short supply on the informal market in return for super profits. Those who caused human suffering by their deeds lacked virtue as their actions did not promote and uphold human dignity.

Since the late 1990s to the present, the antithesis of it all has been the meteoric growth of the market share of the informal employment sector and the collapse of the formal industry. According to Coltart (2008), by 2005 the informal economy had effectively become the primary source of income for the majority of Zimbabweans. Nearly 3 million Zimbabweans earned their livelihood from informal-sector employment and supported some 5 million people. The formal sector employed only about 1.3 million people. The vibrancy of the informal sector saw mainly Zimbabwean women crossing the country's borders into South Africa, Botswana Zambia, and Mozambique to sell arts and craft and to purchase scarce essential commodities for reselling back home. More often than not, these wares were sold at very exorbitant prices. However, as the country's currency astronomically weakened against that of its neighbors, some such women often resorted to selling not only arts and craft, but in some cases, their bodies as well to survive.

The economy's domination by the informal sector also resulted in the contraction of the government's revenue base. This is primarily because most informal traders easily evaded paying taxes to the government. At the country's entry ports where import duties might have been easier to collect from informal traders, the latter bribed some corrupt customs officers or smuggled their wares using long-distance truck drivers. This further weakened the government's ability to meet vital national obligations such as the importation of fuel, electricity, food, and debt servicing. This was until the formation of Zimbabwe's Government of National Unity (GNU).

*After the GNU: Cultivating Ethical Relativism and Virtue Ethics for Economic Survival.* The above has explored the flawed nature of business conduct during Zimbabwe's crisis.The formation of the GNU at the beginning of 2009 and the dollarization of the Zimbabwe economy resulted in economic stability. Subsequently some of the abovementioned immoral and corrupt activities that had beset the country's economy equally ebbedand some have resiliently persisted. Post the GNU; this researcher contends that Zimbabwean government, business, and people follow a moral agenda. What follows, therefore, argues that the proper cultivation of good traits particularly in individuals involved in the industry will eventually translate in the ethical conduct and operation of Zimbabwean businesses to the benefit of Zimbabweans and the country's image as a whole.

General morality might not approve of the strictly competitive nature of the modern market-oriented economic systems, and business organizations may use cunning methods to outdo each other on the marketplace. However, Carr (2003) argues that such is the nature of a healthy business environment. He compares business with a game of poker whose personal "ethics" allow, among others, deception and cunning that eventually brings victory to the clever over their rivals. For this reason, the general ethics of society are seen as unnecessary in business. This is because evaluating business practices from the perspective of the public ethics would fundamentally strip a company of the competitive edge that makes it what it is. Stripping business of its competitive edge would render business people philanthropists who give away the products and proceeds of their investments to customers at prices that make the business breakeven or even make loses. Such a scenario defeats the purpose of going into business.

Maclntyre (1966) also argued that it is paradoxical to talk of virtue ethics in business. In his opinion, this is because the tenets of marketing and virtue are utterly contradictory to such a point that having virtue ethics as the foundation of business operations would question the competitiveness of such a business. This is because virtue theory opposes such business practices as aggressive and false advertising as well as the selling of goods with structural defects without adequately informing consumers of such shortcomings. To MacIntyre, smuggling virtue theory into the realm of business is "a myth sustained by those who have vested interests in sustaining it" (MacIntyre, 1966). MacIntyre's main point here is that it would be pointless to predicate business practices on virtue ethics because it destroys the whole essence of competitive business. However, one wonders as to what vested interests virtue ethicists would possibly hope to "sustain" by smuggling virtue ethics into the realm of business. As for aggressive advertising and goods with structural defects, surely these would not be necessary where virtue ethics have been instilled and are being cultivated.

On the other hand, virtue ethicists like Aristotle and Freeman were very critical of the supposed separation of business from the rest of society. To Freeman, the idea that business and morality are independent of each other ought to be outrightly rejected because:

> We cannot divorce the concept of a moral community or a moral discourse from the ideas of the value-creation activity of a business. To do so entails the acceptance of a principle, the Separation Thesis, which has for too long been used to close off discussion and to silence conversation. (2008:213)

According to Abela (2001), the Separation Thesis argues that:

> Business decisions have no moral content, and moral choices have no business content. In other words, business decisions are neutral as far as ethics is concerned, and while ethical guidance or constraint can be *added* to a business decision, such advice always comes from "outside," since the business decision is ethically neutral, to begin with. (Sandberg 2008:224)

Given these schools of thought, the question then arises: Is the classical virtue theory of Aristotle still relevant to the widespread immoral business practices in the business sector in Zimbabwe and elsewhere on the continent and indeed, the globe? Since the times of MacIntyre, it is now widely agreed that there is no neutrality as far as business actions are concerned. While chiefly driven by economic motives, in the twenty-first century ethical considerations have increasingly become important in determining businesses' bottom-line.

In Zimbabwe, as the country moves away from the post-GNU era, the supposed dichotomy between business and virtue ethics cannot continue to be used to justify morally scandalous business practices. Instead, there is the need to respect and abide by the general moral codes of society (Masaka, 2007). This is especially if friendly relations between the two are to continue to thaw and not return to their frozen state of 2007 and 2008. Only when Zimbabweans trust business and the latter feels obliged to reciprocate, then will an environment conducive for business to succeed and continue to grow have been put in place.

For that to happen and continue to be strengthened moving forward, I recommend an amalgamation of both schools in the form of ethical relativism and virtue ethics, especially the latter. This is because it would not be practical and fair on free enterprise to take a too moralistic view of business activities. At the same time, I believe in the relevance and timelessness of Aristotle's business ethics in modern business and to Zimbabwe's business environment. So, without criminalizing trade for profit (Solomon, 1999, p.82), what is pivotal is to attune trade and profit to virtue as business understands it, and secondly, as proffered by Aristotle without it being too much of a deterrent to the free market system.

For the sake of political and business expediency, some business people and organizations during Zimbabwe's crisis by any evaluation inarguably imbibed the separation of business from the realm of good morality. Between 1999 and 2009, this state of affairs in the country's business sector was accomplished by its insulation into a self-contained unit answerable to only itself. Assessment and evaluation measures based on sound business standards, ethics fell away, and immoral and unethical "easy money" business practices took root. However, if such businesses are to move past their previous conduct, akin to Albert Z. Carr (2003, pp.100–107) firstly, I urge ethical relativism in business.

According to Carr (2003) and Shaw (1999:15), ethical relativism is the view that business should have and has its own unique moral codes of conduct governing the practice of business. These ethical codes may be at variance with those of society. Therefore, general morality ought not to override the business' moral codes. As such, business's actions should and can only be evaluated by those standards and not what society believes to be the standards of human conduct. In Zimbabwe, there is, therefore, an urgent need to resuscitate, recapitalize, and strengthen organizations such as the Standards Association of Zimbabwe (SAZ) and Consumer Council of Zimbabwe (CCZ) to monitor, assess, and evaluate the practices and standards of business.

With regards to Aristotle's virtue ethics and more good approaches to business, what Zimbabwean business people need is a moral education that annihilates the belief that business is separate from society and its ethical standards. However, given the pervasiveness of corruption and other forms of immoral business practices in both the public and private sectors over the last 13 years of this millennium, the inculcation of noble traits is desperately needed in both areas. The education of such characteristics as integrity, trustworthiness, truthfulness, and fairness could be the panacea to immoral business conduct in Zimbabwe.

However, this inculcation and cultivation of moral virtues should not just be once-off, but periodical and continuous if the country is to stem corporate malpractices that have been bedeviling Zimbabwe. For instance, both private and public sector employees ought to have the character trait of integrity if they are not to execute morally questionable business assignments or what their conscience tells them to be ethically inappropriate (Beauchamp and Bowie, 1997). During the crisis, the lack of integrity helped deepen Zimbabwe's economic crisis. Alongside the absence of an economy, lacking were "honesty, trustworthiness and integrity" (*Standard*, 7–13 January 2007). However, now that the country's crisis has ebbed, the lack of honesty and integrity in business practices and actions ought to end. This can only be achieved by the inculcation, cultivation, and exhibition of commendably good traits in and by all ourpersonnel in both the public and private sector service.

It is incumbent upon us all to uphold and display virtue ethics if we are to improve the generality of Zimbabwe's population. Indeed, Zimbabwe should look forward to a time when for the sake of both the country and business an employee can refuse to be a "team player" in doing wrong and have their moral conviction to override corrupt practices commended (Solomon, 1999:86). Integrity so conceived would promote ethical practices in others to the benefit of both business organizations and the community at large.

The challenge is how to implement such an exercise. Aristotle argues that virtue is neither a feeling nor innate. Instead, it is a disposition that can be bred from an "innate capacity properly trained and exercised" (Boylan, 1995, p.9). Thus, just as one can acquire such skills as playing football, making pots and baskets, so too can one also acquire good character traits. This could be done through Moral or Life Skills education in primary, secondary, and tertiary institutions. Corrupt public and business people can also be reformed by being taught how to conduct themselves virtuously in their business dealings. Where necessary, it could be made mandatory for business organizations to have refresher virtue ethics courses at the beginning of the year. Such initiatives would assist to put the nation on the road to a morally prudent people who conduct their affairs in a manner that is ethically commendable not only for their benefit but also for the benefit of those they transact. Once this has been instilled in Zimbabwean business people, then the battle will just have been half won.

Instituting virtue ethics education would, however, be only the beginning. This is because it is not enough for people to be virtuous just because it has been inculcated in them. They must also have the desire to do so. The goal must be a person with an inherent motivation and willingness to perform right actions (Velasquez, 2002, p.134) and who is characteristically concerned about morally appropriate and desirable practices. In the words of Solomon (1999, p.87) "one is just if she/he is willing always to ensure that everyone else gets a fair share." Real trustworthiness and truthfulness so crucial to the execution of business contracts and transactions are more admirable when inherent. Confronted with a dishonest situation, such a person shows a moral concern and desire to act in such a manner that does not give them an unfair advantage over others. A just businessperson or public servant is just by the just works s/he does in business interactions with their fellows.

In this vein, it was Aristotle's view that "one has to think of oneself as a member of the *Polis* (larger community) and endeavor to excel, to bring out what is best in ourselves and our shared enterprise" (Boylan, 1995). A member of a larger community should, therefore, seek to achieve what is best for oneself and the community at large (Solomon, 1999, pp.82, 85). To act in this way is to act virtuously. As such, a virtuous individual would never work towards the fulfillment of his self-interest only but would also contribute to society's total good. A social order that is beneficial not only to the specific moral agent but the community at large is essential to Zimbabwe given the corporate deceit, self-interest, and side-trading of basic human requirements at the height of the economic meltdown.

The German philosopher Kant (2002) taught that a moral agent has to do to others what he/she expects others to do to him; otherwise, the principle that underlies his action cannot be a universal moral law. His first formulation was the categorical imperative that "Act as if the maxim of your action were to become through your will the universal law of nature" (2002, p.18). To Kant, the hallmark of morality is that principles that underlie our actions be universal for them to have moral value. Also, such activities are necessary because they are right in themselves and not because of other external considerations.

Virtue ethics in business do not, however, mean that people should go into business to promote social utility. Instead, as Adam Smith "the father of economics" argues, and rightly points out, it is economically suicidal for business to be driven primarily by a desire to promote social utility. In the pursuit of personal interest one should also indirectly (Newton and Ford, 2002) or in the case of Zimbabwe directly encourage those of society as well. Thus, for the sake of both the business person and the consumer, public interest must also be intentionally achieved in the pursuit of business interests. However, by implementing business ethics those doing so must be aware that it is not the most cost-effective way of doing business. As Velasquez warns, this does not mean that occasions never arise when doing what is ethical will prove costly to a company (2002, p.5). What is important to note, however, is that it is not the most cost-effective way to do business only in the shortterm. It is, in fact, a long-term investment and the most profitable business route to take for those entities that wish to grow sustainably. This is because although unethical behavior is not "always punished and sometimes pays off, and the good guy sometimes loses" (Velasquez, 2002, p.5); there are lesser long-term risks to following ethical business practices. This can indeed be attested to by two countries, in particular, Germany and Japan.

Both Germany and Japan were once themselves pariah states of the world. The stigma of defeat in the Second World War hung around them. Akin to Zimbabwe after the crisis, their economies lay ruined, and trade relations were challenging to make. Almost seventy years later, both are economic giants whose technological precision, innovation, and ethical business practices are the envy of many and are held as standards for the rest of the world. Today both the German and Japanese economies are partly dependent on the goodwill their business ethics have earned them. The two countries are a testimony to how ethical behavior in business is crucial to long-term business sustainable growth. This is mainly because of the strategic advantage their ethical business practices have given them over other industrialized countries that are synonymous with morally and technologically scandalous business practices.

The intentional inculcation and cultivation of ethically sound moral fiber in both the public and private sectors can equally hold Zimbabwe in good stead. As the country approaches its fortieth year of self-rule in the year 2020, the inculcation and cultivation of virtue ethics should be a deliberate aim. Businesses should set out with the objective of producing quality and more durable products predicated on morally appropriate practices. Beauchamp and Bowie (1997) highlight that such business practices are possible when persons whose characters manifest truthfulness, justice, compassion, respect, and patience are part and parcel of the business.

However, this does not entail merely knowing the provisions of the law or moral precepts and acting moralistically in some instances. Beauchamp and Bowie (1997) also agree that virtue ethics must go beyond just on-going training and its implementation; it must be genuinely a culture of the organization. In the end, employees genuinely displaying good traits add real value and potential to the company's balance sheet than those who merely feign them out of "sheer obligation"and duty (Boss, 1999, p.25). Zimbabweans must similarly aspire to add to the country's balance sheet.

Lastly, if virtue ethics are to continue to grow and have firm roots, a display of ethical behavior must be reinforced by appropriate and motivational responses. In this regard, the government must recognize and incentivize those who demonstrate virtue ethics. One who is disposed to act virtuously deserves to be praised if their exemplary behavior is to be emulated by others. So, much as Adam Smith famously declared:

> I have never known much good done by those affected to trade for the public good. It is an affectation, indeed, not very common among merchants, and very few words need be employed in dissuading them from it. (2002:10)

It is time that Zimbabwean businesses proved Smith wrong by demonstrating that it is possible to conduct business ethically, to "trade for the public good"and remain competitive and profitable. This is because when businesses base their activities on a sound foundation of virtue ethics, they in the medium- to long-term business will still benefit, while at the same time remaining sustainably profit-oriented. Any economic system that extols morally scandalous business practices is poised for collapse in comparison to one that extolls them. It, therefore, makes economically and socially sound sense to predicate Zimbabwe's business practices on sound business ethics explicitly.

## *Conclusion*

The modern state that is Zimbabwe today was colonially founded on unethical promises and dealings. As this chapter has shown, it was the unethical dispossession of land that later spawned numerous other unethical practices in the nation's postcolony. Postindependence, such practices once again stemmed from the country's land issue, but this time, with Zimbabwe's neo-colonialist black taking the lead. After that, as the nation's postcolonial economy deteriorated, the situation steadily provided a fertile breeding ground for unethical business practices. Business people entangled themselves in profiteering, resulting in corrupt tendencies generally in the marketplace.

It is in light of what went on during the crisis and the observation that business malpractices which had gripped the country then, continue to do so, that the chapter has argued for the inculcation and cultivation of virtue ethics in the country's private and public sectors as well as among the general population. This has been based on the premise that persons who cherish and genuinely exhibit the virtues of ethics and integrity lead to honorable business dealings to the benefit of the Zimbabwean economy in particular, and society in general. Thus, in spite of the perceived short-term limitations associated with ethical business practices, this chapter has argued that the inculcation of virtue ethics is most relevant to a post-GNU business environment that mostly continues to be predicated on the desire to self-serve and maximize profit. Lastly, such an intervention ought not to be seen as interference in the country's free market system. Instead, it should be seen as stemming from the need to protect business from itself, guard its clientele and indeed Zimbabwe from the sector's rational and at times insatiable desire to unjustifiably maximize profits at the expense of future business.

## Note

1. Affiliation: Department of Philosophy and Religious Studies, Great Zimbabwe University.

## References


Aristotle. (1995). Nichomachean ethics.In M. Boylan (Ed.), *Ethical issues in business.* Philadelphia: Harcourt Brace College Publishers.

Beauchamp, T. L., & Bowie, N. E. (Eds.). (1997). *Ethical theory and business.* Upper Saddle River, NJ: Prentice Hall.

Biti, T. (2009). *The Zimbabwe 2010 budget* (pp. 1–72). Harare: Ministry of Finance.

Bond, P. (1998). *Uneven Zimbabwe: A study of finance, development, and underdevelopment.*Trenton: Africa World Press, Inc.

Bond, P. (2001). Radical rhetoric and the working class during Zimbabwean nationalism's dying days. In B. Raftopoulos & L. Sachikonye (Eds.), *Striking back: The labour movement and the post-colonial state in Zimbabwe 1980–2000.* Harare: Weaver Press.

Bond, P., & Manyanya, M. (2003). *Zimbabwe's Plunge. Exhausted nationalism, neoliberalism and the search for social justice.* London: Merlin Press.

Boss, J. A. (1999). *Analyzing moral issues.* Belmont, CA: Mayfield Publishing Company.

Boylan, M. (Ed.). (1995). *Ethical issues in business.* Philadelphia: Harcourt Brace College Publishers.

Bracking, S., & Sachikonye, L. (2009). *Development finance, private and public sectors in Zimbabwe: Sustainability or odious debt?* (BWPI working paper 84, pp. 1–22). Manchester: Brooks World Poverty Institute.

Carr, A. Z. (2003). Is business bluffing ethical?. In L. P. Hartman (Ed.), *Perspectives in business ethics.* New Delhi: Tata McGraw-Hill Publishing Company Limited.

Coltart, D. (2008). *A decade of suffering in Zimbabwe: Economic collapse and political repression under Robert Mugabe* (pp. 1–24). Washington, DC: Center for Global Liberty and Prosperity Development Analysis, CATO Institute, March 24, 5.

Dobson, J. (n.d.). *Virtue ethics as a foundation for business ethics: A "Maclntyre-Based" critique.* California Polytechnic State University. http:www.stthomas.edu/cathstudies/cstm/Antwerp/p30.htm-top. Date Retrieved: February 17, 2010.

Hartman, L. P. (Ed.). (2003). *Perspectives in business ethics.* New Delhi: Tata McGraw-Hill Publishing Company.

Herbst, J. (1990). *State politics in Zimbabwe.* Harare: University of Zimbabwe Publications.

Kant, I. (2002). Grounding for the metaphysics of morals. In L. P. Hartman (Ed.), (2003) *Perspectives in business ethics.* New Delhi: Tata McGraw-Hill Publishing Company.

MacIntyre, A. (1966). *A short history of ethics: A history of moral philosophy from the homeric age to the twentieth century.* London: Routledge. Keegan Paul.

Makochekanwa, A., & Kwaramba, M. (2009). *State fragility: Zimbabwe's horrific journey in the new millennium. Accra: A research paper presented at the European Report on Development's (ERD)* (pp. 1–36).

Masaka, D. (2007). Whistleblowing in the context of Zimbabwe's economic crisis. *EJBO Electronic Journal of Business Ethics and Organization Studies, 12*(2), 32–39. http://ejbo.jyu.fi/

Masiwa, N. (1999). The Congo wilderness. In I. Mandaza (Ed.), *Reflections of the crisis in the democratic republic of Congo.* Harare: SAPES Books.

Moore, D. S. (2005). *Suffering for territory: Race, place, and power in Zimbabwe.* Harare: Weaver.

Moyana, H. V. (2002). *The political economy of land in Zimbabwe.* Gweru: Mambo Press.

Newton, L. H., & Ford, M. M. (Eds.). (2002). *Taking sides: Clashing views on controversial issues in business ethics and society.* Guilford: McGraw-Hill/Dushkin.

Raftopoulos, B., & Sachikonye, L. (Eds.). (2001). *Striking back: The labour movement and the post-colonial state in Zimbabwe 1980–2000.* Harare: Weaver Press.

Sachikonye, L. M. (2002). Whither Zimbabwe? Crisis &democratisation. *Review of African Political Economy, 9*, 13–20.

Sandberg, J. (2008). Understanding the separation thesis. *Business Ethics Quarterly, 18*(2), 213–232.

Shaw, W. H. (1999). *Business ethics.* Belmont: Wadsworth Publishing Company.

Smith, A. (2002). An inquiry into the nature and causes of the wealth of nations. In L. H. Newton & M. M. Ford (Eds.), *Taking sides: Clashing views on controversial issues in business ethics and society.* Guilford: McGraw-Hill/Dushkin.

Solomon, R. C. (1999). Corporate personal virtues: An Aristotelean approach to business ethics. In T. Donaldson & P. H. Werhane (Eds.), *Ethical issues in business: A philosophical approach.* New Jersey, Upper Saddle River: Prentice Hall.

Tekere, E. Z. (2007). *A lifetime of struggle.* Harare: SAPES Books.

Velasquez, M. G. (2002). *Business ethics: Concepts and cases.* Delhi: Pearson Education Inc.

# *Conclusion*

C. Luthuli Mhlahlo

How does one write a conclusive conclusion for a phenomenon as complex and seemingly mutating and unraveling as the Zimbabwean crisis? Much as this might be, however, this volume has sought to disrupt the crisis' transmutation by mainly focusing on and sharing its contributors' perspectives and perceived paradoxes of the twenty years in question and the prospects beyond them. To do so, the four-part multidisciplinary volume has, to some extent, linearly engaged with Zimbabwe's not so distant past and present socioeconomic and political situation from 1997 to 2017.

Hypotheses and debates abound around the origins or causes of the Zimbabwean crisis. From both the Global South and Western perspectives, Part One traced, explored, analyzed, and theoretically explicated what its contributors perceive to be the origins of the crisis. Chapter One revealed that at the root of the Zimbabwean crisis is the pre-lapsarian cause of the fall of humankind—disobedience. Since then, most of humanity's suffering has emanated from one disobedience or another. From an Africanist and Western theoretical perspective, the chapter explicated the cause of the Zimbabwean crisis to be, among others, some Zimbabweans' postindependence existentialist disobedience of an order reportedly issued by the country's foremost spiritual ancestor, Nehanda Nyakasikana, during the 19th century. In this regard, it posited and demonstrated how this disobedience or disregard of Nehanda's warning during the First *Chimurenga* subsequently led to the country's ancestors falling silent and turning their backs on their descendants in a kind of ancestral abandonment or *kufuratirwanevadzimu*. One that also became an international one, as sanctions and ostracization followed and plunged the country deeper into crisis. In the light of which Chapter One concluded that some knowledge and understanding of Zimbabwe's precolonial traditions and beliefs regarding the country's land, its people's relations with it, and their ancestors is pivotal to an appreciation and understanding of the country's past, present, and future as, it is these that, to some extent, have shaped and, in some respects, continue to influence the course of the country's past and present.

Ways of seeing and thinking are different, and the world is intellectually richer for it. In its own search for what lay behind the Zimbabwean crisis, based on the view maintained by Meredith (2005, pp. 634–635) Chapter Two analyzed Samuel P. Huntington's (1968) thesis about modernization and political consciousness against what characterized Zimbabwe from 1999 to 2009. While Huntington's (1968) position on stages of development as they obtained in Europe and America may not precisely apply to either an African or a Zimbabwean situation, his theory, however, has quite successfully illuminated the situation that unfolded during the decade of crisis the chapter covered. It has demonstrated how events which unfolded in Zimbabwe between 1999 and 2009 illustrated the stage the country had achieved according to Huntington's (1968) theorization of political modernization. The ZANU-PF government's use of the land redistribution program as a weapon on a literate population by the Mugabe government only made its party widely unpopular, especially in the urban areas. Coupled with the globalization of Zimbabwe's domestic politics by the participation of external forces such as South Africa and Britain in it, the result was the socioeconomic and political instability that has characterized to 2009.

Over the years, some Western governments have been accused and borne the brunt for the general underdevelopment as well as negative socioeconomic and political developments on the African continent. However, Chapter Three argued that they have been wrongfully so. Instead, it laid the blame squarely on what it called the Zimbabwe government's blatant flirtation with a paternalistic command economic system. As a result, the years 2000–2009 proved that a paternalistic approach to an economy is suicidal and does not bring about a sustainable solution to skyrocketing inflation. Price controls caused the flight of existing investors and scared potential foreign direct investment away as the paternalistic and populist government of the day arbitrarily disregarded market forces and tempered with free-market economic efficiency.

Commodities disappeared from store shelves, the country's manufacturing industries drastically slumped and shortages set in. The greatest paradox of which was the hardship, suffering, and near collapse of the same Zimbabwean consumers and economy the paternalistic price controls were trying to protect from exorbitant prices, profiteering, wide-spread shortages, parallel-market trading, and the specter of corruption and decline. All of which bore true to the fact that individual business organizations are not motivated to employ their economic and human resources to the fullest when faced with economically unviable price decrees. Of those businesses that remained, the prevailing situation forced them to compromise quality to remain viable, and the absence of competition did not justify improvement. This aptly demonstrated the short-term political gains and long-term consequences that accrue from controlling an economy in the absence of government, business, and labor concurrence on a social contract administered along free-market economic principles.

From a Global South theoretical perspective, the last chapter of Part One deployed concepts of Yoshiko Herrera's imagined economies thesis and explored how the authoritarian-inclined ZANU-PF government, in the name of nationalism, employed social constructions of the economy to centralize power. It demonstrated this by juxtaposing Herrera's imagined economies framework's notions of *doxa*, *orthodox*, and *heterodox* to explicate the cause and course of the Zimbabwean crisis. Akin to Herrera's *heterodox*, the ruling party resorted to its ability to draw multiple historical and cultural understandings of the economy to rally the peasantry and war veterans to retake their land from postcolonial economic domination. The state's invocation of the past and a possible return to that past convinced and mobilized some in the country that despite the ruling party's flaws, it was better than the specter of foreign intervention, regime change, and loss of sovereignty. The culmination was land seizures that restored some of the country's land to the black majority, however skewed its redistribution. In response, both local and external political and economic interests mutually constituted and mobilized some internal and largely external pressure against the Mugabe regime. Thus, escalating the crisis.

By the end of Part One, what is clear is that theoretical analyses of the causes of the Zimbabwean crisis are intimately entwined with the country's past, its citizenry, in particular the war veterans of the Second *Chimurenga* and opposition parties, State governance and economic policies, especially around economic structural adjustment, price controls, land reform and, as we see later, monetary policy. In essence, both the Zimbabwean public and the State feature prominently are implicated against the backdrop of some regional and international foreign powers in causing the country's socioeconomic and political crisis. No one cause can be attributed to causing the Zimbabwean crisis. Instead, a myriad of factors originating from the Zimbabwean public, the State, and some foreign powers played their part in causing the crisis. However, much as the chapters in Part One implicated the Zimbabwean public, the State and some foreign powers for their part in causing the socioeconomic and political crisis, those of Part Two also demonstrated that neither the Zimbabwe government nor some of its people were passive victims of the socioeconomic and political crisis, albeit complicit in its entrenchment.

At times, the world forgets that while the Zimbabwean crisis has been a monumental historical event on the African continent and arguably affected the whole world, in one way or another,it has also been largely about the people it has both affected and effected. The chapters in Part Two of the collection observed and analyzed some citizens' and the State's responses and survival strategies to the socioeconomic and political crisis that engulfed the Zimbabwean nation-state. Chapter Five of the volume's second segment chronicled how the country's shortage of housing notably heightened the crisis for home-seekers and yet provided a survival strategy for those with access to housing who were willing to let it out. For such ones, house ownership proved an economic asset and an essential aspect of wealth-creation, self-empowerment, and poverty alleviation. This was especially so, when, during the crisis, the Mugabe regime activated Operation *Murambatsvina* and credit deficiency spiked a high demand for shelter. The insatiable demand for private rental shelter and private rental rooms that culminated was filled by small-scale landlordism, as the letting out of rooms by some landlords became a major source of regular income. Small-scale landlordism became a critical economic survival strategy not only for landlords but also for their lodgers and tenants who equally devised their own survival strategies. For the less fortunate, the low-income earners and unemployed, slum-dwelling or squatting became the only means of escape. For those Zimbabweans whom the crisis drove beyond the country's borders, survival strategies took on more creative forms.

Chapter Six revealed how the steady decline of the Zimbabwean economy from 2000 saw a spike in immigrants from Zimbabwe and how some ordinary South Africans' response to the influx revealed a resilient prejudicial past and ignorance of the historical ties between the two countries. It explored how in contrast to some of their countrymen and women from other tribes, some Zimbabwean immigrants of Ndebele origin manipulated their close ancestral ties to South Africa and adorned "Zulu masks" by mimicking Zulu identity and culture. Thus, when discriminatory identification practices reminiscent of South Africa's apartheid years emerged, such immigrants enacted what they traditionally already knew, at times, exaggeratedly mimicked and feigned Zuluness as a survival strategy. The result was not only the literal survival of such ones but also the promotion of monoculturalism and emergence of ambivalent, flexible, and fluid identities among sections of Zimbabwean immigrants.

In the face of its ostracization and the imposition of "smart sanctions" by most Western nations, the then Mugabe-led government equally embarked on strategically defensive foreign and domestic policies for both its own and the country's survival. Chapter Seven adopted the Systemic theory to analyze the problems that the country faced due to the poor public policy of the government in power till 2017. The chapter posited that the result was the internationalization of Zimbabwe's internal affairs and dispute with the West as the EU and UN contended with China, Russia, and the AU when it came to the African country. It illustrated how as the world tangled over the internal politics of the country, the Mugabe government capitalized on the situation, and went into diplomatic survival mode for historical, economic, and political reasons by embarking on a "Look East" policy mainly with the Chinese government. This rendered the UNSC divided over the government in Harare and proved one of its lifelines.

Chapter Seven also revealed how survival for the then Mugabe-led government also stemmed from some African countries' pan-Africanist stance and the need to find "African solutions to African problems" when it came to Zimbabwe. In this respect therefore, in order to break internal political deadlocks over the future of Zimbabwe, the organs of both the AU and SADC facilitated mediation and negotiation between the political parties concerned. ZANU-PF and the opposition MDCs assented with the SADC which led to the formation of the Government of National Unity (GNU) from 2009 to 2013. However, as Chapter Eight exposed, the GNU was to prove a palliative yet painful solution for the two political rivalries forced into a paradoxical marriage of both convenience and inconvenience.

Chapter Eight assessed the workability of Zimbabwe's GNU from 2009 to 2013 in the context of the divergent views of its partners. It demonstrated how, to some extent, the political formation was paradoxically a marriage of both convenience and inconvenience to both those in the government and the Zimbabweans. This is especially insofar as the political settlement provided an opportunity to mend Zimbabwe's decade-old economic decline and stagnation, on the one hand, and,on the other hand, fleeced limited resources in a search to be workable. The result was that it only proved to be an expedient temporary panacea for a crisis that was, in fact, a cancer.

Besides, Chapter Eight also castigated the concept of political belligerents forming a government of national unity. This is particularly as it set a bad precedent and entrenched a system of governance whereby whenever elections are disputed, either the incumbent or defeated party eventually insinuates itself into the new government by way of a negotiated settlement. Consequent to which, even in the event of a credible electoral process, all the losing political party must do is dispute the result and threaten violence until a government of national unity is proposed. As the chapter demonstrated, in Zimbabwe, such a system of governance became problematic as it turned into a continuous struggle of political gladiators at the expense of the people and the full democratization of African institutions difficult. The hurdles faced by Zimbabwe's GNU were further proof, not only of the redundancy of a government that is a product of negotiations rather than a credible election, but also its unworkability.

While Part 2 commended the innovation, creativity, and strategic acumen of both some Zimbabweans and then Mugabe-led government,respectively, it also simultaneously chastised their agency. This is because no matter how innovative and strategic some Zimbabweans and the State's economic and political survival strategies, respectively,were, however, there is the need for them both to objectively scrutinize and atone for those which specifically led to the manipulation, virtual cannibalization, and suffering of other Zimbabweans, on the one hand, and compromised the country's socioeconomic and political future, on the other hand.

Of the perceived causes of the Zimbabwean crisis, its political past, political parties' factionalism, the State's economic policies vis-à-vis economic fundamentals entrenched and perpetuated it. The chapters in Part Three of the volume scrutinized the mechanisms behind and personalities of some of the major players of the crisis. Chapter Nine's exploration of the mechanisms and course of the crisis concluded that it was the history of factionalism in both the ruling and opposition parties which both fanned and paradoxically finally doused the crisis. According to the chapter, an analysis of the black nationalist movement in Zimbabwe suggests that it and the history of the country have revolved around factionalism brought about by conflicts in personality clashes and leadership styles in both the ZANU-PF and opposition parties. In the ZANU-PF party, the political ascendance of Grace Mugabe resulted in a trichotomy of Gamatox, Lacoste, and Generation 40/G40. It eventually took the emergence of a fourth insidious faction in the military to bring about Mugabe's departure.

Conversely, Chapter Nine also argued and demonstrated how it was the Mugabe government's expedient response to the crisis by uncontrollably printing the Zimbabwe dollar that ultimately was not only the most irresponsible economic mismanagement of that administration but also its most destructive and deadliest. It effectively engrained hyperinflation and corruption as a *topos* of the Zimbabwean socioeconomic landscape and left the people of Zimbabwe to bear the brunt of it the parties' factional fighting. Despite it all, some still managed to see the humor of it all.

Social and cultural phenomenon is sometimes determined or driven by history. In this vein, Chapter Ten noted how from 2007 to 2009, the rapid development and rise in the popularity of electronic mail, digital technology, and media within the context of Zimbabwe's socioeconomic and political crisis gave impetus to new forms of sociological imagination that were shared as what the chapter called ZForwards. Rich in creativity and reflective of the country's experience of crisis, ZForwards captured some significant moments of Zimbabweans' lives as impacted by their leaders' governance of them. This is such that akin to most postcolonial literary, sociological imagination, some of these ZForwards gave a sociohistorical perspective, analysis, understanding, and explanation to what was happening in the country. In most cases, the result of this was running satirical commentary and humor in the context of crisis. Subsequently, ZForwards not only revealed some Zimbabweans' sentiments about the goings-on in their country, they also brought out the comic in the tragic as well as helped their recipients empathize and stay informed.

Since biblical times, women and particularly wives have held sway over the course of human history. Chapter Eleven explored and showed that, while two women in Mugabe's life, his mother, Bona and his first wife, Sally, significantly contributed to the promising leader and statesman he became soon after Zimbabwe's independence, it also demonstrated the widely held conjecture that it was his second wife, Grace, who later reduced him from the preponderant figure of his younger days to the authoritarian yet tacitly emasculated leader identity he cut in his later years. This is such that when parliament later sought to impeach the aged president, Grace would be implicated and held complicit for the negative developments in the country. That as it may be, however, the same chapter also demonstrated that it was also Mugabe's paradoxical flirtation with African modernity and his increasingly radical Africanization agenda that coupled with his advanced years finally added to his demise and eventual removal from power.

With President Robert Mugabe's 2017 resignation in mind, Chapter Twelve explored and analyzed what occurred from 13 to 24 November 2017 in Harare, Zimbabwe. It concluded that occurred was the climax of the factional fighting at play in the ZANU-PF party. However, it also posited that by "stepping in and intervening" to dislodge a rival faction that was intimately supported by the country's president, the officers commanding the defense forces had inadvertently staged a coup d'état. As such, to rid themselves of the stigma of it, those who had staged the coup had attempted to reverse it by turning it into a constitutional transition. Consequently, aided by the Zimbabwe National Liberation War Veterans Association, the ruling ZANU-PF party and the cooperation of the main opposition, the MDC-T, constitutional processes were orchestrated and set in motion, culminating in Robert Mugabe's resignation. In this way, Chapter Twelve concludes was a coup d'état turned into a constitutional change of power worthy of the Zimbabwe High Court's endorsement. It is primarily for this reason that Part 3 concluded on the premise that by the end of 2017, the crisis had reached a watershed, one that could either abate or exacerbate after Zimbabwe's elections on July 30, 2018.

Hope is a powerful dynamic, and for both the eternal optimists and pessimists alike, the events of November 2017 sparked and promised a hopeful future. Consequently, Part 4 audaciously looked beyond the crisis and its chapters proffered and charted prospective paths open to the country as it progressed into a promising future. After an examination of Zimbabwe's experiences of democracy between the years 2000 and 2009 and finding how the majority rule principle of electoral democracy caused rather than solved problems of political violence and disputed elections as political parties pursued the majority of votes, Chapter Thirteen advocated a non-party consensual democracy that is more compatible with both Zimbabwe and the continent's past. It warned that the failure to do so would only ensure the perpetuation of political bickering, economic stagnation, and unnecessary human suffering that have characterized Zimbabwe and many other African nations since the dawn of the specter that is Western democracy.

Conversely, Chapter Fourteen called for restorative justice if the country is to heal its festering wounds and finally move into the future. To do so, the chapter advised that the country should draw from its indigenous knowledge systems, some of which resonate with biblical scripture and modern understandings of justice. Otherwise, to neglect the country's traditional values, knowledge systems, and biblical principles would be to do so at the country's peril. Also, given the ruling ZANU-PF government's disconnect with the citizenry and its strained to severed relations with the international community, the chapter also advocated instituting a Government Relations strategy and other innovative governance developments to might help any new government connect specifically with its citizenry and the international community generally. It concluded that going forward, it was necessary for Zimbabwe's nation-building, development, and growth to rest on a syncretic mix of traditional, humanist values; competent leadership; innovation; open dialogue; and transparency with itself and indeed the world if the country is to solve and move beyond its past.

Based on the historic understanding that modern-day Zimbabwe was colonially founded on unethical promises and dealings and neo-colonialist black corruption, and, as the nation's postcolonial economy deteriorated, unethical business practices, Chapter Fifteen recommended for the inculcation and cultivation of virtue ethics in the country's private and public sectors as well as among the general population. This is especially as post-2017 Zimbabwean business community and some enterprising individuals have continued on a course self-serving aggrandizement and profit maximization. However, as the chapter explicated, such an intervention ought not to be seen as interference in the country's free-market system. Instead, it should be seen as stemming from the need to protect business from itself, guard its clientele and indeed Zimbabwe from the sector's rational and at times insatiable desire to unjustifiably maximize profits at the expense of future business. It optimistically concluded on the understanding that persons who cherish and genuinely exhibit the virtues of ethics and integrity undertake honorable business dealings which will ultimately benefit the Zimbabwean economy in particular, and society in general.

As the volume optimistically closes, one cannot help but wonder whether the military intervention will be able to surmount the Zimbabwean crisis and indeed move the country forward to new possibilities and above all, socioeconomic and political stability. And if so, what supportive function technological innovations such as blockchain, cryptocurrencies, and crowdfunding can play alongside the roles the collection has scripted for the Zimbabwean public, its leadership, and the international community? I believe that, respectfully, constructively, strategically and mutually coordinated, the prospects are endless for all concerned.